Women
IN SPORTS

Women

IN SPORTS

The Complete Book on the
World's Greatest Female Athletes

By Joe Layden

Foreword by Donna A. Lopiano, Ph.D.,
Executive Director, Women's Sports Foundation®

General Publishing Group GPG

Publisher: W. Quay Hays
Editorial Director: Peter Hoffman
Editor: Amy Spitalnick
Art Director: Kurt Wahlner
Production Director: Trudihope Schlomowitz
Color and Pre-Press Director: Bill Castillo
Production Artist: Gaston Moraga
Production Assistants: David Chadderdon, Tom Archibeque, Gus Dawson
Copy Editors: Mark Lamana, Dianne Woo

For information:
General Publishing Group, Inc.
2701 Ocean Park Boulevard
Santa Monica, CA 90405

Library of Congress Cataloging-in-Publication Data

Layden, Joseph, 1959–
    Women in sports: the complete book on the world's greatest female
athletes/ by Joe Layden.
        p.   cm.
    Includes bibliographical references and index.
    ISBN 1-57544-064-4
    1. Women athletes—Biography.   I. Title.
GV697.A1L35 1997
796.092'2—dc21
[B]   97-6666
                                                    CIP

Printed in the USA
by RR Donnelley & Sons Company
10 9 8 7 6 5 4 3 2 1

General Publishing Group
Los Angeles

Very special thanks to:
Wendy Day, U.S. Speedskating; Lars Dietrich, BAA; Tricia Downing, United States Swimming;
Lorene Graves, USA Volleyball; Shirley Ito and the staff at AAF; Karen Johnson, Nyra/Aqueduct Press;
George Kirkman, Museum of Flying; Bruce Levy, USTA; Kelly Lovell, Harlem Globetrotters International, Inc.;
Valerie Miller, PVA Publications; Zoy Parkinson, FAMJOY Enterprises, Inc.; Elaine Scott, LPGA;
Evelyn Valenti, U.S. National Ski Hall of Fame; and Carolyn Williams, USA Basketball

Table of Contents

Acknowledgments

Any author who undertakes a project of this magnitude requires considerable help. From the outset, I was fortunate to have the cooperation of the Women's Sports Foundation. My most sincere thanks go to director of public relations Rachel Zuk, who returned every phone call and honored every request (sometimes on ridiculously short notice), and whose office provided a wealth of historical and statistical information. Without the foundation's assistance, my job would have been much more difficult, and this book would not be nearly as comprehensive as it is.

I am also indebted to the media relations staffs of numerous organizations, most notably the following: USA Gymnastics, United States Swimming, USA Basketball, U.S. Figure Skating Association, U.S. Skiing, U.S. Speedskating, U.S. Tennis Association, USA Track and Field, Women's Tennis Association, Ladies Professional Golf Association, Women's International Bowling Congress, New York Racing Association, U.S. Cycling Federation, National Baseball Hall of Fame and Museum, Naismith Memorial Basketball Hall of Fame, National Bowling Hall of Fame and Museum, International Tennis Hall of Fame, and National Track and Field Hall of Fame.

Finally, special thanks to Frank Coffey, an extremely nimble collaborator and agent, and to Quay Hays of General Publishing Group, who provided a first-class home for this project.

Preface

There was a time, not so long ago, when women had no place in the world of sports. The athletic arena was the exclusive domain of males; women, when allowed through the door at all, were restricted to the sidelines. They were cheerleaders, nothing more.

At the first Olympic Games of the modern era, in 1896, all of the athletes were men. Four years later, however, at the 1900 Summer Games in Paris, the first of many barriers fell, as twelve women competed in tennis and golf. Twelve out of 1,330 competitors was a small but significant number. It marked the beginning of one of the most important cultural changes of the 20th century: the participation of women in competitive sports.

While the playing field today is not exactly level, it is more balanced than at any time in history. In gymnasiums and stadiums around the world, women of all ages are testing themselves—against each other, against the clock, against history. And their numbers are swelling. Twenty-five years ago fewer than 300,000 girls participated in interscholastic athletics in the United States. But the passing of Title IX of the Educational Amendments Act in 1972 caused an explosion in women's sports. Today more than two million girls are playing interscholastic sports. And the opportunities for them to continue playing after high school are increasing as well: A decade ago, 60 U.S. colleges offered women's athletic scholarships; today, more than 650 do so.

At the 1996 Summer Olympics in Atlanta, nearly 4,000 women participated—a Games record. And, increasingly, there are opportunities for women to compete as professionals, both in the United States and abroad. Granted, there are still far more opportunities for male athletes—and both media coverage and financial compensation are generally slanted in favor of men—but there is no question that the tide is turning. Slowly, perhaps. But it is turning. As each new generation demands in greater numbers its right to play, to participate, and to compete, the inexorable march toward gender equity will continue.

Women In Sports celebrates this sporting revolution by recognizing 250 of the most important and compelling figures in athletic history, from pioneers such as Babe Didrikson Zaharias

and Althea Gibson to modern superstars like Steffi Graf and Jackie Joyner-Kersee. As is always the case with this type of compilation, the list of people selected for inclusion is highly subjective. Generally speaking, the women on these pages are uncommonly gifted athletes who have achieved remarkable success in their chosen sports. They are Olympic gold medalists, hall of fame inductees, national champions, and world record holders. Some cases were innovators whose willingness to challenge traditional notions of femininity and athleticism resulted in opportunities for those who followed in their footsteps. Others had marginal athletic careers but went on to achieve greatness in other areas, such as coaching, administration, or journalism. And a few, it could be argued, are more infamous than famous. But they all have one thing in common: in one way or another, through their actions and accomplishments, they helped advance the cause of women's sports.

I don't doubt that some readers will take issue with this list, that they will point out notable omissions or question the merit of some of the athletes who have been included. That's all right. Obviously there have been far more than 250 exceptional female athletes throughout history. If *Women In Sports* sparks debate and conversation about this topic, then it has clearly accomplished one of its goals.

In addition to biographical sketches, *Women In Sports* includes sidebars on some of the more significant, memorable, and amusing moments in women's sports. Although these sidebars describe events that are among the most important in women's sports, they are certainly not intended to be a definitive listing. Rather, they are snapshots—some well-known, some obscure. All, I hope, are interesting.

—Joe Layden

Foreword

For as long as I can remember, I wanted to play for the New York Yankees. The smell of the grass, the feel of the dirt, the roar of the crowd—I wanted to be Mickey Mantle.

I know I am far from alone in those feelings. There are many girls around the globe who have dreamed of becoming their sports heroes. The difference today is the names of some of these heroes. Instead of girls aspiring to "be like Mike," they are hoping to be the next Sheryl Swoopes or Rebecca Lobo; instead of Babe Ruth, they are looking to be like Lisa Fernandez or Toni Stone; and instead of Wayne Gretzky, they are emulating Manon Rheaume. With more girls and women playing sports than ever before, there is a plethora of athletes to serve as role models for young girls. Many of these athletes are showcased in *Women In Sports: The Complete Book on the World's Greatest Female Athletes.*

As you look through this book, you will see many of the heroines who have broken barriers and paved the way for today's athletes. These athletes competed during a time when sports were not a socially acceptable activity for females. We have come a long way since those days. Nineteen ninety-six was a monumental year for women's sports, with record numbers of female athletes participating in the Olympic Games, the creation of two new women's professional basketball leagues, a new women's professional fast-pitch softball league, and now, potentially, a women's professional soccer league. The future looks bright for women's sports.

I wonder if I was a young girl today whether playing for the Yankees would still be my dream, or if I would be aspiring instead to be a member of the Colorado Silver Bullets, the all-women's professional baseball team.

Donna A. Lopiano, Ph.D.
Executive Director,
Women's Sports Foundation®

For Mom, who has always been a fan.

Women
IN SPORTS

Michelle Akers

Born February 1, 1966

Michelle Akers, the all-time leading scorer for the U.S. women's national soccer team, was born in Santa Clara, California. She moved to Seattle as a child and began playing soccer at an early age. She is known for her work ethic as well as for her love for the game. But there was a time, early in her career, when Akers wasn't sure if she wanted to embrace the training necessary for success in any sport. Tired and frustrated after losing a youth league game, she walked off the field in tears. Her father stopped her and asked an interesting question—"Did you have fun?"

The answer was yes. And it was then that Akers discovered the real reason that she liked soccer: It was fun. She remained a fierce competitor but learned to enjoy everything about the game, win or lose. In fact, she is now considered one of the most devoted athletes ever to wear a soccer uniform.

"When I was growing up, I just played a lot," Akers has said. "I was different from other players. I was more competitive and I had a strong desire to win. That continues today. I usually play harder than anyone else on the field, and that gives me an advantage. But I don't play for awards. I play because I love the game and I love to compete."

That attitude makes Akers a coach's dream. "Her work ethic is phenomenal," said Anson Dorrance, a former U.S. national team coach. "She puts more time in the development of her game than any player at a high level. She's always asking for extra sessions and more shooting work."

A three-time high school All-America player at Shorecrest High in Seattle, Akers earned a scholarship to attend the University of Central Florida in Orlando. In college she became one of the most dominant players in the country. She was a four-time All-America winner who set UCF records in career goals, assists, and points. In 1987 she was named Most Valuable Player of the NCAA soccer championships, and in 1989 she was named UCF's Athlete of the Year.

After graduating from UCF with a degree in liberal studies, Akers joined the Orlando Calibre Soccer Club. She also spent three seasons playing for the Tyreso Football Club in Sweden. In 1992 she scored 43 goals and was the leading goal scorer—male or female—in any of Sweden's professional divisions. That same year she led Tyreso to its first championship.

Over the years, Akers' leg strength became so impressive that people outside of soccer took notice. She even spent a week training with the kicking coach of the Dallas Cowboys. Akers booted several field goals 50 yards or more, but never got the chance to put on a uniform. No matter. She had other worlds to conquer. In 1991 she not only was the leading scorer in the first Women's World Championships, but she also helped the United States capture the team title. In that tournament Akers scored 10 goals, including five in one game. She scored both goals in the United States' 2–1 victory over Norway in the title game.

In 1994 Akers was named MVP of the Confederation of North, Central America, and Caribbean Association Football Qualifying Championships in Montreal. She scored six goals in that tournament, earning the United States the right to defend its title at the 1995 world championships in Sweden. In 1996 Akers helped lead the United States to a gold medal at the Summer Olympics in Atlanta.

Accomplishments

    U.S. women's national team all-time leading
        scorer
    Three-time high school All-American
    Four-time NCAA All-American
    Offensive MVP, NCAA championships: 1987
    Leading goal scorer, FIFA Women's World
        Championships: 1991
    MVP of U.S. Cup Tournament: 1996
    Olympic gold medalist: 1996

Tenley Albright

Born July 18, 1935

An Olympic medalist and two-time world figure skating champion, Tenley Albright was born in Newton, Massachusetts. Her father, a surgeon who had a passion for sports, flooded the yard behind their home every winter so that Albright and her friends would have a place to skate. By the time she was nine, Albright was cutting neat figure eights into the ice. Two years later she won the U.S. Eastern Junior Championship—the first in a long string of figure skating victories. At the age of 11, Albright contracted polio, a mild case that nonetheless left her muscles weak and withered. As part of her rehabilitation, she began training at the Skating Club of Boston. She did not consider this a chore; rather, she found it exhilarating.

"Did you ever notice how many athletes my age once had polio?" Albright has said. "I think it's because being paralyzed makes you aware of your muscles, and you never want to let them go unused again."

Albright was 14 years old when she won the U.S. National Junior Championship and 16 when she captured the first of five consecutive U.S. titles in 1952. That same year she took the silver medal at the Winter Olympics in Oslo,

Norway. In 1953 she not only won the U.S. and North American titles, but also became the first American woman to win a world figure skating championship.

After settling for a silver medal at the world championships in 1954, Albright came back to record another triple the following year, winning the U.S., North American, and world championships. That accomplishment was made even more impressive by the fact that she was a full-time student at Radcliffe College, majoring in premed.

In 1956 Albright capped a brilliant career by winning a gold medal at the Winter Olympics in Cortina d'Ampezzo, Italy. Less than two weeks earlier she had been injured while practicing; she was forced to compete in the Olympics with a substantial cut on her ankle. If it bothered her, she didn't let on. Albright skated wonderfully and was rated first by 10 of 11 judges. Later that month, at the world championships, she finished second to her 16-year-old teammate

and archrival, Carol Heiss. But in their final meeting, at the U.S. championships, it was Albright who finished first.

At the conclusion of the 1956 season, Albright retired from competitive figure skating to concentrate full-time on her studies. She was an outstanding scholar as well as an athlete, as demonstrated by her ability to graduate from Harvard Medical School at the age of 24. Not surprisingly, Dr. Albright chose sports medicine as her specialty. She became a general surgeon at Boston Deaconess Hospital and is the founder of Sports Medicine Resource, Inc., in Brookline, Massachusetts. In 1976 she was chief physician for the U.S. Winter Olympic team. That same year she was presented with the Golden Plate Award by the American Academy of Achievement. In 1983 she was inducted into the International Women's Sports Hall of Fame.

Today, Albright lives near Boston with her husband, Gerald Blakeley, and their three children.

Accomplishments

First place, U.S. championships: 1952, 1956
First place, world championships: 1953, 1955
First place, North American championships: 1953, 1955
Olympic gold medalist: 1956
Inducted into International Women's Sports Hall of Fame: 1983

Amy Alcott

Born February 22, 1956

Amy Alcott, who was born in Kansas City, Missouri, became one of the most successful players on the Ladies Professional Golf Association circuit. But her introduction to the sport was somewhat unusual. When Alcott was a child she loved to watch television on Saturday mornings. An instructional golf program followed her favorite cartoons, and she often continued to tune in. She was fascinated enough to express an interest in learning to play the game and ambitious enough to take matters into her own hands.

Alcott was not born into the privileged world of country clubs and caddies. Instead, she dug holes in her backyard, inserting empty tin cans in the holes and setting up her own private course. To practice, she used her mother's old clubs, which had been gathering cobwebs in the garage.

"I guess I had it tougher than the kids who grew up around country clubs," Alcott said. "But I had something more important. I had desire."

Alcott won the United States Golf Association's Junior Girls title in 1973, at the age of 17. She turned professional two years later. Her first victory came at the Orange Blossom Classic in Miami, one day after her 19th birthday. Since then she has been one of the biggest winners on the LPGA tour. From 1975 through 1986, she won at least one tournament each year, tying JoAnne Carner's record; she has never failed to finish in the top 10 of at least one tournament. For nine consecutive years, from 1978 through 1986, she was among the top 10 money winners on the tour and in 1980 was *Golf* magazine's Player of the Year.

In 1983 Alcott became the sixth LPGA player to crack the $1 million mark in career earnings. In 1979, 1980, and 1984 she won at least four tournaments in one season. Her most successful season was in 1988, when she accumulated more than $292,000 in earnings and won the Nabisco Dinah Shore title. It was her second Dinah Shore victory—she had also won in 1983. In 1991 she added a third. Alcott's other major LPGA victories came at the 1979 Peter Jackson Classic and the 1980 U.S. Women's Open.

Alcott has also been honored for her work off the golf course. In 1986 she was awarded the Founders Cup, which recognizes altruistic contributions to the betterment of society by an LPGA member. In 1984 Alcott, who runs her own tournament to benefit multiple sclerosis research, won the LPGA Good Samaritan Award and the National Multiple Sclerosis Achievement Award. She is on the advisory board of the Women's Sports Foundation and has donated $50,000 to the Women's Athletic Department at UCLA to establish golf scholarships.

Accomplishments

Nabisco Dinah Shore champion: 1983, 1988, 1991
Peter Jackson Classic champion: 1979
U.S. Women's Open champion: 1980
U.S. Junior Girls champion: 1973

Constance Applebee

June 4, 1873—January 26, 1981

Constance Mary Katherine Applebee introduced the sport of field hockey to the United States at the turn of the century. Born at Chigwall, Essex, England, she spent most of her childhood in Devonshire. A somewhat fragile girl, she developed an interest in physical education, thinking that it might improve her health. While studying at the British College of Physical Education, Applebee became intrigued by the subject of anthropometry—the study of human body measurements. She later took a course on the subject at Harvard University in Cambridge, Massachusetts. One day in class, talk turned to women's exercise. Such sedentary and frivolous activities as musical chairs and drop-the-handkerchief were mentioned. "We play those games at parties," Applebee said. "For exercise we play hockey."

Her American classmates knew nothing about the game, so Applebee demonstrated. On a summer day in 1901, she borrowed men's ice hockey sticks and a baseball, and introduced the sport of field hockey to a group of Harvard students. Her simple demonstration was a major step forward in women's athletics in the United States.

At the time, women interested in sports had few options. They played croquet or lawn tennis, which was nothing like the rigorous tennis of today. Competitive sports were solely for men. Proper American women did their best to avoid sweating. But at Harvard, Applebee met Harriet Ballantine, director of physical education at Vassar College. Ballantine asked Applebee to teach the new game to some of her students. For the next three years Applebee traveled the United States to conduct clinics and seminars in field hockey. In 1903 she accepted the position of director of outdoor sports at Bryn Mawr College in Pennsylvania. Five years later she founded the school's Department of Health.

Applebee coached field hockey at Bryn Mawr for more than 60 years and became a pioneer in the field of women's health and fitness. During a discussion with college president M. Carey Thomas, Applebee said, "You want all these students to go out and do something in the world, to get the vote. What's the good of their having the vote if they're too ill to use it?"

Applebee's influence on field hockey was felt well beyond Bryn Mawr. In 1922 she and 12 other women founded the U.S. Field Hockey Association. Each year she ran a children's field hockey camp in the Pocono Mountains, hoping to foster a new generation of aficionados; frequently, she enlisted the assistance of her British friends, who were happy to share their expertise.

In 1980 the Association of Intercollegiate Athletics for Women presented Applebee with its Award of Merit for giving "depth and value to participation in sport." She was inducted into the International Women's Sports Hall of Fame in 1991.

Accomplishments

Introduced field hockey to the United States: 1901
Founding member of the U.S. Field Hockey Association: 1922
Presented with AIAW Award of Merit: 1980
Inducted into International Women's Sports Hall of Fame: 1991

Debbie Armstrong

Born December 6, 1963

Skier Debbie Armstrong, a surprise gold medalist in the giant slalom at the 1984 Winter Olympics, was born in Salem, Oregon. The popular, charismatic daughter of a Seattle psychologist, she was a natural athlete who first tried on a pair of skis when she was a toddler and took her first trip down the slopes when she was just three years old. As a teenager she was one of the best junior skiers in the country, although she refused to concentrate exclusively on that sport.

There was, after all, soccer in the fall and basketball in the winter—Debbie played both in high school.

But after she graduated, Armstrong turned her full attention to skiing, and it wasn't long before she was one of the best racers in the nation. Unfortunately, it also wasn't long before she began to have trouble staying healthy. In 1980 she earned a spot on the U.S. national team, but a broken leg prevented her from competing. Through rehabilitation she eventually regained her status as an elite skier, managing a

second-place finish in the alpine combined at the 1983 U.S. national championships and a third-place finish in the Super G (supergiant slalom) in the 1984 World Cup event.

Nothing prepared the skiing community for what Armstrong accomplished in Sarajevo on February 13, 1984. Only 20 years old, with a résumé that could only charitably be called "modest," she stunned many of the finest skiers in the world. In the first of two runs down the giant slalom course, Armstrong had the second fastest time, a scant one-tenth of a second behind teammate Christin Cooper. Cooper recalled being appropriately nervous about the whole experience but was struck by Armstrong's effervescence. "She kept telling me to have a

good time," Cooper said. "She would say, 'I'm just going to have fun out there.'"

And she did. Although her second run was slower than her first, Armstrong held on to win the gold medal. Cooper was the silver medalist, and another American, Tamara McKinney, was fourth, just .43 seconds behind bronze medalist Perrine Pelen of France.

"About halfway through her second run, we knew that unless she fell down onto her behind Debbie would win," said Harald Schoenhaar, alpine director of the U.S. Ski Coaches Association. "And everyone was numb for a brief period, maybe a couple of minutes. Happy, yes, of course, but also kind of not believing it."

Armstrong never recaptured the form that she had displayed that magical day in Sarajevo. In 1985 she finished 20th in the World Cup standings, and in January 1986 she seriously injured her left knee during a practice run. "The crummy part was that I was in the best shape of my life," she said. "I really was ready."

Armstrong won the giant slalom at the national championships in 1987 and qualified for the U.S. Olympic team in 1988. After failing to win a medal, she retired from competitive skiing and turned to coaching. She later resumed her studies at the University of New Mexico.

Accomplishments

Silver medalist, combined, U.S. nationals:
  1983
Olympic gold medalist, giant slalom: 1984
Inducted into U.S. National Ski Hall of Fame:
  1984
U.S. national champion, giant slalom: 1987

Evelyn Ashford

Born April 15, 1957

Evelyn Ashford, one of the greatest track-and-field athletes the United States has ever produced, was born in Shreveport, Louisiana. She first came into prominence as a sprinter during her freshman year at UCLA in 1976. She made the U.S. Olympic team that year, and in the first of her four Olympic appearances, she finished fifth in the 100 meters at Montreal. Among the women she defeated in the Olympic final was Marlies Gohr of East Germany, with whom Ashford would have a long and heated rivalry.

The U.S.-led boycott of the 1980 Olympic Games in Moscow robbed Ashford of what might have been her finest international performance. She was 22 years old that year, and perhaps the best sprinter in the world. Still, she came back strong after that disappointment, winning the 100- and 200-meter competition at the World Cup in 1981. Two years later, at the inaugural International Amateur Athletic Federation World Championships, Ashford was favored to win a pair of gold medals. But in the 100, she pulled a hamstring and failed to finish the final, which was won by Gohr; she later withdrew from the 200.

At the 1984 Summer Olympics in Los Angeles, Ashford won two gold medals. In the 100 she set an Olympic record (10.97 seconds), and in the 4 x 100 relay she anchored the U.S. team to victory. But there was a hollowness to the victories because they had come against lesser competition. East Germany had joined a Soviet-led boycott of the Los Angeles Games, thus preventing Ashford from again competing against Gohr. Their rivalry was renewed, however, shortly after the Olympics, when they raced at a meet in Zurich. There, Ashford broke her own world record with a time of 10.76.

Ashford took a year off after the Olympics so that she could begin raising a family. On May 30, 1985, she and her husband, Ray Washington, who was a basketball coach at Mount San Jacinto College, became the parents of a baby girl, Raina Ashley. By 1986, Evelyn was fit and ready to resume competition. She defeated East Germany's sensational young sprinter and long jumper, Heike Drechsler, at the Goodwill Games; later, she turned in the year's fastest time, 10.88, in beating Gohr. By year's end she was, for the fourth time, the world's top-ranked sprinter. Still, she was approaching her 30th birthday, and there was speculation that she might retire. Rumors to that effect, however, were squelched.

"Oh, no," Ashford said. "I'm going to run until these legs fall off."

In the summer of 1988, Ashford's title as World's Fastest Woman was taken over by teammate Florence Griffith Joyner, who won the 100 meters at the Seoul Olympics with a time of

10.54. Ashford settled for the silver at 10.83. "Her time was phenomenal, but records are made to be broken," Ashford said. "She's been chasing my records for more than four years now." Ashford later brought the crowd at the Seoul Olympic Stadium to its feet with a stirring performance in the 4 x 100 relay. Running anchor, she took the baton from Griffith Joyner and led the United States to a gold medal. In 1992, at the age of 35, Ashford added a final Olympic medal to her trophy case, helping the United States take the gold in the 4 x 100 relay at the Barcelona Games.

In addition to her achievements on the track, Ashford has worked as a television reporter and served as co-chairperson of Athletes for Literacy.

Accomplishments

Olympic gold medalist, 100 meters: 1984
Olympic gold medalist, 4 x 100 relay: 1984, 1988, 1992
Olympic silver medalist, 100 meters: 1988

Juliette Atkinson
April 15, 1873–January 12, 1944

Juliette Atkinson, one of the most important players in women's tennis during the latter part of the 19th century, was born in Rahway, New Jersey. The daughter of physician Jerome Gill Atkinson and Kate McDonald, she was a diminutive woman (just 5 feet tall) whose size belied her gift for athletics. She excelled at swimming, bowling, golf, cycling, and basketball. But it was in tennis that she made her mark.

Juliette and her younger sister, Kathleen, were self-taught players who honed their games on the public courts of Fort Greene Park in Brooklyn. Juliette won her first public tournament, a local handicap event, in 1893. The following year she entered the national championships at Philadelphia, and came away with titles in women's doubles and mixed doubles. She lost the singles final after coming within a point of victory.

In 1895 Atkinson returned to the national tournament. Her strength and confidence carried her to a second consecutive doubles title and to her first singles title. At that time the defending champion was required to play only one match—against the winner of the singles tournament. Atkinson defeated Bessie Moore in the final of the singles tournament, and then knocked off Helena Hellwig, her doubles partner, in the challenge round. The next year, playing with a badly sprained ankle (the result of an equestrian accident), Atkinson lost her title to Moore. From that point on, Atkinson wore leather shoes adorned with tiny spikes, rather than the traditional canvas sneakers.

Atkinson recaptured her national title in 1897 with a five-set victory over Moore. The next year, she achieved another five-set triumph, this time over Marion Jones Farquhar of California. In both 1897 and 1898 Atkinson teamed with her sister to win the U.S. women's doubles title. In 1898 Atkinson was named North American Athlete of the Year by the Citizens Savings Bank Hall Board of Brooklyn. She did not compete in the national championships again until 1901. That year and the next she won the women's doubles title and lost in the semifinals of the singles competition.

Men's tennis star Fred B. Alexander said that Atkinson was "probably the first girl able to volley successfully. She was also able to do a good job of smashing lobs. Her ground strokes were not severe, but were well placed. Her disposition was beyond criticism. In her day I think that she was undoubtedly the brainiest tennis player in the United States."

Atkinson married George B. Buxton in 1918. She died on January 12, 1944, at her home in Lawrenceville, Illinois, after a severe bout with influenza. She was inducted into the International Tennis Hall of Fame in 1974.

Accomplishments

U.S. singles champion: 1895, 1897–1898
U.S. doubles champion: 1894–1898, 1901–1902
Inducted into International Tennis Hall of Fame: 1974

Tracy Austin

Born December 12, 1962

The youngest woman ever to win the U.S. Open, Tracy Austin was a tennis prodigy whose brilliant career was cut short by a series of nagging injuries. Born in Palos Verdes, California, she was the youngest of five children, three of whom became professional tennis players. Her sister, Pam, played on the women's circuit; brother John played on the men's tour; brothers Jeff and Doug played in college.

In 1980 Tracy and John became the first brother-and-sister team to win the mixed doubles title at Wimbledon. Their interest and proficiency in tennis can be attributed to their mother, Jeanne Austin, who was a ranked player in California. Their father was a nuclear physicist.

Tracy was just two years old when a tennis racket was first placed in her hand. At four she was receiving instruction from noted teaching professional Vic Braden at the Jack Kramer Tennis Club in Rolling Hills Estates. Later she worked with Robert Lansdorp. Both men saw in Tracy a potential champion. She was talented, determined, and focused. She hated to lose—and rarely did.

"The only person I've seen who has come close to my determination was Tracy," said Chris

Evert, one of the game's greatest players. "She was tough. I could see it in her eyes."

Martina Navratilova put it another way—"One cannot think of Tracy as a child. If you do, she will beat you."

Indeed, Austin won 25 national junior titles. She was just 14 when she recorded her first professional victory, at the Avon Futures of Portland in 1977. That same year she faced Evert in the second round at Wimbledon. Austin, in pigtails and braces, charmed the Centre Court crowd. The spectators did not realize that Evert had taken Austin aside in the locker room before their match and taught her how to properly curtsy in front of the Royal Box, a Wimbledon tradition. Despite the final score, 6–1, 6–1, it was a difficult victory for Evert, who felt she was in a no-win situation—beat a child or lose to a child.

As Navratilova had pointed out, Austin did not play like a child. That same year she reached the quarterfinals of the U.S. Open; in 1979, at age 16, she defeated Evert, 6–4, 6–3, to become the youngest player ever to win the U.S. Open. The tennis world was stunned by Austin's success, but she took it in stride. "I can still remember driving to the Open from Long Island for the final against Chris," she said later in an interview. "I was with my family and I was so relaxed. I didn't know how important the Open was."

Austin finished 1979 as the No. 3–ranked player in the world. The following year she went over the $1 million mark in career earnings and was named Sportswoman of the Year by the Women's Sports Foundation. She was 17 years old and had everything. Or so it seemed. In late 1980 she began suffering from back pain and was forced to take eight months off. She came back to win the U.S. Open in 1981, defeating Navratilova in the final, but less than a year later the back problems recurred, and she was forced to the sidelines again. This time, however, she never really recovered. There were several attempts, but the back and neck pain frequently resurfaced, forcing Austin to take time off. In 1989 she was involved in an automobile accident that left her with a broken leg. Although she has played team tennis and appeared in numerous tournaments over the years, she has not won an event on the women's tour since 1982. Essentially, she retired at the age of 19.

Today, Austin works as a television commentator and motivational speaker and also donates considerable time and energy to charitable organizations. Her autobiography, *Beyond Center Court*, was published in 1992. That same year she became the youngest player inducted into the International Tennis Hall of Fame.

Accomplishments

Youngest U.S. Open champion in history: 1979
U.S. Open champion: 1979, 1981
Wimbledon semifinalist: 1979–1980
Winner of 25 national junior titles
Inducted into International Tennis Hall of Fame: 1992

B

Shirley Babashoff

Born January 31, 1957

Shirley Babashoff, who won eight Olympic medals in swimming, was born in Whittier, California. Though she never won an individual gold medal, she is one of the most successful athletes in U.S. Olympic history.

Babashoff grew up in a family devoted to swimming. Her father, Jack, a machinist at a steel plant in Vernon, California, took on second jobs to provide his kids with some of the finer things in life—like swimming lessons. Vera Babashoff, Shirley's mother, handled the family finances; she watched every penny so that there would be enough to ensure first-class instruction for her talented brood. Indeed, there was no shortage of athletic ability in the family. Jack Jr. went on to be a silver medalist in the 100-meter freestyle at the Montreal Olympics; Billy Babashoff swam collegiately at UCLA; Shirley's younger sister, Debbie, became national champion in the 1,500 freestyle in 1989.

But the best swimmer in the family was Shirley. During the first half of the 1970s she was the most dominant swimmer in the United States and one of the best in the world, winning 27 Amateur Athletic Union titles. In 1975 she won gold medals in the 200- and 400-meter freestyle at the world championships. In 1972, at the Summer Games in Munich, West Germany, at the age of 15, she won silver medals in the 100- and 200-meter freestyle, and a gold medal in the 4 x 100 freestyle relay.

Four years later, 19-year-old Babashoff won five medals at the Montreal Olympics. She helped lead the United States to gold medals in the 4 x 100 freestyle relay and 4 x 100 medley relay. She also won silver medals in the 200-meter freestyle, 4 x 100 freestyle relay, and 800-meter freestyle. In each event, Babashoff was beaten by an East German swimmer. It was a frustrating experience for her. Like many athletes from the West, Babashoff suspected the East Germans of using steroids to gain an unfair advantage. None of the East Germans had tested positive; however, in 1991, after the Berlin Wall came down, several prominent East German coaches went public with statements supporting Babashoff's contention. They said doping was common among East German athletes in the 1970s. Babashoff's response was straightforward and simple—"What is the statute of limitations on cheating?"

After the 1976 Summer Games, Babashoff entered UCLA. She competed on the swimming team, but found that her heart was no longer in the sport. After one year, she left school. She then accepted a personal services contract with a swimsuit company. She later became a swimming instructor and a mail carrier for the U.S. Postal Service. She is a member of the U.S. Olympic Hall of Fame.

Accomplishments

Olympic gold medalist, 4 x 100 freestyle relay:
  1972, 1976
Olympic silver medalist, 100-meter freestyle:
  1972
Olympic silver medalist, 200-meter freestyle:
  1972, 1976
Olympic silver medalist, 400-meter freestyle:
  1976
Olympic silver medalist, 800-meter freestyle:
  1976
Olympic silver medalist, 4 x 100 medley relay:
  1976
Inducted into U.S. Olympic Hall of Fame: 1987

Oksana Baiul

Born November 16, 1977

Born in Dnepropetrovsk, Ukraine, Oksana Baiul overcame a tragic childhood to become one of the youngest gold medalists in the history of Olympic figure skating. Her parents separated when she was a toddler; she never really knew her father. Her grandmother, who had helped raise her, and to whom she felt close, died when Baiul was eight. Five years later, she watched her mother, Marina, a French teacher, wither and die of ovarian cancer.

During those years her grandfather, who had bought Baiul her first pair of skates when she was just three years old, also died. And when she was 14 she lost a friend and mentor, Stanislav Korytek, her first coach. They had worked

Momorable Moment: August 6, 1926

Gertrude Ederle Swims the English Channel

In 1925, when Gertrude Ederle announced her intention to become the first woman to swim the English Channel, the public response was hardly supportive. The *London Daily News* had this to say: "Even the most uncompromising champion of the rights and capacities  of women must admit that in contests of physical skill, speed, and endurance, they must remain forever the weaker sex."

The concern was understandable though misguided. Harsh currents and cold temperatures made swimming the Channel a particularly difficult and dangerous stunt—for men and women. But Ederle, who had been an Olympic gold medalist in 1924, paid no attention. After failing on her first attempt to swim the Channel in 1925, she continued to train in preparation for what she believed would be a landmark event. Early on the morning of August 6, 1926, she stepped into the water off the coast of France. Fourteen hours and 31 minutes later, she completed her journey.

Ederle instantly became an international hero. Not only was she the first woman to successfully swim the English Channel, but her time was the fastest in history—faster, even, than any man had achieved. It was a spectacular effort, especially because she had survived a storm that dragged her off course, which tacked on an additional 14 miles to the 21-mile route.

Weaker sex, indeed!

Ederle's time was broken by a man later that year, but it remained the women's standard for nearly four decades.

together for nine years, until she was on the cusp of greatness. Then, suddenly, he left the Ukraine for a better opportunity in Canada. She was alone again.

Through all this adversity, Baiul endured. She was taken in by Galina Zmievskaya, who had coached, among others, a future world champion named Viktor Petrenko. Baiul moved to Odessa and became part of the Zmievskaya family. She took comfort in having a secure home and began to spread her wings. In 1993, at age 15, she became an international star, taking first place at Skate America, the Ukrainian nationals, and, most surprisingly, the world championships. In a matter of months she had stepped out of the shadows and into the spotlight.

At the 1994 Winter Games, however, Baiul's story was lost amid the controversy surrounding Americans Nancy Kerrigan and Tonya Harding. Several weeks before the Olympics began, Harding had been implicated in an attack that left Kerrigan with a badly bruised knee, but through some clever legal maneuvering she won the right to compete in Lillehammer, Norway. Their tabloid showdown was the highest-rated sporting event in television history. But it was Baiul who stole the show. The 5-foot 4-inch, 103-pound skater turned in a mesmerizing performance. She was graceful, charming, and flawless, which ultimately helped her overcome the tidal wave of sympathy for Kerrigan. Baiul won the gold medal by one-tenth of a point over Kerrigan, the smallest margin possible, becoming the youngest woman to win an Olympic gold medal in figure skating since Sonja Henie more than six decades earlier. Her victory was nothing less than a triumph of the spirit.

Baiul skipped the world championships in 1994, but emerged later in the year to participate in a made-for-TV event known as *Ice Wars—the USA vs. the World*. She also skated with Petrenko in a production of *The Nutcracker* on ice. Wherever she went, she captivated audiences not only with her skating, but with her wide smile and a natural flair for the dramatic. Observers noted that she resonated happiness when performing on the ice.

"I like when people are watching," Baiul once said. "What's the reason for figure skating without spectators?"

Accomplishments

World champion: 1993
First place, Skate America: 1993
First place, Ukrainian nationals: 1993
Olympic gold medalist: 1994

Iolanda Balas

Born December 12, 1936

Iolanda Balas, a two-time Olympic gold medalist in high jumping, was born in Timisoara, Romania. Tall and lean, even as a child, Balas seemed ideally suited to the sport that would one day make her famous. But she was so tall (6 feet 1 inch) that she was actually at something of a disadvantage. Balas competed in the 1950s and 1960s, long before the advent of the Fosbury flop, a move that proved advantageous to tall athletes. Because of her unusually long legs, however, Balas had difficulty mastering the high-jumping techniques that were popular in her day—the straddle and western roll. Instead, she was forced to adapt a modified form of the outdated scissors.

That considered, Balas' accomplishments were particularly impressive. She was the first woman ever to clear 6 feet in competition. And before her long and illustrious career was over, she had soared over that height more than 50 times. Before any other woman could clear the 6-foot height even once, Balas had cleared it 46 times. She shattered the world record 14 times. Balas' first world-record performance came in July 1956, when she cleared 5 feet, 8¾ inches. In December of that year she competed in her first Olympiad, in Melbourne, Australia. As the world record holder, she was considered one of the favorites. But her youth and inexperience took their toll, as she fell three inches short of her record and finished fifth.

But that loss apparently served only to motivate Balas, for over the next decade she put together one of the most remarkable winning streaks in all of sports—140 consecutive meets without a defeat.

At the 1960 Summer Olympics in Rome she easily won the gold medal with an Olympic-record leap of 6 feet, ¾ inch; her closest competitor was more than 5 inches behind. Balas won the European championship in 1962; in 1964 she again won an Olympic gold medal, setting a new Olympic record with a jump of 6 feet, 2¾ inches. As in Rome, no one came close to challenging her at the Tokyo Games—her margin of victory was more than 3 inches.

Another indication of Balas' dominance of her sport is the fact that she set her final world record—6 feet, 3¼ inches—in 1961. At the time, her record was 7 centimeters above any height cleared by her competitors. Balas' record stood for nearly 10 years, finally falling in 1971, when Austria's Ilona Gusenbauer added a mere centimeter to the world record.

Injuries brought Balas' incredible career to an end in 1966. The following year she married her coach, Ion Soeter.

Accomplishments

Olympic gold medalist, high jump: 1964, 1968
European champion, high jump: 1958, 1962
First woman to clear 6 feet in the high jump
Won 140 consecutive high-jump competitions

Ann Bancroft

Born 1955

Ann Bancroft, the first woman to reach the North Pole by dogsled, grew up in rural Minnesota. She learned at an early age to appreciate the outdoors, and to embrace rugged individualism and the frontier spirit. In the fourth grade she started camping outdoors alone in the middle of winter. With the help of her older brother, a mountain climber, she learned in the seventh grade how to rappel off frozen waterfalls. She was a fearless child whose parents instilled in her the strength and desire to take risks—her father was a photographer who spent time in Central America, chronicling war atrocities; her mother was a social activist who spent time in jail for her protests.

It was no surprise, then, that Ann grew to be a passionate young woman who wanted to live life to its fullest. She did that through her job as a teacher and through her outdoor activities. She climbed Mount McKinley in 1983. In July

1985, when she was offered a chance to join the Steger International North Pole Expedition—a dogsled expedition to the North Pole—she was faced with the challenge of her life. She decided to quit her job and devote all of her energy to the project.

That fall she and the seven other members of the expedition began training in Ely, Minnesota. They camped for days in the woods, without running water or electricity, and worked out on dogsleds. On March 8, 1986, the team set out from Canada's Ellesmere Island. With five loaded sleds and a team of 49 dogs, they hoped to complete the first confirmed dogsled trek to the North Pole without adding new supplies along the way.

Bancroft knew the trip would be difficult, but it surpassed all of her expectations. For the first two weeks the group covered only about two miles a day. The temperature routinely hovered around 70 degrees below zero. As physically challenging as the expedition was, it was even more grueling from an emotional and mental standpoint. Members of the team slept in two tents, so privacy was nonexistent.

"We'd cook in the tent, change in it, sleep in it, eat in it, and because of the freezing temperatures outside, even go to the bathroom in it," Bancroft wrote when she returned. "In this regard, my being a woman wasn't an issue. We were definitely asexual up there."

In her heart, though, she knew that gender was an issue, albeit an unspoken one. She felt compelled not merely to carry her share of the workload, but to actually do a bit more than the men on the expedition, just so that no one could accuse her of being the weak link. By the end of the 55-day trip, no one questioned her courage or determination. She had proven herself beyond all doubt. On May 1, six members of the original expedition reached the North Pole; two others had been forced to abandon the quest, one because of broken ribs, the other because of frostbite.

Ann Bancroft, however, had endured.

Accomplishments

Climbed Mount McKinley: 1983
First woman to reach the North Pole by dogsled: 1986

Maud Barger-Wallach

June 15, 1870–April 2, 1954

One of the oldest players ever to win the U.S. Open tennis championship, Maud Barger-Wallach came to the game relatively late in life. Born in New York, she spent the summers with her family in Newport, Rhode Island, when—among the tennis aficionados who populated the resort community—she became interested in the sport. Barger-Wallach was approaching her 30th birthday; that she was capable of competing on a world-class level just a few years later is testament to her natural skill and competitive desire. Once she began playing, there was no stopping her.

She reached her first singles final at the U.S. championships in 1906, losing to Helen Homans in straight sets, 6–4, 6–3. But that was no embarrassment—Barger-Wallach was already 36 years old, and while she was, comparatively speaking, a neophyte, she was well past her physical prime. Then as now, women's tennis at its highest levels was a game dominated by youngsters.

Barger-Wallach was hardly discouraged by the setback. Two years later, at the 1908 U.S. championships, she became the oldest singles titlist in the tournament's history. Barger-Wallach defeated Marie Wagner, 4–6, 6–1, 6–3, in the all-comers final, then stunned defending champion Evelyn Sears, 6–3, 1–6, 6–3, in the challenge round. She was 38 years old; not until Molla Mallory's remarkable championship run in 1926, at the age of 42, did Barger-Wallach relinquish her record.

In 1909 Barger-Wallach was no match for Hazel Hotchkiss Wightman, who rolled through the all-comers tournament, then dispatched the defending champion with ease, 6–1, 6–0. If that match should have indicated to Barger-Wallach that it was time to consider retirement, she didn't pay attention. Instead, she continued to excel. In 1915 she was the fifth-ranked female player in the country. In 1916, at the age of 46, she made one final run at a national title, advancing to the quarterfinals of the U.S. championships before losing to Louise Raymond, the eventual winner. No player that age had ever advanced to the quarterfinals before, and no one has matched that feat since. Barger-Wallach was also a respectable doubles player. Though she never won a national title, she did team up with Mrs. Frederick Schmitz to reach the final of the U.S. championships in 1912. Barger-Wallach and Schmitz lost in three sets to Dorothy Green and Mary Browne.

Despite her late entry into the world of tennis, Barger-Wallach enjoyed a successful career that spanned nearly two decades. As she once said, "Mine was not a great career, but a long and happy one."

Barger-Wallach died in Baltimore at the age of 83. She was inducted into the International Tennis Hall of Fame in Newport in 1958.

Accomplishments

U.S. singles champion: 1908
U.S. singles runner-up: 1906, 1909
U.S. doubles runner-up: 1912
Inducted into International Tennis Hall of Fame: 1958

Laura Baugh

Born May 31, 1955

In the early 1970s Laura Baugh used her charm and talent to become one of the top performers on the Ladies Professional Golf Association tour; however, she failed to realize the enormous potential that she had displayed as an adolsecent. Taking instruction from her father, Baugh learned to play as a child and eventually became one of the top junior players in the world. But the most important period in her development came when she was 12 years old. It was then that her parents divorced. She and her mother moved from their home in Gainesville, Florida, to California. The trauma of that event galvanized Baugh. She worked harder than ever to become a good golfer and spent nearly all of her free time practicing. It was, she later acknowledged, emotional and physical therapy, a way to deal with the scars of divorce and the pain of loneliness.

Baugh graduated from school a semester ahead of time and immediately turned profes-sional. At the time, she had already captured the U.S. Women's Amateur Championship, and she wanted nothing so much as independence.

"I was really anxious to earn my own living," she said. "I don't want to owe anyone anything. I think that a woman should have some skill of her own, and not just be dependent."

Baugh's girlish features and well-scrubbed looks belied an intensity that made her one of the best young players in the game. In her professional debut in 1973, she tied for second in the Lady Tara Tournament in Atlanta. Baugh led for much of the tournament but lost by a single stroke; it was a stunning performance for one so young—she was only 17—and it put her on the fast track to success. In short order Baugh became one of the hottest players on the tour, winning LPGA Rookie of the Year honors; several endorsement deals helped her achieve the financial security she had sought. A charming young woman, Baugh was a favorite with fans and advertisers. She was named *Golf Digest*'s Most Beautiful Golfer in 1972; the *Los Angeles Times* named her Woman of the Year.

For much of the next decade Baugh was a steady but unspectacular performer on the LPGA tour. She was runner-up in several tournaments, but never did claim a victory. In 1982 she and husband Bobby Cole, a professional golfer, welcomed a baby girl into their lives. Baugh returned to the tour in 1983 and played reasonably well over the next five years; however, in 1988 she gave birth to a second child and again sat out the year. After the birth of each of her six children, Baugh eventually returned to competition. She had her best financial season in 1991, when she had six top-20 finishes and won more than $70,000 in prize money.

Accomplishments

U.S. Women's Amateur champion: 1971
Southern Amateur champion: 1970–1971
Member of U.S. Curtis Cup and World Cup teams: 1972
Named *Los Angeles Times* Woman of the Year: 1971
LPGA Rookie of the Year: 1973

Patty Berg

Born February 13, 1918

A charter member of the Ladies Professional Golf Association and one of the most important athletes the sport has known, Patricia Jane Berg was born and raised in Minneapolis, Minnesota. On the golf course Berg was her own toughest critic. If she missed a putt or hooked a tee-shot, she could be overheard saying, "Patty, you bum." Berg, with 57 LPGA tournament victories, was one of the greatest golfers in history.

She was a natural athlete and a fierce competitor, as evidenced not only by several outstanding performances as a high school track-and-field star—or even by a second-place finish at the national girls' speed skating championships when she was 15—but also by her status as quarterback of the 50th Street Tigers, a local boys' football team headed by Berg's brother and Bud Wilkinson, who would later achieve greatness as a player and coach.

Her father bought her a golf membership and a set of secondhand clubs when she was 13. Just three years later, she won the 1934 Minneapolis City Championship. That same year she reached the semifinals of the U.S. Women's Amateur. By the time she was 20 she had won every major amateur title in the United States. Berg turned professional in 1940. She missed 18 months of golf after being involved in a serious automobile accident in 1941, but five years later she became a founding member of the Women's Professional Golf Association, which in 1948 became the LPGA. That year alone, Berg won seven titles.

Berg served as a lieutenant in the Marine Corps during World War II. In 1949 she assumed the newly created role of LPGA president, a position that she held for three years, and in 1951 she became one of four original inductees into the LPGA Hall of Fame. Berg was the LPGA's leading money winner in 1954, 1955, and 1957. Her hole in one at the 1959 U.S. Women's Open at Churchill Valley Country Club in Pittsburgh was the first ever recorded by a woman in a United States Golf Association competition. She was voted Associated Press Athlete of the Year in 1938, 1943, and 1955. In 1978 the LPGA established the Patty Berg Award to be presented to a person for outstanding contributions to women's golf.

Berg is considered one of the finest ambassadors the world of golf has ever known. In 1963 she was named the Bob Jones Award winner, given to a person who emulates the sportsmanship of the award's namesake. She is a successful author, having written three books on golf, and in 1976 she became the first woman to receive the Humanitarian Sports Award from the United Cerebral Palsy Foundation.

Berg underwent cancer surgery in 1971, hip surgery in 1980, and back surgery in 1989. But she continued to lead an active life, teaching and promoting the game of golf to women and children. In the summer of 1991, at the age of 73, she recorded a hole in one.

Accomplishments

U.S. Women's Open champion: 1946
Charter member of the LPGA: 1948
One of four original inductees into LPGA Hall of Fame: 1951
LPGA money leader: 1954, 1955, 1957

Pauline Betz

Born August 16, 1919

Pauline Betz, a member of the International Tennis Hall of Fame, was born in Dayton, Ohio. The daughter of Immanuel George Betz and Stella McCandless Betz, she began playing tennis at age nine. The game at first presented no special appeal to Pauline. She played occasionally, without any great zeal. It wasn't until her mother, a high school physical education teacher and national archery champion, began tutoring her that Pauline excelled. She was 14 years old when she started to take the sport seriously, and from then on she improved rapidly.

Betz was an agile young woman who possessed not only the heart of a true competitor, but considerable athletic ability as well. She was one of the quickest players of her time; she often tracked down balls that seemed to be well out of her reach, winning points and surprising and demoralizing her opponents. A trademark of Betz's game was her refusal to give up—on a point, a game, or a match. Because of that competitive fire, she was one of the most popular players of her time. Spectators and competitors alike admired and respected her. They might have felt differently if they could have seen her in private practice sessions, when she sometimes became so angry and frustrated that she would break her racket. Such outbursts, however, were reserved for practice. In public and especially in tournament play, she was a gracious woman, dignified in victory and defeat.

Betz attended Rollins College in Florida on a full athletic scholarship. Until 1943, when she graduated, she played on the men's tennis team. By that time she had already established herself as one of the finest players in the world, having won the U.S. singles championship in 1942. That was the first of three consecutive U.S. titles Betz would win. Her greatest year was 1946, when she won the women's singles titles at the U.S. Open and Wimbledon, and was runner-up at the French Open. Because the ranks of men's tennis—and most other sports—were depleted by World War II, women's tennis enjoyed a surge in popularity in the mid-1940s. At that time, Betz was one of the most successful and famous athletes in the world. Still, she saw little financial reward for her efforts, and in the postwar years the spotlight quickly returned to the men's game.

"In my era we just accepted everything docilely, felt privileged to play, made no money, and didn't care," she once told a reporter. "It was not an age of rebellion."

In 1947, as she was getting ready to defend both her U.S. and Wimbledon titles, Betz was suspended from amateur competition because of her role in helping to form a women's professional tennis tour. She later joined the Kramer tour and conducted public clinics and demonstrations. After retiring from tennis, she married Bob Addie, a sportswriter for the *Washington Post*. Her autobiography, *Wings on My Tennis Shoes*, was published in 1949. In 1965 Pauline Betz Addie was inducted into the International Tennis Hall of Fame.

Accomplishments

> U.S. Open champion: 1942–1944, 1946
> Wimbledon champion: 1946
> Inducted into International Tennis Hall of Fame: 1965

Bonnie Blair

Born March 18, 1963

Bonnie Blair, winner of five Olympic gold medals, is widely regarded as the best female speed skater in history. From the beginning, the sport was in her blood. On the day she was born, her father, a civil engineer from Champaign, Illinois, who had a lifelong love for speed skating, was working as an official at a competition in Yonkers, New York. This was not unusual. Charlie Blair had five children, all but one a competitive skater. As it happened, Eleanor Blair was back in Champaign, about to give birth to Child No. 6; Charlie felt he could make it home in time. He was wrong. In the middle of a race, with Charlie holding a stopwatch, an announcement crackled over the public address system— "Looks like Charlie's family has just added another skater."

Not just another skater. Child No. 6, Bonnie Blair, would become the most successful woman in speed skating. In a sport dominated by athletes in their 20s, she was an anomaly, a 30-something marvel who seemed to grow stronger and more determined with each passing year.

At the 1988 Winter Olympic Games in Calgary, Blair won a gold medal in the 500 meters and a bronze in the 1,000 meters. Her story captured national interest, in part because much was made of the fact that Blair's hometown police department had dubbed her "Champaign's favorite speeder." For the previous six years, the Champaign police department had offered moral and financial support to Blair, writing checks and raising money when local businesses were reluctant to do so.

Following the 1988 Olympics, against the advice of everyone who knew her, Blair, hungry for a new challenge, put away her skates for a while and gave cycling a try. The experiment failed. A short time later she returned to skating, as determined and spirited as ever. By 1992 it was apparent that Blair had lost nothing; if anything, she was more mature, both physically and mentally. At the 1992 Olympic Games in Albertville, France, she finished first in the 500

and 1,000 meters. The latter gold medal she dedicated to her father, who had died in 1989. She was supported in her efforts by the group known as the Blair Bunch, numbering more than 50, which included aunts, uncles, nephews, and cousins, ranging in age from 4 months to 80 years. Each night they sat together in the stands, proudly applauding Champaign's favorite speeder as the world looked on.

Although tempted by retirement, Blair decided to continue training after the Albertville Games. Like many winter athletes, she was motivated by a change in the Olympic calendar—for the first and perhaps only time, the gap between Winter Olympic Games would be only two years. In 1994, she decided to go to Lillehammer, Norway, to again represent the United States—and prove that she was still the fastest woman on ice.

And she did. Despite a controversial split with her longtime coach—Peter Mueller, a former Olympian and the head coach of the U.S. speed skating team—Blair's performance was mesmerizing. Just a few weeks short of her 31st birthday, she won gold medals in the 500 meters and 1,000 meters, as well as the bronze in the 1,500 meters, solidifying her reputation as one of the greatest athletes in Olympic history. She was named Sportswoman of the Year by *Sports Illustrated*, and in both 1994 and 1995 she was named Individual Sportswoman of the Year by the Women's Sports Foundation.

Accomplishments:

- Olympic gold medalist, 500 meters: 1988, 1992, 1994
- Olympic gold medalist, 1,000 meters: 1992, 1994
- Olympic bronze medalist, 1,500 meters: 1994
- Olympic bronze medalist, 1,000 meters: 1988
- Women's Sports Foundation Individual Sportswoman of the Year: 1994, 1995
- *Sports Illustrated* Sportswoman of the Year: 1994

Jane Blalock

Born September 19, 1945

Jane Blalock, one of the most successful golfers in the world during the 1970s and early 1980s, was born in Portsmouth, New Hampshire. The daughter of a newspaper editor, she didn't pick up a club until she was 13 years old, but in 1963, at the age of 17, she won the New Hampshire and New England junior championships, a sure sign that she was destined to make her mark in the sport. For four consecutive years—from 1965 through 1968—she was the New Hampshire Amateur champion; she also won the New England Amateur championship in 1968.

Despite her success, Blalock was not sure that she wanted to devote her life to golf. She attended Rollins College, a prestigious liberal arts school in Winter Park, Florida. After graduating in 1967 with a degree in history and economics, she returned to Portsmouth and took a job as a teacher at her old high school. She continued to play golf, and in the back of her mind she entertained thoughts of one day joining the Ladies Professional Golf Association tour. In 1968, when she finished fifth as an amateur in the LPGA Burdine's event, she began to seriously consider trading the security of a teaching job for the nomadic but exhilarating life of a professional golfer. Blalock finished second in the North-South Classic, and by 1969 she was ready to take the plunge. It seemed to her a logical step—if she was good enough to compete against professionals, she might as well get paid for it.

Blalock's decision turned out to be the right one. She won her first tour event, the Lady Carling, in 1970. The next year she won two tournaments and finished third on the LPGA money list. In 1972 she won five events, including the Colgate Dinah Shore Winner's Circle, and finished second on the money list. But that year also brought distress to Blalock, who was accused by the LPGA of moving her ball to gain a more favorable lie. Blalock was shocked and angry—she had been branded a cheat. Rather than suffer that indignity, she fought back. She sued the LPGA and won $13,000 in damages; the LPGA was also ordered to pay more than $95,000 in legal fees.

"It's only a matter of time before I end up on top," Blalock said at the time. "There's no reason I can't. I'm playing well, I'm happy, and my troubles are all behind me now."

Blalock never did make it to the very top. But she was one of the most consistent and successful players on the tour for more than a decade. Between 1970 and 1985 she won 29 tournaments; from 1971 to 1980 she finished among the top 10 money winners each year and was the first player in LPGA history to win more than $100,000 in each of four consecutive seasons.

Blalock retired from full-time tournament competition in 1986 and founded her own sports consulting firm, the Jane Blalock Company.

Accomplishments

New Hampshire Amateur champion:
  1965–1968
New England Amateur champion: 1968
LPGA Rookie of the Year: 1969
Winner of 29 career LPGA tour events

Theresa Weld Blanchard

August 21, 1893–March 12, 1978

Theresa Weld Blanchard, the first American woman to win a medal at the Winter Olympics, was born in Brookline, Massachusetts, near Boston. Her father, A. Windsor Weld, was a founding member of the Skating Club of Boston, which helped pioneer the smooth, artistic style of figure skating that became popular in international competition.

Tee, as Theresa was often called, began driving her pony cart to the skating rink for lessons when she was 12 years old. She loved practicing the new, freer form of skating. It wasn't as rigid as the traditional English technique, which Theresa and many other skaters found terribly restrictive.

Blanchard began competing in 1914, at age 21, and she quickly established herself as one of the best in the sport. That year she became the first U.S. ladies' champion at New Haven, Connecticut. From 1920 through 1924, she won the title each year. But Blanchard was more than a talented individual performer. She also knew how to work with a partner. She and Nathaniel W. Niles won the waltz event in 1914 and also finished second to Canadians Jeanne Chevalier and Norman Scott in the pairs competition. Blanchard and Niles went on to win nine gold medals in the U.S. pairs competition. They also won the North American title in 1925.

Blanchard was the first American skater to incorporate a series of jumps into her routines. Most skaters of that era attempted nothing more daring than a simple toe hop. But because her style bucked tradition, Blanchard was frequently penalized for being "unladylike."

One of Blanchard's greatest performances came at the 1920 Winter events in Antwerp, Belgium. She skated wonderfully and athletically, and received a raucous ovation from the crowd, which included hundreds of U.S. soldiers stationed in the region. Although Blanchard had to settle for a bronze medal, that was no small accomplishment—no American had ever won a medal of any kind at the Winter Olympics. Blanchard became a regular on the Olympic scene. She represented the United States as a competitor in 1924 and 1928, and later became an official.

Blanchard continued to compete until 1934 and remained a strong advocate for the sport for many years afterward. Her father was the first president of the U.S. Figure Skating Association, and Theresa edited the organization's official publication, *Skating* magazine. Blanchard served as editor until shortly before her death. The magazine remains in circulation today.

Blanchard was also a respected figure skating judge who served on the USFSA executive board for 13 years. She was inducted into the World Figure Skating Hall of Fame in 1976 and the International Women's Sports Hall of Fame in 1989.

Accomplishments

U.S. ladies' champion: 1914, 1920–1924
U.S. pairs champion: 1918, 1920–1927
Olympic bronze medalist: 1920
Inducted into World Figure Skating Hall of
  Fame: 1976
Inducted into International Women's Sports
  Hall of Fame: 1989

Fanny Blankers-Koen

Born April 26, 1918

Francina Blankers-Koen, winner of three Olympic gold medals in track and field, was born in Baarn, Netherlands. Her father enjoyed a moderate degree of success in local track-and-field meets; he specialized in the weight events, primarily shot put and discus. It took Fanny some time to follow her father's lead into the world of track and field, but from the beginning she was a capable athlete. She preferred swimming, both recreationally and competitively, but at age 16, when told by her coach that the Netherlands had an abundance of talented swimmers, she began to explore other sports. Not surprisingly given her family history, she decided to give running a try.

Fanny turned out to be a natural. After only two years of intense training, she qualified for the Dutch Olympic team in 1936. At the Summer Games in Berlin she finished sixth in the high jump and was a member of the Dutch 4 x 100 relay team, which took fifth.

Koen married her track coach, Jan Blankers, shortly after the 1936 Olympics. She continued to train, maturing and improving. But like many other athletes of her time, she was deprived of competing on the world's biggest stage during her prime—World War II wiped out the Olympic Games in 1940 and 1944, when Blankers-Koen was in her 20s.

By the time the Summer Games resumed, in 1948, Blankers-Koen was a 30-year-old mother of two who happened to hold world records in six different events—the 100-meter dash, 80-meter hurdles, long jump, high jump, and two relay events.

It was presumed by most observers that she was too old and too far removed from world-class competition to contend for a gold medal at the Summer Games in London. But Blankers-Koen didn't think so. She trained fiercely in the months leading up to the Olympics, often with her children by her side. In the Netherlands, which had been devastated by five years of Nazi occupation, she became an image of strength and courage that persists to this day.

By the end of the London Games, she was an international star whose popularity transcended the boundaries of sport. For starters, she won the 100-meter dash. Then, in her toughest race, she came from behind to win the 80-meter hurdles, defeating, among others, Great Britain's Maureen Gardner. In a trial heat of the 200, she set an Olympic record but nearly withdrew from the final because of exhaustion. Her husband talked her into continuing, and shortly before the gun went off he reportedly stoked her competitive fires with the following words—"Remember, Fanny, you're too old."

She wasn't, of course. Blankers-Koen went on to win the 200 by a wide margin. At an age when most athletes, especially in track and field, have hung up their spikes, she won three gold medals. Four years later, at the age of 34, she returned to the Summer Olympics. But this time she was unable to overcome the nagging aches and pains that come with being the oldest competitor in the race. In her only event, the 80-meter hurdles, she knocked over the first two barriers and failed to finish. She continued to compete for several more years, often at a world-class level. Blankers-Koen was inducted into the International Women's Sports Hall of Fame in 1982 and now lives a quiet life in the Netherlands.

Accomplishments

Olympic gold medalist, 80-meter hurdles: 1948
Olympic gold medalist, 100 meters: 1948
Olympic gold medalist, 200 meters: 1948
Inducted into International Women's Sports
  Hall of Fame: 1982

Carol Blazejowski

Born September 29, 1956

One of the most prolific scorers in the history of women's college basketball, Carol Blazejowski was born in Elizabeth, New Jersey. Raised in Cranston, New Jersey, she embraced the work ethic demonstrated by her father, Leon, a laborer, and her mother, Grace, who worked at a bank. Neither parent ever pushed Carol to participate in sports, but her father said that he occasionally offered a few words of parental wisdom.

"She played softball before basketball, and all I told her was that whenever the guys call batting practice, she should be the first to grab the bat," Leon Blazejowski said. "If she waits for the rest to show up at practice, she may get only a few licks at the ball and time will run out."

Carol took his advice to heart. When playing pickup basketball games at the playground, she was always the first to arrive. She'd spend hours working on her moves and her shooting, so that when the boys showed up, she'd be ready to play. Of course, for a long time they never wanted her to play. Like many girls attempting to infiltrate a male-dominated world, she was at first shunned. Once given an opportunity, however, she quickly proved that she could play.

"At first I was always the last one chosen," Blazejowski said. "But once I learned the right moves and perfected my one-handed jumper from watching pro basketball on TV, I was accepted. But it wasn't easy."

After graduating from high school, the 5-foot 11-inch Blazejowski decided to stay close to home and attend Montclair State, hardly a national basketball powerhouse. But the lack of competition and name recognition didn't deter Blazejowski. She was a three-time All-American at Montclair State, leading the nation in scoring in 1976–77 (33.5) and 1977–78 (38.6). In her senior year she was one of the most dominant players the game had ever known. She scored more than 40 points in each of her last three games and set a Madison Square Garden record—for male and female college players—by racking up 52 points in a game against Queens College. She led Montclair State to a No. 4 ranking in the Associated Press final women's college basketball poll in 1978 and was the first winner of the Wade Trophy, given annually to the finest women's collegiate player.

In four years Blazejowski scored 3,199 points, but like most female basketball players in the United States in the 1970s, she found few opportunities to ply her trade after graduation. She led the United States to a world championship in 1979 and qualified for the U.S. Olympic team in 1980; unfortunately, because the United States led a boycott of the 1980 Summer Games in Moscow, Blazejowski never had a chance to win an Olympic medal.

She played with an Amateur Athletic Union team in Allentown, Pennsylvania, for two years, and in 1980 she signed a three-year contract (reportedly worth $150,000) to play for the New Jersey Gems in the Women's Basketball League. Blazejowski was the highest-paid player in the league, which went out of business after a single season.

Accomplishments

Leading scorer in college basketball: 1976–77, 1977–78
Wade Trophy winner (Collegiate Player of the Year): 1978
Member of U.S. Olympic team: 1980
Led U.S. to world championship: 1979

Ila Borders

Born February 18, 1975

Ila Borders, the first woman to pitch in a men's college baseball game, grew up in La Mirada, California. She was one of four children born to Phil and Marianne Borders. Phil taught Ila how to throw an overhand pitch when she was just 10 years old. Even then she was breaking down barriers as the only girl on her Little League team.

Borders continued to play with the boys as she got older. And as she progressed, it became clear that she was no mere token. As a senior at Whittier Christian High School in La Mirada, she was named Most Valuable Player on the boys' team, as well as first-team all-league. In four years of varsity baseball she compiled a record of 16–7 with a 2.37 earned run average. There was just one problem—what would Borders do for an encore?

"My ultimate goal," she said, "is to pitch in the major leagues."

To be on the safe side, however, Borders decided to continue her education. She enrolled at Southern California College in Costa Mesa and began working out with the baseball team. Her presence, naturally, created a stir. But, as she had done at every stop along the way, Borders quickly proved that she belonged. "People think I took her for the publicity," coach Charlie Phillips told a reporter. "I don't need the publicity. I took her because she can pitch and she can help this team."

On February 15, 1994, Borders made her first appearance in a Southern California College uniform. It was a historic event, but she took it in stride. She pitched a complete game, picking up the victory and limiting her opponent, Claremont-Mudd, to just five hits in a 12–1 rout. In her second start, a 10–1 victory over Concordia University, she did not give up a single earned run. As had happened on numerous occasions throughout her career, Borders took a fair amount of abuse during those first few games. Early in the game against Concordia, she pitched herself into a jam, loading the bases in the third inning. The Concordia players cursed her mercilessly from their dugout, but Borders simply dug down and worked her way out of the mess.

A 5-foot 10-inch, 160-pound athlete with a variety of pitching weapons (fastball, curveball, split-finger, and screwball), Borders preferred to think of herself simply as a baseball player, not a trailblazer. "I'm not trying to prove anything about women," she said. "This has nothing to do with women's rights. I love the game, nothing else."

Borders finished her freshman season with a record of 2–4 and an ERA of 2.92. She started seven games and pitched 49⅓ innings. She later sent a jersey, hat, glove, and autographed baseball and photograph to Cooperstown, home of the National Baseball Hall of Fame. The items were used in the museum's "Women in Baseball" exhibit.

Accomplishments

First woman to pitch in a men's college baseball game
Included in "Women in Baseball" exhibit at the National Baseball Hall of Fame

Hassiba Boulmerka

Born 1968

Middle-distance runner Hassiba Boulmerka, the first Algerian woman to win a world championship, was raised in Constantine, a small city located more than 300 miles east of Algiers, in the Atlas Mountains. The town was planned and settled by the French; Boulmerka's father spent more than 10 years working in France as a truck driver.

Memorable Moment:
August 1928

The First Olympic Track-and-Field Competition for Women

The Olympic Games of the modern era were inaugurated in Athens, Greece, in 1896. But women did not compete until 1900, and even then their participation was limited to tennis and golf. It wasn't until 1928, in Amsterdam, that women were allowed to compete in the rigorous sport that is most closely identified with the Olympic experience—track and field.

The first women's Olympic track event was the 100 meters. Far from being the purely athletic spectacle that it is today, the first race to determine "the world's fastest woman" was a strange and wonderful event. As David Wallechinsky writes in *The Complete Book of the Summer Olympics*, "The entrants were unusually nervous, as was the primarily male audience. The men found it particularly unsettling when the three Canadian finalists hugged and kissed each other before the race."

In the end, Betty Robinson, a 16-year-old high school student from Riverdale, Illinois, won the first Olympic gold medal in women's track and field. In light of her age and limited experience (the 1928 Summer Olympics represented only the fourth track meet of her career), it was a stunning performance. And one of the most dramatic moments of the Olympiad.

Hassiba benefited from the rugged terrain of her native land—it helped make her strong and fit. She was an active child, with no limit to her energy. All she needed was an outlet. As a teenager, she won a race at her school. That success, coupled with the inability to sit still for any length of time, led her from recreational running to serious training. But as an Arab girl in a country dominated by the Muslim faith, Boulmerka faced great resistance in her bid to become a world-class athlete. She lived in a land where women were expected to be subservient to men; they were not expected to embrace the spirit of competition. At one point there was even a movement in Algeria's parliament to ban female participation in sport. It failed, but the sentiment was felt nonetheless.

Fortunately, Boulmerka's family wanted her to chase her dreams, regardless of public opinion. "My parents supported me all they could, emotionally and financially," she has said.

The first indication of Boulmerka's talent came at the 1988 African Games, where she won both the 800- and 1,500-meter races. But at the Summer Olympics in Seoul, Boulmerka was a disappointment. She failed to get past the first round of either race. Far from being discouraged, she and her coach mapped out a plan that would culminate in her winning an Olympic gold medal in 1992. "You can't be a champion in a week or a year," she said. "You must accept a time of suffering."

Boulmerka's quest for the gold included considerable sacrifice. She left her family and moved to Algiers, where she trained as much as eight hours a day. Her diligence paid off at the 1991 World Track and Field Championships in Tokyo, where she sprinted into the lead on the final turn and held on to win the 1,500 meters with a time of 4:02.24. She beat a talented field that included Olympic 3,000-meter champion Tatyana Samolenko of the Soviet Union. Boulmerka's effort was considered heroic in some circles, embarrassing in others. Because devout Muslim women were supposed to be covered from head to toe in public, she was sharply criticized by Muslims for "running with naked legs in front of thousands of men." She defended herself by arguing that she was a practicing Muslim but also an athlete. And as an athlete, she had to dress appropriately for competition.

In 1992 Boulmerka was one of the brightest stars of the Summer Olympics in Barcelona. She successfully completed her plan of four years earlier by winning the 1,500 meters with a time of 3:55.30. In 1995, at the World Track and Field Championships in Sweden, she again captured the 1,500-meter title.

Accomplishments

World champion, 1,500 meters: 1991, 1995
Olympic gold medalist, 1,500 meters: 1992
First Algerian woman to win a world championship: 1991

Pat Bradley

Born March 24, 1951

Pat Bradley, a member of the Ladies Professional Golf Association Hall of Fame, was born in Westford, Massachusetts, and began playing golf at the age of 11. Her first instructor was John Wirbal, head pro at Nashua Country Club in Nashua, New Hampshire. He taught Bradley the basics, and under his tutelage she began to accept the notion that her athletic future might be on the golf course.

Bradley graduated from Florida International University in 1974. By that time she had compiled an impressive amateur résumé that included victories in the New Hampshire Amateur (1967, 1969) and the New England Amateur (1972, 1973) competitions. She was an NCAA All-American in 1970. Although it took her more than two years to achieve her first professional victory, she made an immediate impact on the LPGA tour. She was strong and blessed with a natural swing, and most observers believed she had the potential to be a great player. She believed it, too.

"When I joined the tour I went right to the sources, right to the great players," Bradley has said. "I didn't hang out with my contemporaries. I wanted to get to know players like Kathy Whitworth, Judy Rankin—the top players. They were winners, and I wanted to see how they operated."

Bradley was a quick study. She won her first tournament, the Girl Talk Classic, in 1976. In the late 1970s she started working with Gail Davis, a former touring pro. Davis turned out to be the perfect teacher for Bradley, who began climbing up the LPGA money list. She finished second in 1978, third in 1981 and 1983, and second in 1985. In 1980 she won the Peter Jackson Classic (later known as the du Maurier Classic), and in 1981 she captured the U.S Women's Open. Bradley's finest year came in 1986, when she won three major titles—the Nabisco Dinah Shore, the LPGA championship, and the du Maurier Classic. Not surprisingly, she was named LPGA Player of the Year.

In 1987 and 1988, Bradley's game was less consistent. She won only one tournament in two years and plummeted from the top of the money list. There was, however, a reason for her slump—she was diagnosed with hyperthyroidism. After receiving treatment, she returned to the tour in 1989 and won the All-Star/Centinela Classic, her first victory in two years. The following year she won three events and finished fifth on the money list, and in 1991 she had one of her best seasons, finishing first on the money list with $763,118. For that comeback performance, the Golf Writers Association of America made Bradley the recipient of its Ben Hogan Award.

"It's a tremendous truth that if you set your mind to something, if the will is there, you will find a way," she has said. "But it's something you have to go through, the trials and tribulations."

Bradley won her 30th title on September 29, 1991, at the MBS Classic and gained induction into the LPGA Hall of Fame. She did not win another tournament until January 24, 1995, when, at age 43, she captured the Health South Inaugural at Daytona Beach, Florida. She has served as honorary director of the Thyroid Foundation of America and was the winner of the LPGA's Samaritan Award in 1992.

Accomplishments

U.S. Women's Open champion: 1981
du Maurier Classic champion: 1980, 1985–1986
Nabisco Dinah Shore champion: 1986
LPGA championship winner: 1986
Inducted into LPGA Hall of Fame: 1991

Lyudmila Bragina

Born July 24, 1943

Middle-distance runner Lyudmila Bragina, an Olympic gold medalist, was born in the city of Sverdlovsk in the Soviet Union. Track-and-field athletes typically develop at a predictable rate. They build strength and stamina over the years, improving steadily as they step up in competition, until, in their late 20s, they hit a peak. With Bragina, however, the change was startling—and quite late. In 1967 her personal best for 1,500 meters was a pedestrian 4:22.2. By 1969 she had lowered that mark to 4:13.2. Two years later she failed to show any marked improvement—her fastest time that season was 4:13.8.

But in 1972, Bragina became a different runner. At the USSR championships on July 18, she shaved 2.7 seconds off the world record for 1,500 meters. Her time of 4:06.9, accomplished in an early-round heat, was nearly seven seconds faster than she had ever run for that distance; so dramatic was her performance that track-and-field fans around the world reacted with disbelief. Not long after that, she made it clear that she was not merely a one-race runner. At the 1972 Summer Games in Munich, the women's 1,500 was contested for the first time in Olympic history. And Bragina was the star.

In a first-round heat she again broke the world record, with a time of 4:06.5. In the semifinals she lowered the record even further, winning her heat in 4:05.1. In the final she completed one of the most dominant performances in Olympic track-and-field history by winning the gold medal in 4:01.4. Over six days she had trimmed more than five seconds off the world record. What made her victory in the final so impressive was the manner in which it was achieved. Bragina, usually a front-runner, laid off the pace for the first half mile, then sprinted to the lead during the final two laps.

Over the next four years, Bragina turned her attention to longer distances. She failed to repeat as a gold medalist in the 1,500 meters in the 1976 Summer Olympics in Montreal; in fact, she could manage only a fifth-place finish, well behind teammate Tatyana Kazankina. But less than a month after the Olympics, the 33-year-old Bragina, in a dual meet between the United States and the Soviet Union, obliterated the record for 3,000 meters. Her winning time of 8:27.1 was an astonishing 18.3 seconds faster than the world record. To put her effort in perspective, it helps to remember that no man ran that fast until 1926.

Accomplishments

Olympic gold medalist, 1,500 meters: 1972
Broke world record for 1,500 meters three times in one Olympiad: 1972
Broke world record for 3,000 meters: 1976
Member of USSR Olympic team: 1972, 1976

Valerie Brisco

Born July 6, 1960

Valerie Brisco, the first athlete to win gold medals in the 200 and 400 meters at a single Olympiad, was born in Greenwood, Mississippi. She was blessed with a strong, muscular body and great natural speed. Those qualities helped

make her an outstanding scholastic runner, despite her reluctance to embrace any real work ethic. As she once told a reporter, "In high school, workouts weren't the thing for me. I'd just jog and go home—that was it."

Talent also carried Brisco to an exceptional college career. As a student at California State University–Northridge, she won the 200 meters at the 1979 Association of Intercollegiate Athletics for Women track-and-field championships. She was a member of the U.S. 4 x 100 relay team that won a gold medal at the Pan American Games.

Brisco's life changed in 1981 when she married professional football player Alvin Hooks, a wide receiver with the Philadelphia Eagles. Within a year their first child, a boy, was born. Motherhood agreed with Brisco, but it took a toll on her body. After giving birth, she was 40 pounds overweight and not the least bit interested in resuming her track career. In fact, she thought her retirement would be permanent. Her husband and Bob Kersee, her coach, convinced her that at 21, she was too young to give up on track and field; she hadn't even scratched the surface.

Kersee compelled Brisco to work hard—perhaps for the first time in her life. She adhered to a grueling workout schedule designed to bring her to a peak performance three years down the road, at the 1984 Summer Olympics in Los Angeles. Brisco didn't complain about the physical discomfort she endured every day. Instead, she concentrated on her goals. She came to understand the brutal nature of her specialty, the 400 meters.

"If you're not ready to take the pain, you won't run it," she said. "Or you'll go slow because you know you're going to 'rig' [as in rigor mortis]."

Endless track sessions, lung-searing interval workouts, two to three hours of weight training every other day, 250 pushups and 1,000 situps every day—Brisco's workouts were grueling. By 1984 she was among the fittest athletes in the world.

In the months leading up to the Olympics, she not only finished first in the 400 meters at the USA/Mobil nationals but also became the first American woman to break 50 seconds. Earlier in the year she had captured the national indoor 200-meter title. She was clearly prepared to launch an assault on the unprecedented 200/400 double at the Los Angeles Games.

At the 1984 Olympics, Brisco won individual gold medals in the 200 and 400 meters and also helped the United States win the 4 x 100 relay. In 1985 she set a world indoor record in the 400 with a time of 52.99 seconds. She was national outdoor 400-meter champion in 1986.

Accomplishments

National outdoor champion, 400 meters: 1986
National indoor champion, 200 meters: 1985
Olympic gold medalist, 200 meters: 1984
Olympic gold medalist, 400 meters: 1984
Olympic gold medalist, 4 x 100 relay: 1984

Mary Browne

June 3, 1891–August 19, 1971

One of the best pre–World War I tennis players in the United States, Mary Kendall Browne was raised in Ventura County, California. Her father, Albert William Browne, was a sheep farmer; her mother, Neotia Rice, a homemaker. Mary became interested in tennis after watching her older brother, Nat, play. In fact, it was through practice sessions with him that Mary became a topflight player.

A rather diminutive young woman, just 5 feet 2 inches, she was an extremely competitive athlete who had an uncanny ability to paint the corners of a tennis court. In 1908 she began playing against the top players on the West Coast, including May Sutton Bundy, Hazel Hotchkiss Wightman, and Elizabeth Ryan. For the better part of three years, Browne found herself overmatched in these encounters. But she was still a neophyte; there would be better times ahead.

In 1912 Browne competed in the U.S. championships for the first time. In one of the most remarkable debuts in the history of the U.S. championships, Browne swept the board, winning three titles in a single day. Not only did she defeat Evelyn Sears to capture the singles title, but she also teamed up with Dorothy Green to win the women's doubles crown, then joined Dick Williams to win the mixed doubles title.

That was the start of a tremendous three-year run in which Browne won nine U.S. titles. In 1913 she defeated Dorothy Green in the singles championship, and in 1914 she beat Marie Wagner. She teamed with Louise Williams to win the women's doubles and with Bill Tilden to win the mixed doubles. She was the top-ranked player in the country at that time.

At the top of her game, Browne took an extended break from competitive tennis. For nearly seven years she concentrated on her work as superintendent of the Los Angeles Humane Society for Children. During that time the only

serious tennis she played was a series of tournaments against Molla Mallory in 1917. Browne shook off the rust and played some impressive tennis, winning more than half of the matches. Her success could be attributed to the fact that she had remained fit and sharp by frequently playing golf. Browne was no weekend hacker. In 1921 she won the Southern California women's golf championships. A few months later, after returning to the women's tennis circuit, she finished second to Mallory at the U.S. championships. With Dick Williams as her partner, she won the mixed doubles title.

In 1924 Browne lost in the semifinals of the U.S. tennis championships, but less than a month later pulled off a surprising upset of Glenna Collett Vare in the semifinals of the U.S. women's amateur golf championships. She lost in the final to Dorothy Campbell Hurd. For the next three years Browne played both tennis and golf at an exceptionally high level. She reached the quarterfinals of the 1925 U.S. amateur golf championships and was a finalist at the French Open in 1926. In the 1930s she concentrated on golf, though she also served as a tennis instructor. She later became a teacher of physical education and a highly regarded painter. The author of several books on tennis, Browne was inducted into the International Tennis Hall of Fame in 1957.

Accomplishments

U.S. Open singles champion: 1912–1914
U.S. Open doubles champion: 1912–1914, 1921, 1925
French Open singles finalist: 1926
Inducted into International Tennis Hall of Fame: 1957

Zola Budd

Born 1966

Distance runner Zola Budd, who became famous not only for racing in bare feet, but also because of several controversial incidents on and off the track, was raised in Blomfontein, South Africa, and educated in racially segregated schools. She was just a child when she began running in the hills near her home. Before long Budd was winning races against women twice her age. When she was 17 she broke the world record for 5,000 meters and set junior records in the 1,500 and 3,000.

But Budd's success as a runner remained limited to her native country. Because of the apartheid policies of the South African government, South Africans were banned from international competition by both the International Olympic Committee and the International Amateur Athletic Federation. Runners from member nations were prohibited from competing in events in which South Africans participated, which meant not only that Budd was not

It didn't help that in the summer of 1984, at the Los Angeles Olympics, the barefooted Budd became entangled with American favorite Mary Decker Slaney in the 3,000 meters. Slaney went down and failed to finish the race. Budd tripped, regained her balance, and struggled home in seventh, practically in tears, as the crowd at the Los Angeles Coliseum showered her with boos. Slaney later charged Budd with causing the accident, but objective spectators ascribed blame to no one.

In 1988 a homesick and emotionally exhausted Budd returned to South Africa, where she had been spending more time. She qualified for the British Olympic team in the 10,000 meters but was not allowed to compete. The ban on South African athletes was lifted in the 1990s, but Budd never again took part in high-level international competition.

Accomplishments

Broke world record for 5,000 meters: 1985
World cross-country champion: 1985–1986
Member of British Olympic team: 1984

Maria Bueno

Born October 11, 1939

Tennis player Maria Bueno won seven Grand Slam singles titles in the late 1950s and early 1960s, and mesmerized audiences with her beauty and athleticism. Her father, Pedro Bueno, was a veterinarian who liked to play tennis in his spare time. He introduced Maria to the game when she was just five years old, and before long she had a membership at a health club near their home in São Paulo, Brazil. But she was not immediately thrown into the pressure-cooker world of private lessons and youth tournaments. Instead, Maria taught herself the finer points of tennis. She studied the moves of players she admired, read books, and analyzed photographs of the game's great athletes. For hours on end she copied the techniques of the older, more experienced players at her club. "I would copy anybody I liked to watch," she said. "Any of the club players."

Despite her unorthodox approach—or perhaps because of it—Maria Bueno turned out

permitted to compete in foreign meets, but also that foreign athletes were not permitted to travel to South Africa to compete against her. Moreover, any records set by South African runners were not recognized. Budd was an outcast.

All that changed in 1984 when Budd moved to Great Britain. Because her grandfather was born in England, she was able to apply for British citizenship. Amid much controversy, and with great speed, her request was granted. She took up residence part-time in England and lived there for the better part of four years. During that time she became one of the finest athletes in her sport, accumulating the international honors previously denied her. There were the world cross-country championships in 1985 and 1986. And on August 26, 1985, she set her first recognized world record, running 14:48.07 for 5,000 meters in the Crystal Palace meet in London.

During this time, however, Budd was under great emotional stress. Wherever she competed, she faced criticism from anti-apartheid protesters. It mattered not that Budd was essentially apolitical. They demanded that she renounce her country's racist policies, but she was a shy young woman, barely 5 feet tall and 90 pounds, and all she wanted to do was run.

to be an original. She won the Brazilian championships when she was 14 years old; at 18 she won the Italian singles and at 19 the Wimbledon doubles championships. The next year, 1959, Bueno became an international star. Seeded sixth at Wimbledon, she put together her finest tournament and found herself in the final against Darlene Hard of the United States. She had lost to Hard in each of their six previous matches. But this time, serving with pinpoint precision and power, Bueno recorded 17 aces and cruised to a 6–4, 6–3 victory. She became the first non-American woman to win Wimbledon in more than 20 years and the first Brazilian ever to win.

Instant celebrity followed the Wimbledon triumph. Bueno brought to the game of tennis a sense of style and artistry that it had never known. She combined the fluid movements and lithe appearance of a ballerina with a subtly aggressive serve-and-volley attack. She also took great pride in the way she looked. Her designer tennis outfits were meant to show off her figure as well as her sense of fashion.

Tennis had never seen a player like her, and La Bueno, as she came to be known, broadened worldwide interest in tennis. But there was substance behind the style. Bueno was a perfectionist, driven not only to win her matches but to do so in a way that was aesthetically pleasing. "I was never satisfied if I did not play beautifully," she said. "I was always going for the impossible shots."

Bueno won the U.S. Open in 1959 and repeated as Wimbledon champion in 1960 with a straight-set victory over Sandra Reynolds of South Africa. That was to be the high point of her career. After winning her second Italian title in the spring of 1961, she contracted hepatitis. It was nearly a year before she was able to return to the women's tour, and even then she was not at full strength. By 1963, however, Bueno became the player she had once been. She won her second U.S. Open title that year, and the following year won both Wimbledon and the U.S. Open. She added a fourth U.S. title in 1966.

Injuries shadowed Bueno throughout her career. She suffered from chronic tendinitis in her right arm and underwent surgery several times. She was forced to retire by the age of 30.

Accomplishments

U.S. Open champion: 1959, 1963–1964, 1966
Wimbledon champion: 1959–1960, 1964
Italian singles champion: 1958, 1961
Inducted into International Tennis Hall of Fame: 1978

May Sutton Bundy

September 25, 1887–October 4, 1975

Tennis champion May Sutton Bundy, who brought power and strength to a game that had previously been quiet and dignified, was born in Plymouth, England. When May was six years old her family moved to a ranch in Pasadena, California. Adele Sutton, the oldest of the five children, had played tennis back in England and still had a fondness for the game, so the family constructed a clay court on their property. It wasn't long before all the girls were playing. May was the youngest; because she was also the heaviest, her sisters often refused to play against her, a fact that angered—and motivated—her. She promised herself that one day she would be the best tennis player in the Sutton family.

The Sutton sisters won every singles title in the Southern California championships from 1899 to 1915. In 1904, May traveled to the East Coast to make her first appearance at the U.S. national championships. To say she caused a stir would be an understatement. May was a confident, 160-pound woman who eschewed the conservative, impractical outfits of her time. She believed tennis clothing should be comfortable and light, allowing for as much movement as possible. To that end she wore skirts and dresses that did not even reach her ankles and rolled up the sleeves on her baggy, oversized shirts.

In the truest sense of the term, May Sutton dressed for success; the fact that she was not as neatly attired as her Eastern counterparts did not bother her in the least. Once the game began she proved she belonged. In fact, she was as innovative with her racket as she was with her wardrobe. Women's tennis in the early part of the 20th century was a delicate game, full of spins and slices and precisely played drop shots. Sutton's favorite shot was a powerful forehand

Memorable Moment: April 2, 1931

Jackie Mitchell Pitches for a Men's Baseball Team

It is common today for girls to compete alongside boys in Little League baseball. Even high school and college teams have opened their doors to females.

But few people remember the woman who helped to pioneer this cause.

Her name was Jackie Mitchell, and she was the first woman to play for a men's professional baseball team. It happened on April 2, 1931. Mitchell, who loved the game of baseball, claimed to have been taught the finer points of big-league pitching by Dazzy Vance. She wanted to pitch in the majors, but was willing to settle for her 15 minutes of fame.

Joe Engel, the manager of the Memphis Lookouts, hired Mitchell to pitch for his team, which played in the minor league Southern Association. The Lookouts were scheduled to face the New York Yankees in an exhibition game, and while many observers believed that Engel had signed Mitchell merely as a publicity stunt, neither the manager nor the pitcher ever confirmed that rumor.

When Mitchell entered the game, her performance was nothing less than mesmerizing. She faced three of the Yankees' best hitters—Babe Ruth, Lou Gehrig, and Tony Lazzeri—and struck out the side. Then, with the crowd standing and applauding, she left the game. The Yankees went on to win by a score of 14–4.

loaded with topspin; she was the first female player who routinely attempted to pound the ball. She also openly displayed her competitive spirit. Sutton liked to win, and she saw no reason to hide that fact. Not surprisingly, this attitude irritated many of her opponents.

"She was very hard for me to play against," the great Hazel Hotchkiss Wightman once said of Sutton. "She was not ladylike. She was rude, she was unsportsmanlike, and it upset me."

In 1904 Sutton overwhelmed her competition at the national championships, losing only 10 games. In the final she defeated Elisabeth Moore, 6–1, 6–2. Sutton found the entire experience so unchallenging and lacking in drama that she declined invitations to compete in the national championships for the next 17 years. Instead, she turned her attention to another tournament. In 1905 she became the second American woman ever to play at Wimbledon. As she had a year earlier, she rolled through the early rounds. In the final she defeated Dorothea Douglass (who later became known as Dorothea Lambert Chambers) in straight sets, 6–3, 6–4, to become the first foreign woman champion at Wimbledon. It was the beginning of a heated rivalry. Douglass beat Sutton in the 1906 final, and Sutton returned the favor in 1907.

Sutton soon retreated from national and international competition; in 1912 she married Thomas C. Bundy, a national men's doubles champion, and they raised four children. She later returned to competitive tennis, reaching the semifinals of the national championships at age 36 and the quarterfinals of Wimbledon at age 44. In 1938, her daughter, Dorothy Bundy Cheney, became the first American woman to win the Australian Open. In 1956, May Sutton Bundy was inducted into the International Tennis Hall of Fame.

Accomplishments

U.S. Open champion: 1904
First foreign woman to win at Wimbledon: 1905
Wimbledon champion: 1905, 1907
Inducted into International Tennis Hall of Fame: 1956

Susan Butcher

Born December 26, 1956

Susan Butcher is a four-time winner of the grueling Iditarod Trail Sled Dog Race. But her childhood was decidedly urban—she grew up in Cambridge, Massachusetts. It was all Susan knew, yet somehow it seemed wrong to her. She pleaded with her parents to buy a house in the country. At the very least, she asked if she could set up a tent in their backyard so that she could live outdoors and sleep under the stars. She had few friends and later admitted that as a child she felt closest to her dogs. When she was in the first grade she even wrote a story called "I Hate Cities."

So it was no great surprise that in the early 1970s, when she was old enough to make her own decisions, she fled the heavily congested northeastern United States and settled in the Rocky Mountains of Colorado, where the air was cleaner and the neighbors fewer. There Butcher learned about racing sled dogs, and she quickly fell in love with the sport.

It wasn't long before even the Rockies seemed too heavily populated for Butcher's tastes. So she moved again, this time to Alaska. "I knew if I went north I'd hit some really good stuff," she has said. "People don't go where it's cold. I wanted to live someplace where I could run my dogs for hundreds of miles." She settled in the town of Eureka, a place not found on any map. She built a compound for herself and her dogs—some one-room cabins, an outhouse, and more than a hundred doghouses. It was in Eureka, where the human population numbers roughly a dozen, that Butcher began training for the Iditarod Trail Sled Dog Race, the most prestigious event of its type in the world.

The 1,100-mile trek from Anchorage to Nome, Alaska, is a brutal and exhausting test of strength and stamina, courage and cunning, instinct and ingenuity. A competitor who hopes to capture the $50,000 first prize not only must be able to withstand brutal winter conditions—high winds, heavy snows, subzero temperatures—but she also must be able to understand the dogs who accompany her on her journey. She might be alone in the wilderness for nearly three weeks, so she must know the difference between a dog that is merely tired and one that is on the brink of collapse. She must be able to work in harmony with her team.

Butcher has repeatedly demonstrated those traits. In 1985, in her first attempt at the Iditarod, she and her team were attacked by a moose and forced to withdraw. Two of her dogs were trampled to death; she sustained a serious shoulder injury and might have been killed had another musher not come along and shot the moose. Between 1986 and 1990, however, Butcher won the race four times. She was not the first woman to win the Iditarod—Libby Riddles won in 1985—but Butcher was easily the most famous, and the fastest. Depending on weather and luck, the Iditarod winner needs anywhere from 10 to 20 days to complete the course. Each of Butcher's victories required less than 12 days. Her 1986 time of 11 days, 15 hours, 6 minutes was a record at the time. She beat her own record in 1987 and again in 1990.

After Butcher's third consecutive victory in 1988, race founder Joe Redington, a fan of Butcher's and a close friend, joked to a reporter, "It's getting pretty damn hard for a man to win anything anymore. Maybe we should start a race especially for them."

Accomplishments

Iditarod Trail Sled Dog Race champion:
  1986–1988, 1990
Fastest woman ever to complete the Iditarod:
  1990 (11 days, 1:53.23)

Mabel Cahill

April 2, 1863–?

A member of the International Tennis Hall of Fame, Mabel Esmonde Cahill was born in Ballyragget, County Kilkenny, Ireland. She was the daughter of Margaret Magan and Michael

Netterville Cahill, a prosperous barrister and the high sheriff of Kilkenny. Little is known of her life in Ireland, though it is presumed that she was the same Mabel Cahill who lost in straight sets to eventual champion May Langrishe at the 1886 Irish championships, and who later captured the Lansdowne Ladies Open Singles Handicap.

Cahill arrived in the United States in 1889, becoming a citizen shortly thereafter. She took up residence in New York and became a regular on the Central Park tennis courts, where she employed a solid baseline game. At 5 feet 4 inches, Cahill had a strong forehand and was quick on her feet. She was lean and deceptively strong; often, she simply overwhelmed her opponent. But her physical condition was tenuous throughout her career, and sometimes forced her to abandon matches that she appeared to have in hand. In 1890, at the national championships in Philadelphia, she was within two points of a semi-final victory over Ellen Roosevelt. But exhaustion got the better of Cahill, and she ultimately defaulted. Roosevelt went on to win the title.

Cahill had established herself as one of the premier players in the game. She won the singles title at the Ladies Club for Outdoor Sports on Staten Island in 1889, and the New Jersey women's singles and Hudson River Valley singles titles in 1890. In 1891, as a prelude to the national championships, she defended her New Jersey crown. At the nationals she fared much better than in her previous appearance. First she defeated Ellen Roosevelt to win the singles title. Then she teamed up with Emma Leavitt Morgan to win the women's doubles and with Marion Wright to win the mixed doubles. In 1892 she defended all three titles, though not without a struggle. In the final of the singles event, Cahill met 15-year-old Bessie Moore. Women played five-set matches at that time, and Cahill, as was often the case, began to tire in the latter stages of the match. After the fourth set she became ill and retreated to the locker room. After an extended period of rest and recovery, however, she returned to the court and won the fifth and deciding set.

Cahill chose not to defend her national title in 1893. According to the published report, she was angry over the way she had been treated the previous year, though she did not offer specific criticism. She won the New York State championship in 1893, but that was the last tournament

she would win in the United States. Without explanation, Cahill's competitive career came to a close. She wrote tennis articles and romance novels and later worked as a riding instructor. She was a spectator at the 1898 All-England championships at Wimbledon, but few details of her life beyond that time are available. The date of her death is not known, though it is believed that she died in her native Ireland. She was inducted into the International Tennis Hall of Fame in 1976.

Accomplishments

> U.S. Open singles champion: 1891–1892
> U.S. Open doubles champion: 1891–1892
> Inducted into International Tennis Hall of Fame: 1976

Donna Caponi

Born January 29, 1945

Donna Caponi, one of the top players on the Ladies Professional Golf Association circuit in the 1970s and early 1980s, was born in Detroit and raised in California. She learned the game of golf from her father, Harry; he apparently taught her well, for she was quite adept at the game even as a youngster. In fact, she captured the Los Angeles junior title in 1956, when she was only 12 years old.

That early success prompted Caponi to pursue a professional career. She decided to forgo college and dive into the competitive world of big-time athletics as soon as she graduated from high school. But success was not immediate—Caponi did not qualify for the LPGA tour until 1965. Once in the big leagues, however, she was a consistent money winner. She finished 20th in the LPGA rankings in her rookie season, and in 1969 she captured the U.S. Women's Open. It was a dramatic achievement—as of 1996, only 12 LPGA members had ever won the U.S. Women's Open during their inaugural tour.

Caponi was no one-hit wonder. She won the Lincoln-Mercury Open in 1969 and came back the following year to successfully defend her U.S. Women's Open title. She added a third major victory in 1976, taking the Peter Jackson Classic. That wound up being one of Caponi's finest seasons—she also finished first at the Portland Classic, the Carlton, and the Mizuno Japan Classic. When the year ended she was second on the LPGA money list with $106,553, more than double the amount she had earned in any previous season.

And better things were to come. In 1979 Caponi won the LPGA championship and earned more than $125,000. The next year, she failed to win a major title but finished first in five other tournaments, including the Colgate Dinah Shore Winner's Circle. She was second on the LPGA money list with $220,619. In 1981 she not only won a second LPGA championship, but also captured the LPGA Desert Inn Pro-Am, the American Defender/WRAL Classic, the WUI Classic, and the Boston Five Classic. Her prize money for the year was $193,916, making her the third woman to surpass the $1 million mark in career earnings.

Caponi's career declined after 1981, though she remained one of the top 50 players in the game until the late 1980s. By 1988 she had reduced the amount of time she spent golfing and had begun to concentrate on her second career—broadcasting. She became a regular on ESPN's telecasts of women's events. In 1988 she was named one of *Golf* magazine's 100 Heroes during the celebration of the Centennial of Golf in America.

While on the tour, the 5-foot 5-inch, red-haired Caponi was regarded as a fun-loving woman with a fondness for dancing, which earned her such nicknames as Watusi Kid and Boogie D. In the 1990s she dusted off her clubs and played in women's senior events.

Accomplishments

U.S. Women's Open winner: 1969, 1970
Peter Jackson Classic winner: 1976
LPGA championship winner: 1979, 1981
Winner of 24 LPGA tournaments

Jennifer Capriati

Born March 29, 1976

Jennifer Capriati made history by becoming the youngest American to play a professional tennis match. She did so on March 5, 1990,

just a few weeks before her 14th birthday. She was a hit with the fans and the media, which tracked her every move. On the court, she handled her new celebrity with surprising grace. One week after turning 14 she reached the finals of a tournament in South Carolina, where she met Martina Navratilova. Capriati lost the match but won more supporters when, with a broad smile, she said it was simply a thrill to have had the opportunity to play a living legend. Navratilova responded by calling Capriati "a legend in the making."

Capriati was born into a tennis-playing family on Long Island. Her mother, Denise, had even played a few sets the day before giving birth to Jennifer. Her father, Stefano, was a former soccer goalie from Italy who had taught himself to play tennis. He became quite good and eventually found work as a teacher.

From an early age, tennis was part of Jennifer's life. She went to the courts with her father, crawled around the ball machines, and played with the equipment. By the time she was three, she had a racket in her hand. She was

handling long rallies by the age of four. The Capriatis lived in Spain at that time but returned to the United States in 1980 so that Jennifer could play tennis year-round and work with some of the finest coaches. They settled in Florida, where she began to take lessons from Jimmy Evert, the father and coach of Chris Evert, one of the greatest players in history. Jimmy Evert refined Jennifer's baseline stroke, and taught her to be patient and determined. He immediately saw that she had the talent to become one of the best.

In 1987, at age 10, Capriati won the U.S. 12-and-under indoor championship. A few months later she won the 14-and-under title. By then the publicity wheels were turning. Capriati was a prodigy, and everyone wanted to know when she would start playing against adults. In March 1988 she became the youngest girl ever to win the U.S. Tennis Association Girls 18-and-Under Hard Court Championships. That same year she was named Junior Player of the Year by *Tennis* magazine. The following year she became the youngest player ever win the junior titles at the French Open and the U.S. Open. In 1990

she became, at age 14, the youngest person ever to win a match at Wimbledon. She also became the youngest player ever to reach the semifinals of a Grand Slam tournament (the French Open). By 1991 Capriati was a top-10 player and had landed on *Forbes* magazine's list of the 40 highest paid athletes in the world. In 1992 she won the gold medal at the Barcelona Olympics, defeating Steffi Graf in the final.

In 1994 Capriati's career took a turn for the worse. Tired and overweight, she faltered badly on the court. Off the court, she ran into trouble. In May 1994 she was arrested for possession of marijuana and decided to take a sabbatical from competitive tennis. She returned to the game in 1996.

Accomplishments

Olympic gold medalist: 1992
Youngest Grand Slam finalist (French Open): 1990
Youngest player to win a match at Wimbledon: 1990
French Open junior champion: 1989
U.S. Open junior champion: 1989

Memorable Moment: June 23, 1931

Lili de Alvarez Introduces Shorts to Wimbledon

Tennis is a traditional game, and nowhere is that tradition embraced with greater firmness than at Wimbledon. Perhaps there is room for creativity and personal expression at some of the game's other major tournaments, but at stodgy old Wimbledon, one is expected to abide by the rules. It is not a place to make a statement.

Imagine the fuss, then, when Lili de Alvarez, a Spaniard who was born in Rome, showed up for the 1931 championships dressed in an outfit that was considered more than a bit provocative. Women in the 1920s had customarily played in skirts and stockings. Often they wore sweaters. These outfits—supposedly a concession to traditional notions of femininity—were hot, constricting, and completely impractical. Still, they were the accepted uniform of the day in women's tennis, and few people were willing to buck the trend.

But Lili de Alvarez was a daring woman of style. She saw no reason to conform to an unreasonable mode of dress. So, on June 23, 1931, she stepped onto the court at Wimbledon wearing shorts. Actually, they were more like trousers. Baggy and comfortable, they fell to her calves. Alvarez had made the outfit herself. The fashion risk didn't help her on the court that year, but it did open the door for other women who wanted to dress practically during athletic competition.

Mary Carillo

Born 1957

Tennis commentator Mary Carillo, one of the best analysts in the business, was raised in the Douglaston section of Queens, in New York City. Her father, Tony Carillo, was an art director at an advertising agency; her mother, Teresa, was a housewife who raised three children.

As a child, Carillo was one of the more promising junior tennis players in the country. But she was not the best player in Douglaston—that honor went to her neighbor, John McEnroe, who would become one of the greatest players in the history of tennis. Carillo often practiced with McEnroe, which helped her become a stronger, more competitive player.

"I was sort of pushed along," Carillo said. "We went to the same tennis academy and had the same coach. If John hadn't been there, I wouldn't have gone so far."

By the time she was an 18-year-old high school senior, Carillo was the top-ranked amateur player in the East and the 10th-ranked player in the country. She seemed to be a young woman with a promising future in professional tennis, so rather than accept an athletic scholarship to a major university, she turned pro. Her parents were dismayed by her decision, but she was determined to make it on her own. She took a job at a tennis academy in Florida and began working toward her goal of surviving on the women's tour.

Carillo's game proved to be far from flawless. She spent three years in the professional ranks, and while she did manage to climb as high as No. 33 on the computer rankings, she never lived up to the potential she had demonstrated as a youth. The high point of her playing career came in 1977, when she teamed up with McEnroe to win the mixed doubles title at the French Open. But her career came to an end in 1980, when she injured her knee while playing at Wimbledon.

"It was no tragedy," Carillo has said of that incident. "It wasn't like I'd left behind this great legacy."

Receiving an invitation from the USA Network to try her hand at broadcasting women's tennis matches, Carillo proved to be a natural. She later became one of the top analysts at CBS, working both men's and women's matches. With her strong, deep voice, she brought a sense of style to the telecasts. As a former player, she knew precisely what was going on in each match; she was witty and opinionated—without being annoying. Over the years viewers have heard Carillo speak her mind on a number of topics—accusing Andre Agassi of throwing a match on purpose and arguing that Jennifer Capriati should not have been allowed to turn professional when she was only 13 years old, an observation that turned out to be prescient in light of Capriati's legal and personal problems.

Carillo's candor angered some players, but reviews of her work were positive. In the mid-1990s she received numerous offers to expand her résumé, but because she wanted to spend as much time as possible with her two young children, she turned most of them down.

Accomplishments

French Open mixed doubles champion: 1977
First female broadcaster to cover Davis Cup tournament: 1988

JoAnne Gunderson Carner

Born April 4, 1939

JoAnne Gunderson Carner, a member of the Ladies Professional Golf Association Hall of Fame, was born in Kirkland, Washington. She taught herself the game of golf by watching the best amateur players and copying their methods. Her sisters ran the snack bar at the local public golf course and her brother watered the greens, but JoAnne worked hardest at the game, becoming the best golfer in the family.

"We played after the customers went home, with old taped-up clubs, wearing gloves until they fell apart," she said. "We played in the moonlight, which is why I'm such a feel player."

Gunderson won her first state title at the age of 14 and her first U.S. Girls' junior title in 1956, when she was 17. That effort helped her land a golf scholarship to the University of Arizona, where she captured the Women's National Collegiate Championship in 1960. She also won her second U.S. Women's Amateur title that year (she'd previously won in 1957). The Great Gundy, as she would come to be known, was one of the game's most decorated amateur players. She won the U.S. Women's Amateur title five times—just one fewer than all-time leader Glenna Collett Vare. Gunderson, with her booming voice and dynamic, wisecracking personality, became a crowd favorite. Fans loved the way she could be a clown one moment, a ferocious competitor the next. Opponents were intimidated not only by her monstrous tee shots, but also by her confidence.

After dominating the amateur ranks for the better part of 15 years, Gunderson turned professional in 1969, at the relatively advanced age of 30. She won the U.S. Women's Open in 1971, but then fell into a terrible slump, failing to win another tournament until 1974. "As an amateur I could hit the ball, but I didn't really know how," she later said. "I didn't know how to break down my swing and find out how to hit every shot. And at the same time I was thinking too much. They tack on *professional* after your name and you're supposed to know something."

With the help of her instructor, golf pro Gardner Dickinson, Gunderson regained her touch. She married Don Carner and began competing under the name JoAnne Carner. The victories came in rapid succession. By 1977, when she won her second U.S. Women's Open, she could consistently be found among the tour's leading money winners. In 1981 she became the second player in LPGA history to reach $1 million in career earnings. In 1982, after winning her 35th tournament, she was inducted into the LPGA Hall of Fame.

While she may have gotten a late start on a professional career, Carner broke records for longevity. In 1991, at the age of 52, she finished eighth in the LPGA championship. As of 1994, she was still a semiregular on the LPGA tour, competing against women half her age. She hopes to become the oldest player—male or female—to win a regular tour event; the record is held by Sam Snead, who won the Greater Greensboro Open when he was 52.

Carner was captain of the U.S. Solheim Cup team in 1994 and served as a playing editor for *Golf Digest* magazine. When not playing on the LPGA tour, she lives in Palm Beach, Florida.

Accomplishments

Women's National Collegiate Champion: 1960
U.S. Women's Amateur champion: 1957, 1960, 1962, 1966, 1968
U.S. Women's Open champion: 1971, 1976
Inducted into LPGA Hall of Fame: 1982
Inducted into International Women's Sports Hall of Fame: 1987

Connie Carpenter

Born February 26, 1957

Connie Carpenter, a great all-around athlete who competed on the U.S. Olympic team in two different sports, was born in Madison, Wisconsin. She was a confident, competitive young woman who grew up in a region known for producing outstanding winter athletes. Speed skating was Carpenter's first love. She was a child prodigy, talented enough to make the U.S. Olympic team as a 15-year-old in 1972. That year, at the Winter Games in Sapporo, Japan, she finished seventh in the 1,500 meters. Not bad for a high school sophomore, but merely a prelude to what she would accomplish as an adult.

In 1976 Carpenter captured the overall title at the U.S. outdoor speed skating championships. But she also suffered an ankle injury, which prevented her from competing in the Winter Olympics. Never one to wallow in self-pity, Carpenter tried to make the best of a lousy situation. Like most skaters, she had routinely used cross-training—primarily cycling—to maintain fitness during the off-season. During her recovery and rehabilitation from her ankle injury, Carpenter trained almost exclusively on a bicycle. The competitive juices began to flow, and as it turned out, she was even more accomplished as a cyclist than she had been as a skater.

In 1976, 1977, and 1979, Carpenter won the U.S. road and pursuit championships. A nasty spill left her with a concussion and prompted her to give up cycling in 1980, and she again decided to switch sports. She enrolled at the University of California at Berkeley and joined the crew team. As usual, success came quickly. She was a member of the Berkeley crew that won the 1980 NCAA championship in the four-oared shell with coxswain.

In 1981 Carpenter decided to end her hiatus from competitive cycling and captured the national road championship. In 1982 and 1983 she was the national criterium champion. In 1983 she set a world record in winning the world pursuit championship, and in 1984, at the Summer Games in Los Angeles, she became the first American in 72 years to win an Olympic medal in cycling. Her breakthrough came in the road race, where she found herself in a sprint to the finish with teammate Rebecca Twigg, who had taken the lead in the final 100 meters. Carpenter caught Twigg at the last possible moment and inched ahead at the finish line to capture the gold medal. Carpenter later thanked the crowds lining the Olympic course and said that their support helped give her the strength to win.

Carpenter, who married fellow cyclist Davis Phinney, spent much of her career competing under the name Connie Carpenter–Phinney. She is a member of the International Women's Sports Hall of Fame and the U.S. Olympic Hall of Fame.

Accomplishments

Olympic gold medalist, road race: 1984
Inducted into International Women's Sports
   Hall of Fame: 1990
Inducted into U.S. Olympic Hall of Fame: 1992
U.S. national road race champion: 1981
U.S. national criterium champion: 1982–1983

Vera Caslavska

Born 1942

Gymnastics champion Vera Caslavska, a member of the International Women's Sports Hall of Fame, grew up in Prague, Czechoslovakia. An athletic, 5-foot 3-inch blonde with striking features, she first exhibited an affinity for figure skating and seemed destined for greatness in that sport. But at age 15, she decided to respond to a nationwide search for promising young gymnasts. She had done some skating, and understood that both sports required grace, balance, and strength. She gave gymnastics a try and proved to be a natural.

During the course of her long and distinguished career, Caslavska won 22 European, world, and Olympic titles. She made her first international appearance at the 1958 world championships. Just 16 years old at the time, and with little more than a year of high-level training under her belt, Caslavska helped Czechoslovakia win a silver medal in the team competition. The next year, she got her first taste of individual success, taking a gold medal in the balance beam at the European championships.

By 1962 Caslavska was one of the most accomplished all-around gymnasts in the world. At the world championships that year she faced reigning Olympic and world champion Larissa Latynina of Russia, perhaps the most successful gymnast in history. Caslavska pushed Latynina to her limit, but still came up short,in the combined exercises and was forced to settle for a silver medal.

Two years later, however, at the 1964 Summer Olympics in Tokyo, Caslavska was approaching her physical and competitive peak. She easily captured the overall title, defeating, among others, Larissa Latynina. She also won gold medals in the balance beam and vault. At the 1965 European championships she won a gold medal in each individual event, as Latynina had done before her. Two years later, in Amsterdam, she repeated her performance note for note, thereby earning a permanent place in the pantheon of great gymnasts.

After winning the combined gold medal at the world championships in 1966, Caslavska won four gold medals and two silver medals at the 1968 Summer Olympics in Mexico City. What made her performance so dramatic was the fact that a few months earlier she had been forced into hiding as a result of the Soviet invasion of her homeland—she went to the Games with little preparation but competed brilliantly. With little access to gymnastics equipment, she had stayed fit by hauling bags of coal. She entered all six events at the Summer Games and earned a medal in each one. She later presented her four gold medals to the four leaders of Czechoslovakia's democratic reform movement. Caslavska was inducted into the International Women's Sports Hall of Fame in 1991.

Accomplishments

Olympic gold medalist, combined exercises:
   1964, 1968
Olympic gold medalist, balance beam: 1964

Olympic gold medalist, vault: 1964, 1968
Olympic gold medalist, parallel bars: 1968
Olympic gold medalist, floor exercise: 1968
Inducted into International Women's Sports
   Hall of Fame: 1991

Tracy Caulkins

Born January 11, 1963

Tracy Caulkins, the most decorated swimmer in history, was born in Winona, Minnesota. At six her family moved to Nashville, Tennessee. Older brother Tim and sister Amy were also swimmers, and by the age of eight Tracy was swimming competitively.

"I was really thin and small, and I would get out of the pool at practice and tell the coach it was too cold, that I was freezing," she has said. "He would tell me to go wrap up in a towel. I hated to practice. But then I realized I had some potential, and I used to cry when my parents couldn't take me to practice."

Caulkins was a gangly kid, 5 feet 8 inches tall and only 105 pounds as a 14-year-old. She had big feet and unusually long arms. But the same physical traits that made her feel awkward helped her to become a brilliant swimmer. Physiologically

speaking, she was perfectly suited for the sport. At the height of her career, she was a solid 5 feet 9 inches, 135 pounds, with a broad wingspan that allowed her to pull through the water with stunning grace and speed.

Caulkins stepped into the spotlight in 1977 at the U.S. Indoor National Championships, where she finished first in the 100-yard breaststroke. The following year, as a 15-year-old, she won five gold medals and one silver medal at the world championships and also became the youngest person ever to receive the Sullivan Award, presented annually to the top amateur athlete in the United States. In 1979 she won five medals at the Pan American Games, and in 1980, as a 17-year-old high school senior, she qualified for the U.S. Olympic team. But the boycott of the Moscow Games prevented her from adding to her burgeoning trophy case.

As a student at the University of Florida, Caulkins continued to improve. She won the Broderick Award as the outstanding female college swimmer in the United States in 1982, 1983, and 1984. In 1982 and 1984 she also won the Broderick Cup, given to the outstanding female college athlete. Even more impressive was her ability to keep up with her classroom obligations. Despite training twice a day, six days

a week, she was an excellent student, as reflected by her status as an Academic All-American in 1983 and 1984.

Caulkins' greatest achievement came at the 1984 Summer Olympics in Los Angeles. On opening day she won the 400-meter individual medley, setting a new American record. Five days later she set an Olympic record by also winning the 200-meter individual medley. She added a third gold medal by helping the United States to a first-place finish in the 4 x 100 medley relay. She was named Swimmer of the Year by the U.S. Swimming Association and Sportswoman of the Year by the U.S. Olympic Committee.

"Any superlatives you can think of apply to Tracy," said Don Talbot, who coached the Nashville Aquatics Club and later took over the Australian national swimming program. "She is the greatest woman swimmer who has ever lived."

Caulkins retired shortly after the 1984 Games, when she was just 21 years old. She graduated from the University of Florida in 1985. In 1986 she was inducted into the International Women's Sports Hall of Fame.

Accomplishments

Sullivan Award winner: 1978
Olympic gold medalist, 400-meter individual medley: 1984
Olympic gold medalist, 200-meter individual medley: 1984
Olympic gold medalist, 4 x 100 medley relay: 1984
Inducted into International Women's Sports Hall of Fame: 1986

Evonne Goolagong Cawley

Born July 31, 1951

Evonne Goolagong Cawley, a member of the International Tennis Hall of Fame and a winner of seven Grand Slam singles titles, was born in New South Wales, Australia. She grew up in the Australian outback, in the farming community of Barellan. She was the third of eight children born to Kenneth Goolagong, a sheep shearer of Aboriginal descent, and his wife, Melinda. They were a poor family, but Evonne's childhood was happy.

Evonne was introduced to tennis in a most unorthodox way—when her father gave her a few tennis balls that he had found in an old used car he had purchased. After watching his little girl play, Kenneth decided to borrow a friend's racket. Evonne spent hours swatting balls against a wall. She developed a natural stroke and eventually joined a junior program at a club near her home. The man who ran the program was immediately impressed by Evonne's talent and contacted Vic Edwards, a respected teaching professional in Sydney. The first time Edwards came to visit, Evonne was only nine years old; nevertheless, he was impressed. When she was 13, Evonne left home and moved to Sydney to train full-time. She moved in with Edwards' family; he became her legal guardian.

It was an exciting but difficult time in Goolagong's life. Although lonely and suffering from culture shock, she was determined to succeed as a tennis player. "I cried every night," she said. "But I knew if I told somebody that I was homesick, I'd be back in Barellan. If I was able to handle that, I must have been tough in other ways, too."

Goolagong won the Australian junior championship when she was 16. Two years later, in 1970, she played at Wimbledon for the first time but lost in the second round. Just a few months later she advanced to the final of the Australian Open before losing to Margaret Smith Court. Then, in the spring of 1971, Goolagong beat Helen Gourlay in the final of the French Open and defeated Margaret Smith Court for the Wimbledon championship. Still a month shy of her 20th birthday, she had won two of the game's most important events. When she went home to Australia, she was given a hero's welcome.

"It was a big thrill, but at the time I didn't realize how important winning Wimbledon was," she has said. "I was just having a good time."

That innocence was part of her appeal. Goolagong never cried when she lost, never gloated when she won. She was a competitor, but she was not obsessed. She believed in having balance in her life, so after she married Roger Cawley in 1975, they decided to raise a family. Her first child was born in 1977. Three years later she defeated Chris Evert, 6–1, 7–6, to capture her second Wimbledon title. In so doing, she struck a blow for working mothers around the world—not since Dorothea Lambert Chambers in 1914 had a mother won the most prestigious tennis tournament.

Goolagong Cawley stopped playing regularly on the women's tennis tour in 1983. She was inducted into the International Tennis Hall of Fame in 1988 and the International Women's Sports Hall of Fame in 1989. In 1993 she published her autobiography, *Home!*, in which she addressed, among other things, her Aboriginal heritage.

Accomplishments

Australian Open champion: 1974–1977
French Open champion: 1971
Wimbledon champion: 1971, 1980
Inducted into International Tennis Hall of Fame: 1988
Inducted into International Women's Sports Hall of Fame: 1989

Florence Chadwick

November 9, 1917–March 15, 1995

Like Gertrude Ederle some 25 years earlier, Florence Mary Chadwick became famous throughout the world by shattering records in the grueling sport of long-distance swimming. She was born in San Diego, California, to Richard and Mary Chadwick. Her father was a police detective who ran a restaurant with his wife after retiring from the force. Florence loved the water and displayed a natural affinity for swimming when she was just a child. At the age of six she became the youngest person ever to swim across San Diego Harbor. Not long after, she began participating in age-group events; she usually won and soon began to race older competitors. She was only 13 when she finished second in the backstroke to Eleanor Holm at the national championships.

Chadwick could have been an Olympic-caliber swimmer, but she chose to pursue long-distance swimming. Between 1929 and 1943 she won the 2.5-mile race in La Jolla, California, one of the most prestigious of its kind, ten times.

Her athletic career was sidetracked when she attended college and gave thought to becoming an attorney and, later, when she agreed to perform in various aquacades during the late 1930s. Chadwick worked with the United Service Organizations during World War II, producing, directing, and performing in shows for servicemen and at veterans hospitals. She also appeared in a movie with the legendary swimmer and film star Esther Williams.

Show business was good to Chadwick, but it had its drawbacks, the most obvious being that it robbed her of her amateur eligibility. Exiled from all national and international competition, she had to find other outlets for her competitive energy. She decided then to make a lifelong dream become reality—she would swim the English Channel.

While working as a statistician for an oil company, Chadwick trained for several hours each day in the turbulent waters of the Persian Gulf. On August 8, 1950, at age 32, she stepped into the water at Cape Gris-Nez, France, to wage an assault on Ederle's record. She reached Dover, England, in 13 hours, 20 minutes, eclipsing Ederle's mark by more than an hour. When she emerged from the water, Chadwick smiled and said, "I feel fine. I'm quite prepared to swim back."

She didn't, of course; not that day, anyway. But Chadwick went on to distinguish herself as one of the finest swimmers to repeatedly tame the English Channel. She even crossed the Channel in reverse—generally considered a much more difficult swim—three times, in 1951, 1953, and 1955. In 1952 she became the first woman to swim the 21 miles of heavy seas between Catalina Island and the California mainland. The next year, perhaps her best, she crossed four channels—the English Channel, the Strait of Gibraltar, the Bosporus, and the Dardanelles—in a span of five weeks.

When her athletic career ended, Chadwick earned a living as a spokesperson and lecturer. She later became a stockbroker on Wall Street. "I'm still swimming, but in the sea of finance," she quipped. No less an authority than Johnny Weissmuller—Olympic champion, long-distance swimmer, and Hollywood star—once said of Chadwick, "She's the greatest woman swimmer of all time—maybe of either sex—and it's time she got credit for it." Chadwick was inducted into the International Women's Sports Hall of Fame in 1996.

Accomplishments

- Broke women's record for crossing the English Channel: 1950
- Broke men's record for crossing the English Channel in reverse: 1955
- First woman to swim from Catalina Island to California mainland: 1952
- Crossed the English Channel, Strait of Gibraltar, Bosporus, and Dardanelles in a five-week period: 1953
- Inducted into International Women's Sports Hall of Fame: 1996

Suzy Chaffee

Born 1947

Suzy Chaffee captained the 1968 U.S. Olympic ski team, and later became an outspoken advocate of fitness and gender-equity legislation. She was, it seems, born to ski. Her father was a ski jumper and her mother an alternate on the 1940 U.S. Olympic team. Their influence on Suzy was obvious—by the age of two, she had strapped on her first pair of boots and bindings. Growing up, she learned not only how to ski but also how to dance. She studied classical ballet, a discipline that would eventually help her become something of a pioneer.

Chaffee qualified for the U.S. alpine ski team in 1965 and remained a member through 1968. In 1966 she represented the United States at the world championships; she had her best season in 1967, winning four consecutive races to become the highest-ranked American woman. That led to Chaffee being named captain of the 1968 U.S. Olympic team in Grenoble, France. After the Winter Games she switched to freestyle skiing, then in its embryonic form. Freestyle combines elements of dance, skiing, and gymnastics, so Chaffee took to it with ease. Freestyle skiing became a professional sport in 1971; since there was no women's division, Chaffee competed against men and won three consecutive world championships. She was one of the first performers to add musical accompaniment to her routines.

Noteworthy as her accomplishments on the slopes were, Chaffee achieved her greatest fame—and financial success—after retiring from competitive skiing. She offered pointed and vocal support for the Amateur Athletic Act, the Equal Rights Amendment, and Title IX, a landmark piece of legislation intended to ensure that young women receive equal funding in high school and college athletics.

Chaffee later turned her attention to promoting health and fitness, especially among women. She served on the Healthy American Coalition and was the chief fundraiser for the first World Women's Sports Festival. She gained notoriety—not all of it positive—as Suzy Chapstick, the ski bunny who appeared in advertisements for Chapstick. She achieved wealth and fame through those ads—and through an infamous seminude photo that appeared in *Town & Country* magazine.

"Afterward, I had to go out and prove I had a brain again," Chaffee said in an interview. "But it made me a household name. It gives you a certain power and gives you the free time to get

involved with causes that you otherwise couldn't afford to be involved with."

Chaffee appeared in a handful of movies and became successful on the lecture circuit. Ski America called her the First Lady of Skiing, and *Ski* magazine dubbed her "the ski industry's best PR." In 1988 she was inducted into the U.S. Ski Hall of Fame.

Accomplishments

> Member of U.S. Olympic team: 1968
> World freestyle champion: 1971–1973
> Inducted into U.S. Ski Hall of Fame: 1988

Dorothea Lambert Chambers

September 3, 1878–1960

One of the finest tennis players ever to come out of Great Britain, Dorothea Lambert Chambers was born Dorothea Douglass, in Ealing, England. The daughter of an Anglican minister, she taught herself the finer points of tennis by spending hours batting a ball against a wall. She even tried to make the exercise more interesting by lining up her dolls nearby and pretending they were spectators.

Douglass was 17 years old when she entered her first tournament and 21 when she made her debut at Wimbledon in 1900. Once she set her mind to becoming a first-rate tennis player, she wasted little time. Less than a year after her first Wimbledon appearance, she was one of the top five players in England.

Douglass' first Wimbledon title came in 1903, but her second was more impressive. In 1904 the field was stronger, including such former champions as Charlotte Cooper and Muriel Robb. In 1905, suffering from a nagging wrist injury, Douglass lost to May Sutton in the championship. It was a dramatic final, played before a standing-room-only crowd of 4,000. In the end Sutton proved too strong and fit for Douglass, and much to the chagrin of the British crowd, she became the first American to win the Wimbledon women's singles title.

By 1906 Douglass had married Robert Lambert Chambers and begun playing under the name Dorothea Lambert Chambers. She met Sutton in a rematch and came away with her third Wimbledon crown. The rivalry between the two women intensified the following year, when Sutton defeated Chambers, 6–1, 6–4, in the final. In each meeting, the defending champion lost, possibly because she was not ready to play. The tournament format of the time dictated that the challenger play numerous matches throughout the tournament; the champion, meanwhile, simply waited for a challenger to emerge from the all-comers field.

"I always felt that my opponent must be playing at the top of her form to have reached the challenge round," Chambers wrote. "And that she must have got so used to the court and the crowds to feel quite at home there, while I was only making my debut of the year."

Chambers won back-to-back Wimbledon titles in 1910 and 1911, each time defeating Dora Boothby in straight sets. After sitting out the 1912 tournament, she won two more titles in 1913 and 1914, bringing her Wimbledon total to seven. Perhaps none of those victories, however, was as impressive as one of her losses. In what is widely regarded as one of the greatest Wimbledon finals ever played, 40-year-old Dorothea Lambert Chambers lost in 1919 to a rising young star named Suzanne Lenglen by a score of 10–8, 4–6, 9–7. When the match was over, both athletes were too exhausted to make the customary trip to the Royal Box. It was the first of six Wimbledon titles for Lenglen, who also defeated Chambers in the 1920 final.

Chambers never won another Wimbledon singles title, but she continued to play there until 1927, when she was 47 years old. She defied time and logic, winning two Wimbledon titles after the birth of her first child, and two more after the birth of her second. She was inducted into the International Tennis Hall of Fame in 1981.

Accomplishments

> Wimbledon champion: 1903–1904, 1906, 1910–1911, 1913–1914
> Wimbledon runner-up: 1919–1920
> Oldest Wimbledon finalist (41): 1920
> Inducted into International Tennis Hall of Fame: 1981
> Wightman Cup captain: 1924–1926

Jennifer Chandler

Born June 13, 1959

Jennifer Chandler, an Olympic gold medalist in diving, grew up in Mountain Brook, a suburb of Birmingham, Alabama. Like many Olympians, the seeds of her success were planted at an early age. While Jennifer's father was out of town on a business trip, her mother, Kay Merril, took her to a country club and placed her on the swim team. By the time her father returned, Jennifer was a competitive swimmer and her mother was the team's chief sponsor. There was, however, one problem.

"We were losing all our meets because we didn't have any divers," Chandler said.

Jennifer's mother decided that her little girl could handle the responsibility. By the time she was six years old, Jennifer Chandler was climbing ladders, spinning in the air, and embracing the acrobatic, exhilarating—and sometimes dangerous—life of a competitive diver. She was not an especially daring athlete; rather, she mastered a handful of simple, elegant dives and performed them flawlessly time after time. She was only 14 when she won her first national title. In 1976, at the Summer Olympics in Montreal, she won a gold medal in the 3-meter springboard event as a 17-year-old junior in high school.

A back injury in 1977 slowed Chandler's development, but she worked hard over the next few years; by the end of the decade she was again among the finest divers in the world. She qualified for the 1980 Olympic team, but was denied the chance to compete when the United States led a boycott of the Summer Games in Moscow in protest of the Soviet Union's invasion of Afghanistan. Like many athletes stung by the boycott, Chandler never got another chance to compete in an Olympic competition. She retired from diving and began channeling her energy into other ventures.

Chandler studied art at the University of Arizona, where she met a sculptor and teacher, Dennis Jones. The two married. Jennifer soon parlayed her athletic success into a career as a popular and successful motivational speaker.

In 1993 Chandler took a job with Health-South in Birmingham, promoting fitness and injury prevention in children. That led to a temporary high-profile job as marketing director of the Birmingham Soccer Organizing Committee, formed to oversee the soccer competition at the 1996 Summer Olympics. The Games were held in Atlanta, but Birmingham's Legion Field hosted the first few rounds of soccer competition. For Chandler, a native of the South, it was not only a personal opportunity, but a chance for her hometown—which had been the center of much racial unrest in the 1960s—to stand proudly in the international spotlight.

"The world is watching us," Chandler said. "It's a chance for Birmingham to be seen in colors other than black and white."

Accomplishments

Pan Am Games gold medalist: 1975
Olympic gold medalist, 3-meter springboard: 1976
U.S. Olympic team member: 1976, 1980
Won first national title at the age of 14

Chi Cheng

Born 1944

The third of seven children, track-and-field star Chi Cheng grew up in Hsinchu, Taiwan. Running came easily to her, and she began competing in track-and-field meets when she was in grade school. By the age of 16 she was among the top sprinters in her country—she even represented Taiwan at the 1960 Summer Olympics in Rome. That trip, her first away from her island nation, left her bewildered. She was surprised, for example, to discover that Westerners found it unusual to see a woman carrying the luggage of her male teammates, as Chi did. The subordinate role of women in traditional Chinese society was an alien concept to the European athletes she met.

"It was my first time out of my country, and I was in shock," Chi later said. "I had never seen eyes different from mine."

Neither had she faced the sort of competition she encountered that summer in Rome. The teenager from Taiwan, running against older, stronger, more experienced women, was

Memorable Moment: August 7, 1932

Babe Didrikson Disqualified in Olympic High Jump

Mildred "Babe" Didrikson Zaharias is arguably the greatest female athlete who ever lived. She excelled in baseball, track and field, golf, and softball, among other sports. Her talent and enthusiasm were boundless.

So inventive and gifted was Didrikson that she occasionally found herself playing outside the rules. Such was the case at the 1932 Summer Olympics in Los Angeles. "I am out to beat everybody in sight, and that's just what I am going to do," she said upon her arrival, and she nearly made good on her promise. Didrikson won the javelin with an Olympic-record throw of 133 feet, 4 inches. Then she set a world record in the 80-meter hurdles. Two events, two gold medals.

In the high jump, where she expected to face the stiffest competition, Didrikson tied with another American, Jean Shiley. Both women cleared 5 feet, 5 1/4 inches, another world record. In a special jumpoff to determine the gold medalist, both women cleared 5 feet, 5 3/4 inches. But the judges determined that Didrikson had used an illegal technique, which was true. She had cleared the bar head first. At the time, the rules required a jumper to go over the bar feet first or sideways. Didrikson settled for a silver medal and tried to take solace in the knowledge that she had pioneered a new technique. Within a year, the rules were changed, and the western roll, as it came to be known, was employed by high jumpers all over the world.

outclassed. Competing in the 80-meter hurdles, she finished dead last in her qualifying heat. But the experience proved beneficial for Chi. Besides gaining exposure to world-class competition, she was introduced to Vincent Reel, the track coach at Claremont–Harvey Mudd College in California and a member of the U.S. coaching staff. Two years later, at the Asian Games, they met again. Chi was 18, a talented young woman who needed nothing so much as first-rate coaching. Reel talked her into coming to the United States to train for the 1964 Olympics, and soon she was in California.

Upon arrival, Chi faced obstacles common to any immigrant—homesickness, the inability to speak the native language, financial hardship. But she persevered. By late 1963 she had been accepted at California State Polytechnic University, where she became a straight-A student majoring in physical education. She also began training with Reel at the Los Angeles Track Club. Despite that grueling training, there was not enough time to properly prepare for the Olympics; Chi fared poorly in Tokyo, where she failed to reach the finals of the hurdles and finished 17th in the pentathlon.

Watching her perform, Reel came up with an idea—perhaps Chi should become a sprinter. They immediately began working toward that goal, and by 1968 the transformation was well under way. Chi reached the finals of the 100 and took a bronze medal in the 80-meter hurdles. She was the only Asian woman to win an Olympic medal in the Mexico City Games, and when she returned to Taiwan, the country treated her as a hero. "They had a parade for me," she said. "Every day for over a month. It was wonderful."

Chi reached a peak in 1970. She dominated women's track in the United States, posting the fastest times of the year in six different events—the 100-yard dash, 220-yard dash, 440-yard dash, hurdles, long jump, and pentathlon. At a meet in Portland, Oregon, she broke the world records in the 100 and 220. She entered 63 races that year and won all of them. The Associated Press named her Female Athlete of the Year.

Chi did not have another opportunity to win an Olympic gold medal. She had been bothered by hip, knee, and thigh injuries for years, and doctors were forced to remove several inches of muscle from each leg. For more than a month she was unable to walk. Chi eventually recovered, but at 26 her running career was over. She retired from competition and settled into a quiet domestic life with her new husband—Vincent Reel.

Accomplishments

> Olympic bronze medalist, 80-meter hurdles: 1968
> Three-time Olympian: 1960, 1964, 1968
> Held five world records in 1970
> Named Associated Press Female Athlete of the Year: 1970

Louise Brough Clapp

Born March 11, 1923

A winner of six Grand Slam singles titles in a 17-year career, Louise Brough Clapp was born in Oklahoma City, Oklahoma, and raised in Beverly Hills, California. Her parents separated when she was young; although she grew up in a broken home, she never was subjected to economic hardship. Louise developed an early interest in sports, which was fueled by her mother. Althea Brough was not an athlete and had little understanding of sports, but she thought that her children would benefit from participating and competing. She eventually became something of a stage mother, living and dying with every point of every tournament, causing Louise a bit of anxiety.

"She was very supportive, but she didn't understand the game," Louise has said. "She was very unhappy when I lost in junior tournaments. I think that drove me. It also made me mad, and a couple times I threatened that I wouldn't play anymore."

Years earlier, Louise and her brother had begun playing tennis on the public courts in their neighborhood, and their attire was quite casual. Once an aunt suggested that Louise wear a long white dress to the courts. After some debate, Louise acquiesced. The experience was so unpleasant that she stopped playing for a while.

By the age of 13, Louise was receiving instruction from Dick Skeen, a top teaching pro whose pupils included former champion Pauline Betz. She blossomed under his tutelage and became one of the best junior players in the United States. She was an exceptionally driven young woman—in 1940 she played in two tournaments simultaneously, the U.S. Women's National Singles Championships at Forest Hills and the National Junior Championships at the Philadelphia Cricket Club. Louise and her aunt commuted back and forth all week. When their car broke down on the way to Philadelphia one day, Louise left her aunt behind and hitched a ride to Philadelphia. "When you're young, things like that don't bother you," she recalled.

Brough reached the finals at Forest Hills five times, but won only once, in 1947. She won consecutive Wimbledon titles in 1948, 1949, and 1950, and, at 32, defeated Beverly Baker Fleitz, 7–5, 8–6, to win a fourth title in 1955. She captured the Australian Open title in 1950. Along with her accomplishments in singles competition, Brough won 21 Grand Slam doubles titles and eight mixed doubles titles. Only four women have won more championships. She might have won even more, if not for a debilitating case of tennis elbow in her right arm. She found it increasingly difficult to toss the ball properly on her serve and was forced to make numerous adjustments in her game. She loved tennis, though, and refused to quit, playing well beyond her physical peak.

Even when she left competitive tennis, Brough did not really retire. Marrying a dentist named Alan Clapp in 1958, she became a teaching professional, a job she held for 20 years. In 1967 she was inducted into the International Tennis Hall of Fame.

Accomplishments

> Wimbledon champion: 1948–1950, 1955
> U.S. Open champion: 1947
> Australian Open champion: 1950
> Inducted into International Tennis Hall of Fame: 1967

Alice Coachman

Born November 9, 1923

Alice Coachman, a high jumper and sprinter, was the first African American woman to win an Olympic gold medal. The third of 10 children born to Fred Coachman and Evelyn Jackson Coachman, she grew up in Albany, Georgia. During her school days at the Monroe Street School, Alice discovered that she had some ability as a runner. She liked to compete against the other children, and usually did quite well. One of her teachers, Cora Bailey, recognized the girl's talent and encouraged her as much as possible.

At Madison High School, Coachman was a standout in both track-and-field and basketball. She later enrolled at Tuskegee Institute, where she continued to play basketball and became one of the premier track and field athletes in the United States. The high jump was her specialty. She won her first national title in 1939 at the Amateur Athletic Union trials in Waterbury, Connecticut. She won a second title in 1941 by clearing a height of 5 feet, 1 inch. She also won the national AAU title in 1945 and 1946. One of the most dominant performers in the sport, she won a total of 25 indoor and outdoor AAU titles.

One of Coachman's best years was 1945, when she finished first in the 100-meter dash, 50-meter dash, and high jump. In the 100 she defeated Stella Walsh, who was regarded as one of the best sprinters in the world. Coachman won the same three events the following year, at the 1946 AAU championships in Buffalo, New York.

But Coachman was denied the chance to perform on an Olympic stage throughout much of her career. She was in her athletic prime in the early to mid-1940s, but the 1940 and 1944 Olympic Games were canceled because of World War II. Coachman had to wait until 1948, when she was 35 years old, to compete in the Olympics. At the Summer Games in London, she won the high-jump competition with a leap of 5 feet, 6⅛ inches—an Olympic record. Not only was she the first black woman to win an Olympic gold medal, but she was also the only American woman to win a gold medal in track and field at the 1948 Games.

Coachman transferred from Tuskegee Institute to Albany (Georgia) State in 1947 to pursue a degree in education. After her competitive career was over, she began teaching and coaching. She later gained recognition as an activist who fought segregation in the South and discrimination against women. She is a member of the Tuskegee Athletic Hall of Fame, the U.S. Track and Field Hall of Fame, and the International Women's Sports Hall of Fame.

Accomplishments

Olympic gold medalist, high jump: 1948
First black woman to win an Olympic medal: 1948
Inducted into U.S. Track and Field Hall of Fame: 1975
Inducted into International Women's Sports Hall of Fame: 1991

Bessie Coleman

January 20, 1893–April 30, 1926

Bessie Coleman, the first African American licensed pilot, was born in Atlanta, Texas, and raised in Waxahachie, Texas, near Dallas. When she was seven years old, her father left the family, leaving her mother to raise five children. Susan Coleman supported the family by picking cotton and doing laundry for neighbors. The children pitched in and helped.

With her mother's support and guidance, Bessie graduated from high school and enrolled at Langston Industrial College in Oklahoma. But after only one semester, she ran out of money and was forced to withdraw. She moved to Chicago and took a job as a manicurist at a barber shop. She later managed a restaurant.

Always an avid reader, Coleman became fascinated with stories and articles about aviation. She decided to learn how to fly and to earn a living as a pilot. First she had to get a license, which proved to be no small task, since all of her applications to aviation school were rejected. Undeterred, she traveled to France to study aviation. She took lessons from French and German pilots and learned to fly the German Fokker airplane. She returned to the United States in 1921, pilot's license in hand. One year

later she had her international license. She was the first black, male or female, to receive a pilot's license.

Coleman went on to become a stunt pilot on the barnstorming circuit. On Labor Day Weekend in 1922, in New York City, she made her first recognized appearance at a U.S. air show. Her reputation blossomed—she came to be known as Brave Bessie—and began to star in air shows across the country. She also lectured on aviation.

Coleman had hoped to establish a flight school for black pilots, but she never realized that dream. On April 30, 1926, at an air show in Jacksonville, Florida, she died while practicing a maneuver. Her controls jammed, and she was ejected from the plane. She was buried at the Pilgrim Baptist Church in Chicago.

In 1990 Coleman was included in a monument recognizing the achievements of African Americans in aviation. Two years later she was inducted into the International Women's Sports Hall of Fame.

Accomplishments

First African American to receive a pilot's
    license
Inducted into International Women's Sports
    Hall of Fame: 1992

Nadia Comaneci

Born November 12, 1961

Nadia Comaneci, the first gymnast to receive a perfect score in Olympic competition, was born in Onesti, Romania. Famed gymnastics coach Bela Karolyi discovered Comaneci by chance, when she was a six-year-old playing with her friends on an elementary school playground. Karolyi watched Nadia jump and run and leap about, and he was struck by her natural athleticism—so much so that he asked her if she might be interested in taking gymnastics lessons. She said yes, and one of the most famous partnerships in sports was born.

Only a year after that meeting, Comaneci became the youngest person ever to compete in the Romanian junior nationals. She finished 13th. In 1970, at age eight, she won the junior

title, clearly establishing herself as a prodigy. Three years later she began competing in international events; by 1975 she was winning them. Her first breakthrough performance came at the European championships, where she won the all-around title. But it wasn't until 1976, at the Summer Olympics in Montreal, that her talent became evident.

It was expected that the women's all-around gold medal would be captured by one of three veteran Soviet gymnasts—Olga Korbut, Lyudmila Tourischeva, or Nelli Kim. Instead, the entire competition belonged to a quiet, wide-eyed 14-year-old from Romania. Comaneci, a waiflike child weighing only 86 pounds and standing 4 feet 11 inches tall, was nothing less than mesmerizing. In winning the all-around title she reached the final of every individual event and walked away with gold medals in the balance beam and uneven bars. She took a bronze medal in the floor exercise and led Romania to a silver medal in the team competition. More impressive than the medals she took home were the scores she recorded. No gymnast had ever received a perfect score of 10 in Olympic competition. But in Montreal, Comaneci received seven 10s—four on the uneven bars and three on the balance beam. Out of a possible 80 points in the all-around competition, she accumulated 79.275. Comaneci was able to accomplish this feat despite a distinct lack of charisma. She was technically flawless, almost mechanical, and rarely smiled or exuded any personality. Nevertheless, the judges and the crowds fell in love with her.

"She has three qualities," Karolyi said after the Games. "The physical qualities—strength, speed, agility. The intellectual qualities—intelligence and the power to concentrate. And Nadia has courage."

That courage would be tested later in her life. Comaneci took a silver medal in the all-around competition at the 1980 Olympics in Moscow; she also won two gold medals and two silver medals in individual events. By 1984 she had retired from competitive gymnastics and was working primarily as a coach. But her life was hardly satisfying. Her friend and mentor, Karolyi, had defected in 1981, and Comaneci was lonely and unhappy. In November 1990 she escaped the despotic rule of Romanian dictator Nicolae Ceauçescu by crossing the border into Hungary under the cover of night. She later defected to the United States, where she was able to start a new life as a spokesperson and fitness consultant. In 1994 she donated $120,000 to the Romanian gymnastics team, and in 1996 she married Bart Conner, a former Olympian from the United States. The two now operate a gymnastics school in Oklahoma.

Accomplishments

Olympic gold medalist, all-around: 1976
Olympic gold medalist, balance beam: 1976, 1980
Olympic gold medalist, uneven bars: 1976
Olympic gold medalist, floor exercise: 1980
First to receive a score of 10 in Olympic competition: 1976

Maureen Connolly

September 17, 1934–June 21, 1969

Maureen Connolly, who won nine Grand Slam singles titles in a short but brilliant tennis career, was born in San Diego, California. Her mother was a musician, her father a naval officer; they divorced when Maureen was three years old. Maureen then lived with her mother and an aunt and developed two distinct passions at a young age—tennis and horses. As a rider she was skilled and graceful; as a tennis player she was brilliant.

Dubbed "Little Mo" by a columnist for the *San Diego Union* (her firepower, he said, was comparable to that of "Big Mo," the battleship *Missouri*), the 5-foot 4-inch Connolly is remembered as one of the greatest tennis players in history. She was not physically impressive and did not have a particularly powerful serve. In fact, she was a rather unspectacular player. But there is no denying that she was an efficient and tireless athlete who routinely wore down the opposition. Accuracy and determination were her greatest assets, and she used them to chisel away at her opponents, slowly and methodically breaking them down.

Connolly stepped onto the world stage at the age of 16, when she won the U.S. Open at Forest Hills in 1951. She traveled to London the

in San Diego. The horse, a jumper named Colonel Mayberry, was frightened by the sound of a passing truck and reared up. The horse fell against the truck, pinning Connolly against its side. Her right leg was crushed in the accident, and despite undergoing several surgical procedures and extensive rehabilitation, Little Mo never played competitive tennis again. At the time of her retirement, she was just 19.

After retiring from tennis Connolly married Norman Brinker, an Olympic equestrian. They had two children, Brenda and Cindy. Connolly became a popular and successful tennis teacher. But tragedy struck again shortly after her 30th birthday, when she was diagnosed with stomach cancer. She fought the disease for three years before succumbing in 1969, at the age of 34.

One year earlier Connolly had been elected to the International Tennis Hall of Fame in Newport, Rhode Island. She was inducted into the International Women's Sports Hall of Fame in 1987.

Accomplishments

U.S. Open champion: 1951–1953
French Open champion: 1953–1954
Australian Open champion: 1953
Wimbledon champion: 1952–1954
First woman to complete Grand Slam: 1953
Inducted into International Tennis Hall of Fame: 1968
Inducted into International Women's Sports Hall of Fame: 1987

Jody Conradt

Born May 13, 1941

Jody Conradt, a member of the International Women's Sports Hall of Fame, was born in Goldthwaite, Texas. She was an exceptional athlete in high school, and her favorite sport was basketball. She went on to play collegiately at Baylor University in Waco, Texas. After graduation she took a job as a high school teacher; later she became an assistant coach at Midway High School in Waco. Her first college coaching assignment at Sam Houston State was followed by a stint at the University of Texas at Arlington. In 1976 she made the move to the big time, taking over as head coach of the women's

following year for her first appearance at Wimbledon. Only 17 years old, she became the youngest Wimbledon champion since Lottie Dod in 1887. The following year was even better for Little Mo. In 1953 she won the French Open, U.S. Open, Australian Open, and Wimbledon championships, becoming the first woman to complete the Grand Slam. That entire year Connolly did not lose a single match. So complete was her dominance of women's tennis that from September 1951 until July 1954 she lost only one match.

The Associated Press selected Connolly as its Woman Athlete of the Year in 1952, 1953, and 1954. She also placed third in AP's 1952 Woman of the Year poll, just behind Queen Elizabeth and Mamie Eisenhower.

Connolly's reign was cut short. In the summer of 1954, while preparing for the U.S. Open, she was injured while riding one of her horses basketball program at the University of Texas at Austin.

At Texas, Conradt built one of the best programs in the country. Her teams dominated the Southwest Conference from 1978 through 1991—in one stretch the Lady Longhorns won 183 consecutive games—and have remained among the best in the country. With a record of 654–178 heading into the 1995–96 season, Conradt boasts a career winning percentage of .822; she is the winningest women's basketball coach in NCAA history, though she claims not to care about such things.

"I didn't keep track of the record, even though a lot of attention was paid to it," Conradt has said.

Conradt's teams have appeared in 12 NCAA postseason tournaments; twice the Lady Longhorns have made it all the way to the Final Four. In 1986 they went 34–0 to become the first women's team to complete an undefeated season; Texas defeated USC by a score of 97–81 to capture the national championship. In Conradt's 20-year tenure at Texas, her teams have finished among the top in Associated Press polls 14 times. The Lady Longhorns were first in 1984, 1985, 1986, and 1987; Conradt was voted Southwest Conference Coach of the Year in 1984, 1985, 1987, and 1988. She was named National Coach of the Year in 1980, 1984, and 1986. Voted on by a panel of coaches, that award is considered the highest honor in women's coaching.

Conradt's success extends internationally as well. In 1987 she led the United States to a gold medal at the Pan American Games. At Texas, she has produced four U.S. Olympic team members, one Broderick Award winner, two Wade Trophy winners, two National Players of the Year, and 19 All-Americans. Her players have a reputation for being true student-athletes, as demonstrated by a graduation rate of better than 90 percent. Despite all of her success, Conradt is quick to point out that the players are the true stars. "I always keep in mind that the game must be played by the players, not the coach," she said.

Conradt serves as athletic director at the University of Texas and contributes time and effort to charitable organizations. She helped establish the Neighborhood Longhorn program, which encourages academic and athletic excellence among the youth of Austin. She started a fantasy basketball camp for women between the ages of 33 and 65.

Accomplishments

Southwest Conference Coach of the Year: 1984, 1985, 1987, 1988
National Coach of the Year: 1980, 1984, 1986
Winningest women's basketball coach in NCAA history
Coached Texas to NCAA championship: 1986
Inducted into International Women's Sports Hall of Fame: 1995

Willa McGuire Cook

Born 1928

Water-skier Willa McGuire Cook, a member of the International Women's Sports Hall of Fame, grew up in Lake Oswego, Oregon. At the urging of her father, who ran a marina, she began skiing in 1942. Willa McGuire, only 14 at the time, was more interested in diving than waterskiing. Once she tried the sport, however, she was hooked for life. It was, in her view, "the greatest of all sports."

In 1945, when a ski show came to Lake Oswego, the show's director spotted McGuire and encouraged her to train for a national competition. The next year, she entered the National Water Ski Championships in Holland, Michigan. She performed flawlessly and took first place in three divisions—slalom, tricks, and overall.

Over the next 10 years McGuire was the most successful woman in her sport. Before her retirement in 1955, she won the national overall title eight times. She won 18 national titles and never lost in the tricks division. She represented the United States at four world tournaments; three times she won the overall title.

As a show skier McGuire was quite an attraction. She formed the Lake Oswego Water Ski Club in 1947 and convinced a group of skiers to join her at regional festivals. In 1948 she graduated to the big time, Cypress Gardens, where for 10 years she was the featured performer. Her

Memorable Moment:
May 1943

Formation of the First
Women's Professional Baseball League

In the spring of 1943, Phillip Wrigley, head of the chewing gum empire, devised a plan to bring professional baseball to a wider audience and to sustain interest in the game during World War II. At the time, more than 40,000 women were playing softball in amateur and semipro leagues. It was Wrigley's idea to bring the best of them together in a single league—and exchange the softball for a baseball.

Hundreds of women showed up for the first tryouts, which were held in Chicago for several days in May 1943. Then, the All-American Girls Professional Baseball League was quickly formed. Originally, there were four teams—the Rockford Peaches, the Racine Belles, the Kenosha Comets, and the South Bend Blue Sox. That number grew rapidly, as teams from Fort Wayne, Minneapolis, Grand Rapids, Battle Creek, and Kalamazoo joined the league's ranks. The women were fine athletes, but Wrigley insisted that they conduct themselves in a way that he considered "feminine." That meant they had to wear skirts, rather than pants, when they played. Off the field, they were required to wear not only skirts, but also high heels and makeup. If they failed to adhere to the dress code, they were fined. Wrigley even hired a cosmetics company to conduct a charm school for his players.

The All-American Girls Professional Baseball League enjoyed tremendous popularity for a while. At its peak, in 1948, it consisted of 10 teams and drew nearly a million fans. Eventually, mismanagement, combined with the popular belief that women should not be playing sports, caused the death of the All-American League. It folded in 1954.

All-American Girls: The Fort Wayne Daisies (top left), Racine Belles (top right), and Rockford Peaches (right).

success there led to appearances in movie and television productions.

McGuire became known as an innovative and thoughtful waterskiing teacher. "My theory is, if you can feel it, ski it," she said. "I do a lot of analyzing and dry-run skiing in my mind, and then I transpose it to the practice session."

McGuire later married Bob Cook. She devoted much of her time to promoting the sport of waterskiing and also became an accomplished painter. In 1990 she was inducted into the International Women's Sports Hall of Fame.

Accomplishments

Won 18 national waterskiing titles
Inducted into American Water Ski Hall of Fame: 1982
Inducted into International Women's Sports Hall of Fame: 1990

Margaret Smith Court

Born July 16, 1942

Margaret Smith Court won 24 Grand Slam singles titles and is considered one of the finest athletes ever to pick up a tennis racket. When she was growing up in the town of Albury in New South Wales, Australia, Margaret Smith joined the neighborhood boys in sneaking into a tennis club. As the story goes, the children were hidden from view as long as they kept the ball in the front half of the court.

"It was my job to stand at the net and volley back every ball," Smith explained. "Whenever anybody tells me I can volley well, I recall those moments I had to volley or get caught."

Eventually she was not only caught, but invited to join the Border Lawn Tennis Association. In exchange for playing time and instruction, Smith did odd jobs around the club—sweeping the courts, chalking lines, painting the net posts. She was a gifted athlete, tall and lean, with natural speed and strength. As a teenager she was a budding track star who gave serious thought to pursuing a spot on the Australian Olympic team. In training for races at 400 and 800 meters, however, she discovered that while gaining speed and strength, she was losing some of the agility and quickness that made her a great tennis player. So she put away her spikes and laced up her sneakers.

Smith won her first Grand Slam event, the Australian Open, in 1960, when she was only 17 years old. That was the first of seven consecutive national titles that she would win in her homeland, and the first of 24 Grand Slam singles titles. No other woman has won even 20 Grand Slam singles titles.

Smith married Barry Court in 1967, when she was at the top of her game, and decided to retire from competitive tennis and open a boutique in Perth. She could not stay away for long, though. In 1969 she won three Grand Slam singles titles, and in 1970 had her greatest year ever, winning the Australian Open, the French Open, the U.S. Open, and Wimbledon, becoming only the second woman to complete the Grand Slam. At Wimbledon, Court defeated Billie Jean King, 14–12, 11–9, in a 46-game marathon that still stands as the longest women's match in Wimbledon history.

Court left the tour in 1972 to begin raising a family, but returned in 1973 after the birth of her first child. That year she came within a breath of capturing a second Grand Slam, winning the Australian Open, the French Open, and the U.S. Open, and losing to Chris Evert in the semifinals at Wimbledon. Her second child was born in 1974; after another year off, she returned to competition. She never won another major title, but in 1975 she did reach the quarterfinals of both the Australian and U.S. Opens, and the semifinals of Wimbledon.

By the time she retired for good in 1976, Court had won 11 Australian Open titles, five U.S. Open titles, five French Open titles, and three Wimbledon titles. She had also become something of a symbol for the budding feminist movement. Not because of anything she said—she was a quiet, almost painfully shy athlete—but simply because of her lifestyle. Twice she had taken time off to have children, and twice she resumed her career. She was a successful athlete and a mother, traveling with her husband and family all over the world. As Billie Jean King said, "Margaret is women's lib in action, even though she doesn't seem to realize it. She earns the bread and her husband baby-sits."

Court was inducted into the International Tennis Hall of Fame in 1979; in 1986 she was inducted into the International Women's Sports Hall of Fame.

Accomplishments

Australian Open champion: 1960–1966,
   1969–1970, 1973
French Open champion: 1962, 1964,
   1969–1970, 1973
U.S. Open champion: 1962, 1965, 1968–1970,
   1973
Wimbledon champion: 1963, 1965, 1970
Inducted into International Tennis Hall of Fame:
   1979
Inducted into International Women's Sports
   Hall of Fame: 1986

Cristl Cranz

Born July 1, 1914

Cristl Cranz, who won a record 12 world alpine skiing championships, was born in Brussels, Belgium. She grew up in a family that loved outdoor sports, and she began skiing when her parents moved to Freiburg, Germany, in 1928, when she was 14 years old. A few years later she entered the University of Freiburg, where she received a degree in physical education. While a student, Cranz continued to train for world-class competition.

The World Alpine Championships were inaugurated in 1931, at Murren, Switzerland; three years later Cranz was the dominant performer. She qualified for the German National Ski Team in 1934, and won gold medals in the slalom and combined at the world championships.

That was the start of a remarkable career in which Cranz won 12 world championship titles, more than any other skier in history, male or female. In 1935 she won the downhill and combined events; in 1937 she won the slalom, downhill, and combined; in 1938 she won the slalom and combined; and in 1939 she won the slalom, downhill, and combined.

Cranz also won a gold medal in the alpine combined at the 1936 Winter Olympics, despite finishing sixth in the downhill portion of the event. She was the best skier in the world at the time and would surely have won more medals.

But alpine combined was the only Olympic skiing event open to women that year.

World War II wiped out the 1940 and 1944 Olympics, so Cranz did not have another opportunity to compete in the Winter Games. She retired and moved to Steibis, Germany, where she opened a ski school and founded the Steibis Ski Club. She married Adolf Borchers and had three children. In 1991 she was inducted into the International Women's Sports Hall of Fame.

Accomplishments

Olympic gold medalist, alpine combined:
   1936
Inducted into International Women's Sports
   Hall of Fame: 1991
12-time world champion
First woman to win an Olympic gold medal in
   skiing

Beth Daniel

Born October 14, 1956

Two-time Ladies Professional Golf Association Player of the Year Beth Daniel was born in Charleston, South Carolina. When she joined the LPGA tour in 1979, she was considered one of the finest prospects the game had ever seen. Daniel had been a collegiate star at Furman University in Greenville, South Carolina. In 1975 and 1977 she captured the U.S. Women's Amateur Championship, and in 1976 and 1978 she was a member of the U.S. Curtis Cup team. At 5 feet 11 inches, she had a fluid swing and was graceful. So promising was her future that she began her rookie season with a writer as her caddie—together they planned to chronicle her first year on the tour.

But the pressure got to Daniel. In her first tournament, in which she finished seventh, she made a lasting impression by heaving her clubs, throwing a temper tantrum, and generally acting in an unprofessional manner. "I had just come out on the tour and all of a sudden I was being compared to [Nancy] Lopez," she later explained. "It was like walking around with a 500-pound weight on my shoulders."

Despite that disappointing start, Daniel won $97,027 and was named LPGA Rookie of the Year in 1979. In 1980 she won four tournaments, accumulated more than $230,000 in earnings, and was named Player of the Year. Although she was the leading money winner in 1981 and was fifth in 1982, her critics questioned both her desire and her ability to withstand pressure. In the 1981 U.S. Women's Open she lost by one stroke to Pat Bradley, a defeat that left her in tears.

The following year at the Open, while addressing a crucial birdie putt on the eighth hole of the final round, Daniel became convinced that her ball had moved—though no one else had noticed—and called a penalty on herself. Instead of taking a two-stroke lead, she fell into second place. It was a stunning and heartwarming display of sportsmanship and honesty, and while it might have cost her the championship, it earned her a legion of new fans.

In 1984 Daniel became the eighth player to exceed $1 million in career earnings. She had become one of the steadiest and wealthiest players on the tour. Still, she had not won a major tournament, a fact that began to bother her in 1986 and 1987, when back problems and mononucleosis forced her to spend time on the sidelines. When she came back in 1989, she was a different player—hungrier, more aggressive. She won a half million dollars that year; in 1990 she earned $863,578—more than any female player in history. Equally important, she won her first major title, the LPGA championship. "I had to show people that I wasn't going to quit, that I could still play this game," Daniel said.

In 1990 she played as well as anyone has ever played. In addition to her Open victory, Daniel shot a record nine consecutive rounds in the 60s, had a career best round of 63 at the Centel Classic, and recorded her second career hole in one. She won the Rolex Player of the Year award, the Vare Trophy for lowest-scoring average, and was named United Press International Female Athlete of the Year. In 1994 Daniel won four tournaments, and was the tour's second leading money winner with $659,426; she was sixth on the money list in 1995.

Accomplishments

U.S. Women's Amateur champion: 1975, 1977
LPGA Rookie of the Year: 1979
LPGA championship winner: 1990
LPGA Player of the Year: 1980, 1990
Shot a record nine consecutive rounds in the 60s: 1990
United Press International Female Athlete of the Year: 1990

Laura Davies

Born October 5, 1963

Laura Davies, the leading money winner on the Ladies Professional Golf Association tour in 1994, was born in Coventry, England. Her parents, Dave and Rita Davies, divorced when she was seven. Dave moved to the United States and settled in Columbia, South Carolina; Rita remained in England with the couple's two children, Laura and Tony. Three years later,

when Rita and her second husband, an aerospace mechanic named Mike Allen, gave Tony a set of golf clubs for his birthday, Laura seemed envious. So Mike and Rita gave the 10-year-old girl a five-iron, figuring she could hack around the backyard while her brother learned the finer points of the game.

As it turned out, Laura was the true golfer in the family. She loved to play and was a natural. In 1983 she won the first of several significant amateur titles, the English Intermediate Championship. She also won the South Eastern Championship that year. In 1984 she won the Welsh Open Stroke Play Championship, repeated as South Eastern champ, and was a member of the Curtis Cup team. By that time Davies was ready to turn professional. In early 1985 she was a talented part-time golfer who had to work a variety of jobs, including grocery store clerk and gas station attendant, to pay her bills. Soon she would have more money than she could spend.

For several years Davies remained a part-time player on the LPGA tour. She became terribly homesick whenever she traveled for extended periods of time, so most of her victories came on the Women Professional Golfers European tour. But in 1987 Davies surprised many observers by winning the U.S. Women's Open, defeating Ayako Okamoto in a play-off. The following year she was named a member of the British Empire by the queen of England. Davies won two tournaments as a rookie on the LPGA tour in 1988 and another tournament in 1989, but it wasn't until 1991 that she became one of the circuit's premier players. At 5 feet 10 inches and 180 pounds, Davies had far more strength than her opponents, and quickly gained a reputation as the longest hitter on the tour. She won more than $200,000 in 1991 and $240,000 in 1993. In 1994 she was the game's most dominant player, capturing the LPGA championship and winning more than $600,000.

Davies' dramatic improvement could be attributed to a natural maturation process. Previously she had been a volatile, unpredictable player who lost both her temper and her concentration when shots began to drift. But as she got older, she learned to accept the inevitable ebb and flow of a long season of professional golf.

One thing that did not change was Davies' aversion to practice. In addition to playing as many as 10 rounds per week, professional golfers typically spend hours a day on the driving range or putting greens. Not Davies. For her, 30 minutes constituted a grueling workout. "You've got to have fun," she has said. "Otherwise this would be too much like a real job. Just hitting balls aimlessly is a complete waste of time."

Davies was the LPGA tour's second leading money winner in 1995 with $530,349. In 1996 she was second again, trailing only rookie star Karrie Webb. Davies won four tournaments that year, including the LPGA championship and the du Maurier Classic.

Accomplishments

U.S. Women's Open champion: 1987
Named a member of the British Empire: 1988
LPGA championship winner: 1994, 1996
du Maurier Classic champion: 1996
LPGA's leading money winner: 1994

Anita DeFrantz

Born October 4, 1952

Anita DeFrantz, the first woman to represent the United States on the International Olympic Committee, grew up in Indiana, where basketball was practically a religion. For DeFrantz, however, there were few opportunities to participate. She spent most of her time sitting in the stands, applauding the efforts of her three brothers.

When DeFrantz enrolled at Connecticut College, she decided it was time to participate; considering her background, she chose basketball. There was just one problem—she didn't know the first thing about the game. Too much time on the sidelines and not enough on the court had left her unprepared for intercollegiate athletic competition. But Connecticut had just started a rowing program when DeFrantz arrived. The sport seemed simple enough to her, and since it consisted almost entirely of novices, she figured she'd have no trouble fitting in.

DeFrantz rowed competitively throughout her college career. After graduation she went

American to serve on the committee. Her primary duty during the 1984, 1988, and 1992 Games was being in charge of housing for Olympic athletes. She quickly developed a reputation for being thoughtful and outspoken, no great surprise to those who had trained or attended school with her. DeFrantz has been president of the Los Angeles Amateur Athletic Foundation, which awards grants to youth sports groups in Southern California.

Accomplishments

Olympic bronze medalist, rowing: 1976
First African American on International
    Olympic Committee
First American woman on International
    Olympic Committee

Shirley de la Hunty

Born July 18, 1925

on to law school. Her choice of schools—the University of Pennsylvania—was based in part on the school's strong rowing program. While in law school DeFrantz qualified for the U.S. Olympic team. She won a bronze medal at the Summer Games in Montreal in 1976, and received her law degree the following year. In 1979 she took a leave of absence from her job at a public interest firm in Philadelphia to concentrate her efforts on training for the 1980 Olympics. But like so many athletes that year, she was denied the opportunity to compete when the United States led a boycott of the Moscow Olympics. Unlike the majority of athletes, however, DeFrantz did not merely complain; rather, she filed a lawsuit against the U.S. Olympic Committee.

DeFrantz lost that battle, but her spirit caught the attention of the International Olympic Committee, which offered her an opportunity to join its ranks. "I stood up to the Olympic Committee and said that athletes ought to be able to make their own decisions," DeFrantz has said. "I think the IOC saw the strength, encouragement, and determination I had." DeFrantz became one of only two American members of the IOC. She was also the first American woman and the first African

Shirley de la Hunty, who won seven Olympic medals in track and field, was born Shirley Strickland in Guildford, Australia. She came to international prominence in 1948, during the Summer Olympics in London. Like so many athletes of her generation, de la Hunty had been forced to postpone her Olympic debut—World War II had wiped out the 1940 and 1944 Games. De la Hunty won three medals at the London Olympics—a bronze in the 100 meters, a bronze in the 80-meter hurdles, and a silver in the 4 x 100 relay. A photo finish in the 200-meter final, not made public until years later, indicated that she should have received another medal. De la Hunty had crossed the line with another runner in a virtual dead heat for third place, but after some deliberation she was placed fourth.

Four years later, at the 1952 Summer Games in Helsinki, de la Hunty turned in another bronze-medal performance in the 100 meters. In the 80-meter hurdles she ran one of the best races of her life, taking the gold medal with a world-record time of 10.9 seconds; no woman had ever broken 11 seconds in that event.

De la Hunty saved her most dramatic Olympic performance for her countrymen. By the start of the 1956 Games in Melbourne, Australia, de la Hunty was hardly the typical world-class runner. She was also a wife, mother, and professor of physics and mathematics. Unlike most of her competitors, she did not have the luxury of concentrating solely on training and racing, and she was older than her competitors.

Not only did de la Hunty defend her title in the 80-meter hurdles, but she did so in record fashion. Her winning time of 10.7 seconds was the fastest in Olympic history. She then ran the opening leg on Australia's 4 x 100 relay team, which took the gold medal in a world-record time of 44.5 seconds. De la Hunty's seven Olympic medals stood as a women's track-and-field record for more than 20 years, until Irena Szewinska equaled the mark in 1976. De la Hunty did not compete in another Olympiad after the 1956 Games but continued to demonstrate the speed that had made her famous. In 1960, at the age of 35, she broke 11 seconds in a 100-yard race. De la Hunty was also a formidable presence in the Commonwealth Games, in which she won two gold medals and two silver medals.

Accomplishments

Olympic gold medalist, 80-meter hurdles:
  1952, 1956
Olympic gold medalist, 4 x 100 relay: 1956
Olympic silver medalist, 4 x 100 relay: 1948
Olympic bronze medalist, 100 meters: 1948,
  1952
Olympic bronze medalist, 80-meter hurdles:
  1948

Donna de Varona

Born April 26, 1947

She grew up to become an Olympic swimming champion, outspoken advocate of women's athletics, and one of the founders of the Women's Sports Foundation, but when Donna de Varona was a child, she often felt that none of the other children wanted her on their team. "As a kid, I can still picture myself being constantly in the wrong playground," she said. "Was it my fault I was so athletic and so full of energy?"

Much of the blame—or the credit—goes to her father, a former college football All-American and a member of the U.S. Rowing

Hall of Fame, who passed along his talent and ambition. "He used to say, 'Realize your potential. If you've got it, work at it,'" de Varona recalled. She heeded his advice.

In the summer of 1958 de Varona joined a recreational swimming program in San Francisco. The girl with energy to burn finally got a chance to compete. A mere two years after her introduction to the sport of swimming, 13-year-old de Varona was in Rome, representing the United States at the 1960 Summer Olympics. Because she was the youngest member of the U.S. team, she attracted considerable media attention. She failed to win a medal, but wound up on the covers of *Life* and *Sports Illustrated*. Afterward, she returned to junior high and was elected president of her eighth-grade class.

By 1964, when it came time for the Summer Olympics in Tokyo, de Varona had broken 18 world records and was one of the fastest sprint swimmers in history. At the Games she won the 400-meter individual medley and helped the United States take a gold medal in the 4 x 100 freestyle relay. So impressive was her effort that both the Associated Press and United Press International named her Outstanding Female Athlete of the Year.

De Varona retired from competitive swimming in the fall of 1964. Within a year she landed a job as an expert commentator for ABC-TV's *Wide World of Sports*, providing insight and observation at the Amateur Athletic Union swimming championships. Although only 17, de Varona was the first woman to appear on network television as a sports broadcaster. The job fit her well—she was smart and graceful in front of the camera. She went on to cover several Olympic Games and served as assistant to the president of ABC Sports.

In addition to her work as a broadcaster, de Varona became a highly visible proponent of women's athletics. She was a consultant to the U.S. Senate from 1976 through 1978, and was a major force behind the 1978 Amateur Sports Act and the landmark Title IX legislation, which guaranteed equal opportunities to women in sports. As a member of President Jimmy Carter's Advisory Committee for Women in 1980, she was publicly commended by Carter for her work in amateur sports. She became the first elected president of the Women's Sports Foundation, a post she held for 10 years. She participated in the International Olympic Congress in 1981, and in 1982 worked as a consultant for the Los Angeles Olympic Organizing Committee. In 1983 she was elected to the International Women's Sports Hall of Fame. De Varona has been an athlete, author, entrepreneur, motivational speaker, pioneer, wife, and mother.

Accomplishments

Olympic gold medalist, 400-meter individual medley: 1964
Olympic gold medalist, 4 x 100 freestyle relay: 1964
Elected first president of Women's Sports Foundation: 1980
Inducted into International Women's Sports Hall of Fame: 1983
Inducted into U.S. Olympic Hall of Fame: 1987

Gail Devers

Born November 19, 1966

An Olympic gold medalist in track and field, Gail Devers was born in Seattle, Washington. Her racing career began with informal contests against her brother. For the longest time, Gail was unable to win those races. Then one day, she decided that she'd had enough of losing. She began working out on her own, training as hard as she could. Eventually, she beat her brother. After that he never challenged her again. "Instead," she said in an interview, "he used to get other little friends in the neighborhood to run against me. I beat them, too. From then on, running and track were all that mattered."

At Sweetwater High School in National City, California, Devers became one of the top prep runners in the country. As a senior she finished second in the 100 meters at the 1984 National Junior Championships; that same year she was third in the 100 at the Pan American Junior Games. Her performances prompted interest from college coaches—Devers chose UCLA, where she worked with renowned sprint coach Bobby Kersee, the husband of heptathlon champion Jackie Joyner-Kersee. As a freshman Devers reached the finals of three events—the 100 meters, the 200 meters, and 100-meter hurdles—at the NCAA championships. The following year she took fourth in the 100-meter hurdles and second in the long jump. In 1987, as a junior at UCLA, she became a world-class competitor. She lowered her personal best in the 100 to 10.97. Concentrating on that event, she finished second at the NCAA championships, fourth at the Athletics Congress championships,

and first at the Pan American Games and Olympic Festival.

In 1988, as a senior, Devers set an American record in the 100 meters and finished first at the NCAA championships. She qualified for the Summer Olympics by finishing second in the 100-meter hurdles at the U.S. trials. At the Summer Games in Seoul, however, things began to go wrong. She felt weak and tired. In her semifinal heat she finished last. Upon returning to the United States, her condition worsened. She suffered from migraine headaches and fainting spells, and her weight fluctuated wildly. Usually Devers carried 115 pounds on her 5-foot 3-inch frame. Suddenly, her weight would drop to 99 pounds or balloon to 130.

After two years and countless trips to physicians, Devers was diagnosed with a thyroid condition known as Graves' disease. Although radiation therapy eventually helped her beat the disease, she experienced painful and potentially crippling side effects, the most serious of which was a severe blistering of the skin. At one point, her feet bled so badly that doctors wanted to amputate both of them. Fortunately, a decision was made to give the healing process more time, and the symptoms eventually faded.

Few people gave Devers much chance of returning to world-class competition. But by the summer of 1991 she was the fastest sprinter in the United States, winning the 100-meter hurdles in 12.83 seconds at the national championships. At the World Track and Field Championships in Tokyo, she took a silver medal. The next year, at the Summer Games in Barcelona, Devers completed her remarkable comeback by winning the 100 meters with a time of 10.82 seconds. She stumbled and fell during the 100-meter hurdles, but that took none of the luster off her gold medal.

In 1993, at the world championships in Stuttgart, Germany, she won both the 100 meters and 100-meter hurdles, becoming the first woman in 45 years to win a sprint-hurdles double in a world-championship event. At the end of 1993 Devers was named Sportswoman of the Year by the U.S. Olympic Committee. Three years later, at the 1996 Summer Olympic Games in Atlanta, she defended her 100-meter title and helped the United States win the 4 x 100 relay.

Accomplishments

Olympic gold medalist, 100 meters: 1992, 1996
World champion, 100 meters: 1993
World champion, 100-meter hurdles: 1993
U.S. Olympic Committee Sportswoman of the Year: 1993
Olympic gold medalist, 4 x 100 relay: 1996

Manuela Di Centa

Born 1962

Italian cross-country skier Manuela Di Centa, an outspoken and rebellious woman who helped bring about much-needed change in her country's national ski federation, won five medals at the 1994 Winter Olympics in Lillehammer, Norway. She was an athletic prodigy who began skiing when quite young; by the time she was 17 she was already a respected and formidable member of the Italian national team. Even then she was not a typical athlete. Di Centa was not content to simply listen to her coaches and do as instructed. Her striking appearance, combined with her tendency to speak her mind, often got her into trouble; more than once she saw her name in the Italian tabloids.

The biggest controversy of her career came quite early. In 1984, at the age of 22, Di Centa angrily walked away from the sport because of an ongoing dispute with the national ski federation over a variety of matters, not the least of which was the treatment of female athletes. In Di Centa's eyes, women were second-class citizens to the federation; they were either abused or ignored. She refused to tolerate such injustice.

"They paid no attention to women," Di Centa said in an interview. "We skied, but we were taught nothing. The world of cross-country skiing used unnatural systems—yes, blood doping went on. I didn't agree with these things, so I quit."

Di Centa remained true to her convictions. For three years she refused to be a part of the old system. In 1987, however, when there were major coaching changes in the Italian ski federation, she returned to the fold. But almost immediately, controversy swirled around her again. This time it was a battle between Di Centa and Stefania Belmondo, the team's newest star, that attracted attention. Their personalities clashed, creating an air of tension on the national team that was never resolved.

For several years Belmondo was the superior skier. At the 1992 Winter Games in Albertville, France, Belmondo captured three medals, while Di Centa took home only one. Di Centa later discovered that she was suffering from a thyroid condition that dramatically affected her physical endurance and emotional stability. She spent more than two months in various hospitals before the malady was properly diagnosed. With daily medication, the illness was brought under control, and Di Centa was able to resume training.

At the 1994 Olympics in Lillehammer, Di Centa was 31 years old. But she had the energy and enthusiasm of a kid. She won gold medals in the 15-kilometer and 30-kilometer races, silver medals in the 5-kilometer race and pursuit, and a bronze medal in the 4 x 5K relay event. Belmondo, her teammate and chief rival, won only two bronze medals. Afterward, Di Centa seemed most proud of the fact that she was able to win on her own terms. "I want little girls to be inspired by seeing that a woman who is not like a man can win in sport," she said. "I think my medals touch all women."

Accomplishments

Olympic gold medalist, 15-kilometer freestyle: 1994

Olympic gold medalist, 30-kilometer classical: 1994

Olympic silver medalist, 5-kilometer classical: 1994

Olympic silver medalist, 10-kilometer freestyle pursuit: 1994

Olympic bronze medalist, 4 x 5K relay: 1994

Lottie Dod

September 24, 1871–October 10, 1962

Charlotte Dod, one of the first great multisport athletes, was born and raised during the Victorian era in Great Britain, when women were expected to be quiet, proper, and restrained. Lottie Dod would have none of that. She preferred the sweat and grit of tennis to the passivity of croquet. She preferred competing to watching. And she preferred winning to losing.

So she copied the style of play popular among male tennis players. Not for her the genteel baseline game—Dod was fiercely aggressive, willing to charge the net and deliver an occasional overhead smash to her opponent.

Dod recorded her first significant tennis victory in 1885, when she defeated two-time Wimbledon champion Maud Watson at Bath, ending Watson's streak of 55 consecutive victories. In 1887 Dod supplanted Watson as the finest tennis player in the world, taking the Ladies All-English title (Wimbledon) for the first time. As a 15-year-old, she was allowed to wear her school uniform, which included a calf-length skirt. This helped Dod—women traditionally played tennis in longer, bulkier skirts that slowed and constricted them. Dod remains the youngest player ever to win a championship at Wimbledon.

She repeated as Wimbledon champion in 1888, again defeating Blanche Hillyard in the final. In 1891 Dod regained the Wimbledon crown, which she wore through 1893; each year her victim in the championship match was Hillyard. Dod won the Wimbledon doubles championship in 1886, 1887, and 1888, and the mixed doubles title in 1889 and 1892.

Toward the end of her tennis career Dod played exhibition matches against male opponents, but even those did not quench her thirst for athletic competition. Tired of tennis, she retired from the game in 1894, at the age of 21. She switched to golf, archery, and field hockey, excelling at all three. At the 1908 Olympics she won a silver medal in archery; she was a member of Great Britain's national field hockey team in 1899; and she was the British Amateur golf champion in 1904. She was the first woman to successfully negotiate the bobsled run at St. Moritz and became an accomplished ice skater. In 1986, 24 years after her death and nearly a century after her first Wimbledon title, Dod was inducted into the International Women's Sports Hall of Fame.

Accomplishments

Wimbledon singles champion: 1887–1888, 1891–1893

Wimbledon doubles champion: 1886–1888

Olympic silver medalist, archery: 1908

British Women's Amateur golf champion: 1904

Anne Donovan

Born November 1, 1961

Anne Donovan, one of the finest—and tallest—players in the history of U.S. women's basketball, was born in Ridgewood, New Jersey. She was the youngest of eight children. Her father was 6 feet 6 inches tall; her mother 5 feet 10 inches. So it was no surprise that Anne was taller than most of her friends. She also liked sports, and it helped to have an advantage in size.

But Donovan's childhood was difficult. Before she got out of elementary school, she was already 6 feet tall; by the time she was 15, she was 6 feet 6 inches. She was taunted by other kids, who called her names and made fun of her. Physical size notwithstanding, Donovan was a sensitive child. "I remember being young enough to still go trick-or-treating, and people would tell me I was too old for that," she has said. "They'd say, 'You're not a little girl.' I remember people calling me 'sir' or 'young man.' People didn't look at me. They looked at my size."

Donovan learned to view her size as a blessing, rather than a curse. She looked at it as a gift from her father, who had died when she was five. If the fact that she was tall made her special, then she felt she had an obligation to develop that gift. So she turned to sports.

Donovan started playing basketball for a Catholic Youth Organization team in fifth grade. At first she was a bit clumsy and slow, but she worked hard at the game and began to cultivate her skills. In seventh grade she was named the Most Valuable Player in a tournament. In high school she became a star player for the Paramus Catholic Paladins. She started as a sophomore, along with her older sister, Mary, who was 6 feet 4 inches. After the season Mary went to Penn State on a basketball scholarship; Anne wound up on the Parade All-America team.

Two years later, as a senior, Anne Donovan was one of the most highly recruited players in the country. She scored 58 points in one game, 61 in another. She became the leading scorer in the history of New Jersey high school girls' basketball with 2,582 points and led Paramus to a third consecutive state championship. She sifted through all the college offers and selected defending national champion Old Dominion University in Norfolk, Virginia.

By the time she arrived at ODU, Donovan had grown two more inches, to 6 feet 8 inches. Though she didn't expect to play much as a freshman, she wound up leading the team in scoring and rebounding. She also helped lead the Monarchs to the 1980 national championship.

One of Donovan's greatest disappointments came in 1980, when the U.S. boycott of the Moscow Summer Games prevented her from achieving her lifelong dream of competing in the Olympics. But there would be other chances. She graduated from ODU in 1983, played professional ball in Japan the next year, and returned to the United States to prepare for the 1984 Olympics. With Donovan at center, and with the Soviet Union boycotting the Games in Los Angeles, the United States easily won the gold medal. Over the next few years Donovan continued to play professionally in Japan, where she became an enormously popular athlete. In 1988, at the Summer Olympics in Seoul, she played an important role in the United States' 77–70 victory over Yugoslavia in the gold medal game. Donovan later played professionally in Italy before returning to her alma mater to begin a coaching career.

Accomplishments

Three-time high school All-American
Olympic gold medalist: 1984, 1988
Naismith Award winner: 1983
Women's Basketball Coaches Association
  Player of the Year: 1983

Jean Driscoll

Born 1966

Jean Driscoll, born with spina bifida, is one of the most successful physically challenged athletes in history. From an early age she was determined not to let her physical disabilities be a handicap. She was an energetic and athletic girl who tried soccer, tennis, football, racquetball, and waterskiing. But it was basketball that gave her an opportunity to explore her potential as an athlete. The University of Illinois at Urbana, Champaign, which has one of the finest wheelchair sports programs in the world, recruited Driscoll to play basketball. There she was exposed to other exceptional athletes with similar physical limitations. They lived and trained together, pushing each other to excel. It was, Driscoll said, one of the best things that ever happened to her.

Driscoll took up wheelchair road racing

while in college, quickly becoming one of the best in the sport. In 1990 she captured the first of seven consecutive Boston Marathon titles, setting a world record with her time of 1 hour, 44 minutes, 9 seconds. She narrowly defeated her training partner, Ann Cody-Morris, who was second at 1:44.32. Their times reflected the rapidly changing nature of wheelchair sports, in which technology as well as physiology play major roles. Just three years earlier, Driscoll's time would have been good enough for a men's world record.

The following year, Driscoll defended her title at Boston, but not without a struggle. Nine days before the marathon, she was helping the University of Illinois women's wheelchair basketball team defend its national title. She did not have time to put in the miles of roadwork typically necessary to compete at the highest levels of wheelchair marathoning. Nevertheless, on April 15, 1991, Driscoll was again the fastest female competitor in Boston. She broke her own world record with a time of 1:42.42, which earned her more than $26,000 in cash and prizes.

In 1992 Driscoll was again at the front of the pack. She captured her third consecutive Boston title with a time of 1:36.52—another world record. In 1993 and 1994 she again finished first, with times of 1:34.50 and 1:34.22. She was also the champion in 1995 and 1996.

On the track Driscoll has been equally successful. She was a silver medalist in the 800-meter wheelchair exhibition race at the 1992 and 1996 Olympic Games, and helped lead the United States to a gold medal in the 400-meter relay in 1992. At the 1996 Para-Olympic Team Trials, she finished first in the 1,500 meters, 5,000 meters, and 10,000 meters. She also won the World Challenge 10K, the Houston Marathon, and the Los Angeles Marathon that year.

Trophies and paychecks notwithstanding, it has been Driscoll's biggest goal to be accepted as an athlete—not an athlete with a handicap. That is why she was so thrilled when the Women's Sports Foundation chose her as its Amateur Sportswoman of the Year in 1991. The award had previously gone to such exceptional athletes as Mary Lou Retton, Jackie Joyner-Kersee, and Janet Evans.

"When women first started going out there and playing sports, people didn't give them credit for having a competitive nature," Driscoll said. "In wheelchair sports, people thought athletes with disabilities were courageous and inspirational. They never give them credit for simply being competitive."

Accomplishments

Boston Marathon champion: 1990–1996
Member of national wheelchair basketball championship team: 1990–1991
Women's Sports Foundation Amateur Sportswoman of the Year: 1991
The Athletics Congress Disabled Athlete of the Year: 1991
National Wheelchair Athletic Association Female Athlete of the Year: 1991

Margaret Osborne du Pont

Born March 4, 1918

One of the great tennis players of the late 1940s and early 1950s, Margaret Osborne du Pont married into society's elite, but her beginnings were humble. She was born in rural Oregon and lived on a farm until the age of 10 when her family moved to Spokane, Washington. In Spokane, Margaret Osborne was introduced to tennis. While walking to her piano lessons in the afternoon, she would occasionally pass a public court and stop to watch the competitors. Her mother learned of her interest in tennis and decided to buy her a racket. Margaret fell in love with the game and displayed an unusual degree of ability.

Still, it wasn't until Osborne was 17 that she first received serious instruction. Working with former Davis Cup player Howard Kinsey, she began to blossom. She also benefited from an encounter with Hazel Hotchkiss Wightman, who had been one of the top players in the world. Wightman observed Osborne working out one day at the Berkeley Tennis Club; while impressed with the girl's physical talent and technique, she found her game lacking in one vital area. "She's too nice," Wightman noted. "She doesn't have the killer instinct."

When Osborne read Wightman's comments in the newspaper the next day, she was furious.

She was more motivated than ever to become a champion, if for no other reason than to prove Wightman—who would eventually become her close friend—wrong. Osborne's first championship came in 1936, when she won the U.S. 18-and-under title. She won her first Grand Slam singles title 10 years later at the age of 28, when she captured the French Open. The following year she won at Wimbledon. In 1948, after marrying millionaire Will du Pont, she won the first of three consecutive U.S. Open titles. She won the French Open in 1949.

During that time du Pont developed a lasting friendship—and rivalry—with Louise Brough, who would also win six career Grand Slam singles titles. The two were virtually inseparable on the tour, often practicing together in the morning, playing against each other in a singles match in the afternoon, and finally teaming up for a doubles match in the evening. Du Pont's first Grand Slam title came in 1941, when she won the U.S. Open women's doubles championship; her last came 21 years later, in the mixed doubles competition at Wimbledon. During that span of time du Pont won five French Open titles, seven Wimbledon titles, and 24 U.S. Open titles in singles, doubles, and mixed doubles. Most of the time her doubles partner was Louise Brough. From 1942 through 1950, they won nine consecutive U.S. Open doubles titles. They also staged wonderful matches on opposite sides of the net. In 1949, Brough defeated du Pont by a score of 10–8, 1–6, 10–8, in the Wimbledon final.

Margaret's marriage to Will du Pont, who was 20 years her senior, ended in divorce in 1964. In 1967 she was inducted into the International Tennis Hall of Fame. She later raised thoroughbred racehorses with Margaret Varner Bloss, another of her doubles partners. The two women gave their horses names that were reflective of their love for tennis. One filly, Mrs. Wightie, was named after Hazel Wightman.

Accomplishments

U.S. Open champion: 1948–1950
Wimbledon champion: 1947
French Open champion: 1946, 1949
Inducted into International Tennis Hall of Fame: 1967
Won 36 Grand Slam titles in singles, doubles, and mixed doubles

E

Amelia Earhart

July 24, 1897–July 2, 1937

Amelia Earhart, the first female pilot to fly solo across the Atlantic Ocean, was born and raised in Atchison, Kansas. She was a gifted and thoughtful young woman but she lacked focus. Though a talented student, she dropped out of school three times and never completed her college degree at Columbia University. For a time she worked as a nurse in a Toronto hospital, and even considered becoming a doctor. But those plans never panned out. She toyed with other careers, including social work. It wasn't until 1921, when she was 24 years old, that Earhart stumbled upon the passion of her life—flying.

In those early days of aviation, only 18 years after the Wright Brothers had made their historic flight at Kitty Hawk, Earhart was one of only a handful of women to hold a pilot's license. Though her reputation has swelled with the passing of time, the truth is that Earhart, in her younger days, was a marginal and sometimes reckless pilot who was fortunate to escape serious injury.

That she earned a place in history can be attributed to luck as well as to talent and courage. After Charles Lindbergh crossed the Atlantic in 1927, there was much debate about who would become the first woman to perform a similar feat. An expedition—led by, among others, Admiral Richard Byrd—was put together, and Earhart was chosen as the pilot. Her selection stemmed largely from the fact that she bore a striking resemblance to Lindbergh, and her personality seemed suited to the intense publicity that the event would generate. It's interesting to note that Earhart was one of three people in the plane that crossed the Atlantic on June 17, 1928, and she was merely a passenger. The navigator and pilot, both men, were virtually ignored by the press.

None of this was lost on Earhart, who, despite the fame and adulation, wanted something more. She wanted to leave her mark on the world; she wanted to be thought of as a pilot. Indeed, she accomplished that feat, eventually becoming one of the best in the business. In late 1928, with money earned from her speaking engagements, she purchased her own airplane and became the first woman to fly solo, round-trip, across the United States. In 1932, Earhart, by then married to publisher George Putnam, became the first woman to complete a nonstop solo flight across the Atlantic. Her plane suffered engine problems, and she was forced to land in an Irish cow pasture.

Earhart's last flight was to be a trip around the world. In a plane provided by Purdue University, Earhart left Miami, Florida, in June 1937. Accompanied by navigator Fred Noonan, she made stops in Puerto Rico, Venezuela, Brazil, French West Africa, Chad, the Sudan, Ethiopia, Calcutta, Singapore, Java, Australia, and New Guinea. After three weeks and 20,000 miles, she headed across the Pacific Ocean, with Howland Island as her destination. A U.S. naval base on the island lost contact with Earhart when she was only a few miles away. It was the last anyone ever heard from her. A massive air and sea search was conducted, but no trace of Earhart, Noonan, or their plane was ever found.

The disappearance of Amelia Earhart has been shrouded in mystery ever since, fueling many rumors. The most popular suggested that Earhart became deliberately lost at sea in order to give the United States a reason to search the area and to investigate the actions of the Japanese military. Others have speculated that she wanted solitude, landed somewhere safely, and lived out her life in seclusion. But the definitive Earhart biography, published in 1989, lends little credence to any theory other than this—her plane went down somewhere in the Pacific, and she was lost at sea. Earhart was a charter member of the International Women's Sports Hall of Fame.

Accomplishments

First woman to fly across the Atlantic: 1928
First woman to fly solo, round-trip, across the U.S.: 1928
First woman to fly solo across the Atlantic: 1932
Set women's speed record of 181 mph: 1930
First person to fly solo from Hawaii to California: 1935
Inducted into International Women's Sports Hall of Fame: 1980

Gertrude Ederle

Born October 23, 1906

Gertrude Ederle, the first woman to swim the English Channel, was born in New York City and raised in a German-American neighborhood. President Calvin Coolidge once referred to her as "America's best gal." It was a term that would surely be deemed condescending and inappropriate today, but was high praise in those days.

Ederle's father was a butcher, her mother a housewife. She learned to swim during summertime trips to the New Jersey shore but was a late bloomer—it wasn't until she was 15 that Ederle joined the Women's Swimming Association of New York and learned proper swimming technique.

Her progress was remarkable. Just three years later, at the 1924 Olympics, she won three medals, including a gold in the 4 x 100 freestyle relay. Between 1921 and 1925, Ederle held 29 world records at distances ranging from 50 yards to a half mile, and was the most successful and decorated woman in the sport of swimming. But she felt something was missing. She wanted a greater challenge, and that challenge was the English Channel.

Ederle's first attempt came in 1925, at age 19. Less than seven miles from the British shore, Ederle, suffering from seasickness, was pulled out of the water by her trainer. She was angry and disappointed but not beaten.

She returned the next year, more determined than ever. Wearing a protective coating of Vaseline, olive oil, and lanolin over her bathing suit, Ederle stepped into the water at Cape Gris-Nez, France, on the morning of August 6, 1926. She was a compact, powerful woman, carrying 135 pounds on a 5-foot 5-inch frame. The Channel is notoriously cold and unpredictable, but Ederle's strength helped sustain her during more than 14 hours of swimming. At 9:40 P.M. she emerged from the water at Kingsdorn. Her time of 14 hours, 31 minutes was nearly two hours better than that of any of the five people—all men—who had previously swum the Channel. In addition to the usual rigors of Channel swimming, she had survived a storm that dragged her off course and tacked on an additional 14 miles to the 21-mile route.

Ederle became an instant celebrity after swimming the English Channel. She was front-page news in the *New York Times*; a ticker-tape parade, attended by more than 2 million people, was held in her honor on the streets of New York.

Ederle's triumph was followed by tragedy. Financial mismanagement caused her to lose much of the money she had earned as a speaker and performer on the promotional circuit. Worse, she suffered permanent damage to her hearing during the Channel swim; by 1933, at age 27, she was completely deaf. A few years later she suffered an emotional breakdown; after that she fell down a flight of stairs and suffered a serious back injury. She later recovered from her ailments sufficiently to teach swimming to children with hearing problems, and even participated—as a swimmer—in Billy Rose's Aquacade at the 1939 World's Fair in New York. Ederle's last public appearance was in 1976, on the 50th anniversary of her remarkable swim across the English Channel.

Accomplishments

Olympic bronze medalist, 100-meter freestyle: 1924

Olympic bronze medalist, 400-meter freestyle: 1924

Olympic gold medalist, 4 x 100 freestyle relay: 1924

First woman to swim the English Channel: 1926

Lyubov Egorova

Born 1966

Russian cross-country skier Lyubov Egorova, one of the most decorated athletes in the history of the Winter Olympics, grew up in Tomsk, Siberia. She was the second child born to a pair of factory workers. As a young girl she loved to dance, and she studied ballet for several years. But in Siberia, children either learn to embrace winter sports or find themselves confined to the house for months on end.

Egorova found cross-country skiing to be a pleasant endeavor, and she was quite good at it. In the Soviet Union at that time, talented athletes—even those who lived in such remote outposts as Siberia—were often spotted at a young age and targeted for greatness. So it was with Egorova, who was encouraged to develop her skill as a Nordic skier. In 1982, at the age of 16, she left her family and moved to Leningrad to train with the country's finest cross-country skiers.

By 1992 Egorova had become one of the best cross-country skiers in the world, as indicated by her performance at the Winter Olympics in Albertville, France. No athlete accomplished more than Egorova did in Albertville. She took home five medals, including golds in the 10-kilometer freestyle pursuit, 15-kilometer freestyle, and 4- x 5-kilometer mixed relay.

Two years later, in Lillehammer, Norway, Egorova was again one of the premier athletes of the Winter Olympics. Over the Olympic fortnight she staged an intense battle with Italy's Manuela Di Centa, another gifted cross-country skier. Di Centa emerged with the most medals (five), but Egorova again won three gold medals, finishing first in the 5-kilometer classical, 10-kilometer freestyle pursuit, and 4- x 5-kilometer mixed relay. Egorova also won a silver medal in the 15-kilometer freestyle.

That brought her medal total to nine, one shy of the all-time record set by Soviet skier Raisa Smetanina. Egorova's six gold medals tied the record held by Soviet speed skater Lydia Skoblikova. Egorova received $15,000 from the Russian Olympic Committee for each of her gold medals and $7,000 for her silver medal.

The money was badly needed, since Egorova and her husband, a former sailor, were hardly born into wealth. Most of the money, Egorova said, would be used to construct the couple's first home.

After the 1994 Games, Egorova decided to take a long break from skiing, perhaps as much as a year. But she was not considering retirement. At the 1998 Winter Games in Nagano, Japan, she would be 31 years old; Di Centa, after all, had won five medals at that age.

Accomplishments

Olympic gold medalist, 15-kilometer freestyle: 1992

Olympic gold medalist, 10-kilometer freestyle pursuit: 1992, 1994

Olympic gold medalist, 4- x 5-kilometer mixed relay: 1992, 1994

Olympic gold medalist, 5-kilometer classical: 1994

Kornelia Ender

Born October 25, 1958

One of several great swimmers to come out of East Germany in the 1970s, Kornelia Ender was the first woman to win four Olympic gold medals. Stepping into the international spotlight at the 1972 Summer Olympics in Munich, 13-year-old Ender won three silver medals—in the 200-meter individual medley, 4 x 100 freestyle relay, and 4 x 100 medley relay. With those performances she made it clear that she wouldn't be swimming in anyone else's wake for long.

Less than a year later, Ender shattered Shane Gould's 100-meter freestyle world record. Only 14, she was easily the finest and fastest swimmer in the world. By the time she was 16, Ender had broken the world record in the 100-meter freestyle eight times. In 1973, at the first swimming world championships, she won the 100-meter freestyle and the 100-meter butterfly, and helped East Germany capture team titles in the freestyle relay and medley relay. In addition to her four gold medals, she won a silver in the 200-meter individual medley.

At the European championships in 1974, Ender won four gold medals; in 1975 she took four golds and one silver. She went to the 1976 Summer Olympics brimming with confidence—she had set 15 world records in the previous three years. At the Montreal Games, the 17-year-old Ender won her first gold medal in the 100-meter freestyle, in which she set a world record with a time of 55.65 seconds. She added a second gold medal—and world record—in the 200-meter freestyle. In her final individual event, the 100-meter butterfly, she equaled the world mark. Before the Olympiad ended, she picked up a fourth gold medal in the 4 x 100 medley relay, anchoring East Germany to victory, and a silver in the 4 x 100 freestyle relay. Afterward, Ender was allowed to meet her grandmother, who had defected when Ender was a baby. Their meeting was closely monitored by East German officials, who were fearful that Ender might also decide to take up residence in the West.

During Ender's rise to prominence, East Germany's athletic programs were strongly criticized by officials from Western nations. The East German swimmers were frequently accused of taking performance-enhancing drugs, such as steroids. East German athletic officials repeatedly denied the charges, and said that the success of their swimmers resulted from intense training and innovative nutritional techniques. Years later, substantial evidence of East German steroid use was revealed, but Ender never tested positive for steroid use in international competition. Her swimming ability was first spotted when she was a child playing in the water during a family vacation. Not long after that, she was recruited into the East German athletic system, in which children spent as much time on athletics as they did on academics.

Ender retired after the Montreal Olympics. She was inducted into the International Swimming Hall of Fame in 1981, and later married Roland Matthes, who had also won eight Olympic medals in swimming.

Accomplishments

Olympic gold medalist, 100-meter freestyle: 1976

Olympic gold medalist, 100-meter butterfly: 1976

Olympic gold medalist, 200-meter freestyle: 1976

Olympic gold medalist, 4 x 100 medley relay: 1976

Inducted into International Swimming Hall of Fame: 1981

First woman to win four gold medals in Olympic competition

Janet Evans

Born August 28, 1971

Janet Evans, the first American woman to win four gold medals in Olympic swimming, was born in Fullerton, California, and grew up in the Los Angeles suburb of Placentia. As a girl she was a talented athlete with a bright smile that belied her competitive zeal. One of her biggest problems as an adolescent was maintaining weight and strength. Swimmers tend to be heavily muscled, but Evans was short and lean. She had virtually no body fat. In fact, as a 15-year-old high school student, she was 5 feet 3 inches tall and weighed less than 100 pounds. It seemed that she could never eat enough food to fuel her raging metabolism.

In some of her early international meets, other swimmers laughed at Evans because she looked more like a runner than a swimmer. Once she hit the water, though, the laughter stopped. As Evans demonstrated many times, appearances can be deceiving.

Evans' breakthrough came at the 1988 Olympic Games in Seoul. Prior to that she had been considered a promising young athlete in need of training and maturity. She had finished first in the 400-meter freestyle and 800-meter freestyle at the 1987 U.S. Open, and had even set a world record in the 1,500-meter freestyle. But whether she would be able to withstand the rigors of Olympic competition against older, stronger athletes was another matter.

As it turned out, there was no reason for concern. At the 1988 Games, Evans, a 17-year-old high school senior, won individual gold medals in the 400-meter freestyle, 800-meter freestyle, and 400-meter individual medley. In the 400 she shattered her own world record; in the 800 she set an Olympic record. When she returned to the United States, she discovered that her life had changed forever.

"When I first got back I was naive," Evans said. "I thought I was going to come home and be just a typical California teenager. That's when it dawned on me the impact the Olympics had on everyone."

There were hundreds of interviews to conduct and endorsement deals to negotiate, and there was the matter of choosing a college. Evans settled on Stanford, which had one of the finest swimming programs in the nation. She entered college in the fall of 1989. That same year, she won the Sullivan Award and was named the U.S. Olympic Committee Sportswoman of the Year. She was also named Amateur Sportswoman of the Year by the Women's Sports Foundation.

As a college student Evans grew to 5 feet 6 inches tall and added a few pounds of muscle to her frame. She won three NCAA titles in 1990 and two more in 1991, but left Stanford to train at the University of Texas. She won two gold medals and a silver medal at the 1991 world championships. The next year, at the 1992 Summer Olympics in Barcelona, she won a gold medal in the 800-meter freestyle and a silver in the 400-meter freestyle. In 1994 she became the first woman outside of East Germany to win consecutive world championship titles, taking the gold medal in the 800-meter freestyle in Rome. But two years later, at the 1996 Summer Olympics in Atlanta, she failed to win a single medal.

Accomplishments

Olympic gold medalist, 400-meter freestyle:
   1988
Olympic gold medalist, 800-meter freestyle:
   1988, 1992
Olympic gold medalist, 400-meter individual
   medley: 1988
Sullivan Award winner: 1989
USOC Sportswoman of the Year: 1989

Cory Everson

Born 1959

Cory Everson, a champion bodybuilder-
turned-entrepreneur, grew up in Deerfield,
Illinois. She was the second of three girls born
to Hank and Chris Kneuer. Hank was a brew-
master by trade, but earlier in life he had been
a successful gymnast; Chris, who worked
as a bus driver, had been a track star in
Germany, where both she and Hank were
born. Cory's parents divorced when she was
in the sixth grade; while the split was amicable,
it had a dramatic effect on the children. Cory
responded by throwing herself into both
schoolwork and sports. She was a straight-A
student at Deerfield High School, from which
she graduated in 1977; she was also an outstanding athlete. Track and field was her sport
of choice; because she was fast, strong, and
versatile, the grueling pentathlon became her
specialty. At the University of Wisconsin, she
was among the finest track-and-field competitors in the United States. Four times she captured the Big 10 pentathlon championship.

While a student at Wisconsin, Cory
Kneuer met Jeff Everson, one of the school's
strength and conditioning coaches. Seven
years older than Kneuer, and an expert in fitness and training, he convinced her that she
had the ability to become a topflight bodybuilder. But shortly after graduating with a
degree in interior design in 1981, Kneuer
developed a serious medical problem. A rare
enzyme deficiency that affects the circulatory
system had caused her left leg to double in
size. She spent two months in a hospital
before the doctors discovered the cause and
prescribed a course of treatment. Within a

year, Kneuer was not only fully recovered, but
also married Jeff Everson.

Working with her husband, Everson transformed herself into a world-class bodybuilder in
just two years. In 1984, on her first attempt, she
won the Ms. Olympia contest, the most prestigious
event in women's bodybuilding. It was one of
many titles that she would win over the next six
years. Everson won the Ms. Olympia contest six
consecutive times—a record—before retiring from
the sport in 1989. At her best, she was a symmet-
rical marvel. She stood 5 feet 8 inches tall and
weighed 145 pounds. Each of her well-muscled

thighs measured 23 inches, exactly the same as her waist.

Everson was successful at parlaying her bodybuilding achievements into a second career. She became a writer, businesswoman, fitness consultant, television personality, and, finally, an actress. In 1991 she appeared in the film *Double Impact* with martial artist Jean-Claude Van Damme. She was among a handful of actresses sought to play strong female roles in action-adventure films.

"Julia Roberts isn't believable as being able to hurdle a truck and not hurt herself, and go and kick two guys in the face. Nor is Meryl Streep," Everson said in a magazine interview. "They're both great actresses, but you have to look believable."

Accomplishments

Four-time Big 10 pentathlon champion
Won Ms. Olympia title on first attempt: 1984
Six-time winner of Ms. Olympia contest

Chris Evert

Born December 21, 1954

Chris Evert, who won 18 Grand Slam singles titles in a long and illustrious tennis career, grew up in Fort Lauderdale, Florida. There was never any doubt that she would be a tennis player. Her father, Jimmy, a teaching pro at the Holiday Park Tennis Center in Fort Lauderdale, had attended the University of Notre Dame on a tennis scholarship; he had won the U.S. National Indoor Championship in 1940 and the Canadian Singles Championship in 1947. All of the Evert children—Chris and her two brothers and two sisters—were playing tennis by the time they were six.

Evert's first big victory came in 1970, when she was 15. At a tournament in North Carolina she defeated England's Margaret Smith Court, who was coming off a sweep of Grand Slam events. Evert was merely the U.S. junior champion; no one expected her to upset the greatest player in the world. After that victory, Evert, known as Chrissie, became a darling of the media, and her clean-cut image made her a favorite with both fans and sponsors. In 1971,

at the age of 16, she competed in the U.S. Open for the first time and advanced as far as the semifinals before losing to Billie Jean King. Some of the tournament competitors expressed envy at the attention Evert was receiving, but King, who went on to win the Open that year, rushed to her defense.

"This is a 16-year-old kid who's beating the best people in the world," King said. "It's

beautiful." In 1974 Evert won her first Grand Slam events—Wimbledon and the French Open. The following year she repeated as French Open champion and won her first U.S. Open title. By the end of the year, she was the top-ranked player in women's tennis, a position that she would hold for the better part of the next six years.

About that same time, Evert was involved romantically with men's tennis star Jimmy Connors. The couple's relationship received intense media coverage but eventually fizzled. If there was any fallout, it didn't show up in Evert's game. Through the early 1980s she continued to perform masterfully, trading places at the top of the women's rankings with Martina Navratilova. Evert won at least one Grand Slam title every year for 13 years, from 1974 through 1986. In 1981 she was named Sportswoman of the Year by the Women's Sports Foundation, and in 1985 the same organization voted her the Greatest Woman Athlete of the Last 25 Years. By the time she retired from the game in 1989, Evert had won 18 major titles—seven French, six U.S., three Wimbledon, and two Australian.

At 5 feet 6 inches, 125 pounds, Evert was a methodical player who liked to hang back on the baseline. Her asset was her stamina, both mental and physical—she could outlast almost anyone in a rally. Rarely, if ever, did she betray any emotion on the court, a trait that led to her being dubbed the "Ice Princess." Evert was a pleasant and sometimes emotional woman away from the court. She felt that in order to be at her best—and she was a fierce competitor—she had to focus entirely on the match.

Evert was married to former tennis pro John Lloyd, then to Olympic skier Andy Mill. Her first child, Alexander James, was born on October 12, 1991. She and her husband host the annual Chris Evert Pro/Celebrity tennis tournament, a charity event that benefits hurricane relief and the fight against drug abuse in South Florida. Evert also works as a commentator for NBC-TV.

Accomplishments

Wimbledon champion: 1974, 1976, 1981
U.S. Open champion: 1975–1978, 1980, 1982
French Open champion: 1974–1975,
    1979–1980, 1983, 1985–1986
Australian Open champion: 1982, 1984
Named Greatest Woman Athlete of the
    Last 25 Years by Women's Sports
    Foundation: 1985
Inducted into International Women's Sports
    Hall of Fame: 1981

F

Mae Faggs

Born April 10, 1932

Dubbed the "human rabbit," Aeriwentha Mae Faggs was one of the world's greatest sprinters. Born in Mays Landing, New Jersey, she was introduced to the sport of track and field as a young teen, when she was recruited by the New York City Police Athletic League. She proved to be a gifted athlete who, at the age of 16, became the youngest member of the U.S. Olympic track-and-field team.

Faggs attended Tennessee State University (where she became a mentor to such outstanding athletes as Wilma Rudolph and Willye White) on a track scholarship and continued to develop as a sprinter. In 1949 she set an American record for 220 yards. In 1952 she set an American indoor record for 100 yards and set a world record for 400 meters (45.9 seconds). At the 1952 Summer Games in Helsinki, she helped the United States win a gold medal in the 4 x 100 relay. She was the U.S. national 200-meter champion in 1954 and 1956, and the 100-yard champion in 1955 and 1956. She qualified for the 1956 Olympics, where she led the United States to a bronze medal in the 4 x 100 relay.

By the time she retired from competitive track and field, Faggs had held every American sprint record—indoors and outdoors. She went on to achieve success in a variety of educational and administrative positions. She worked for many years as a teacher and as assistant athletic director in Cincinnati, Ohio, and Princeton, New Jersey. After leading her team to a state track-and-field championship in 1989, she was named Ohio Coach of the Year.

Faggs became an outspoken advocate for female athletes. She believed not only that young girls should have opportunities to participate in sports, but also that they should have the encouragement of their parents. She targeted

Memorable Moment: 1944

Ann Curtis Wins the Sullivan Award

When Ann Curtis was 11 years old she won her first major swimming championship, the Amateur Athletic Union girls freestyle—her only coaches having been the Sisters of the Ursuline Convent in Santa Rosa, California.

Over the years Curtis would win many more races. She began swimming in seniors competition in 1943 and quickly became one of the most dominant performers in the sport. She won the AAU national outdoor championship in the 100 meters four times, and in the 400 and 800 meters six times each. She won two medals at the 1948 Olympic Games.

Of all her honors, perhaps the most prestigious was the Sullivan Award, which Curtis won in 1944. The James E. Sullivan Memorial Trophy is presented annually to the outstanding amateur athlete in the United States. The odds against Curtis receiving the award were great. First, no swimmer had ever won; second, no woman had ever won. There had, of course, been women who deserved serious consideration—including the great Babe Didrikson Zaharias—but none had been able to overcome the extreme bias against women's sports that existed at the time. Curtis did. In 1944 not only did she win the Sullivan Award, she was also named Female Athlete of the Year by the Associated Press.

the mothers of young athletes in many of her remarks, pleading with them to support their daughters' efforts to compete in sports—just as they would support their sons.'

Faggs, who remained an avid golfer despite a protracted battle with breast cancer, was inducted into the Tennessee State University Sports Hall of Fame and the U.S. National Track and Field Hall of Fame in 1965. In 1996 she was inducted into the International Women's Sports Hall of Fame.

Accomplishments

Olympic gold medalist, 4 x 100 relay: 1952
Olympic bronze medalist, 4 x 100 relay: 1956
Inducted into U.S. National Track and Field
   Hall of Fame: 1965
Inducted into International Women's Sports
   Hall of Fame: 1996

Heather Farr

March 10, 1965–November 20, 1993

Heather Farr, whose promising career as a professional golfer was cut short by cancer, was born in Phoenix, Arizona. She played in her first tournament when she was only nine years old and became Arizona amateur champion at the age of 13. That was the beginning of a brilliant amateur career in which Farr won two Junior World Championships and two PGA National Junior titles. She was a three-time winner of the Future Legends and also captured the 1982 United States Golf Association Junior Girls tournament. In 1981 she tied for medalist honors at the U.S. Women's Amateur and in 1983 was low amateur scorer at the U.S. Women's Open. At Arizona State University she was a two-time All-American.

When she qualified for the Ladies Professional Golf Association tour on her first attempt, at the tender age of 20, Farr seemed destined for wealth and celebrity. Just 5 feet 1 inch, she had strength, control, and a work ethic that was second to none. "When she first came on the tour, nobody worked harder," former LPGA regular Mary Bryan said. "Heather was determined to do well."

Farr soon became one of the better young players on the pro tour. By 1988 she was 41st on the LPGA money list, and climbing steadily. But that was the year Farr discovered a lump in her breast. The tumor was malignant, and she immediately began radical and aggressive treatment for breast cancer. It was the beginning of a courageous battle that would last nearly five years. Farr endured a mastectomy, chemotherapy, radiation therapy, spinal surgery, and a bone marrow transplant. Throughout this horrific course of treatment, she remained a spirited young woman with a zest for life.

"Life's not fair to anybody," Farr said during a 1992 interview, shortly after learning of yet another recurrence of cancer. "Sometimes you just have to get a grip. Do you know what's not fair? My second year on the tour I didn't make a check for eight weeks. And the ninth week, when I did make a check? It was for $500. You just play through."

Farr's spirit and sense of humor lifted those around her, and they responded in kind. Players on the PGA and LPGA tours held several fund-raisers to help Farr and her parents, Gerald and Sharon, defray the cost of medical treatment. In 1992, after a bone marrow transplant and another round of radiation therapy, Farr felt strong and confident enough to predict her return to the LPGA tour. She married Goran Lingmerth, a former National Football League placekicker, and began working on her game.

But Farr never made it back to the tour. On November 20, 1993, after undergoing several medical procedures, her body gave out. She died as she had lived—surrounded by friends, family, and fellow golfers. She was 28 years old.

In her honor, the LPGA began awarding the Heather Farr Player Award in 1994. The award recognizes the LPGA tour player "who, through her hard work, dedication, and love of the game of golf, has demonstrated determination, perseverance, and spirit in fulfilling her goals as a player."

Accomplishments

USGA Junior Girls champion: 1982
U.S. Women's Amateur medalist: 1981
Two-time NCAA All-American
Two-time PGA National Junior champion

Peggy Fleming

Born July 27, 1948

Olympic figure skating champion Peggy Fleming was born in San Jose, California, and raised in Pasadena. With her long dark hair, slender build, and delicate features, she

sometimes appeared frail on the ice. But Fleming was an artist, fragile but spirited, and if she was less athletic than many figure skaters, she was still an undeniably mesmerizing performer. And for a time she was the best in the world.

Fleming's rise to prominence began at the age of nine, when she laced up her first pair of skates. By 11 she was competing, and by 12 she had captured the Pacific Coast Juvenile Figure Skating Championship. In January 1964, when she was 15, Fleming won the first of her five national titles. No one had ever done that at such a young age. A month later, at the Winter Olympics in Innsbruck, Austria, she finished a respectable sixth in her first international competition.

The daughter of Albert and Doris Fleming was clearly a prodigy. But her talent was not necessarily considered a blessing. Albert Fleming was a pressman who changed jobs often. The Flemings had three other children, and they did not have much money. Nevertheless, they were committed to helping Peggy realize her potential; they moved to Colorado Springs in 1965 so that Peggy could work closely with Carlo Fassi, a former European champion who had graduated to coaching. To make ends meet, Albert worked extra hours; Doris sewed Peggy's costumes. It was a strain on the entire family, but the sacrifice paid off. In February 1966 Fleming captured first place at the world championships in Davos, Switzerland. While there, she learned that her father had died of a heart attack. Fleming was devastated, but she continued to skate.

Fleming defended both her U.S. and world titles in each of the next two years, and in 1968 won the gold medal at the Winter Olympics in Grenoble, France. Winning the gold medal was the greatest achievement of her career—her beauty, elegance, sensitivity, and artistry were put on display for the world to see, and she defeated runner-up Gabriele Seyfert of East Germany.

After winning her third world title in March 1968, Fleming announced her retirement from amateur figure skating. It was time to help support her family, so she became a professional skater. She signed a network television contract in April of that year and in November appeared in her own special, *Here's Peggy Fleming*. She later went on tour with the Ice Follies.

In 1971 Fleming married Greg Jenkins, a doctor. The first of their two children was born in 1977, a year after Fleming had retired from the pro circuit. She has since become a polished and respected figure skating commentator on U.S. television.

Accomplishments

First place, U.S. championships: 1964–1968
First place, world championships: 1966–1968
Olympic gold medalist: 1968

Dawn Fraser

Born September 4, 1937

Born in Balmain, a suburb of Sydney, Australia, Dawn Fraser dominated women's swimming for nearly a decade, capturing three individual Olympic gold medals and setting 27 world records. But she is remembered as much for her exploits out of the water as for her achievements in the water.

Fraser was, by the age of 19, the fastest female swimmer in the world. At the 1956 Olympics she won a gold medal in the 100 meters, with a world-record time of 1:02.0. At the 1960 Games in Rome she repeated as 100-meter champion with a time of 1:01.2, a new Olympic record. She broke that record four years later at the 1964 Games, when she took her third 100-meter gold medal with a time of 59.5.

For all her success, Fraser also had her share of tragedy and controversy. When she was a teenager her brother, Don, who was her first swimming instructor, died of leukemia; he was only 21. Then, in March 1964, her mother was killed in an automobile accident. Dawn had been the driver of the car, and she suffered a chipped vertebra in her neck. Less than six months later, at the Tokyo Olympics, she came back to win her third 100-meter gold medal.

Sports Illustrated once wrote of Fraser, "She boldly and gaily dominates a sport that commonly verges on asceticism." A free spirit whose talent and exuberance were appreciated by the vast majority of her countrymen, Fraser nonetheless provoked the anger of Australian swimming officials. In 1960 she refused an 11th-hour request to swim on a relay team. She said she had been out late celebrating her 100-meter victory the night before and was not prepared to race.

Two years later, at the British Commonwealth Games, she stunned team officials by announcing to a reporter that she planned to celebrate her first sub-one-minute performance at 100 meters by having a few beers.

At the 1964 Olympics, against the orders of Australian Swimming Union officials, who said that they wanted her to rest and conserve energy, Fraser took part in the opening-day parade. She later refused to wear a regulation swimsuit. Then, she was arrested for stealing a Japanese flag from the grounds of the emperor's palace. To Fraser, it was a harmless practical joke. She wanted a souvenir, so she jumped into the moat surrounding the palace and went after the flag. Police later released her, and the incident was considered a harmless bit of fun by most Australians. Fraser was even named Australian of the Year by the Australian Day Council in 1964. But swimming officials viewed her as something less than a hero. Because of her antics in Tokyo, they decided to ban her from competition for the next 10 years. Her suspension was lifted in 1968, after only four years, but she never returned to competitive swimming.

Accomplishments

Olympic gold medalist, 100-meter freestyle: 1956, 1960, 1964
Olympic silver medalist, 400-meter freestyle: 1956
Olympic gold medalist, 4 x 100 freestyle relay: 1956
Olympic silver medalist, 4 x 100 freestyle relay: 1960, 1964
Olympic silver medalist, 4 x 100 medley relay: 1960

Gretchen Fraser

February 11, 1919–February 18, 1994

The first athlete from the United States to win an Olympic medal in skiing, Gretchen Kunigk Fraser was born in Tacoma, Washington. Her mother was a native Norwegian whose affection for the sport of skiing was passed on to Gretchen. Young Gretchen never lacked for opportunities to hone her skill on the slopes— the Kunigk family owned a ski resort near Mount Rainier, Washington. In that nurturing environment Gretchen became one of the first great American alpine skiers.

In 1936 Kunigk married Donald Fraser, a member of the U.S. Olympic ski team. The pair trained together, hoping to become husband-and-wife Olympians in 1940. But they were denied the opportunity to compete. With the outbreak of World War II, the Olympic Games were put on hold for more than a decade.

Rather than bemoan her fate, Gretchen Fraser continued to ski. In 1941 she captured the U.S. national downhill and alpine combined championships; the following year she was the national slalom champion. Retirement followed, but she stayed active by offering lessons in skiing, riding, and swimming to disabled veterans in U.S. Army hospitals. Her husband served in the U.S. Navy.

When the war ended, Gretchen Fraser had no intention of returning to competitive skiing. She was 26 years old, and several years removed from world-class competition. But her husband talked her into giving the sport one last try; he even volunteered to be her coach. Together, they worked toward one goal—an Olympic medal. In 1948 Fraser surprised many by qualifying for the U.S. Olympic ski team. She was only a few weeks shy of her 29th birthday when the

Winter Games began in St. Moritz, Switzerland. Even by the more relaxed standards of her day, she was an old-timer.

Fraser's age and her underdog status made her a favorite with the crowd. She had waited 12 years for the opportunity to compete on the biggest stage in amateur athletics; leaving retirement behind, she proved that skiing was not the exclusive domain of teenagers. On the day Fraser won the gold medal in the slalom, she overcame another bit of adversity. She was in first place after her first run, and needed only to ski smoothly and safely on her final run to win the gold. But a last-second technical glitch caused a 17-minute delay, during which she had to stand, shivering nervously, in the starting gate at the top of the run. When it was finally time to ski she negotiated the course cleanly, thus becoming the first American to win a medal in Olympic skiing. She later added a silver medal in the alpine combined.

Fraser was inducted into the U.S. National Ski Hall of Fame in 1960. She died in 1994, on the eve of the Lillehammer Winter Olympics, little more than a month after the death of her husband of 54 years.

Accomplishments

First American to win an Olympic medal in skiing
Olympic gold medalist, slalom: 1948
Olympic silver medalist, alpine combined: 1948
Inducted into U.S. National Ski Hall of Fame: 1960

Jane Frederick

Born 1952

Jane Frederick, who won five national pentathlon championships in the 1970s, grew up in Berkeley, California. Her father, Harland Frederick, was a political science professor at the University of California at Berkeley; a former competitive runner, he also officiated track meets at the school. Harland's fondness for the sport was passed on to each of his four children. Jane was the youngest and the most eager to take part in their backyard track meets. She first learned to hurdle by using a sawhorse in her driveway. She was always busy doing something athletic—jumping, climbing, running. This pleased her father and didn't exactly bother her mother, who had been a field hockey player in college. The Fredericks understood the importance of physical fitness, and they were not overly concerned that the finest athlete among their children was their baby girl.

Jane began competing in Amateur Athletic Union track meets when she was only 11 years old. The long jump was her specialty, but it wasn't long before she took up the shot put and the high jump. She was lean and muscular, and blessed with talent rarely seen in children her age. That year she equaled the national age-group record in the high jump.

Because Frederick was so versatile, her coach at the Orinda Track Club, Larry Pilcher, steered her toward the pentathlon, an event with competition in five areas—high jump, shot put, long jump, 200-meter run, and hurdles. She distinguished herself almost immediately. At the age of 13 she received special permission to compete in the national pentathlon championships. There, against women nearly a decade older, Frederick finished fifth. She even won two events—the hurdles and the 200 meters. When she wasn't training, she liked to paint or work on ceramics. As a senior at Miramonte High School, she played basketball and volleyball and also became a cheerleader.

After graduating from high school, Frederick enrolled at the University of Colorado. She injured her hamstring as a freshman and missed the better part of two track seasons. By 1972 she had recovered completely. She finished first at the national pentathlon championships, and later qualified for the U.S. Olympic team. But she was not prepared for the intensity of international competition and finished 21st. She defended her national pentathlon title in 1973, broke the American record by winning it again in 1975, and won the gold at the World University Games. In 1976 she captured a fourth national title; she also won the 100-meter hurdles title in both 1975 and 1976. But at the Summer Olympics in Montreal, Frederick competed only in the pentathlon. Nervous and tired, she finished seventh with

4,566 points, more than 100 points below her American record.

Frederick bettered her U.S. mark in 1977 and won her fifth national pentathlon championship in 1979. At 28, she figured to be among the leaders at the 1980 Summer Olympics, but the United States led a boycott of the Moscow Games. As it turned out, Frederick did not qualify for the U.S. team anyway; she suffered an injury during the Olympic trials and was forced to withdraw after three events.

Accomplishments

U.S. national pentathlon champion:
  1972–1973, 1975–1976, 1979
World University Games pentathlon champion:
  1976
Member of U.S. Olympic team: 1972, 1976
Former American record holder in
  pentathlon

Fu Mingxia

Born 1979

By the time she was 17 years old, Fu Mingxia was already recognized as one of the greatest divers in Olympic history. A prodigy who thrived in China's rigorous youth diving program, she trained more than 40 hours per week and made her first Olympic appearance at the age of 13, at the 1992 Summer Games in Barcelona. Only 5 feet tall and weighing slightly more than 90 pounds, Fu became one of the Games' most surprising and endearing performers. While it is common for prepubescent girls to win gold medals in gymnastics, diving is a sport better suited to young women. But Fu proved herself to be one of the most graceful and daring athletes in the sport by winning the gold medal in the women's platform.

Four years later, in Atlanta, Mingxia bore little resemblance to the waifish girl of Barcelona. At 17, she was two inches taller and 30 pounds heavier. But her growth had not been just physical. In 1992 she was confident and composed enough to win a gold medal. At the 1996 Games, Fu, no longer a girl, defended her Olympic title in the women's platform. A few days later, she went after a second gold medal in the springboard competition. The favorite was Fu's teammate, Tan Shuping, who had finished first at the world championships in 1994. But Tan botched her third dive—it was nearly a belly flop—and fell from third to 25th in the standings. Suddenly, Fu's primary competition was her own psyche—and the partisan American crowd.

She turned out to be unflappable. After the second of her five dives in the final, Fu moved into first place and never relinquished the lead. She was the only diver in the competition to receive at least 60 points from the panel of judges on each of her dives. By winning the springboard competition, she became only the second woman (the first was East Germany's Ingrid Kramer in 1960) to win both diving events in a single Olympics; with three career gold medals she was only one shy of the record held by Americans Pat McCormick and Greg Louganis. She promised to be back four years later, for the 2000 Olympics in Sydney, Australia.

Accomplishments

Olympic gold medalist, women's platform
  diving: 1992, 1996
Olympic gold medalist, women's springboard
  diving: 1996

G

Zina Garrison-Jackson

Born November 16, 1963

Zina Garrison-Jackson, one of only two African American women tennis players ever to reach the final of a Grand Slam singles event, was born in Houston, Texas. The youngest of seven children, she sprouted from the hard courts of Houston's public parks. She began playing when she was 10 years old. She became one of the best junior players in the city and would become one of the best junior players in the world—a remarkable accomplishment considering the lack of resources available to her. But Garrison was driven; she loved sports, and played softball as well as tennis in high school. Garrison gained national attention in 1978, when she reached the final of the U.S. national 14-and-under tournament. In 1981 she was named International Tennis Federation Junior Player of the Year after winning the junior titles at both Wimbledon and the U.S. Open; no one had achieved that double win since Natasha Chmyreva of the Soviet Union in 1975.

The next year, at the age of 19, Garrison entered the professional ranks. She reached the quarterfinals at the French Open in 1982 and the fourth round at Wimbledon and the U.S. Open. At year's end she was the 16th-ranked player in the world. The next year she was a semifinalist at the Australian Open—and the 10th-ranked player in the world.

What most people did not know was that while her professional life was soaring, Garrison's personal life was crumbling. Her mother died in 1983, and the loss was devastating. Mary Garrison was not only Zina's mother, but also her best friend. It was the third time that Zina's life had been touched by tragedy. Her father, Ulysses, died when she was only 11 months old.

An older brother, Willie, died when she was a toddler. To deal with the pain of her mother's death, Garrison turned to food. "I was eating all the time," she later explained. "Basically, I kind of felt like I had an empty hole after my mother died. The only thing I had to comfort me was food."

Garrison developed bulimia, an eating disorder marked by bingeing and purging. She

suffered from physical problems common among bulimics—exhaustion, skin problems, tooth decay, depression—but somehow she managed to play tennis at a world-class level. At the 1988 Olympics in Seoul, she teamed up with Pam Shriver to win a gold medal in doubles and took a bronze in singles. In 1989 she reached the semifinals of the U.S. Open before losing to Gabriela Sabatini, and in 1990 she posted back-to-back victories over Monica Seles and Steffi Graf—two of the best players in the world—to reach the final at Wimbledon. There she became the first black woman since Althea Gibson 32 years earlier to reach the final of a Grand Slam tournament. In the championship, Garrison lost to Martina Navratilova.

Two years later Garrison finally confronted her illness. With the help of professional therapy and the support of her husband, Willard Jackson, she overcame bulimia and continued to be one of the best tennis players in the world. In the summer of 1992 she founded Zina Garrison's All-Court Tennis, a program for inner-city children. Garrison was ranked among the top 25 players in women's tennis for 15 consecutive years, from 1981 through 1995.

Accomplishments

> International Tennis Federation Junior Player of the Year: 1981
> Olympic bronze medalist, singles: 1988
> Olympic gold medalist, doubles: 1988
> Wimbledon finalist: 1990

Althea Gibson

Born August 25, 1927

Born in Silver, South Carolina, and raised in Harlem, tennis champion Althea Gibson was not only an exquisite athlete, but also an agent of social change. By her own assessment, Gibson was a difficult and arrogant child prone to getting into trouble. One of her first passions was pool, and she often skipped classes to hustle a few games. By the age of 13 she had dropped out of school. She helped support her family by taking on a number of jobs, including elevator operator and waitress.

A naturally gifted athlete, Gibson excelled in basketball and handball. Her skill at paddle tennis caught the eye of a Police Athletic League instructor who introduced her to Fred Johnson, a tennis pro at the Cosmopolitan Club in New York. At the time, the Cosmopolitan was one of the few tennis clubs that permitted blacks on the premises; there Gibson received the personal and professional instruction that helped transform her into one of the great pioneers of women's tennis.

When she was 19 years old, Gibson was befriended by Dr. Herbert Eaton, a longtime tennis fan. Eaton and his wife welcomed her into their Tennessee home. They took care of her, encouraged her to complete her education, and supported her budding tennis career. At 22 she graduated from high school and went on to attend Florida A&M on an athletic scholarship. There she played both basketball and tennis. She graduated in 1952, at the age of 25.

At that time Gibson played in few racially integrated tournaments. In 1948 she captured the first of nine consecutive American Tennis Association singles championships. She was one of the finest players in tennis, but she was not allowed to participate in the most prestigious tournament in the country—the U.S. Open.

That all changed in 1950, when Gibson became the first African American—male or female—to play at Forest Hills. With the aid of an editorial by former tennis star Alice Marble, which appeared in *American Lawn Tennis Magazine*, Gibson gained entry into the U.S. Open. She was beaten in the second round, but her accomplishment was nonetheless remarkable. A barrier had been shattered. One year later, in 1951, Gibson traveled to London and became the first black to compete at Wimbledon.

Gibson's career soared to new heights in 1956, when she won the French Open and Wimbledon doubles titles with partner Angela Buxton. The following year Gibson won both Wimbledon and the U.S. Open. She repeated as champion of both tournaments in 1958. In both years the Associated Press named her its Woman Athlete of the Year.

Gibson played tennis at a time when prize money was virtually nonexistent, so she signed a $100,000 contract with the Harlem Globetrotters, playing tennis exhibitions during halftime at their basketball games. She joined the Ladies Professional Golf Association, and while she never became a star, she was moderately successful.

When her athletic career ended, Gibson worked as a teaching pro, appeared in a film with John Wayne, and wrote her autobiography. Most recently she has served as manager of the Department of Recreation for the city of East Orange, New Jersey, where one of her primary goals is to promote tennis to inner-city children.

Accomplishments

Wimbledon singles champion: 1957–1958
U.S. Open singles champion: 1957–1958
Wimbledon doubles champion: 1956–1957
Australian Open doubles champion: 1957
Associated Press Woman Athlete of the Year: 1957–1958

Kathleen McKane Godfree

May 7, 1896–June 19, 1992

Kathleen "Kitty" McKane Godfree, a member of the International Tennis Hall of Fame, and one of the finest players ever to come out of Great Britain, was born in London. Once, when her father, John McKane, had to attend a business meeting in Germany, he convinced the entire family to join him. There was a catch, however—they would all travel the entire 600 miles by bicycle.

Kitty McKane liked sports from the time she was a small girl. But her first love was skating, not tennis. She even earned a bronze medal from the British Skating Association at the age of 10. It wasn't until she and her sister attended a Scottish school that Kitty began thinking seriously about tennis. There the girls received a heavy dose of tennis instruction, and Kitty took to it naturally. She later joined a club in London, and spent nearly all of her free time perfecting her game. In 1919, when the Wimbledon championships resumed after World War I, McKane was invited to compete in the most prestigious tournament in the world. She won three matches before running into Suzanne Lenglen, who was also playing at Wimbledon for the first time. The two would meet many times over the years, and McKane would have her share of victories. But in that initial match Lenglen was superior; she lost only a single game to McKane. Both players had performed so well that they were asked to join the British team that would compete in the World Covered Court Championships. At that tournament McKane won the women's doubles, the first of more than 100 doubles and mixed doubles titles that she would win during her career.

At the 1920 Olympic Games, McKane won three medals—a bronze in the singles, a silver in the mixed doubles, and a gold in the women's doubles. In 1923 McKane won the doubles title at the World Hard Court Championships in Paris, and reached the finals of the singles and mixed doubles. That same year she was runner-up to Lenglen at Wimbledon and represented Great Britain in the first Wightman Cup match. In 1924 she not only won a silver medal in doubles and a bronze in singles at the Summer Olympics, but also captured her first Wimbledon singles title. Trailing 4–1 in the second set to Helen Wills, McKane came back to win, 4–6, 6–4, 6–4. It was Wills' only loss in nine trips to Wimbledon.

Two years later McKane won her second Wimbledon title, beating Lili de Alvarez, 6–2, 4–6, 6–3, in the final. She became the first Brit to win a pair of Wimbledon singles title after World War I. At the U.S. championships, McKane was a singles finalist in 1925, and a doubles champion in 1923 and 1927. In the latter appearance she was known as Kitty Godfree, having married Leslie Godfree, also a fine tennis player, in 1926. In fact, in 1926 the Godfrees became the first married couple to win the mixed doubles title at Wimbledon.

Kitty McKane Godfree died in London at the age of 96. She was inducted into the International Tennis Hall of Fame in 1978.

Accomplishments

Wimbledon singles champion: 1924, 1926
Wimbledon mixed doubles champion: 1924, 1926
U.S. Open doubles champion: 1923, 1927
Inducted into International Tennis Hall of Fame: 1978

Diana Golden

Born March 20, 1963

Native New Englander Diana Golden began skiing as a child and became one of the most accomplished disabled athletes in the world. She was a free-spirited 12-year-old when her leg first gave out from under her. At first she paid no attention. But then it happened

It was a remarkable transformation for Golden. "I was the last one picked on every team when I was a kid," she has said. "I was a klutz. If you had ever told me that I would make being an athlete my profession, I would have laughed at you, and my family would have laughed at you."

At Dartmouth College, Golden was an athlete and a scholar of skill and perseverance. She did not think of herself as disabled—and neither did anyone who knew her. At Dartmouth she became a born-again Christian; the energy and emotion that she previously devoted to skiing was directed toward her religion. She began to spend less time training, and by her junior year she had retired. After graduating she took a sales job. Soon she began to think about skiing. Her friends went off to the slopes on weekends, and they pestered her to join them. Eventually she relented and became hooked again.

It took more than a year for Golden to achieve a level of fitness suitable for world-class competition. Between 1986 and 1990, Golden won 10 gold medals at the World Handicapped Championships. She also won 19 U.S. titles. In 1988 she won an Olympic gold medal in the giant slalom for disabled skiers. But of all her accomplishments, the one she is most proud of is when, in 1987, she cracked the top 10 in an open slalom race—she was the only disabled skier in the field.

In 1986 Golden won the Beck Award as the best U.S. skier in international competition. Two years later, after winning a gold medal in downhill skiing at the Winter Para-Olympics, she was named U.S. Female Alpine Skier of the Year by *Ski* magazine. That same year the U.S. Olympic Committee named Golden its Female Skier of the Year. She retired from competitive skiing in 1991, and turned her attention to coaching and rock climbing.

again. And again. When the doctors told Diana and her family that she had cancer, and the leg would have to be amputated immediately to prevent the disease from spreading, she was sure they were wrong. She felt so strong and healthy.

Golden permitted herself a brief flirtation with self-pity. Within days after her surgery she asked a doctor if it was possible to ski with only one leg. The answer was yes. A few months later she laced up a single boot and went back to the slopes. She remained a recreational skier until her junior year at Lincoln-Sudbury (Massachusetts) High School, when the varsity skiing coach, impressed by her talent and determination, asked her to start practicing with the team. The workouts were difficult, but Golden devoured them. She grew stronger, more confident. Within a year she qualified for the World Games for Disabled Athletes in Geilo, Norway. That same year, as a 12th grader representing the U.S. Disabled Ski Team, she finished first in the downhill at the World Handicapped Championships.

Accomplishments

Olympic gold medalist, giant slalom: 1988
Named Female Skier of the Year by U.S.
   Olympic Committee: 1988
Winner of 10 career gold medals at the
   World and Handicapped Championships
Winner of 19 national championships
Flo Hyman Award winner: 1991

Steffi Graf

Born June 14, 1969

Steffi Graf, one of only three women to win the Grand Slam of tennis, was born in Mannheim, West Germany, the older of Peter and Heidi Graf's two children. Both parents were tennis players, and Steffi received her first racket when she was four years old. From that moment on, life in the Graf household revolved around Steffi's tennis career. Peter, who had been a car dealer, sold his share of the business and moved the family to Bruhl, West Germany, where he opened a tennis school. Steffi quickly became his top pupil.

In 1983, at the age of 13, Graf turned professional. By the end of that year she was ranked among the top dozen women players in West Germany. In 1984 she was ranked as high as 22nd in the world on the Women's Tennis Association computer. The following year she reached No. 6, and in 1986, thanks to her first Grand Slam title, at the French Open, she hit No. 3.

But all of that was merely a prelude to what Graf would accomplish in the coming years. By 1987 she was maturing physically and emotionally. She was 5 feet 9 inches and 132 pounds, a strong and quick athlete with a powerful forehand and seemingly unlimited stamina. She won 11 of 13 tournaments in 1987 and finally reached the top of the WTA rankings. She won the French Open that year, and reached the finals at Wimbledon and the U.S. Open. In 1988 she became the third woman to win the Grand Slam of tennis, capturing the French Open, Australian Open, U.S. Open, and Wimbledon titles. Only Maureen Connolly (in 1953) and Margaret Smith Court (in 1970) had ever accomplished that feat. Graf's achievement was even more impressive because each title came on a different court surface. On top of that, she won a gold medal at the 1988 Summer Olympics in Seoul.

Graf hardly slowed down in 1989. If not for a loss to clay-court specialist Arantxa Sanchez Vicario of Spain in the final of the French Open, she would have won another Grand Slam. That year the Women's Sports Foundation selected Graf as its Professional Sportswoman of the Year.

From June 26, 1989, to May 20, 1990, Graf did not lose a single match. Her 66-match winning streak is the second longest in the modern tennis era, surpassed only by Martina Navratilova's 74-match streak. Graf's winning streak included a dry spell during which she was recovering from a broken thumb sustained on a skiing trip.

Graf held the No. 1 ranking for a record 186 weeks, from August 17, 1987, through March 10, 1991, longer than anyone in tennis. She fell to No. 2, behind Monica Seles, in late 1991 and in 1992, then reclaimed the top spot in 1993 and 1994.

But Graf's ascent was tinged with tragedy. Seles stopped playing for more than two years after she was stabbed during a match in Hamburg, Germany, in April 1993. The assailant turned out to be a deranged fan of Steffi Graf. Moreover, even as she reclaimed her position as the world's greatest player, Graf had to deal with the negative publicity surrounding her father, who was arrested on charges of tax evasion. But she nonetheless won the French Open, Wimbledon, and the U.S. Open in 1995, then repeated that feat in 1996.

Graf tends to be publicity-shy, though she has done some modeling and product endorsement. She is the founder of the Steffi Graf Youth Tennis Center in Leipzig, Germany.

Accomplishments

Wimbledon champion: 1988–1989, 1991–1993, 1995–1996
French Open champion: 1987–1988, 1993, 1995–1996
U.S. Open champion: 1988–1989, 1993, 1995–1996
Australian Open champion: 1988–1990
Olympic gold medalist: 1988
Grand Slam winner: 1988

Ann Moore Gregory

July 25, 1912–1990

Like Jackie Robinson in baseball and Althea Gibson in tennis, golfer Ann Moore Gregory had the courage, talent, and determination to break down the racial barriers that existed for so long in the world of athletics. On September 17, 1956, at the U.S. Women's Amateur at Meridian Hills Country Club in Indianapolis, she became the first African American woman to play in a United States Golf Association–sponsored national competition. Another black player, Renee Powell, said of Gregory, "Not enough people know about Ann. She set the stage for every black female who came into golf after her."

More than once, Gregory was mistaken for a maid by her fellow competitors. In her hometown of Aberdeen, Mississippi, she was denied access to the public golf course. At the U.S. Women's Amateur in 1959, she was not allowed to take part in the dinner before the tournament. Despite those insults, Gregory rarely revealed a sense of bitterness.

"Racism works best when you let it affect your mind," she said. "For all the ugliness, I've gotten nice things three times over. I can't think ugly of anybody."

She was born Ann Moore. Her parents died when she was a small child, so she grew up with a white family. They provided her with clothes, food, and a comfortable home. But in return, she was expected to serve as their maid. In 1938, when she was 26 years old, Ann Moore married Percy Gregory, left Aberdeen, and moved to Gary, Indiana. There she won not only the Chicago Women's Golf Association title (in 1943), but also the Gary city tennis championship. Most of her golf victories in those years came in segregated tournaments. Her first experience outside that world came in 1947, when she participated in the Tam O'Shanter in Chicago.

In 1954 Ann Gregory became the first black to hold a seat on the Gary Public Library Board. Her husband had a job with U.S. Steel, and she was active on civic committees. But she needed more. Gregory was an accomplished golfer who had been denied the chance to prove herself in national competition. She was in her early 40s and wanted to test herself against the best. That opportunity came in 1956, when the CWGA became the first all-black organization to join the USGA. Gregory could no longer be prevented from playing in USGA-sanctioned tournaments. She entered the U.S. Amateur and made the trip to Indianapolis.

Most of the players, officials, and spectators treated Gregory with respect, but some did not. Racial epithets were thrown about, as were harsh words for Gregory and her playing partners. Moreover, Gregory was criticized by some black golfers for abandoning them to play with whites. But she withstood the storm of controversy with grace and dignity, winning two matches before losing in the third round. Gregory, who died in 1990, never did win a major integrated tournament, but she came close, finishing second in the 1971 U.S. Women's Senior Amateur.

Accomplishments

First black woman to play in a USGA-sponsored national championship: 1956

U.S. Women's Senior Amateur runner-up: 1971

Winner of several all-black tournament titles, including the Joe Louis Invitational, CWGA championship, and the U.S. Golf Association

Janet Guthrie

Born March 7, 1938

Auto racer Janet Guthrie, the first female to compete in the Indianapolis 500, was born in Iowa City, Iowa, and grew up in Miami, Florida. The eldest of five children, she attended the Harris Florida School for Girls, where, as Guthrie once said, "Our main objective was not to sweat."

But Guthrie didn't mind sweating. In fact, she was an adventurous girl who dreamed of following in the footsteps of her father, an airline pilot. She actually wanted to be a fighter pilot. As a teenager, she made her first solo flight in a small plane. She tried skydiving long before it became popular. By the time she had graduated

from the University of Michigan in 1960 with a degree in physics, she had received her commercial pilot's license.

The summer after she graduated from college, Guthrie hitchhiked through Europe. She then worked for a New York company specializing in aerospace projects, but found the job boring. The exciting part of space exploration, she thought, was being in space. So she applied to NASA's astronaut training program. Guthrie survived the first few rounds of testing, but because she lacked an advanced degree, she was eventually eliminated from consideration. But her quest for speed remained. She

began competing in weekend road races, using a Jaguar coupe modified for racing. In 1966, after five years of amateur competition, she entered the Daytona 24-hour International Manufacturer's Championship.

That was the beginning of a 13-year professional career. Guthrie competed in the Daytona race again as well as in the Sebring's 12-hour Classic. She turned to oval track racing in 1976, and the following year made her historic appearance at Indianapolis. On May 23, 1977, Guthrie became the first woman to qualify for the Indy 500. "I want to thank my folks for not bringing me up thinking I couldn't do something because I was a woman," she said afterward. "Over the last year I've given a lot of thought to the symbolism of being the first woman here. I think it's important to credit the women's movement with creating the climate that made this possible."

On Sunday, May 29, 1977, the famous starter's call at Indy was modified—"In company with the first lady ever to qualify at Indianapolis, gentlemen, start your engines." Although she had technical problems and finished 29th, Guthrie's accomplishment was not diminished. The next year, she returned to Indianapolis and placed a respectable ninth. She also qualified in 1979.

After retiring from auto racing, Guthrie became a public speaker and a proponent of women's athletics. In 1980 she was a member of the first group of athletes to be inducted into the International Women's Sports Hall of Fame.

Accomplishments

North Atlantic Road Racing champion: 1976
First woman to race in the Indianapolis 500: 1977
Inducted into International Women's Sports Hall of Fame: 1980

Nicole Haislett

Born December 16, 1972

Nicole Haislett, winner of three gold medals in swimming at the 1992 Summer Olympics in Barcelona, grew up in St. Petersburg, Florida.

A 5-foot 8-inch, 153-pound woman with extraordinary strength and lung capacity, she was just a high school senior when she was asked to take part in a physiological test measuring stroke efficiency. She stunned her instructors and teammates alike by recording a nearly perfect score. She accomplished this feat through a combination of hard work, talent, and ambition. While most endurance athletes shun weight work, Haislett trained for hours on end. After swimming countless laps in the pool, she would towel off, retreat to the weight room, and work up a real sweat, frequently bench pressing more than 200 pounds. While some of her training partners found her fascination with iron a bit odd, Haislett considered it perfectly normal. When growing up, her hero was not a swimmer, but a bodybuilder-turned-actor. "Arnold Schwarzenegger," she once said. "He is God!"

Haislett's breakthrough performance came in 1990, when she won a gold medal in the 100-meter freestyle and a silver medal in the 200-meter freestyle at the Goodwill Games. She swam anchor on the United States' gold medal-winning 4 x 100 medley relay team, which set a U.S. record. In 1991 she won her first collegiate title, capturing the 200-yard freestyle. She also set an American record in winning the 100-meter freestyle at the world championships.

In 1992 Haislett not only defended her 200-yard freestyle title at the NCAA championships, but also shattered the longest-standing American record with her winning time of 1:43.28. That time was nearly a full second better than Sippy Woodhead's record, which had stood since 1979. At the Summer Games in Barcelona, Haislett was the only U.S. athlete to win three gold medals. In the 200-meter freestyle she broke another of Woodhead's American records, taking the gold in 1:58.23. And she helped the United States win gold medals in the 4 x 100 freestyle relay and 4 x 100 medley relay.

The next year, Haislett dominated the NCAA championships, finishing first in three events—the 200-yard individual medley, 200-yard freestyle, and 100-yard freestyle. She added two more NCAA titles—in the 500-yard freestyle and 100-yard freestyle—in 1994. But at the world championships, she finished in fifth place.

In 1995 Haislett was one of several swimmers invited to be part of the first U.S. Resident National Team. Athletes were given free room and board at the Olympic Training Center, along with a monthly stipend of $1,200. This allowed them to concentrate on training, without having to hold part-time jobs. Haislett took part in the program for several months, but left abruptly in July, saying she no longer had the "motivational drive to put myself through what it takes to be one of the best." She retired from the sport at the age of 24.

Accomplishments

NCAA champion, 200-yard freestyle: 1991–1994
NCAA champion, 200-yard individual medley: 1993
NCAA champion, 100-yard freestyle: 1993
NCAA champion, 500-yard freestyle: 1994
Olympic gold medalist, 200-meter freestyle: 1992
Olympic gold medalist, 4 x 100 freestyle relay: 1992
Olympic gold medalist, 4 x 100 medley relay: 1992

Dorothy Hamill

Born March 12, 1956

Olympic figure skating champion Dorothy Hamill grew up in Riverside, Connecticut. She spent her entire adult life in the public eye, but her greatest obstacle to fame and success was a nearly debilitating case of stage fright. It hit her frequently when she was in her athletic prime, causing her to run from the ice in tears or to drop difficult moves from her program. But like most of the hurdles she faced, Hamill eventually cleared this one. She became a graceful and confident athlete who charmed fans and judges alike at the 1976 Olympics, then combined her business and skating skills to forge a professional career.

As a young girl, Hamill had no family ties to the sport and lived in an area that had never produced a figure skating champion. Still, when her parents presented her with a pair of skates for Christmas when she was eight years old, Hamill ran to the nearest pond and gave the blades a workout. Not long after, she convinced her father to allow her to take lessons at a public rink. She quickly distinguished herself as a prize skater and left school at the age of 14 to devote her time to skating. Training sessions took up roughly 50 hours each week; at night she worked with a private tutor so that she could earn her high school equivalency diploma.

Hamill became a fine figure skater, but she was not sharp enough to compete against the best women in the world. To reach that level she trained with Carlo Fassi, the renowned coach who had worked with Olympic gold medalist Peggy Fleming. Under Fassi's tutelage Hamill began to blossom. In 1974, at the age of 17, she won the first of three consecutive titles at the U.S. Figure Skating Championships. She finished second at the world championships in 1974 and 1975.

In 1976 Hamill competed in her first and only Olympic Games. Skating to background music from Errol Flynn movies, Hamill performed magnificently. She held the lead for two-thirds of the competition—the compulsory figures and the short program—then ran away with the title after the free skating program. Her trademark was a move that became known as the Hamill Camel, and when she ended her program with it, the audience stood and roared with delight, and showered her with flowers. The judges made Hamill the Olympic gold medalist.

After winning a gold medal at the world championships in 1976, Hamill retired from amateur skating. She began a long career as a professional skater and spokesperson, signing lucrative contracts with the Ice Capades, the ABC television network, and Bausch and Lomb. Hamill sought a greater challenge, so in 1993 she purchased the Ice Capades, which by that time had become financially strapped. Under her direction the traveling show was revamped and revitalized, becoming less like a circus and more like a Broadway show on ice.

Accomplishments

U.S. figure skating champion: 1974–1976
World figure skating champion: 1976
Olympic gold medalist: 1976
Purchased Ice Capades: 1993

Memorable Moment:
September 7, 1953

Maureen Connolly Wins Tennis' Grand Slam

In 1953 Maureen Connolly, the great American tennis player, decided that she would devote all of her effort to winning the four major tournaments in tennis. Known as the Grand Slam, it was one of the rarest of athletic accomplishments. In fact, no woman had ever won the Grand Slam; the last man to have done so was Don Budge, in 1938.

But Connolly set her mind to it. She began with the Australian Open, defeating her doubles partner, Julie Sampson, in the final round. Then, at the French Open, Connolly lost just one set on the way to a championship. Next up was Wimbledon, where Connolly, in what is generally regarded as one of the greatest tennis matches ever played, defeated Doris Hart, 8–6, 7–5, in the final.

That set the stage for the U.S. Open. By now, Connolly was at the top of her game. No one could match her. She breezed through the field and eventually met Doris Hart again in the final. But this time, there was no high drama. At Forest Hills, on September 7, 1953, Connolly defeated Hart by scores of 6–2, 6–4, in a match that lasted only 43 minutes. Unfortunately, her remarkable accomplishment was given little publicity. The *New York Times* ran a photo of men's winner Tony Trabert on the front page, but relegated Connolly's historic achievement to the sports page.

Suzy Hamilton

Born August 8, 1968

Suzy Hamilton, the first athlete to win four consecutive NCAA outdoor championships at the one mile or 1,500 meters, was born Suzanne Favor in Stevens Point, Wisconsin. She started running when she was young and became a national age-group champion as well as a high school star. She had her choice of colleges, but decided to stay close to home and attend the University of Wisconsin. There she majored in graphic arts.

As a collegiate runner, Favor was one of the best in the history of the sport. She was a ferocious competitor, a trait that manifested itself whenever she stepped on a track. In her specialty, the mile (and its metric cousin, the 1,500), she won 54 of 56 races; she also won 40 consecutive finals. As a freshman in the winter of 1987, she won the NCAA indoor mile championship. That spring she won the first of her four NCAA outdoor 1,500-meter titles. As a junior she won the indoor mile title again along with the outdoor 800-meter title; as a senior she won the indoor 3,000-meter title.

Favor finished her career with nine NCAA championships and also 23 Big 10 Athletic Conference titles. In 1990 she was named the winner of the Honda Broderick Cup as the nation's outstanding female collegiate athlete. She was named the Big 10's female athlete of the year three times, and was voted the conference's female athlete of the decade (1981–1991).

At 5 feet 3 inches and 100 pounds, Favor did not give the appearance of being a tiger. While track is not generally considered a contact sport, she often emerged from races with an assortment of bumps and bruises; more often than not, it was she who had initiated the contact.

"I like the body contact," she explained. "And I don't believe in being boxed in. I can always get out of a crowd in a second, no matter what. Sometimes I say to an opponent, 'Move over.' And they're usually extremely cooperative. But if they don't move, I use my elbows to let them know I'm coming through."

After graduating from college, Favor married Mark Hamilton, and they moved to Los Angeles, where he studied law. They later settled in Eugene, Oregon. Postgraduate success proved elusive for Suzy Hamilton. Injuries and other factors seemed to conspire against her; in her biggest meets, such as the 1991 world championships and 1992 Olympic Games, she failed to reach the finals. But in 1996, Hamilton surprised many track-and-field observers by qualifying for the U.S. Olympic team at 1,500 meters.

Accomplishments

Winner of nine NCAA championships
Winner of 23 Big 10 Athletic Conference titles
Broderick Cup winner (outstanding female collegiate athlete): 1990
Member of U.S. Olympic team: 1992, 1996

Ellen Hansell

September 18, 1869–May 11, 1937

Ellen Forde Hansell, the first U.S. female tennis champion, was born in Philadelphia. The daughter of Samuel Robb Hansell, a manufacturer of upholstery supplies, and Jane Martin Hansell, she was not an athletic child. In fact, she later described herself as being an anemic little girl. But because she displayed a measure of ability with a tennis racket in her hand, doctors advised her parents to encourage the girl. Exercise, they suggested, might help her thrive. Ellen spent as much time playing tennis as she did studying at Miss Gordon's School in Philadelphia. By the age of 13 she was a serious, determined player. In 1885, at 16 years of age, she joined the Belmont Club, where she had the opportunity to train and practice alongside such talented performers as Louise Allderdice, Margarette Ballard, and Bertha Townsend Toulmin.

Like most women of that time, Hansell was expected to play tennis in outrageously heavy, frilly outfits that, by modern standards, were thoroughly impractical. She personalized her attire by adding a red felt hat. Her game was steady, with a sidearm serve and firm, reliable groundstrokes.

Hansell explained, "We did now and then grip our overdraped, voluminous skirts with our left hand to give us a bit more limb freedom when dashing to make a swift snappy stroke every bit as well placed as today, but lacking the force and great physical strength of the modern girl."

Hansell became the first U.S. singles champion in 1887, when she won the Chestnut Hill Lawn Tennis Club open tournament at the Philadelphia Country Club. The field included only seven women. Hansell, 18 years old, defeated Jessie Harding, Mrs. Alan Harris, and Laura Knight to win the championship. In doubles, she teamed up with Knight to finish first, although that portion of the event had not yet been designated a national championship. The next year, Hansell attempted to defend her title. In holding with tradition, she did not compete in the open portion of the tournament, but sat back and waited for a winner to emerge. That person was Bertha Townsend, who had missed the 1887 tournament. Townsend defeated Hansell in the challenge round. Hansell was also unable to defend her doubles title; she and Knight lost to the Roosevelt sisters, Ellen and Grace, in an early round.

Hansell played her final match at the U.S. championships in 1890, losing a first-round mixed doubles match; her partner was Charles Cowperthwait. A few months later she married Louise Allderdice's brother, Taylor. She retired from competitive tennis and settled into a life as a wife and mother. She raised six children, including Mary Taylor, who became an accomplished golfer. Hansell continued to play tennis and golf recreationally for many years. She died in Pittsburgh in 1937 and was inducted into the International Tennis Hall of Fame in 1965.

Accomplishments

First U.S. singles champion: 1887
Finalist, U.S. championships: 1888
Inducted into International Tennis Hall of Fame: 1965

Darlene Hard

Born January 6, 1936

Darlene Hard, a member of the International Tennis Hall of Fame, was born in Los Angeles, California, into a family that played tennis. Darlene's mother, Ruth Hard, had gained a substantial amount of weight during her pregnancy; after Darlene was born, Ruth turned to exercise as a way to regain fitness. Tennis was the sport she chose, and she immediately fell in love with it. That tennis passion was handed down to Darlene, who first volleyed with her mother when she was six years old. By the time she was 13, Darlene was a promising young player with a taste for competition. She won her first doubles tournament that year, and in 1955 won her first major title, teaming up with Beverly Fleitz to win the women's doubles championship at the French Open. That was the first of 13 Grand Slam titles that she would win.

The 5-foot 6-inch, 145-pound Hard was talented and competitive, rarely displaying anger when she lost. In victory, she seemed to revel in the theatrical nature of her business. After receiving the second-place trophy from Queen Elizabeth at the 1957 Wimbledon, Hard performed a brief "victory" dance for the crowd, which applauded warmly. She was offered a scholarship in premed from Pomona College, but decided to major in physical education. She played tennis at Pomona, but because she held jobs as a waitress and a camp counselor, she missed many tournaments. She endured criticism for these actions, as well as for her tendency to wear shorts, rather than skirts, in competition.

In 1957, in addition to finishing second in singles at Wimbledon, Hard won the doubles title there and at the French Open. She also played on the U.S. Wightman Cup team for the first time. In 1958 she won the U.S. Open doubles title and the U.S. Intercollegiate title. Two years later she became one of the best singles players in the world, winning the U.S. Open and the French Open, and finishing second at Wimbledon. She repeated as U.S. champ in 1961, despite missing three months of training due to hepatitis.

Hard stopped playing competitive tennis in 1964. During a brief comeback in 1969, she teamed up with Francoise Durr to pull off a stunning doubles victory in the finals of the U.S. Open. A last-minute substitute, Hard looked out of place at the start of the final; she and Durr lost the first set, 6–0, but came back to win the next two sets, 6–3, 6–4. In 1973 Hard was inducted into the International Tennis Hall of Fame.

Accomplishments

U.S. Intercollegiate champion: 1958
French Open champion: 1960
U.S. Open champion: 1960–1961
Inducted into International Tennis Hall of Fame: 1973

Tonya Harding

Born November 12, 1970

Born in Portland, Oregon, Tonya Harding was a talented figure skater who will be remembered less for her victories than for her role as a featured player in one of the great tabloid stories in sports. Harding was the fifth child born to LaVona Harding, a waitress, and Al Harding, a day laborer and truck driver. She was introduced to the sport when she was just three-and-a-half years old, during a trip to a shopping mall. Tonya saw the other children gliding around an indoor rink, became enthralled, and asked her parents if she could join them. For Christmas that year she received a pair of figure skates. A few weeks later she was taking lessons at a public rink. It didn't take long for her instructors to recognize her talent and determination. She stayed late after practice, worked harder than the other children,

and never worried about falling or getting hurt. By the time she was four, Harding was receiving private lessons from coach Diane Rawlinson. Her parents paid what they could, but it wasn't enough to cover the expenses; Rawlinson, seeing such promise in Harding, donated her time.

In the world of figure skating, known for its style and elegance, Harding was an acrobat, a wildly athletic woman who believed figure skating was less art than sport. In 1989 she finished in first place in the Skate America competition. In 1990 she was second at the Olympic Festival; the following year she captured first place in the senior nationals. She stunned the audience at the Target Center by becoming the first American woman to successfully land a triple Axel in competition. One month later, at the world championships, she finished second behind teammate Kristi Yamaguchi.

But the following year was a disappointment for Harding. At the senior nationals, which served as the U.S. Olympic trials, Harding fell twice during her long program and had to settle for third place. At the Albertville Olympics, where she was one of the favorites, she skated badly and failed to earn a medal. Later that month she finished sixth at the world championships.

In the winter of 1994, Harding was implicated in a conspiracy plot against one of her chief rivals, Nancy Kerrigan. After a practice session for the U.S. Figure Skating Association championships in Detroit, Kerrigan was attacked and struck on the knee by an unidentified man. As it turned out, the assailant had been hired by Jeff Gillooly, the ex-husband of Tonya Harding. The intent was to injure Kerrigan and force her out of the competition, thereby opening the door for Harding, who went on to finish first.

Gillooly eventually pleaded guilty to a count of racketeering, and he and others in the case served jail time. Despite Gillooly's claims that Harding knew about the plot from the beginning, she maintained her innocence. She fought—and won—the right to compete in the Lillehammer Olympics. Kerrigan recovered from her injury, and her February 1994 showdown with Harding turned out to be one of the highest-rated television events in history. Kerrigan skated well and finished second behind Oksana

Baiul; Harding came home without a medal. In March, Harding pleaded guilty to charges of conspiring to hinder an investigation and was stripped of her 1994 U.S. title. Shortly thereafter she left skating to pursue a career in television and film.

Accomplishments

U.S. national champion: 1991, 1994
First place, Skate America: 1989, 1991
Silver medalist, world championships: 1991
First American woman to land a triple Axel in competition

Lucy Harris

Born February 10, 1955

Lucy Harris, the first woman ever drafted by a men's professional basketball team, was born in Minter City, Mississippi. The seventh of nine children, she grew up on a Mississippi farm. Basketball was a way of life in the Harris household; all of Lucy's siblings enjoyed the sport, but for a while she was left out of the fun.

"My older brothers and sister played basketball out back, where they had set up nets and goals," she explained. "But they wouldn't let me play until I was good enough to score against them. I had to be good."

As it turned out, Lucy was the most successful athlete in her family, a gifted basketball player who was recruited to play for Delta State University in Mississippi. While there, she put her team on the college basketball map, leading the Lady Statesmen to a 50-game winning streak over three years. She was a three-time All-American—in 1975, 1976, and 1977; each of those years Delta State won the Association of Intercollegiate Athletics for Women national championship. In her final year, Harris, a 6-foot 3-inch center, averaged more than 31 points per game and scored more than 1,000 points. In a single game against Tennessee Tech, she scored 58 points. In addition to her scoring prowess, Harris thrived in the grittier aspects of basketball, averaging 15 rebounds per game.

In 1975 Harris became Delta State's first black homecoming queen. That same year she represented the United States in both the Pan

American Games and the World University Games. In 1976, at the Summer Olympic Games in Montreal, women's basketball became a medal sport. Harris scored the first basket of Olympic competition and helped lead the United States to a second-place finish behind the Soviet Union.

In 1977 Harris was recognized as one of the finest athletes in the country. In addition to guiding Delta State to a third-straight national title, she won the Broderick Award as the nation's outstanding female college basketball player and the Honda Broderick Cup as the best collegiate athlete in any sport. But after graduating from college, Harris, like most female basketball players of her time, found few opportunities to continue her career. The New Orleans Jazz selected her in the seventh round of the National Basketball Association draft, but that move was little more than a publicity stunt. She did not report to tryout camp and never played for the men's team.

Harris played briefly for the Houston Angels of the Women's Professional Basketball League, but in 1980, when she became pregnant, she decided to end her playing career. She later accepted a job in the admissions office of Delta State while she worked on a graduate degree. In 1992 she was inducted into the Basketball Hall of Fame in Springfield, Massachusetts.

Accomplishments

Three-time All-American at Delta State: 1975–1977
College Player of the Year: 1977
College Athlete of the Year: 1977
First woman drafted by an NBA team: 1977
Inducted into Basketball Hall of Fame: 1992

Doris Hart

Born June 20, 1925

Born in St. Louis, Missouri, Doris Jane Hart overcame a serious childhood illness to become one of the finest tennis players in the world. Doris was less than two years old when, after playing in her backyard, she developed a mysterious infection in her right kneecap. The joint became badly swollen, prompting her par-

ents, Robert and Ann Hart, to seek medical help. With the family's physician out of town at the time, the Harts turned to another doctor for advice. He gave them the worst possible news—in order to save the girl's life, her leg would have to be amputated. The Harts refused. Instead, they waited for the return of their doctor, who,

upon arrival, decided that surgery was a more prudent course of treatment. The infection was drained, and the leg was saved.

"One of the first newspaper stories on me described me as having recovered from polio," Hart later said. "It was a good story that caught on, but it wasn't so."

Hart eventually regained nearly full use of her leg, but not without considerable effort. Her mother performed daily massage therapy, and Hart herself worked diligently to rehabilitate the damaged limb. When she was 10 years old, after the family had relocated to Coral Gables, Florida, Hart underwent surgery for a bilateral hernia. While recuperating, she passed the time by sitting at her hospital window and watching the tennis games being played on the public courts below. She was intrigued by the game, and her interest increased when she received an old racket as a gift. Before long she was playing every day against her brother, Bud, and taking lessons on the public courts at Henderson Park.

At the age of 13, Hart competed in the National Junior Championships for the first time. Twice she won that tournament. Hart was bowlegged and gangly, and did not look like an athlete. But her appearance was deceptive, and she worked hard to develop a solid all-around game. By the time she was 17, Hart was ranked among the top 10 players in the United States. For 14 consecutive years—from 1942 to 1955—she never fell out of the U.S. top 10. In 1954 and 1955, she was ranked No. 1.

Hart won her first major singles title in 1949, when she captured the Australian Open. She also won three French singles titles, two U.S. titles, and one Wimbledon title. In women's doubles she won 14 Grand Slam titles, usually with Shirley Fry Irvin as her partner; in mixed doubles she won 15 titles. Her greatest performance came in 1951 at Wimbledon, where she completed a rare triple by winning the singles, doubles, and mixed doubles titles. In 10 years of Wightman Cup play, she was unbeaten in the singles competition.

In 1954 Doris was named one of *Women's Home Companion* magazine's most outstanding women. A year later she published her autobiography, *Tennis With Hart*. In 1969 she was inducted into the International Tennis Hall of Fame.

Accomplishments

Australian Open champion: 1949
French Open champion: 1950–1952
Wimbledon champion: 1951
U.S. Open champion: 1954–1955
Inducted into International Tennis Hall of Fame: 1969

Judy Devlin Hashman

Born October 22, 1935

Judy Devlin Hashman, winner of 56 national championships in the United States, England, and Canada, is generally acknowledged as the most accomplished player in the history of women's badminton. She was born in Winnipeg, Canada. Her father, J. Frank Devlin, an Irish native and a former English singles champion, was her coach and mentor. A skilled and versatile athlete, Judy dabbled in a variety of sports while growing up, including tennis, field hockey, basketball, and lacrosse (she was a member of the U.S. national team for five years), but it was badminton that brought her international acclaim.

Presented with her first racquet at the age of seven, Devlin quickly proved herself to be a prodigy. By the time she turned 13 she had won every junior title in badminton. From 1949 through 1954 she captured six consecutive junior singles titles. She was only 14 when she won her first major adult title, defeating Ruth Jett and Patsey Stephens in the Mason Dixon Tournament, and just 17 when she played in her first U.S. national championship. She won the English women's doubles championship with her sister, Susan, in 1953.

In one month in 1954, Devlin not only captured national junior and senior titles—and the world singles title—but also combined with her sister to win the All-England and U.S. doubles crowns. She repeated as U.S. national singles champion in 1954 and held the title through 1963. She failed to win in 1964, but recaptured the championship in 1965, 1966, and 1967. From 1953 through 1967, Devlin won 31 national women's singles and doubles championships. She won 17 All-England titles (including 10 singles titles), the last coming at the age of 31. She won the national mixed doubles title eight times, and the Canadian singles and doubles titles three times each.

In 1963 Devlin was inducted into the Helms National Badminton Hall of Fame. She was a member of the World Championship National

U.S. Uber Cup team from 1957 through 1969. In 1966 she was given the International Badminton Federation Distinguished Service Award and the National Ken Davis Sportsmanship Award from the American Badminton Association. Valued for her leadership as well as for her talent, Devlin served as captain of both the U.S. and English national badminton teams. During the 1960s she served as coach of several Thomas Cup (men's) and Uber Cup (women's) championship teams.

Devlin, who married her coach, Dick Hashman, in 1960, continues to work as a badminton, tennis, and squash instructor. She has two sons, Geoff and Joe, and lives in Wootton, England. In 1995 she was inducted into the International Women's Sports Hall of Fame.

Accomplishments

U.S. national singles champion: 1954,
   1956–1963, 1965–1967
All-England singles champion: 1954,
   1957–1958, 1960–1964, 1966–1967
Inducted into Helms National Badminton Hall
   of Fame: 1963
Inducted into International Women's Sports
   Hall of Fame: 1995

Sandra Haynie

Born June 4, 1943

Sandra Haynie, a member of the Ladies Professional Golf Association Hall of Fame, grew up in Fort Worth, Texas. She started playing golf at the age of 11 and improved steadily through her teenage years. In 1957, at the age of 14, she won the Texas State Public title; she defended that title in 1958. That same year she won the first of two consecutive Texas State Amateur championships. In 1990 she capped her career by winning the Trans-Mississippi title.

Haynie turned professional in 1961; over the next 20 years she was one of the most consistent and successful players on the LPGA tour, winning 42 tournaments and accumulating more than $1 million in earnings. As a rookie, she had cracked the top 10 in only one tournament and had earned just $3,709 for the entire year. But in 1962 she picked up her first victories, at the Austin Civitan Classic and the Cosmopolitan Open; she doubled her prize money for the year and wound up 16th on the LPGA money list. That was the first of 14 consecutive seasons in which Haynie would win at least one LPGA event. Her game became more well-rounded with each passing season. There were two victories in 1964 and two more in 1965, including one at her first major tournament, the LPGA championship.

In 1966 Haynie won the Buckeye Savings Invitational, the Glass City Classic, the Alamo Open, and the Pensacola Invitational. She ended the year as the No. 2–ranked player on the LPGA tour, with more than $30,000 in prize money—a huge sum for that time. In 1970 she again finished second on the money list and was voted the LPGA Player of the Year. Four years later, in 1974, she became only the second player to win both the LPGA championship and the U.S. Women's Open in the same year; she also won four other tournaments that year.

From 1977 through 1980, Haynie was bothered by arthritis and forced to play a reduced LPGA schedule. But she rejoined the tour full-time in 1981 and showed few signs of rust, winning nearly $100,000. The following year was one of her best—she won two events, including the Peter Jackson Classic, and piled up more than $245,000 in prize money, second best on the tour. In 1988 she became the 16th woman golfer to crack $1 million in career earnings, despite having again been forced to play a reduced schedule because of her arthritis.

Haynie's last full season on the LPGA tour was 1989, when she played in 23 events. She now devotes time to charitable efforts, including the Swing Against Arthritis tournament, of which she is the chairperson.

Accomplishments

LPGA championship winner: 1965, 1974
U.S. Women's Open champion: 1974
Peter Jackson Classic champion: 1982
Inducted into LPGA Hall of Fame: 1984

Carol Heiss

Born January 20, 1940

Figure skater Carol Heiss, a member of the International Women's Sports Hall of Fame, was born in New York City. Like most world-class figure skaters, she first stepped onto a sheet of ice when she was barely old enough to walk, and intense tutelage began shortly thereafter. Carol was an enthusiastic little girl who loved nothing so much as lacing on a pair of skates. By the age of seven she was taking lessons from Pierre and Andre Brunet at the Skating Club of New York. There she was surrounded by other gifted children, many of whom dreamed of winning Olympic medals and performing in front of thousands of fans. The coaches watched Carol practice her figures; they assessed her drive and athletic skill. They came to the following conclusion, which they shared with Carol's mother—"In ten years, she can be the best in the world."

In less time than that she would be the best in the United States. But if the journey was shorter than expected, it was nonetheless difficult. The nurturing of a top-notch figure skater is an expensive proposition, so Carol's mother helped defray some of the costs. A freelance fabric designer, she worked on her drawings at the Skating Club of New York while Carol practiced. She was Carol's most ardent supporter, but she never got the chance to see her daughter reach the pinnacle of her sport. She died of cancer in October 1956, after watching Carol lose to Tenley Albright at the Winter Olympic Games. Before her death, she had extracted an emotional promise from her daughter—Carol would continue to compete until she won a gold medal.

Albright was one of the greatest skaters in history, and Heiss had the misfortune of being one of her contemporaries—she spent much of her career standing in a long shadow. Heiss finished second to Albright in the 1953, 1954, 1955, and 1956 U.S. championships; the 1953, 1954, and 1955 North American championships; the 1955 world championships; and the 1956 Olympics.

But two weeks after the 1956 Games, Heiss defeated Albright at the world championships. Albright then retired. For the next five years, Heiss was the most successful athlete in figure skating. She won U.S. and world titles from 1957 through 1960, and was the North American champion in 1957, 1958, and 1959. At the 1960 Winter Olympics she kept her promise to her mother by finally winning that elusive gold medal.

After retiring from amateur competition, Heiss skated as a professional for a short time. She married Hayes Alan Jenkins, also a skater, in 1961 and was inducted into the International Women's Sports Hall of Fame in 1992.

Accomplishments

Olympic silver medalist: 1956
World champion: 1957–1960
U.S. champion: 1957–1960
Olympic gold medalist: 1960
Inducted into International Women's Sports
 Hall of Fame: 1992

Gladys Heldman

Born May 13, 1922

Gladys Heldman, an ambitious, innovative woman who helped found the Women's Tennis Association, was born Gladys Medalie in New York City. She was fortunate to grow up in an environment that fostered intellectual development. Her father, George Medalie, was a prominent New York lawyer; her mother, Carrie, was a Latin and Greek scholar. Gladys was a Phi Beta Kappa graduate of Stanford University—she completed her degree in only three years.

Medalie was a late bloomer when it came to tennis. Marrying Julius Heldman—who not only earned a doctorate in physical chemistry from UCLA by the age of 22, but also was a national-class tennis player—she fell in love with the sport after she fell in love with Heldman. After her second child was born, she decided she no longer wanted to be merely a spectator. Her athletic development was remarkably swift for one who had started so late. In the early 1950s Gladys Heldman was the top-ranked player in Texas; in 1954 she qualified for the main draw at Wimbledon. Her debut was unimpressive—she failed to win a game—but that did not diminish her accomplishment.

Heldman founded *World Tennis* in 1953. The

Memorable Moment: April 19, 1967

Katherine Switzer Becomes the First Official Female Entrant in the Boston Marathon

Katherine Switzer was fully aware of the Boston Athletic Association's long-standing policy of barring women from competing in the Boston Marathon. Nevertheless, as an idealistic and head-strong 20-year-old Syracuse University student, she was determined to break the gender barrier. And not merely as a "bandit" runner. Other women had participated in the world's most prestigious 26.2-mile race, but none had ever been granted an official entry. Switzer wanted to be the first. So she submitted her application under the name K. Switzer. Race officials, thinking Switzer was a male, accepted the entry.

She showed up in Hopkinton, Massachusetts, on race day wearing heavy sweats and a hooded sweatshirt. Only when the race began did she peel off some of the clothing. Two miles after the start, horrified race officials realized that they had been duped. Race director Will Cloney stopped the press bus and, along with Jock Semple, a longtime marathon trainer and BAA official, tried to physically force the woman wearing bib No. 261 off the course. This did not go over well with Thomas C. Miller, a sturdily built hammer thrower from Syracuse who was running with Switzer—and who happened to be Switzer's boyfriend. Miller rushed to her defense, shoving both men away. Switzer went on to finish the race, but BAA officials refused to record her time or acknowledge her effort.

magazine lost money at first, but soon became the most successful publication of its kind. Heldman wrote for the magazine, edited most of the copy, and ran the business office. She became an outspoken advocate for the sport, and especially for women's tennis. She criticized the game's elitist attitude; she chastised officials for their reluctance to change. Long before it became fashionable, Heldman championed the cause of "open tennis." She hated the fact that most players were forced to accept under-the-table payments in order to perpetuate the myth of amateurism.

Tournament directors often felt the sting of Heldman's pen, especially those who offered significantly more prize money to men than to women. In 1970 she sharply criticized the Australian Open, where the men's doubles champion received more money than the women's singles champion. Today, prize money at major tournaments is distributed more evenly between men and women than it was then, and Gladys Heldman deserves much of the credit.

In 1970 Jack Kramer, promoter of the Pacific Southwest Tournament, announced that his tournament would offer $12,500 to the men's champion and $1,500 to the women's champion. Heldman, on behalf of several top female players, asked him to increase the women's purse. He refused. So Heldman hosted her own tournament, the Virginia Slims of Houston. It featured an eight-woman field and $5,000 in prize money. The tournament was a success, and the publicity gave Heldman the impetus to expand that single event into a full-fledged women's tennis tour. Virginia Slims agreed to sponsor eight tournaments the first year, and the players asked Heldman to run the tour.

"I think women's tennis received more media coverage in that one week than it had in the entire previous year," Heldman said. "And if it hadn't been for people like Jack Kramer, the Virginia Slims tour never would have gotten that early recognition. When people ask me who founded the tour, I always say Jack Kramer."

Gladys Heldman was inducted into the International Tennis Hall of Fame in 1979.

Accomplishments

Competed at Wimbledon: 1954
Founded *World Tennis* magazine: 1953
Helped found Women's Tennis Association: 1970
Inducted into International Tennis Hall of Fame: 1979

Sonja Henie

April 8, 1912–October 13, 1969

Sonja Henie, born in Oslo, Norway, was perhaps the greatest figure skater in history. She was an innovator whose belief that skating was

equal parts artistry and athleticism put her years—if not decades—ahead of her time. Henie's father, Wilhelm, was not only a successful businessman, but also a former world champion in cycling, and an accomplished skater and skier. Her mother loved to dance and encouraged Sonja's early interest in ballet. Henie began participating in speed skating events when she was five; by the age of eight she had won her first figure skating competition. She was 10 years old when she won her first Norwegian women's figure skating title in 1923, and 11 when she qualified for the first Winter Olympics, in 1924. But at Chamonix, France, Henie finished last.

In 1927 she won the first of 10 consecutive world championships. The following year, at the Winter Olympics in St. Moritz, the 16-year-old Henie won her first gold medal. Her graceful approach, which featured an assortment of ballet moves, impressed the judges, each of whom placed Henie first. Figure skating had previously been a slow and awkward sport, with an emphasis on technical skills. Henie turned the event inside out—she was a dancer on skates, a performer. While her approach may be common today, it was revolutionary in 1928.

Henie dominated the sport of figure skating for the better part of a decade. She captured Olympic gold medals at the 1932 Winter Games in Lake Placid and at the 1936 Games at Garmisch-Partenkirchen. Seven times she entered the Norwegian national championships, and seven times she came away the winner.

In 1936, at the age of 34, Henie retired from amateur figure skating. While performing as a professional in touring ice shows, her ambition was to become a movie star. She first found work as an actress in 1936, sharing the screen with Don Ameche in the hit *One in a Million*, which grossed more than $25 million. By the early 1940s she was among the leading Hollywood box office attractions, rivaling such stars as Clark Gable and Shirley Temple. She made 11 feature films, and while critical reception of her work was lukewarm, the public adored her.

Henie lived extravagantly—she married three times and collected furs, antiques, jewelry, and art. Much of her collection is on display at an Oslo museum, which she helped establish. Estimates of her career earnings range from $37 million to $50 million, an extraordinary sum for that time. Of figure skating, which provided her with so much wealth and happiness, Henie once said, "Ours is not simply a sport, but an art."

Henie died in the autumn of 1969, after a long battle with leukemia.

Accomplishments

Olympic gold medalist: 1928, 1932, 1936
World champion: 1927–1936
Norwegian champion: 1923–1929
European champion: 1928–1936
Inducted into International Women's Sports
     Hall of Fame: 1982

Martina Hingis

Born September 30, 1980

Tennis prodigy Martina Hingis was born in Czechoslovakia, but moved to Switzerland at the age of seven, after her parents divorced. She was raised by her mother, Melanie Molitor, once an accomplished junior tennis player. Martina also inherited athletic ability from her father, Karol Hingis, who was a tennis coach in Czechoslovakia.

With her mother as her coach, Martina (named after another Czech tennis star Martina Navratilova) began developing the skills that would one day make her a world-class player. She entered her first tournament when she was only five years old and turned professional at the age of 13. Three years later she was ranked No. 4 in the world. To avoid burnout she practiced only 90 minutes each day, and continued to dabble in horseback riding, soccer, and basketball.

"People ask me if I miss normal life," Hingis told *Tennis* magazine in the fall of 1996. "And my answer is always the same—I feel I have a normal life, even if it's not the same life as other kids have. It is maybe even better than a normal life, because my life actually is like always being on holiday. That's because I like tennis."

In the spring of 1993 Hingis became the youngest player to win the French Open junior singles title (she was 12). Four months later, in her professional debut, she won an International Tennis Federation Women's Circuit satellite tournament in Langenthal, Switzerland. In 1994 she was the junior singles champion at both the French Open and Wimbledon.

Hingis joined the Women's Tennis Association tour in October 1994. Within a year she was one of the top 20 players in the world. In January 1995, at the age of 14, she became the youngest female player in the open era to win a singles match at the Australian Open; seven months later she reached the fourth round of the U.S. Open, upsetting No. 8–seed Magdalena Maleeva.

By 1996 Hingis had grown to 5 feet 6 inches and 115 pounds. Lean and strong, with exceptional court sense, she was suddenly capable of playing anyone on the WTA tour. She finished first in three tournaments, accumulated more than $1.3 million in prize money, and became one of the most popular players in women's tennis. Although erratic over the course of the season, she displayed grace and confidence in some of the biggest tournaments. She was a quarterfinalist at the French Open and a semifinalist at the U.S. Open; she also won the women's doubles titles (with Helena Sukova) at Wimbledon. She was the youngest Wimbledon champion ever, breaking the record set by Charlotte "Lottie" Dod in 1887.

Accomplishments

French Open junior champion: 1993, 1994
Wimbledon junior champion: 1994
Youngest female player to win a singles match at Australian Open: 1995
U.S. Open semifinalist: 1996
Wimbledon doubles champion: 1996

Nancy Hogshead

Born April 17, 1962

Born in Iowa City, Iowa, and raised in Jacksonville, Florida, swimmer Nancy Hogshead overcame asthma to win three gold medals at the 1988 Summer Olympics. She grew up in a supportive family that stressed academic as well as athletic achievement. In 1975 she became the second youngest person to compete in the Amateur Athletic Union Indoor National Championships. In 1977, at 14, she set American records in the 100-yard butterfly and 200-meter butterfly. She was the only U.S. swimmer that year to be ranked first in an international event.

In 1978, at age 15, Hogshead moved to Gainesville, Florida, to train full-time for the Summer Olympics. She lived alone in an apartment, like an adult, and devoted her time to swimming. She was considered one of the toughest athletes on the U.S. team, in part because she pushed herself so hard during workouts. At least twice a year Hogshead would pass out during practice sessions; she suffered from exercise-induced asthma, although she would not be diagnosed until much later in her career.

In 1980 Hogshead was one of many athletes whose dream of Olympic competition was shattered by the United States' boycott of the Summer Games in Moscow. She entered Duke University in the fall and swam competitively for one year before retiring to devote her energy to academics. But her retirement lasted only two years. In 1983 she left Duke, and began an intensive training program. A private coach and a sports psychologist helped her work toward her goal—a gold medal at the 1984 Summer Olympics in Los Angeles.

In the opening event of the 1984 Games, the 100-meter freestyle, Hogshead tied for first place with 16-year-old teammate Carrie Steinseifer. Hogshead then won gold medals in the 4 x 100 freestyle relay and the 4 x 100 medley relay, and a silver medal in the 200-meter individual medley. On August 8, as Hogshead attempted to tie the record for most medals won by a female swimmer in a single Olympics, something strange happened. Midway through the 200-meter butterfly, she had trouble breathing, and felt that her lungs were blocked. Hogshead struggled to a fourth-place finish, after which she was examined by a physician. He administered a treadmill test and offered his diagnosis.

"He told me I had asthma," Hogshead said. "I thought it was a mistake. I didn't think you could be an athlete and have asthma. That test changed my life."

Hogshead retired from swimming after the 1984 Olympics and returned to Duke, where she graduated with honors in 1986. She became a motivational speaker; wrote a book, *Asthma and Exercise*, in 1990; and became the national spokesperson for the American Lung Association. She has served as a contributing editor to *Fitness* magazine and became president of the Women's Sports Foundation. In 1994 she was inducted into the International Swimming Hall of Fame.

Accomplishments

  Olympic gold medalist, 100-meter freestyle: 1984
  Olympic gold medalist, 4 x 100 freestyle relay: 1984
  Olympic gold medalist, 4 x 100 medley relay: 1984
  Named U.S. Comeback Swimmer of the Year: 1983
  Inducted into International Swimming Hall of Fame: 1994

Eleanor Holm

Born December 6, 1913

Eleanor Holm, the finest American swimmer of her time, was born in Brooklyn, New York. Her specialty was the 100-meter backstroke, an event in which she finished fifth at the 1928 Olympics—she was only 14 years old at the time. Four years later, at the 1932 Olympics, she won a gold medal in the 100-meter backstroke. In a preliminary heat, Holm set a world record, shattering the old mark by seconds. Between 1928 and 1932 she set world backstroke records at every recorded distance.

Holm was not one to live quietly. She worked as a showgirl when she was 16; shortly after her Olympic triumph she signed a contract with Warner Bros., which wanted to capitalize on her swimming fame. The studio asked her to perform as a swimmer in its movies. If she had accepted, Holm would have been considered a professional athlete and been ineligible for further amateur competition. She turned down the offer; the studio promptly upped the ante; again she declined.

In 1933 Holm married Art Jarrett, a musician who had also grown up in Brooklyn. She became a nightclub singer, traveling from one performance to another, training in the morning and jumping on stage at night. It was an incredibly hectic—and conflicting—lifestyle. As she once said, only half jokingly, "I train on cigarettes and champagne."

Despite her unusual training regimen, Holm continued to compete at a world-class level. In the months leading up to the 1936 Olympic Games she set two more world records—in the 100-meter backstroke and 200-meter backstroke. The nightclub singer headed to Berlin as a heavy favorite to win another gold medal. But she never made it to the pool. On the transatlantic voyage aboard the SS *Manhattan*, Holm was, as usual, the life of the party. She played craps and drank well into the night. Upon her arrival in Berlin, Holm learned that the U.S. Olympic Committee, headed by Avery Brundage, had banned her from competition for her misbehavior. A rule in the Olympic team handbook was cited as an explanation—"It is understood of course that all members of the American team refrain from smoking and the use of intoxicating drinks and other forms of dissipation in training."

It was not the first time that the USOC had tried to ban Holm. Her unusual lifestyle had long been a source of irritation to Brundage, who had tried, unsuccessfully, to strip Holm of her amateur status in 1934. But in 1936 he succeeded. Holm was banned from all future amateur and Olympic competition. That did not, however, prevent her from enjoying an extended party in Berlin, where she became a huge celebrity, even though she did not swim a single lap.

Holm went on to star on the vaudeville circuit and also appeared in the movie *Tarzan's*

Revenge. In 1938 she divorced Art Jarrett. A year later she married Billy Rose, founder of the long-running Aquacade, and became the show's featured performer. In 1954 her marriage to Rose ended in divorce. In later years she moved to Florida, where she became an interior decorator.

Holm was inducted into the International Swimming Hall of Fame in 1966 and the International Women's Sports Hall of Fame in 1980.

Accomplishments

Olympic gold medalist, 100-meter backstroke: 1932
Held world records for the backstroke at every recorded distance
Inducted into International Swimming Hall of Fame: 1966
Inducted into International Women's Sports Hall of Fame: 1980

Flo Hyman

July 29, 1954–January 24, 1986

Flo Hyman is remembered not only as a great volleyball player whose life and career were cut tragically short, but also as a woman of uncommon dignity and generosity. She was raised in Inglewood, California, one of eight children. Her parents were not athletes, but were caring, determined people who wanted a better life for their children. Flo's mother was a housecleaner who saved enough money to open her own cafe; her father was a janitor with the Southern Pacific Railroad. Hyman grew up near an area that was wild about volleyball. But basketball was her first choice. From the time she was in elementary school, Hyman was always the tallest kid in the class.

"When they were three feet tall, I was four feet tall," she said. "When they were four feet tall, I was five."

As a child, Hyman tried to hide her size. She slouched when she walked and slid down in her chair. She wanted to be like everyone else. But her mother would not allow self-pity; she convinced her that God had made her special and that she had nothing to be ashamed of.

"Either you benefit from being tall like that," Hyman said, "or you hide. Fortunately, I got involved in volleyball."

Two of Hyman's older sisters had played the sport, and they recruited her. Like most volleyball players, she began with two-on-two games at the beach. Hyman's partner was usually her sister Suzanne.

Flo Hyman was 6 feet 5 inches tall by the time she graduated from Morningside High School. The University of Houston offered her a volleyball scholarship, and she accepted. She led the Cougars to two top-five finishes in the national tournament of the Association of Intercollegiate Athletics for Women.

One of Hyman's dreams was to participate in the Olympic Games. For a while it seemed that her dream might never be realized. The U.S. volleyball team failed to qualify for the Summer Olympics in 1976, and in 1980 the United States led a boycott of the Moscow Games. But by 1984, Hyman was one of the premier players in the world. At the Summer Games in Los Angeles, she led the United States to a silver medal.

After the 1984 Games, Hyman moved to Japan to play professional volleyball. She was a superstar there, beloved for her talent and charm. After a few years she branched out into modeling, acting, and coaching. On January 24, 1986, Flo Hyman collapsed and died during a volleyball match in Matsue City, Japan. The cause of death was cardiac failure caused by a ruptured aorta. It was later discovered that Hyman suffered from Marfan syndrome, a congenital disorder of the connective tissue that affects the bones, ligaments, eyes, and heart. It typically strikes extremely tall, thin people. Hyman's condition had never been diagnosed.

After her death Hyman was inducted into the International Women's Sports Hall of Fame. Since 1987 the Women's Sports Foundation has annually presented an award to a female athlete "exemplifying dignity, spirit, and commitment to excellence." The award is named after Flo Hyman.

Accomplishments

Led University of Houston to two top-five finishes in AIAW tournament.
Member of U.S. Olympic team: 1980, 1984
Olympic silver medalist: 1984
Inducted into International Women's Sports Hall of Fame: 1986

I

Juli Inkster

Born June 24, 1960

The only golfer to win two Ladies Professional Golf Association tournaments in her rookie season, Juli Inkster was born Juli Simpson in Santa Cruz, California. During the early 1980s, she was one of the best amateur players in the world—perhaps one of the best amateurs in the history of the game. As a student at San Jose State she earned All-American honors for four consecutive years (1979–1982). Ranked No. 1 amateur player by *Golf Digest* in 1981 and 1982, she was a member of the U.S. Curtis Cup team in 1982 and the World Cup team in 1980 and 1982. Inkster won the U.S. Amateur tournament three consecutive times—1980, 1981, and 1982. The only other golfers to do so were Virginia Van Wie and Glenna Collett Vare.

Inkster joined the LPGA tour at the end of the 1983 season; almost immediately she proved that her string of amateur victories was no fluke. In her fifth professional tournament she was a winner. She finished first at the SAFECO Classic. Because she competed in only eight tournaments in 1983, Inkster was still considered a rookie in 1984. But she did not play like a rookie. She won $186,501 in prize money, good enough for sixth place in the LPGA rankings. Her biggest victory came at the Nabisco Dinah Shore, one of the four major tournaments on the women's tour. Inkster beat veteran Pat Bradley on the first hole of a sudden-death playoff. That same year she captured another major tournament, the LPGA's du Maurier Classic. The first rookie ever to win two major tournaments, Inkster was voted LPGA Rookie of the Year in 1984.

Two years later, Inkster won four tournaments—the Women's Kemper Open, the McDonald's Championship, the Lady Keystone Open, and the Atlantic City Classic. Her prize money for the year was $285,293, third best on the tour. In 1988 she won more than $235,000 and again finished among the top 10 money winners. The following year she captured her third major title, winning the Nabisco Dinah Shore for the second time.

Inkster gave birth to her first child, daughter Hayley, on February 4, 1990, and played a limited schedule that year. She came back strong the following year, winning the LPGA Bay State Classic. In 1992 she accumulated nearly $400,000 in prize money, and came close to winning two more major tournaments. In the U.S. Women's Open she lost to Patty Sheehan in an 18-hole playoff; in the Nabisco Dinah Shore she lost to Dottie Pepper in a sudden-death playoff.

Considered one of the steadiest players on the LPGA tour, Juli is married to Brian Inkster, a golf pro. She resides in Los Altos, California.

Accomplishments

Collegiate All-American: 1979–1982
U.S. Amateur champion: 1980–1982
Nabisco Dinah Shore champion: 1984, 1989
du Maurier Classic champion: 1984
LPGA Rookie of the Year: 1984

Shirley Fry Irvin

Born 1927

Shirley Fry Irvin, a member of the International Tennis Hall of Fame, was born in Akron, Ohio. She grew up during the Great Depression, but her parents believed in the importance of athletics and made sure that she had the proper equipment.

"I was lucky to be able to play tennis," Irvin said. "It wasn't a cheap sport at the time. When I started to play tennis my dad started restringing tennis rackets. When we went and played ice hockey, he got the grindstone and sharpened skates for everyone."

Lester Fry managed his daughter's early career. When Shirley was just eight years old he brought her to the clay courts at the University Club in Akron to practice. There she learned the fundamentals of the sport. When she was nine years old she was put on a bus and sent to the Cleveland Exposition—alone. Her father

thought it would help her become self-reliant; she returned without any problems. A year later Shirley played in a tournament in Philadelphia. Again she made the trip alone. At an age when most children are concerned only with having fun, Shirley was setting goals. In 1936, when she was nine years old, she wrote the following words in a scrapbook: *Wimbledon—1945.*

Fry did not have the formal instruction that some of her more famous peers had received. Because she grew up in the Midwest, she could play only six months out of the year, which put her at a disadvantage. But she was a quick, smart player who won many matches against superior players.

"I never thought that someone wasn't beatable," she said. "I knew my talents weren't as good, but that didn't mean I couldn't luck through a match if I hung in there."

Fry was 14 years old the first time she played in the U.S. championships at Forest Hills; she was the youngest competitor the tournament had ever known. She reached the quarterfinals the next year, in 1942, losing to Pauline Betz, and it was presumed that it would be only a matter of time before she won a title. But Fry did not win a Grand Slam singles championship until she was 24, when she captured the 1951 French Open. Three years later, at age 27, she retired and moved to St. Petersburg, Florida. She said she was tired of practicing for hours each day and was tired of the travel and competition. And her elbow ached. Physically and mentally, she needed a break. So she took a job with the *St. Petersburg Times* and tried to forget about tennis. Two years later, however, Fry was asked to replace Maureen Connolly on the U.S. Wightman Cup team; she wasted little time in accepting the invitation.

Fry's hiatus had reinvigorated her. Over the next four years she played the best tennis of her life. In 1956 she won singles titles at Wimbledon and the U.S. Open. In 1957 she won the Australian Open. During that trip she met Karl Irvin, a U.S. Tennis Association umpire. They eventually married and raised four children. Shirley Fry Irvin was inducted into the International Tennis Hall of Fame in 1970 and in 1987 received the USTA's Service Award.

Accomplishments

French Open champion: 1951
Wimbledon champion: 1956
U.S. Open champion: 1956
Australian Open champion: 1957
Inducted into International Tennis Hall of Fame:
  1970

J

Barbara Jacket

Born December 26, 1935

Track-and-field coach Barbara Jacket, a member of the International Women's Sports Hall of Fame, was born in Port Arthur, Texas. A 1958 graduate of Tuskegee Institute in Alabama, Jacket, like many great coaches, was a modestly talented athlete who found her true calling only after her own competitive career had ended. The school that came to be synonymous with Jacket's name, Prairie View A&M University in Prairie View, Texas, had no track program when she arrived in 1964. Jacket happily accepted a position as a physical education teacher and swimming instructor. Two years later she started a track-and-field program.

Jacket's tenure lasted 27 years. During that time her teams won 19 conference championships. Prairie View captured the National Association of Intercollegiate Athletics outdoor team title for nine consecutive years, starting in 1982, and won the NAIA indoor team title three times—in 1984, 1987, and 1991.

Jacket was a talented, ambitious woman, and as Prairie View continued to win national championships, her reputation blossomed. In the 1970s she was an assistant coach for the U.S. junior Amateur Athletic Union team. In 1981 she served as an assistant coach for the U.S. team at the World University Games and the Pan American Games; she later became a head

coach for the U.S. team at the World University Games and Pacific Conference Games.

By 1983, whenever the United States needed a coach for an international assignment, Jacket was among the leading candidates. She was a head coach at the 1983 Sports Festival, the 1985 World University Games, the 1987 World Track and Field Championships, and the 1991 World University Games. In 1991 she retired as coach at Prairie View A&M but stayed on as athletic director. She would devote her time and energy to her next assignment—head coach of the U.S. women's track-and-field team at the 1992 Summer Olympics in Barcelona. Under Jacket's guidance the team won four gold medals, three silver, and three bronze.

The measure of Jacket's success can be seen not only in the team titles awarded to Prairie View A&M, but in the number of All-Americans the school produced during Jacket's tenure—27. She was honored as the NAIA Coach of the Year six times and was inducted into the Prairie View A&M University Sports Hall of Fame in 1992. She was inducted into the South Western Athletic Conference Hall of Fame in 1993 and the International Women's Sports Hall of Fame in 1995.

Accomplishments

Six-time NAIA Coach of the Year
Coach of the 1992 U.S. Olympic women's
  track-and-field team
Led Prairie View A&M to nine consecutive
  NAIA outdoor titles
Inducted into International Women's Sports
  Hall of Fame: 1995

Nell Jackson

July 1, 1929–April 1, 1988

Track-and-field pioneer Nell Jackson, the first African American head coach of a U.S. Olympic team, was born in Athens, Georgia. A talented athlete and accomplished student, Jackson attended Tuskegee Institute. As a student there, she represented the United States at the 1948 Summer Olympics in London. Three years later she took a silver medal in the 200 meters at the Pan American Games and also

Memorable Moment:
August 15, 1970

Patricia Palinkas Becomes the First Woman to Play in a Professional Football Game

Football has always been the exclusive province of men. Very large, powerful men. For the same reason that small men do not typically play professional football, women generally choose not to play.

But there are always a few exceptions to the rule, and the very first was Patricia Palinkas of Tampa, Florida. Palinkas was a fan of the game for several reasons, not the least of which was the fact that her husband was a player (Steve Palinkas was a placekicker for the semipro Orlando Panthers of the Pacific Coast League).

When Patricia got the idea that it might be fun to actually play in a game, rather than merely sit on the sidelines, she and Steve came up with a solution that seemed relatively harmless—Patricia would enter the game only briefly. She would take the snap from center, place the ball on the ground, and hold it while Steve kicked an extra point. Hers would be the safest job on the field. There would be no blocking, no tackling—no contact.

That was the plan, anyway. As Patricia discovered, kicking an extra point is not automatic. The snap from center was off target, and she did not have time to place the ball properly. So she did what any self-respecting football player would do—she tried to run with the ball. But she didn't get very far. Palinkas, who weighed 122 pounds, was brought down by Wally Florence, a 235-pound defensive lineman for the Bridgeport Jets. Unfazed and unharmed, Palinkas simply bounced up after the hit and jogged off the field. Before the game ended, she held for two more extra point attempts, both of which were successful.

helped the United States win a gold medal in the 4 x 100 relay. Jackson held the American 200-meter record for six years—from 1949 through 1954. She was the Amateur Athletic Union national champion in the 200 meters and the 4 x 100 relay from 1949 through 1951.

As impressive as those credentials were, Jackson made her mark as a coach. Her first job was at her alma mater, where she worked for more than a decade. In 1963 she moved to Illinois State, and in 1965 she accepted a head coaching position at the University of Illinois. While the University of Illinois had greater resources than Illinois State, it did not have a women's track program—it was Jackson's job to create one from scratch.

Jackson had already won several championships and produced two Olympians. One of her star athletes, high jumper Mildred McDaniel, won a gold medal at the 1956 Summer Games in Melbourne, Australia. In 1956 Jackson became the first black person—

male or female—to be appointed head coach of a U.S. Olympic team. During her time at Illinois, she continued to maintain a high profile on the international track scene. She coached the U.S. Olympic women's track-and-field team again in 1972, and served as chair of the U.S. Olympic Track and Field Committee from 1968 through 1972.

In 1973 Jackson moved to Michigan State. In addition to her athletic achievements, Jackson was an exceptional teacher and scholar. She conducted more than 50 workshops and clinics in track and field, and was, at the time of her death, director of physical education at SUNY-Binghamton.

Jackson served as vice president and secretary of the Athletics Congress and was one of the first women to be named to the U.S. Olympic Committee's board of directors. She is a member of the National Track and Field Hall of Fame, the Black Athletes Hall of Fame, and the International Women's Sports Hall of Fame.

Accomplishments

Head coach of U.S. Olympic women's track-
and-field team: 1956, 1972
Set U.S. record in the 200 meters: 1949
Inducted into U.S. Track and Field Hall of
Fame: 1989
Inducted into International Women's Sports
Hall of Fame: 1990

Helen Hull Jacobs

Born August 8, 1908

Helen Hull Jacobs, who won four consecutive U.S. tennis championships in the 1930s, was born in Globe, Arizona. Her father was a mining engineer. The family moved to San Francisco when she was a child, then relocated to Berkeley, where they purchased the home in which tennis champion Helen Wills had lived. In fact, despite her numerous accomplishments, Jacobs would spend most of her career in Wills' shadow.

Like Wills, Jacobs had refined her game at the Berkeley Tennis Club under renowned teaching professional Pop Fuller, and attended the University of California, Berkeley. While Wills was quiet and introspective, Jacobs was outgoing, friendly, and popular among fans and players. During their long and sometimes heated rivalry, Jacobs was usually the crowd favorite, a fact that led many observers to suggest that the two were enemies.

"During all the years in which we both were playing, we never once exchanged an unpleasant word," Jacobs said.

The first time the two players met, in a practice set, Jacobs was 14 years old. Wills, three years older, needed just seven minutes to thrash Jacobs, 6–0. Even then, Jacobs' resiliency was evident—she asked Wills for another set, but Wills declined. In 1928 the two women met in the finals of the U.S. championships at Forest Hills. Wills emerged victorious, 6–2, 6–1. The next year, they met in the final at Wimbledon, and again Wills won, 6–1, 6–2. Wills won their matches in the finals of the 1930 French Open and the 1932 Wimbledon.

It wasn't until 1933 that Jacobs was able to prove herself a worthy adversary. She had won the U.S. title the previous year; she was 25 years old and in peak physical condition when the two women met in the final of the U.S. championships. Jacobs won the first set, 8–6; Wills won the second, 6–3. In the third set, after falling behind by a score of 3–0, Wills, complaining of back pain, defaulted. She failed to appear at the awards ceremony and was roundly criticized for her behavior. In the press it was suggested that Wills was not seriously injured but merely wanted to avoid the indignity of losing to Jacobs.

Jacobs won the U.S. title in 1934 and 1935.

In 1936, 1939, and 1940 she lost to Alice Marble in the final. Jacobs lost to Wills in the Wimbledon final in 1935 but won the tournament the following year. Jacobs represented the United States in the Wightman Cup from 1927 to 1938, and was considered one of the toughest and most competitive women ever to play the game.

"She had more will to win, more drive and guts than anyone else," Alice Marble wrote of Jacobs. "She never gave up."

Helen Hull Jacobs was inducted into the International Tennis Hall of Fame in 1962. After retiring from tennis she spent time in the U.S. Navy and later turned to a career in writing. She wrote several children's books, three historical novels, and more than a dozen books on tennis.

Accomplishments

U.S. Open champion: 1932–1935
U.S. Open runner-up: 1928, 1936, 1939–1940
Wimbledon champion: 1936
Wimbledon runner-up: 1932, 1934–1935, 1938
Inducted into International Tennis Hall of
   Fame: 1962

Andrea Jaeger

Born June 4, 1965

Andrea Jaeger, whose injury-plagued professional tennis career spanned just a few years, was born in Chicago. Her father, Roland, a boxer from Germany, had compiled a 66–3 record during his amateur career; he later worked as a mason. He was a spirited, driven man, and those traits were passed on to his younger daughter, Andrea.

"I was brought up never to give up," she said. "I don't think I ever will."

In 1956 Roland Jaeger and his wife, Ilse, moved to Chicago, where he found work first as a laborer, then as a foreman. He also worked long hours managing a bar, and Ilse operated a beauty shop. In his spare time Roland took up tennis. Captivated by the game, he eventually became a certified teaching professional. Among his students were his daughters, Susy and Andrea. Susy, three years older than Andrea, became a good college player whose career was cut short by injuries; Andrea became one of the finest players in the world.

At the age of 12, Andrea weighed only 75 pounds and had trouble seeing her opponent over the top of the net. Nevertheless, she was the best player in her age bracket in the United States. By 14 she was frequently winning against older girls. In 1979 she won the national 18-and-under title, and the following year she turned professional. Jaeger was only 14 in 1980 when she won 13 consecutive matches to capture the Avon Futures title in Las Vegas. Later the same year she became the youngest player ever to be seeded at Wimbledon, a record that stood for 10 years until it was broken by Jennifer Capriati. With pigtails flying, Jaeger faced 35-year-old Virginia Wade of Great Britain. A former Wimbledon champion, Wade was the crowd favorite, but Jaeger earned the admiration and respect of the partisan fans. After her upset of Wade, Jaeger was referred to by the British tabloids as Miss Marvelous and the Teenage Tornado. She lost in the quarterfinals to Chris Evert, but her reputation had been established. Later that summer, at the age of 15 years and five months,

Jaeger became the youngest U.S. Open semifinalist in history.

From 1981 through 1983 Jaeger was one of the top five players in the world. Although she never won a Grand Slam title, she consistently finished among the leading money winners on the women's tour. In 1981 she was a quarterfinalist at the Australian Open and a semifinalist at the French Open. By 1982, when she was 17, Jaeger was ready to challenge for the No. 1 ranking. She stood 5 feet 6 inches and weighed 133 pounds; she was strong enough and fit enough to compete against anyone. She was a semifinalist at the Australian Open and U.S. Open, and a finalist at the French Open. In 1983 she lost in the semifinals of the French Open and in the final of Wimbledon.

In 1984 Jaeger lost matches that she was expected to win and seemed preoccupied while on the court. As it turned out, she was bothered by a nagging shoulder injury that interfered with her ability to play. She tried to ignore the pain and continued to compete.

"Andrea was No. 3 in the world, and people were coming to her, asking her to play," Susy Jaeger later explained. "Tennis needed her to play some of these events. She was not mature enough as an athlete to say, 'I'll take some time off.'"

At the 1984 Los Angeles Olympics, Andrea Jaeger barely won her first-round match. Afterward she couldn't lift her arm. On the advice of the team physician, she defaulted and began six months of rest and therapy. She had shoulder surgery for the first time; the damage that had been done was considerable. Over the next six years she would have five more surgical procedures on her shoulder. She played sporadically in 1986 and 1987, but was unable to return to the women's tour full-time.

Jaeger now lives in Aspen, Colorado. She is the founder of the Kid's Stuff Foundation, a not-for-profit organization dedicated to educating children around the world.

Accomplishments

U.S. 18-and-under champion at the age of 14: 1979
Youngest U.S. Open semifinalist (15 years, 5 months, 1 day): 1980
French Open finalist: 1982
Wimbledon finalist: 1983

Betty Jameson

Born May 19, 1919

A charter member of the Ladies Professional Golf Association and the LPGA Hall of Fame, Betty Jameson was born in Norman, Oklahoma, and grew up in San Antonio, where she became the first in a long line of outstanding Texas golfers. Her first love was painting, and she spent much of her time at the canvas. But she was a tall, athletic girl who possessed a strong golf swing. She was a smart player who studied the nuances of the game; she understood the importance of developing both power and touch. Jameson was 13 when she won the Texas Public Links title in 1932. Two years later she won the Southern Women's Amateur Championship. She put together back-to-back U.S. Amateur titles in 1939 and 1940. In 1942, still playing as an amateur, she won her first major tournament—the Western Open.

It wasn't until 1945, when she was 26 years old, that Jameson decided to turn professional. In her third year on the tour she won the U.S. Women's Open. At the Starmount Forrest Country Club in Greensboro, North Carolina, Jameson recorded a winning score of 295, becoming the first woman to shoot below 300 in a 72-hole tournament. In 1954 she achieved another first by winning a second Western Open title; she was the first person to win the Western as both an amateur and a professional.

Jameson was one of the four original inductees in the LPGA Hall of Fame. In May 1949, Jameson, Patty Berg, Babe Didrikson Zaharias, Bettye Mims Danoff, Helen Dettweiler, and Betty Hicks met at the Eastern Open in Essex Falls, New Jersey, and formally appointed Fred Corcoran as director of the new Ladies Professional Golf Association (the organization had previously been known as the Women's Professional Golf Association). Another meeting was held that same year at the U.S. Women's Open in Wichita, Kansas, and Jameson was elected LPGA treasurer.

Jameson won four LPGA tournaments in 1955. Her last full season on tour was 1956; she had won 10 events in her career. In 1952 Jameson decided that the LPGA should present a trophy each year to the professional with the season's lowest scoring average. So she donated the Vare Trophy, named after her close friend, Glenna Collett Vare. The Vare Trophy is now one of the most cherished awards on the LPGA tour.

Jameson presently lives in Delray Beach, Florida.

Accomplishments

> U.S. Amateur champion: 1939–1940
> Western Open champion: 1942, 1954
> Western Amateur champion: 1942
> U.S. Women's Open champion: 1947
> Inducted into LPGA Hall of Fame: 1951

Lynn Jennings

Born July 1, 1960

Lynn Jennings, an Olympic medalist in track and field, and one of the most accomplished cross-country runners in history, was born in Princeton, New Jersey. She began her running career in Harvard, Massachusetts, where she discovered not only the joy of a long, quiet run in the New England woods, but also the thrill of athletic competition. She attended the Bromfield School, where she trained and raced with members of the boys' team. When she competed against girls, she usually ran uncontested. When in high school she won three girls' cross-country state championships, won the Boston Bonne Bell 10K—one of the most competitive road races in the world—and finished third in the Boston Marathon, with a time of 2 hours, 45 minutes.

Jennings received scholarship offers from the major college track and cross-country programs. But she decided to attend Princeton, a school that did not offer athletic scholarships. "I think subconsciously I knew there was a lot more to life than running," she said. "I was going to be forced to find out what those things were by attending an Ivy League school."

In college Jennings had trouble adjusting to being a member of an all-girls team for the first time in her life. She trained inadequately, ate too much, and attended many parties. As she once wrote in a diary for a national magazine, "Princeton expected a champion, but it got a chump."

Jennings left Princeton in the fall of her

Memorable Moment: June 24, 1972

Bernice Gera Umpires a Professional Baseball Game

Bernice Gera was 40 years old when she graduated from a certified umpiring school. Her goal was to work a professional baseball game, and she thought she had earned the right to take her place behind the plate. But to her chagrin, she discovered that it wasn't such a simple matter. She applied to the New York–Pennsylvania Professional Baseball League, a minor league consisting primarily of Class A affiliates of major league franchises. In response, Philip Piton, president of the National Association of Professional Baseball Leagues, told Gera that she didn't meet the physical requirements for being an umpire—a minimum height of 5 feet 10 inches, and a minimum weight of 170 pounds.

Gera, who was 5 feet 2 inches and 129 pounds, decided to fight back. She took her case to court, and on January 13, 1972, a decision came down in her favor. On June 24 of that year, Gera umpired her first professional baseball game. Unfortunately, it was a traumatic evening. Gera blew a call in the fourth inning of a game between the Auburn Phillies and the Geneva Rangers. She acknowledged her mistake and reversed her decision, which prompted an on-field confrontation with one of the managers. After the game, Gera broke down and cried in front of reporters. The stress, she said, was simply too much to handle. She resigned on the spot.

Gera's professional umpiring career lasted just one game, but her willingness to fight made it possible for other women to pursue the same dream.

junior year. She later returned, rejoined the track team, and graduated in 1983. But in the spring of 1984, at the U.S. Olympic trials, Jennings finished last in her 3,000-meter heat. After that, she hung up her spikes, intending never to run again. She returned to her parents' house in Harvard, wallowed in self-pity for a while, put on 20 pounds, and fought the urge to run. Then, one fall morning in 1984, she stepped outside for a gentle run.

"I just said to myself, 'This is ridiculous. You're 24 years old, you have a talent, and you're not using it,'" she said.

For a time Jennings lived in a small cabin in rural New Hampshire, thinking of almost nothing but training and racing. It was an intense, somewhat eccentric approach, but it worked. She won six consecutive national cross-country championships in the late 1980s and early 1990s. On March 25, 1990, Jennings became the first American in 15 years to win the World Cross-Country Championships; she later won that event two more times.

Although she never considered herself much of a road racer, Jennings won several national championships at 5 kilometers and 10 kilometers. On the track she was nearly as impressive, finishing first in the 10,000 meters at the national championships in 1987, 1991, and 1993. In 1992 she took a bronze medal in the 10,000 meters at the Summer Olympics in Barcelona, setting an American record of 31:19.89. She also represented the United States at the 1996 Summer Olympics in Atlanta.

Accomplishments

Three-time Massachusetts high school cross-country champion
Six-time national cross-country champion
Three-time world cross-country champion
Olympic bronze medalist, 10,000 meters: 1992
Set American record for 10,000 meters: 1992

Ann Haydon Jones

Born October 7, 1938

Adrianne Shirley Haydon Jones, a member of the International Tennis Hall of Fame, grew up in Birmingham, England. She never really had a choice about becoming proficient in racket sports—both of her parents were outstanding table tennis players. In fact, her father, Adrian, once reached the semifinal round of the world championships. Ann began playing table tennis when she was a child and knew her way around a tennis court by the time she was 12.

In 1957, at the age of 18, Jones, like her father, reached the semifinals of the world championships in table tennis. She even outdid him, advancing to the final before losing by only points. That is how Jones is usually remembered—as an accomplished athlete who often played for a championship but rarely won. She reached the semifinals at Wimbledon seven times during an 11-year period in the 1950s and 1960s. But only once did she emerge triumphant. Despite all of her accomplishments, Jones was overshadowed throughout her career by the likes of Virginia Wade and Christine Truman, two popular and successful British tennis players.

Not that Jones minded being relegated to the edge of the spotlight's glare. She was never a glutton for publicity. "I was quite happy playing on court 92 somewhere, with only a half-dozen spectators," she said.

Jones' first major victory came in 1961, when she captured the French Open. She won a second French title in 1966, defeating Nancy Richey in straight sets, 6–3, 6–1. During those years she became a fixture in the late rounds at Wimbledon, the tournament she most wanted to win, but it wasn't until 1967 that she reached the final. That year Jones lost to Billie Jean King, 6–3, 6–4. Jones had had numerous chances to win that match, but blew 14 of 15 break-point opportunities. Once again she found herself graciously applauding for someone else when the winner's trophy was presented.

"That had been the story of my Wimbledon life," Jones said. "When it came to the crunch, I didn't have that little something more."

Not until 1969. At age 30, Jones was one of the oldest players in the Wimbledon draw, but she was also as sharp as she had ever been. Among the favorites was 23-year-old Wade, who had captured the U.S. Open the previous summer. But Wade was upset in an early-round match; in the semifinals Jones stunned Margaret Smith Court, the most dominant player in tennis at the time. In fact, Wimbledon was the only Grand Slam singles event that Court failed to win in 1969. Jones' victory gave her the confidence she needed to defeat Billie Jean King, who was seeking her fourth consecutive Wimbledon title. In a dramatic three-set championship match, Jones beat King, 3–6, 6–3, 6–2, to win her first and only Wimbledon title.

Jones never won another Grand Slam singles title, but in the early 1970s she became one of the most important and reliable members of the fledgling Women's Tennis Association professional tour.

Accomplishments

  French Open champion: 1961, 1966
  Wimbledon runner-up: 1961, 1967
  Wimbledon champion: 1969
  Inducted into International Tennis Hall of
    Fame: 1985

Joan Joyce

Born August 1, 1940

Joan Joyce grew up in Waterbury, Connecticut, and was just 13 years old when she became a member of the Raybestos Brakettes, one of the finest women's amateur softball teams in the country. By that time she was already something of a veteran, having spent several hours a day as a child throwing balls against the back of her parents' house. She came from a sporting family—her father was a baseball coach, and Joan often tagged along when he went to practice. She learned at an early age how to run the base paths and to shag fly balls. She also liked basketball, volleyball, bowling, and golf.

In 1957, at the age of 17, Joyce became the Brakettes' star pitcher, assuming that position from Bertha Tickey, who had compiled a record of 757–88 during her two-decade career. Considerable pressure was put on Joyce to fill Tickey's shoes. For 19 consecutive years—from 1957 through 1975—Joyce was an Amateur Softball Association All-American. That streak ended only when she left the amateur ranks to become a professional.

With Joyce on the mound, the Brakettes won 12 national championships. Joyce spent time in California in the mid-1960s, pitching for the Lionettes of Orange County. Benefiting from Joyce's powerful arm, the Lionettes won the national title in 1965. The secret to Joyce's success was obvious to anyone standing in the batter's box with Joyce 45 feet away. She threw the ball with incredible speed—116 miles per hour—and was practically unbeatable. At the 1973 Women's National Fast Pitch Championships, she went 9–0, with eight shutouts. Two years later she won all 36 games that she pitched, led the Brakettes to another title, and was named play-off MVP for the eighth time. Her lifetime record was 507–33, with more than 100 no-hitters and a minuscule earned run average of 0.21.

And while considered the greatest pitcher in the history of women's softball, Joyce was also a fair offensive player. She hit .414 in the 1973 nationals and had a lifetime batting average of .327.

When her amateur career ended, Joyce helped found the Women's Professional Softball League. She was the owner and manager of the Connecticut Falcons, which won the Women's Pro World Series each year from 1976 through 1979—she pitched for the team.

The twilight of Joyce's softball career became the dawn of her golf career. She began playing seriously again in 1975; two years later she became a member of the Ladies Professional Golf Association. She has finished as high as sixth in LPGA tournaments and remains a semi-regular on the LPGA tour. In 1989 she was inducted into the International Women's Sports Hall of Fame.

Accomplishments

  Amateur Softball Association All-American:
    1957–1975
  Lifetime pitching record of 507–33
  Eight-time MVP of Women's National Fast
    Pitch Championships
  Inducted into International Women's Sports
    Hall of Fame: 1989

Florence Griffith Joyner

Born December 21, 1959

Florence Griffith Joyner, who has held the title of World's Fastest Woman since 1988, was raised in the Watts section of Los Angeles. Her mother, also named Florence, had left a bad marriage in 1964 and moved with her 11 children from their home in the Mojave Desert. Together they settled into a housing project located in a neighborhood that would be ravaged by one of the most notorious race riots in U.S. history.

The elder Florence set down strict rules for her children, but she also showered them with love and affection and told them that one day life would be better. The younger Florence was a quiet, introspective child who wrote poetry, kept a diary, and liked to fix her hair in unusual ways—sometimes she styled the hair of friends and family members. When she was given the opportunity to have a pet, she chose a boa constrictor.

But if there was an animal that Florence Griffith came close to imitating, it would have been a cheetah or a jackrabbit. At the age of seven she won her first race, in an event sponsored by the Sugar Ray Robinson Youth Foundation. She went on to star for Jordan High School, setting school records in the sprints and long jump. When her sprint coach at California State University–Northridge, Bob Kersee, took a job at UCLA, Griffith followed him there.

At UCLA, Griffith improved dramatically, winning the 200 meters at the NCAA championship in 1982. In 1984 she earned a spot on the U.S. Olympic team. At the Los Angeles Summer Games she took a silver medal in the 200. She also received a lot of attention by sporting long, brightly colored fingernails and wearing shimmering bodysuits that earned her the nickname Fluorescent Flo.

After the Olympics, Griffith stopped training and took a 9-to-5 job. It wasn't until she began dating and training with Al Joyner—an Olympic gold medalist in the triple jump, world-class hurdler, and the older brother of Olympic champion Jackie Joyner-Kersee—that Griffith received the one-on-one training she needed to resume her career. In 1987 she married Joyner. That same year she finished second in the 200 meters, and helped the United States win the 4 x 100 relay at the World Track and Field Championships in Rome.

In 1988, at the U.S. Olympic trials in Indianapolis, Florence Griffith Joyner set records in the 100 meters and 200 meters; she did so in literally stunning fashion. She wore an assortment of daring outfits during the trials, including one-legged bodysuits that she designed and a white lace bodysuit, which she called the athletic negligee. At the 1988 Summer Games in Seoul, Griffith Joyner, by now nicknamed Flo-Jo, was compelled by Olympic rules to tone down her taste in fashion. But she still cut an impressive figure on the track, taking a gold medal in the 100 meters. She set a world record in the 200 meters with a time of 21.56 seconds in the semifinals. She went on an hour later to break her own record with a time of 21.34 seconds in the finals to win her second gold medal. She won the hearts of millions of fans by flashing a huge smile in the final meters of both races. She helped the United States take a gold medal in the 4 x 100 relay and a silver medal in the 4 x 400 relay. In doing so, Griffith Joyner became the first American woman in track and field to win four medals in a single Olympiad.

Griffith Joyner was named Female Athlete of the Year by the Associated Press in 1988 and also Athlete of the Year by the Soviet news agency Tass. She retired from track and field in 1989 and has since worked as a model, actress, and spokesperson. In 1993, she was appointed the first woman ever to co-chair the President's Council on Physical Fitness and Sports.

Accomplishments

Olympic silver medalist, 200 meters: 1984
Olympic gold medalist, 100 meters: 1988
Olympic gold medalist, 200 meters: 1988
Olympic gold medalist, 4 x 100 relay: 1988
Olympic silver medalist, 4 x 400 relay: 1988
Sullivan Award winner: 1988
International Jesse Owens Award winner: 1989
USOC Olympia Award winner: 1992

Jackie Joyner-Kersee

Born March 3, 1962

Two-time Olympic heptathlon champion Jackie Joyner-Kersee was raised in East St. Louis, Illinois. Born into poverty, she was a study in determination. Her mother named her after Jacqueline Kennedy because she believed the little girl would one day be "the first lady of something." Jackie eventually became one of the greatest all-around athletes in history.

Her father, Alfred, worked two hours from home as a railroad switch operator and was only able to see his family on weekends. Her mother, Mary, was an aide at a hospital. Jackie and her two sisters and brother had a hard life. They were rarely treated to new clothing, and food was sometimes hard to come by. Some days Jackie took to school nothing more than a mayonnaise sandwich. But the Joyners were a tight family, and they took care of each other. Jackie was particularly close to her brother, Al, who would make his own mark as an athlete. They promised each other that they would work hard, concentrate on school and sports, and avoid the trouble that was so easy to find on the streets of East St. Louis.

Jackie was only nine years old when she entered her first race. By 12 she was beating all the boys in her neighborhood; by 14 she was working on her long-jump technique. Coaches at a recreation center told her about the pentathlon, a five-sport event that included the long jump, 100-meter hurdles, shot put, high jump, and 800-meter run. A year later she won the AAU national junior pentathlon championship. She also found time to play basketball for Lincoln High School. In 1980, as a high school senior, she earned an invitation to the U.S. Olympic Track and Field trials. She failed to earn a spot on the team, but the experience proved invaluable.

Joyner accepted a scholarship from UCLA. The death of her mother so devastated her that she nearly dropped out in her freshman year, but she stayed, determined to leave her mark on the world. She became a starting forward on the UCLA basketball team and found a friend and partner in assistant track coach Bob Kersee. Kersee suggested that Joyner concentrate on the heptathlon (which adds the javelin and the 200-meter run to the pentathlon) rather than the long jump, her favorite event. She agreed.

Led by Joyner, UCLA won the NCAA Women's Track and Field Championships in 1982. The following year a hamstring injury prevented Joyner from earning a medal at the world championships in Helsinki, Finland. In 1984, despite suffering from chronic asthma, she took a silver medal in the heptathlon at the Los Angeles Olympics. Her brother took a gold medal in the triple jump.

Kersee became Joyner's husband as well as her coach in 1986, and they worked together to make her the finest heptathlete in the world. She shattered the world record in that event twice in the summer of 1986 and was named the winner of the Sullivan Award, given annually to the top amateur athlete in the United States. Two years later, at the Summer Olympics in Seoul, Joyner-Kersee won gold medals in both the heptathlon and the long jump. She was named Woman of the Year by the *Sporting News*, as outstanding athlete of 1988. That publication had previously honored only male athletes. In 1992 Joyner-Kersee repeated as gold medalist in the heptathlon; she also took a bronze in the long jump.

Four years later, at the 1996 Summer Olympics in Atlanta, Joyner-Kersee suffered a hamstring injury and was forced to withdraw from the heptathlon; however, she did win a bronze medal in the long jump. In the fall of 1996 she joined the Richmond Rage of the newly formed women's American Basketball League.

Accomplishments

Olympic gold medalist, heptathlon: 1988, 1992
Olympic gold medalist, long jump: 1988
Olympic silver medalist, heptathlon: 1984
Olympic bronze medalist, long jump: 1992, 1996
Sullivan Award winner: 1988
Sporting News Woman of the Year: 1988

K

Nancy Kerrigan

Born October 13, 1959

A two-time Olympic medalist, Nancy Kerrigan's fame and celebrity stemmed less from her talent than from her unfortunate role in the biggest scandal ever to hit the sport of figure skating. In January 1994, at the U.S. Figure Skating Association Championships—which served as the Olympic trials—Kerrigan was brutally attacked after a practice session. An unidentified man struck Kerrigan on the knee with a club, knocking her out of the competition. What at first appeared to be a random act of violence turned out to be a calculated attempt to prevent Kerrigan from competing in the Olympic Games. The plot was devised by Jeff Gillooly, the ex-husband of figure skater Tonya Harding, Kerrigan's chief rival at the national championships. Harding eventually pleaded guilty to charges of conspiring to hinder the investigation into the attack, but insisted that she learned of the plot only after it had been executed.

As it turned out, the physical damage done to Kerrigan was minimal. Though she was forced to withdraw from the national championships—thus opening the door for Harding, who finished first—Kerrigan was placed on the U.S. Olympic team by the U.S. Figure Skating Association. Her knee healed quickly, and by February, when she traveled to Lillehammer, Norway, for the Winter Games, she was strong and healthy. There, the world witnessed the conclusion to one of the more bizarre stories in the annals of sport. Harding, distracted and not in shape, skated badly; Kerrigan turned in the performance of her life. With one of the largest television audiences in history watching, Kerrigan skated flawlessly.

But her effort wasn't enough. The gold medal went to 16-year-old Oksana Baiul of the Ukraine; Kerrigan settled for the silver. Making matters worse for Kerrigan, television cameras captured her after the defeat behaving in a manner that wasn't entirely gracious, prompting a flood of negative publicity. Nevertheless, after the Olympics, she landed numerous endorsement deals that made her one of the wealthiest women in sports.

Kerrigan grew up near Boston and fell in love with figure skating at an early age. She was a quiet, serious girl who got up at four in the morning to practice before going to school.

Her father, Dan, a welder, worked extra jobs and took out loans to pay for Nancy's lessons. Kerrigan graduated from Stoneham High School in 1987. She was a bronze medalist at the 1989 U.S. Olympic Festival and a gold medalist in 1990. In 1992 she took a silver medal in the world championships and a bronze medal in the Albertville Winter Olympics. *People* magazine dubbed her one of its 50 Most Beautiful People in 1993.

Just as it seemed as though everything was coming together for Kerrigan, she began to have trouble on the ice. Suffering from acute anxiety and nervousness, she finished fifth in the 1993 world championships; while awaiting her scores, she was overheard saying, "I just want to die."

But with the help of a sports psychologist, Kerrigan overcame her fear of losing and became a stronger athlete. After the 1994 Winter Olympic Games she performed in a series of ice shows, including a 16-city tour called *Christmas on Ice.*

Accomplishments

Olympic silver medalist: 1994
Olympic bronze medalist: 1992
Silver medalist, world championships: 1992
Silver medalist, U.S. championships: 1992
Bronze medalist, world championships: 1991
Bronze medalist, U.S. championships: 1991

Betsy King

Born August 13, 1955

Betsy King, the Ladies Professional Golf Association's all-time leading money winner, was born in Reading, Pennsylvania. The daughter of Dr. and Mrs. Weir King had an exceptional amateur career that included participation in the semifinals of the 1972 United States Golf Association Junior Girls' Championship. After graduating from high school King accepted an athletic scholarship from Furman University. In 1976 she helped lead Furman to the NCAA championship. That same year she was low amateur at the U.S. Women's Open (her eighth-place finish remained the best by an amateur for nearly two decades). King graduated from Furman in 1977 with a degree in physical education. She was named the school's Athlete of the Year and Woman Scholar-Athlete of the Year.

King joined the LPGA tour in the spring of 1977, but managed to win only $4,008 in her rookie season. It wasn't until her eighth year on the tour that King finally won a tournament. In 1984 she won her first LPGA event, the Women's Kemper Open, then won the Freedom Orlando Classic and the Columbia Savings Classic. By the end of the year she had accumulated more than $266,000 in prize money—nearly triple her previous best year—and was the tour's leading money winner. *Golf Digest* presented her with its Most Improved Player Award; she was also named Rolex Player of the Year.

For the next decade King was one of the most successful golfers in the world. In 1987 she won four tournaments, including her first major, the Nabisco Dinah Shore. She was named Player of the Year by both *Golf Illustrated* and *Golf* magazine, and won the LPGA's Samaritan Award for her humanitarian and charitable efforts. King won three more events in 1988 and six the following year, including the U.S. Women's Open. In 1989 she set an LPGA record for season earnings with $654,132 and became the sixth player to surpass $2 million in career earnings. For the second time she was named Rolex Player of the Year.

A third Player of the Year honor came in 1993, a season in which King was again the LPGA's leading money winner. She concluded that year with a victory in the Toray Queens Cup in Japan. It was the 29th victory of her career, one short of the number she needed for inclusion in the LPGA Hall of Fame. After nearly 20 months she achieved win No. 30. On June 25, 1995, at the ShopRite LPGA Classic in Somers Point, New Jersey, King came from behind to post a two-stroke victory over Beth Daniel and Rosie Jones. She won a $97,500 paycheck and inclusion in the Hall of Fame.

Accomplishments

U.S. Women's Open champion: 1989–1990
LPGA Championship winner: 1992
Nabisco Dinah Shore champion: 1987, 1990
Rolex Player of the Year: 1984, 1989, 1993
Inducted into LPGA Hall of Fame: 1995

Billie Jean King

Born November 22, 1943

Billie Jean King was born Billie Jean Moffitt in Long Beach, California, and grew up to become not only a tennis champion, but also one of the most important and influential sports figures in the world. She won 12 Grand Slam tournament titles and nearly $2 million in prize money. As a writer, publisher, and commentator, she has been an outspoken advocate for women's rights, and one of the people most responsible for the financial and athletic success enjoyed by today's female tennis players.

The daughter of Willard and Betty Moffitt first fell in love with baseball—she played often with her brother, Randy, who would one day become a relief pitcher for the San Francisco Giants. By the age of 11, Billie Jean had been introduced to the game of tennis. Her parents arranged for her to take lessons, and she demonstrated a natural affinity. As a teen she said that she hoped to play someday at Wimbledon.

Moffitt achieved that goal in 1961, when she and Karen Hantze became the youngest pair ever to win the women's doubles title at Wimbledon; they repeated in 1962. In 1963 Moffitt reached the Wimbledon finals but lost to Margaret Smith in straight sets. After training in Australia with Mervyn Rose, Moffitt improved her game even more. She lost in the finals of the U.S. Open in 1965. But, competing as Billie Jean King (she had married lawyer Larry King, a friend from her college days at California State University–Los Angeles, in September 1966), she won the singles title at Wimbledon in 1966, 1967, and 1968; the U.S. Open in 1967; and the Australian Open in 1968. After failing to win a Grand Slam singles title in 1969 and 1970, she came back strong in 1971, winning her second U.S. Open. The following year she captured the U.S. Open, the French Open, and the Wimbledon titles. In 1971 she became the first woman to accumulate $100,000 in prize money.

But for all of her achievements in the traditional world of tennis, Billie Jean King will most likely be remembered for her participation in a thoroughly nontraditional event. In 1973 she was challenged to a Battle of the Sexes match against Bobby Riggs, a 55-year-old man who had been, in his day, a pretty fair player but who by then was more self-promoter than anything else. King, a fiery competitor, accepted the challenge. They met at the Houston Astrodome, in front of more than 30,000 spectators and another 40 million tuned in on closed-circuit television. The 29-year-old King demolished Riggs in straight sets, 6–4, 6–3, 6–3.

Before retiring from active singles competition in the mid-1980s, King was named Associated Press Woman Athlete of the Year in 1967 and 1973, *Sports Illustrated* Sportsperson of the Year in 1972, and *Time* Woman of the Year in 1976. She has twice served as president of the Women's Tennis Association, of which she is a founding member, and helped establish both the Women's Sports Foundation and *Women Sports* magazine. She published her autobiography, *Billie Jean*, in 1982, and wrote *We Have Come a Long Way* in 1988.

In 1981 King's life was touched by scandal when she acknowledged having a brief affair with Marilyn Barnett, her former secretary and companion. Barnett sued King for lifetime support, but King received a favorable judgment in the case. Shortly thereafter, she and her husband began laying the groundwork for a project that would become World Team Tennis.

Accomplishments

Wimbledon singles champion: 1966–1968, 1972–1973
U.S. Open singles champion: 1967, 1971–1972, 1974
Australian Open singles champion: 1968
French Open singles champion: 1972
First female athlete to earn $100,000 in a season: 1971
Founder of Women's Sports Foundation: 1974
Inducted into International Women's Sports Hall of Fame: 1980

Micki King

Born July 26, 1944

Maxine J. King, an Olympic gold medalist in diving, was born in Pontiac, Michigan. She was not the sort of girl who was content to play quietly with dolls; rather, she was an exuberant youngster who preferred the thrill of competition.

"I wasn't the one the boys asked to dance," King said. "For me, it was always, 'Let's go out and play catch.'"

Micki began diving when she was 10 years old. She quickly displayed a natural aptitude—and a fearlessness—that compelled people to take notice. But in high school she gave up diving in favor of other sports. Diving, for her, was too solitary a pursuit, too quiet and precise. She concentrated on water polo, a team sport ideal for someone with great energy and competitive fire. Water polo is an exhausting contact sport—above the water it appears elegant, but below the surface bodies become entangled and the rules are frequently bent.

As a member of the Ann Arbor Swim Club, King played on two national championship water polo teams. As a goalie at the University of Michigan, she was twice awarded All-America honors. Dick Kimball, water sports coach at Michigan State, convinced King that she should resume her diving career. By the time she graduated, she had won three NCAA diving titles. She entered the Air Force, but continued to train with Kimball. Her improvement was steady. She won national outdoor 3-meter championships in 1965, 1967, 1969, and 1970. She captured the 1-meter title in 1967 and the platform title in 1969. Indoors, she was nearly as successful, winning 3-meter titles in 1971 and 1972, and platform titles in 1965 and 1971.

King's Olympic experience was both devastating and thrilling. In 1968, at the Summer Games in Mexico City, she was in first place after the first eight dives in the springboard competition. But, on the ninth dive, King struck the board and fractured her left arm. She went on to complete the competition but was clearly not her usual self. When the final standings were announced, King was in fourth place, one spot away from a medal.

Four years later, at the Summer Games in Munich, King took the lead on her eighth dive and capped her performance with a reverse one-and-a-half somersault—the same dive on which she had broken her arm. But this time, she executed the dive flawlessly and won the gold medal. Typically a stoic competitor, King let her emotions flow on the medal stand. She cried openly and, in noting her longevity (she was 28 years old), said, "I've been diving longer than the girl who came in second has lived."

King retired from competition and became diving coach at the U.S. Air Force Academy. She was the first woman to coach an all-male team, a fact that did not intimidate her in the least.

King left the Air Force Academy to become director of women's athletics at UCLA. She returned to the academy in 1983, the same year she was inducted into the International Women's Sports Hall of Fame.

Accomplishments

Olympic gold medalist, springboard: 1972
National 3-meter champion: 1965, 1967, 1969, 1970
Inducted into International Women's Sports Hall of Fame: 1983
Inducted into U.S. Olympic Hall of Fame: 1992

Marita Koch

Born 1957

Marita Koch, one of the finest sprinters in the history of track and field, was born in Wismar, East Germany, near the Baltic Coast. She was an athletic child who came to track and field only after a brief fascination with team handball. Under the rigid East German sports system, in which children were targeted for particular athletic endeavors at a very young age, Koch was deemed too short to be a team handball player. So, before she reached her 12th birthday, she chose a new sport—running.

By 1975 Koch was counted among the most promising sprinters in the world. She was scheduled to run the 400 meters at the 1976 Summer Olympics in Montreal, but a nagging leg injury caused her to run badly in the early heats, and she withdrew from the semifinals. But within two years, she was the outstanding performer in her sport, according to *Track & Field News*. The 400 remained her specialty—on three occasions she shattered the world record; she also broke the world record for 200 meters. In 1979 she set a new mark of 21.71 seconds in the 200, becoming the first woman to run faster than 22 seconds. That same year she also became the first woman to break 49 seconds for 400 meters.

Because the 400 is such a physically demanding event, Koch decided to skip the 200 at the 1980 Olympic Games in Moscow; the quarter, as it is often called, would take all of her concentration. Koch's strongest challengers in the final were teammate Christina Lathan and Czechoslovakia's Jarmila Kratochvilova. Koch won the gold medal with an Olympic-record time of 48.88 seconds. In the 4 x 400 relay, East Germany was upset by the Soviet Union and had to settle for a silver medal, although Koch nearly wiped out a 10-meter deficit on the anchor leg.

In 1983, at the first World Track and Field Championships, Koch decided to pass on her favorite, the 400 meters, and run the other sprints. In the 200 she defeated Jamaica's Merlene Ottey to win the gold medal; in the 100 she finished second behind teammate Marlies Gohr; and in the 4 x 100 relay and 4 x 400 relay, she helped East Germany win gold medals.

"The sprints are all connected for me," Koch said. "In order to run fast in the 400, I need to have good performances in the 100 and 200. The starts in the 100 help my 400, and the endurance in the 400 helps my 100 and 200."

Koch did not have the chance to defend her Olympic title in 1984 because of her country's participation in a boycott of the Los Angeles Games, but in 1985 she recorded the fastest 400 of her life—and the fastest 400 in history—when she ran .7 in 47.60 seconds. As of 1995, that mark still stood as a world record.

Koch's accomplishments are even more impressive considering the fact that during her time as a world-class athlete, she was also a medical student at the University of Rostock.

Accomplishments

UPI International Athlete of the Year: 1979, 1982
Olympic gold medalist, 400 meters: 1980
Olympic silver medalist, 4 x 400 relay: 1980
World champion, 200 meters: 1983
World champion, 4 x 100 relay: 1983
World champion, 4 x 400 relay: 1983

Olga Korbut

Born May 16, 1955

Olga Korbut, who won three gold medals in gymnastics at the 1972 Summer Olympics, was born in Grodno, a town in the Soviet Union near the Polish border. Her father, Valentin, a World War II veteran, and her mother, Valentina, a cook, raised four girls. Like many promising young athletes in the USSR, Korbut was enrolled in a special school. She worked with trainer Renald Knysh, a quiet but driven man who was one of the finest gymnastics coaches in the country. Korbut, a fearless little girl with boundless energy, responded well to Knysh's methods, quickly becoming a world-class gymnast.

In 1969, 14-year-old Korbut received an invitation to compete in the Soviet championships, even though the entry guidelines stated that contestants had to be at least 16 years of age. But Korbut's gifts were known throughout the country, and it was agreed that she was among the most talented gymnasts. Korbut stunned and delighted the crowd by performing a backward somersault on the balance beam, a move that had previously been considered too dangerous to attempt in competition. Knysh, an innovative coach, was criticized in some circles for tampering with tradition, but Korbut's daring techniques were soon copied by gymnasts all over the world.

In the summer of 1972, through sheer talent and her stage presence, Korbut brought the sport of gymnastics to a vast international audience. Only 4 feet 11 inches tall and weighing 85 pounds, she was the darling of the Olympic Games in Munich. She was 17 years old, but, with pigtails flying, looked no more than 13. Television audiences around the world fell in love with her as she laughed, smiled, and cried. Gymnastics had previously been the province of mature women who performed graceful ballet-like movements; now here was Korbut, bounding from one piece of equipment to the next, flying through the air like some innocent daredevil. Detractors said she was more acrobat than gymnast, but the judges didn't seem to care. Korbut won gold medals in the floor exercise and the balance beam, and as a member of the Soviet Union's all-around team. Only a surprising slip on the uneven parallel bars prevented her from capturing the individual all-around title. In the aftermath of the Summer Games, Korbut became an international celebrity, particularly in the United States, where she visited both the White House and Disneyland. She found the attention overwhelming.

"I look at that little girl now and see that it was a shame she wasn't prepared for any of this," Korbut told an interviewer more than 20 years later. "She couldn't comprehend what was happening. She was thinking, *Why are these people bothering me?*"

As is often the case in gymnastics, fame was fleeting. At the 1976 Olympics, Korbut won a gold medal in the team event and a silver in the balance beam, but was no longer the star of her sport; she had been supplanted by 14-year-old Nadia Comaneci of Romania. Korbut retired after the Montreal Games and married Soviet musician Leonid Bertkevich in 1978. In 1982 she was inducted into the International Women's Sports Hall of Fame. She later moved to Atlanta, Georgia, opened a gymnastics school, and became head of the American Child Health Foundation, which helped support victims of the Chernobyl nuclear disaster in her native land.

Accomplishments

Olympic gold medalist, balance beam: 1972
Olympic gold medalist, floor exercise: 1972
Olympic gold medalist, all-around team: 1972, 1976
Olympic silver medalist, balance beam: 1976

Jarmila Kratochvilova

Born 1951

Jarmila Kratochvilova, perhaps the finest middle-distance runner ever, grew up in Golcuv Jenikov, a small town in rural Czechoslovakia, some 60 miles east of Prague. Her father, Antonin, was a police officer; her mother, Bozena, a farmhand. When she was a small girl Jarmila wanted to be a stewardess or a teacher. She was a quiet and shy child who did nothing to draw attention to herself.

But as she grew, Kratochvilova distinguished herself in a number of ways, most of them physical. She had great strength, which allowed her to be as productive as any adult when she worked in the fields. In gym class she always seemed to be one step ahead of her classmates, so a friend convinced her to try competitive running. Kratochvilova turned out to be one of the most successful late bloomers in the history of track and field.

Kratochvilova endured a succession of injuries and illnesses that slowed her development for many years. It wasn't until she was 27 that she first broke 50 seconds in the 400 meters. At the 1980 Summer Olympics in Moscow, 29-year-old Kratochvilova took a silver medal in the 400, finishing second behind East German Marita Koch. In 1982 Kratochvilova set an indoor world record for 400 meters with a time of 49.59. Thirteen years later that mark still stood. One year later, at a race in Munich, she broke the outdoor world record for 800 meters with a time of 1:53.28. As of 1995 that record had not been threatened. In Helsinki in 1983, Kratochvilova won both the 400 meters and the 800 meters at the inaugural World Track and Field Championships.

Her performances in those races were mesmerizing, and her modesty off the track was refreshing. But Kratochvilova could not escape criticism. Because her body was thickly muscled and her features somewhat masculine, she faced accusations of steroid use wherever she went, particularly in the West. Dr. Leroy Perry, a Los Angeles chiropractor who worked with many top female runners, made no effort to mask his suspicions.

"I've never seen a body like that," he said in a newspaper article. "I think there is something chemically different about her physiological makeup, and it had to happen in the last five years. And I'm sure it hasn't come from weightlifting."

Kratochvilova and her coach flatly denied using steroids or any other performance-enhancing drugs, and she passed every drug test that she ever took. But the rumors dogged her to the end of her career. Kratochvilova was 32 years old when she ran her best races; she would have been 33 at the 1984 Summer Olympics in Los Angeles. But Czechoslovakia joined the Soviet-led boycott of the Games that year, preventing her from competing for a gold medal.

Accomplishments

Olympic silver medalist, 400 meters: 1980
World champion, 400 meters: 1983
World champion, 800 meters: 1983

Ingrid Kristiansen

Born March 21, 1956

Born Ingrid Christiansen in Trondheim, Norway, Ingrid Kristiansen became one of the greatest female long-distance runners. She grew up in a snowy climate, so she naturally gravitated toward skiing. She and her older brother often traveled with their parents to cross-country ski races on weekends; there the whole family embraced the rugged outdoors and the spirit of competition. Christiansen was a talented endurance athlete who improved with each passing season. By the time she was in her late teens she was one of the most accomplished cross-country skiers in Norway. She became a member of the national team, and by 1976 was good enough to finish second in the national championships. She was runner-up three times between 1976 and 1980.

After graduating from college, Christiansen took a job as a researcher in Stavanger, located some 500 kilometers south of her hometown. The warmer climate and her hectic schedule prevented her from skiing as much as she would have liked, so to stay in shape she tried running. The sport appealed to her—it was challenging but simple, and required less equipment and preparation than skiing. In 1981 Ingrid Christiansen married Arve Kristiansen, an engineer and a marathon runner. They moved to Oslo and raised a family, starting with a boy named Gaute, who was born in 1983.

Less than two weeks after Gaute's birth, Ingrid Kristiansen resumed training. Within a year she would win marathons in Houston and London, the latter with a time of 2 hours, 24 minutes, 26 seconds. "She is an enigma," Cliff Temple, a noted British writer and coach, said of Kristiansen. "She is a woman who keeps her intense dedication successfully segregated from the rest of her life, shrugs off setbacks, and belies her strength with a genuine happy-go-lucky demeanor."

Kristiansen first raced, and won, in Boston, in the world's most famous marathon, in 1986. Her goal was to become the first woman ever to break 2:20. In one of the most daring races ever run, she forced a grueling pace. At the 5-mile mark she was 11 seconds ahead of Joan Benoit's course record, set in 1983. She was on pace to run 2:17, nearly four minutes faster than the world record. But Kristiansen slowed considerably in the second half of the race, finishing in 2:24.55, more than two minutes off Benoit's course record.

Though she never cracked 2:20 and never won an Olympic gold medal, Kristiansen won both the Boston Marathon and the New York City Marathon in 1989. In 1988 she was the world cross-country champion. She is the only person, male or female, to hold world records in the 5,000 meters (14:37.33, set in 1986), 10,000 meters (30:13.74), and marathon (2:21.06, set in 1985).

Accomplishments

Boston Marathon champion: 1986, 1989
New York City Marathon champion: 1989
World cross-country champion: 1988
Only person to hold world records for 5,000 meters, 10,000 meters, and marathon

Julie Krone

Born July 24, 1963

Julie Krone, the most successful female jockey in the history of thoroughbred horse racing, was raised in Benton Harbor, Michigan. As a toddler, she practiced bareback riding first on her father, Donald, then on her dog, Twiggy. When she was only three years old, she climbed aboard her first Shetland pony, Daisy. That same year a woman visited the Krone farm, hoping to buy a horse. Krone's mother, Judi, a trainer and rider, wanted to demonstrate to the prospective buyer that the animal was gentle and playful, so she hoisted little Julie onto its back. To her dismay, the horse trotted off with the child. Julie did not panic; she simply reached down, grabbed hold of the reins, and steered the horse back in the proper direction.

Such rides eventually became commonplace. Krone and Daisy would gallop for miles without incident. As Krone grew, her fondness

for riding became a passion. She took part in equestrian competitions; she learned how to perform acrobatic tricks. It wasn't long before she realized that she wanted to ride thoroughbred racehorses.

Krone went to Churchill Downs in Kentucky when she was only 15, having convinced her mother to forge her birth certificate so that she could get work as an exercise rider. Two years later she moved to Florida to live with her grandmother. At Tampa Bay Downs, on January 30, 1981, she made her first mount; less than two weeks later, on a horse named Lord Farkle, Krone reached the winner's circle for the first time.

In the summer of 1983 Krone was suspended from racing for 30 days after track officials in New Jersey discovered a small amount of marijuana in her car. It was, she said, one of the lowest moments of her life.

A diminutive 4 foot 10½ inch, 100-pound woman with an impish grin and a childlike voice, Krone possessed a competitive fire that belied her appearance. She hated to lose and refused to accept the notion that being a woman in a man's world gave her an excuse to lose. In a literal sense (for on more than one occasion she came to blows with another rider), she fought for her place in the sport. Over the years, she accumulated more than 2,500 victories and nearly $50 million in earnings. She rode six winners in a single day on August 19, 1987, at Monmouth Park in New Jersey, equaling the track record. In 1992 she became the first woman to win a New York Racing Association riding title. And on June 5, 1993, she became the first woman to win a Triple Crown race when she guided Colonial Affair to victory in the Belmont Stakes.

Like most jockeys, Krone experienced the pain and frustration of injury. Less than three months after her historic performance in the 1993 Belmont Stakes, she was nearly killed when she was thrown from a horse and trampled during a race at Saratoga. Her right ankle was shattered, her chest severely bruised, and her elbow punctured; doctors questioned whether she would ever be able to ride again. But on May 25, 1994, after three operations and nine months of intense rehabilitation, Krone returned to the track.

The Women's Sports Foundation selected Krone as its Sportswoman of the Year for 1993. In January 1994 she was one of five Women of the Year honored by CBS (also on the list were Hillary Clinton and astronaut Kathy Thornton). In March 1994, ESPN named Krone the outstanding female athlete of 1993.

Accomplishments

First woman to win a Triple Crown race (Belmont Stakes): 1993
First woman to win a NYRA riding title: 1992
Women's Sports Foundation Sportswoman of the Year: 1993
All-time money leader (victories and earnings) among female riders

Michelle Kwan

Born July 7, 1980

Figure skating champion Michelle Kwan was born in Torrance, California. Known to her family and friends as Little Kwan, Michelle is the youngest of three children. Her interest in skating was piqued when she began attending her older brother's hockey practices. Soon Michelle and her older sister, Karen, took up figure skating, and everyone in the Kwan family found their lives revolving around trips to various rinks in Southern California. Michelle entered her first skating competition when she was six years old. Within a year she had decided that someday she would compete in the Olympic Games.

In 1990, at the age of 10, Kwan began training with Frank Carrol and choreographer Lori Nichol at the Ice Castle International Training Center in Lake Arrowhead, California. She practiced for three hours a day, seven days a week. The schedule was rigorous, but not unusual for a skater with Olympic aspirations. Within a few years her work began to pay off. In 1994, 14-year-old Michelle finished third at the U.S. national championships, becoming the youngest medalist in the event's history; she later finished eighth at the world championships.

By 1995 Kwan was one of the top figure skaters in the world. She finished second at the U.S. national championships, first at Skate America, and fourth at the world championships. The next year, at age 15, she captured a gold medal at the world championships, becoming, at the time, the third youngest world champion in history (only Sonja Henie and Oksana Baiul were younger).

An outstanding student and a world-class athlete who has an enormous following among young fans, Kwan has twice been voted Figure Skater of the Year by the readers of *Skating* magazine.

Accomplishments

U.S. national champion: 1996
World champion: 1996
First place, World Junior Championships: 1994
First place, Skate America: 1995

L

Marion Ladewig

Born October 30, 1914

Marion Ladewig, the greatest woman bowler of all time, was born in Grand Rapids, Michigan. She was introduced to the sport as a child and became fascinated with it as a teenager, when she took a job at a bowling center. Ladewig worked the cash register, cleaned up after patrons had gone home, and once in a while set pins—for $2.50 a day.

Ladewig captured the Bowling Proprietors Association All-Star event seven more times—in 1950–1952, 1954, 1956, 1959, and 1963. She won the Women's International Bowling Congress All-Events title in 1950 and 1955; the 1955 WIBC doubles title; and the 1950 WIBC

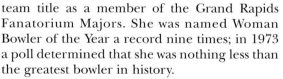

team title as a member of the Grand Rapids Fanatorium Majors. She was named Woman Bowler of the Year a record nine times; in 1973 a poll determined that she was nothing less than the greatest bowler in history.

Ladewig is also remembered for her efforts behind the scenes. She helped form the first professional women's bowling organization and continued to stay involved in the sport long after her retirement from competition. She became co-owner of a bowling center in her hometown and bowled recreationally. In 1982, at the age of 68, she put together a remarkable string of games, averaging better than 190—less than 10 points off her career mark of 204.

Ladewig played a vital role in elevating the popularity of bowling among mainstream sports fans in the United States during the late 1950s and early 1960s. She was at her best then, and people outside the bowling community were taking notice. In the voting for the 1963 Associated Press Female Athlete of the Year, Ladewig finished third behind golfer Mickey Wright and tennis player Maria Bueno. No bowler had ever come so close to winning that award.

Ladewig retired in 1965, after winning the World Invitational for the fifth time. One year earlier she had been inducted into the WIBC Hall of Fame. She was inducted into the International Women's Sports Hall of Fame in 1984.

Accomplishments

Woman Bowler of the Year: 1950–1955, 1958–1959, 1963
Women's All-Star Tournament champion: 1949–1952, 1954, 1956, 1959, 1963
Inducted into Women's International Bowling Congress Hall of Fame: 1964
Inducted into International Women's Sports Hall of Fame: 1984

Francie Larrieu

Born November 23, 1952

Francie Larrieu, a five-time Olympian in track and field, was born in Palo Alto, California, the sixth of nine children. One of her older brothers, Ron Larrieu, made the U.S. Olympic team in 1964 and finished 24th in the 10,000 meters. Francie was then 11 years old, and she was motivated by her brother's success. She began running recreationally and within two years had decided that she, too, would compete in the Olympics one day.

Larrieu was 16 years old in 1969 when she ran 4:16.8 in the 1,500 meters, tying the American record. Her performance was so impressive that she was invited to travel around Europe that summer, representing the United States in international competition. For the next decade Larrieu was the premier female middle-distance runner in the United States and one of the best in the world. Competing at distances ranging from 1,500 meters to two miles, indoors and outdoors, she established 36 American records and 11 world records. In 1974, as a student at UCLA, she won NCAA titles in the 800, 1,500, and 3,000 meters, but she failed to achieve her dream of Olympic gold. At both the 1972 and 1976 Summer Olympics, she was unable to reach the finals of the 1,500 meters.

Larrieu enjoyed the nomadic life of the world-class runner and was blessed with a body that could absorb punishment without breaking down. In 1976 she married sprinter Mark Lutz, but they divorced two years later. In 1980 she married exercise physiologist Jimmy Smith. Throughout this period of personal upheaval, her athletic career endured. She won the Athletics Congress 1,500 in 1979 and 1980. If

Memorable Moment: September 20, 1973

Billie Jean King Defeats Bobby Riggs

It was supposed to be a joke, but it turned out to be much more. Bobby Riggs, a 55-year-old tennis hustler who wore his chauvinism on his sleeve, challenged Billie Jean King to a tennis match. He was spotting her 26 years, but he believed he would win anyway. Male athletes were superior, he said, even those of advancing age. And there was a precedent: Just a few months earlier Riggs had shredded Margaret Court in a similar encounter. This Battle of the Sexes turned out to be much different.

King and Riggs met on the floor of the Astrodome in Houston, in front of 30,472 people (millions more watched on closed-circuit TV). At stake was a winner-take-all purse of $100,000. And, of course, much more. To some this was a perversion of the ideal of sport—a contest between an old man and a woman in her prime would prove nothing; it was demeaning to both. But King saw it differently. She saw an opportunity to strike a blow for women, to prove that she was stronger not only physically, but mentally and emotionally as well. So she played along. She contributed to the carnival atmosphere, entering the Astrodome on an Egyptian litter and presenting Riggs with a live pig wearing a large pink bow. Eventually they played tennis, and on this night King ruled the court. In one of the great performances of her career, she routed Riggs in straight sets, 6–4, 6–3, 6–3.

"This is the culmination of 19 years of work," King said afterward. "Since the time they wouldn't let me in a picture because I didn't have on a tennis skirt, I've wanted to change the game around. Now it's here."

not for the U.S.-led boycott of the 1980 Moscow Summer Games, she would have competed in her third Olympiad.

After falling short in her bid to qualify for the 1984 Olympic team, Larrieu turned to road racing, at the time a lucrative business. She became a star on the road racing circuit, usually competing at 10,000 meters. In 1986 the former miler decided again to move up in distance. At her first marathon, in Houston, she finished in second place at 2 hours, 33 minutes, 36 seconds. She ran the 10,000 at the 1988 Olympics in Seoul, finishing fifth. In 1990 she finished in second place at the highly competitive London Marathon with a time of 2:28.01. In 1991 she finished second in the World Cup marathon with a personal-best time of 2:27.35.

Larrieu's greatest accomplishment came in 1992, when, just a few months short of her 40th birthday, she finished third in the marathon at the U.S. Olympic trials, a performance that qualified her for her fifth Olympic team. That summer, in Barcelona, Larrieu finished 12th in the Olympic marathon.

Accomplishments

NCAA champion, 800 meters: 1974
NCAA champion, 1,500 meters: 1974
NCAA champion, 3,000 meters: 1974
U.S. champion, 1,500 meters: 1970, 1972–1973, 1976–1977, 1979–1980
U.S. champion, 3,000 meters: 1979, 1982
U.S. champion, 10,000 meters: 1985
Member of U.S. Olympic team: 1972, 1976, 1980, 1988, 1992

Larissa Latynina

Born 1934

Russian gymnast Larissa Latynina has won more Olympic medals than any other athlete in history. In her unparalleled career, she dominated women's gymnastics, winning 18 medals over the course of three Olympic Games. She captured nine gold medals, five silver, and four bronze; no other woman has come close to matching that feat. The record for medals won by a male Olympian is 15, a mark held by another Russian gymnast, Nikolai Andrianov (from 1972 to 1980).

Latynina was 18 years old when she traveled to Melbourne, Australia, for the 1956 Summer Games. Far from being intimidated by her introduction to the high-pressure world of Olympic competition, she felt right at home, summoning all of her talent and competitive zeal to leave her opponents awestruck. Latynina finished first in the floor exercise, vault, and all-around competition. She led the Soviet Union to the team title, and took a silver medal in the uneven bars and a bronze in the portable-apparatus team event. A year later, in 1957, she won a record five gold medals at the European Gymnastics Championships. In 1958 she won five more gold medals at the world championships.

By 1960 Latynina was in a league of her own. At the Summer Olympics in Rome, she won a gold medal in the all-around competition, a gold medal in the floor exercise, and silver medals in the uneven bars and balance beam, and helped the Soviet Union defend its team title.

But by 1962 Latynina was feeling pressure from a promising Czechoslovak gymnast named Vera Caslavska. At the world championships that year, Latynina barely held off Caslavska to defend her all-around title. Two years later, at the 1964 Summer Olympics in Tokyo, Caslavska assumed her place as the best gymnast in the world. At the comparatively advanced age of 30 (Caslavska was only 22), Latynina settled for a silver in the all-around competition, but finished first in the floor exercise and team competition. She took bronze medals in the uneven bars, balance beam, and vault.

At the 1966 world championships, Latynina finished 11th in the all-around competition. She retired from competition shortly thereafter, becoming a coach in the Soviet Union. In 1985 she was inducted into the International Women's Sports Hall of Fame.

Accomplishments

Won more Olympic medals (18) than any other athlete
Olympic gold medalist, floor exercise: 1956, 1960, 1964
Olympic gold medalist, vault: 1956
Olympic gold medalist, all-around: 1956, 1960
Olympic gold medalist, team: 1956, 1960, 1964

Inducted into International Women's Sports Hall of Fame: 1985

Andrea Mead Lawrence

Born April 19, 1932

An Olympic gold medalist in alpine skiing, Andrea Mead Lawrence learned at an early age to adapt to the long, cold winters of New England. Her parents ran a resort at Pico Peak in Vermont, so she discovered skiing when she was just a child. Mead first tried on a pair of skis at the age of three. By grade school she was spending long hours on the slopes, training with Carl Acker, a Swiss ski instructor who worked at the resort.

Andrea Mead qualified for the U.S. Olympic team when she was just 14, making her Olympic debut at the 1948 Winter Games in St. Moritz, Switzerland. Although she finished eighth in the slalom, 21st in the alpine combined, and 35th in the downhill, it was an important introduction to the intensity of international competition.

By 1950 Mead was a mature, confident athlete who finished first in the downhill, slalom, and combined at the U.S. nationals. One year later, at 17, she won 10 international events on what would later become the World Cup circuit. She married another skier, David Lawrence. In 1952 Andrea Mead Lawrence represented the United States at the Winter Olympics in Oslo, Norway. She won her first event, the giant slalom, by a wide margin. Six days later, in the slalom, she turned in a courageous performance. After a poor first run left her in fourth place, she was compelled to go for broke in her second and final run down the course. This time she skied magnificently; her combined time for the two runs was 2 minutes, 10.6 seconds, more than a half second better than runner-up Ossi Reichart.

After winning her double-gold in the 1952 Games, Lawrence moved to California to raise a family. She had five children. She competed in the 1956 Games in Cortina d'Ampezzo, Italy, but failed to earn a medal.

Lawrence was selected to light the flame at the 1960 Squaw Valley Olympics in California. She divorced in 1967 and went to work as a

ski instructor to support her children. Lawrence became an environmental activist and, at the age of 50, was elected to public office as a county supervisor.

Accomplishments

Olympic gold medalist, slalom: 1952
Olympic gold medalist, giant slalom: 1952
U.S. champion, downhill, slalom, alpine
  combined: 1950
Inducted into International Women's Sports
  Hall of Fame: 1983

Suzanne Lenglen

March 24, 1900–July 4, 1938

Suzanne Lenglen, who won six Wimbledon titles in the early part of the 20th century, was born in Compiègne, France. Her parents had the means and the good sense to cultivate her athletic ability. They saw early on that she had talent as a tennis player, so they arranged for the proper schooling.

In 1914, at the age of 14, Lenglen won the women's singles and doubles titles at the World Hard Court Championships in Paris. World War I put her career on hold for a while, but she made her Wimbledon debut in 1919, meeting 41-year-old Dorothea Lambert Chambers, a six-time champion, in the final. Lenglen prevailed in three sets, 10–8, 4–6, 9–7. For the better part of the next six years, Lenglen dominated women's tennis, winning the Wimbledon singles titles in 1920, 1921, 1922, 1923, and 1925. During that time she won 66 of the 68 sets she played and also won the French Open six times. She won the gold medal in singles and mixed doubles at the 1920 Olympics.

Lenglen is remembered at Wimbledon not only for her performance on the court, but also for her choice of attire. In her first appearance, she wore a calf-length, one-piece dress that exposed her arms. At the time, it was a shocking fashion statement, but it allowed her to move freely on the court and to play as aggressively as she wanted. She donned a headband that came to be known as the Lenglen Bandeaux. To her it was merely a matter of practicality, but it became popular in fashion salons across Europe.

Between 1919 and 1926, when she turned professional, Lenglen lost only one match—when she withdrew in the second set against Molla Mallory at the 1921 U.S. Open. Lenglen was roundly criticized by the U.S. media, which dubbed her a quitter, but the truth was, she withdrew because of a severe case of whooping cough. Lenglen suffered from maladies ranging from asthma to jaundice (the latter caused her to miss the 1924 championships at Wimbledon), and her career was frequently interrupted by injuries and illnesses. The biggest match of her career was in February 1926, shortly before she turned professional, when she met 19-year-old Helen Wills of the United States in Cannes, France. Lenglen defeated Wills in straight sets, 6–3, 8–6.

Lenglen was among the first tennis players to display a volatile temperament and a flair for the dramatic. She sometimes warmed up in a fur coat and was notorious for disputing calls that displeased her. She understood that great tennis was like great theater and that she was an entertainer as well as an athlete. For that reason she is credited with transforming tennis from a participant sport into a spectator sport. In 1926, during a tour of the United States, she drew a crowd of more than 13,000 to Madison Square Garden. But by the next year, poor health forced

her into retirement. Lenglen returned to France, becoming an author, celebrity, and instructor. She died at the age of 38.

Accomplishments

Wimbledon champion: 1919–1923, 1925
French Open champion: 1920–1923, 1925–1926
Olympic gold medalist: 1920

Lisa Leslie

Born July 7, 1972

Lisa Leslie, who helped lead the U.S. women's basketball team to a gold medal at the 1996 Summer Olympics in Atlanta, grew up in Inglewood, California. By the time she reached seventh grade she was already 6 feet tall. But it wasn't until a friend became captain of their junior high school team that Lisa decided to give basketball a try.

Besides being tall, Leslie was also graceful and athletic. Basketball came easily to her and she soon became a prep star. By the time she graduated from high school Leslie was 6 feet 5 inches tall and one of the top high school players in the United States—she was named national player of the year in 1990. Virtually unstoppable when she got the ball, she once scored 101 points in the first half of a game.

Leslie was recruited by just about every major Division I basketball program in the country. But she decided to attend college close to home, at the University of Southern California. She was a three-time All-American for the Trojans and was named college player of the year in 1994.

Leslie might have spent the next decade playing professional basketball in Europe if not for an offer to represent the United States in Olympic competition. She and 10 others were offered $50,000 in the spring of 1995 to train full-time in preparation for the 1996 Summer Olympics. Leslie accepted, despite the fact that she could have earned far more money playing overseas. Over the next 14 months she helped lead the United States to an incredible 60–0 record in international competition, culminating with a gold-medal performance in Atlanta. In the

final game of the Summer Olympics, a 111–87 rout of Brazil (a team that had defeated the United States at the 1994 World Championships), Leslie played spectacularly. After suffering from a case of nerves in the opening minutes and finding herself benched by coach Tara Van Derveer, she recovered quickly and finished with 29 points.

The success of the Women's Dream Team (as it was often called) helped spark interest in the sport of women's basketball in the United States. In fact, two first-rate professional women's leagues were quickly formed—the American Basketball League, which played its games during the winter, and the Women's National Basketball Association, scheduled to begin play in the summer of 1997, with the financial backing of the NBA. After the Olympics, Leslie announced that she would be playing in the WNBA. She also devoted time to her blossoming career as a fashion model but she made it clear that she was, first and foremost, an athlete.

Accomplishments

National High School Player of the Year: 1990
National College Player of the Year: 1994
NCAA All-American: 1992–1994
Olympic gold medalist: 1996

Nancy Lieberman

Born July 1, 1958

Nancy Lieberman, one of the greatest players in women's basketball, grew up in Far Rockaway, New York. Her fascination with basketball began when she was seven years old, but it didn't go over well in her home. Her mother, Renee, tried to convince her that girls were supposed to play with dolls, not basketballs; once she even punctured one of Nancy's balls with a screwdriver to discourage her.

"Mom," Nancy told her mother, "it's OK. I'm going to make history."

By the time she was in junior high school Lieberman was a regular on the outdoor courts not only in her neighborhood but also in Harlem. The games were New York City tough, and girls were not welcomed. But it didn't take

Lieberman long to prove that she belonged. When elbows began to fly, she never backed down. "I'm a very physical player," she acknowledged in an interview.

The basketball court was where Lieberman could express herself, both physically and emotionally. It was where she could take out the frustrations of living in a house divided by divorce. And on the basketball court she could escape the shadow of her brother, a straight-A student.

Lieberman played basketball with males only until her sophomore year in high school, when she joined the Rockaway Seahorses. They were one of the best teams in New York City. At the same time, Lieberman played for an Amateur Athletic Union team. High school basketball was not competitive enough for her; she was always the best player on the court, years ahead of her opponents and teammates. When she was a 17-year-old high school junior, Lieberman played for the United States in the Pan American Games. In 1976, just a few months after graduating from high school, she became the youngest member of the U.S. Olympic women's basketball team, which won a silver medal.

More than 75 Division I colleges and universities recruited the 5-foot 10-inch, 150-pound Lieberman. She chose Old Dominion University, quickly helping the school to become the best in women's college basketball. ODU won two national championships while Lieberman was there; she was a four-time All-American and two-time Player of the Year. She averaged 18.1 points and 8.7 rebounds per game in her college career.

After graduation Lieberman hoped to pick up another Olympic medal, but her dream was shattered when the United States boycotted the 1980 Moscow Summer Games. She later became the featured performer in the short-lived Women's Basketball League, a point guard for the Washington Generals—nightly opponent of the Harlem Globetrotters—and the personal trainer of tennis star Martina Navratilova. In 1986, as a member of the Springfield Fame of the U.S. Basketball League, she became the first woman to play in a men's professional basketball league. In 1997 she became the seventh woman to be inducted into the Basketball Hall of Fame.

Accomplishments

Olympic silver medalist: 1976
Member of U.S. Olympic team: 1976, 1980
Member of NCAA championship team:
    1979–1980
College Player of the Year: 1979–1980
First woman to play in a men's professional
    basketball league: 1986
Inducted into Basketball Hall of Fame: 1997

Hilary Lindh

Born May 10, 1969

Hilary Lindh, who overcame two career-threatening knee injuries to become one of the top downhill skiers in the world in the 1990s, was born in Juneau, Alaska. Growing up in an area with some of the harshest weather in North America, Lindh learned to adapt to the snow and ice. She got her first pair of skis when she was a child and wasted no time giving them a workout. She liked all types of skiing—cross-country, downhill, slalom. She was only seven years old when she began to enter races on Eaglecrest, an island near Juneau.

By her early teens Lindh was one of the best junior downhill racers in the United States. In 1984, at age 15, she won a national junior title; a year later she finished 11th in the downhill at the World Junior Championships. In 1986 Lindh captured the U.S. senior downhill title and the world junior title. That same year she joined the U.S. ski team.

Over the years it was Lindh's resolve, rather than her talent, that would be most severely tested. In the spring of 1987 she tore cartilage in her right knee; she spent more than two months on crutches and several more months in rehabilitation. She resumed racing in December and gradually began to improve. By 1989 Lindh was once again the top downhill skier in the United States, though she finished 15th at the world championships. In 1992 she tuned up for the Olympics with another first-place finish in the combined and a second in the downhill at the U.S. championships. Then, in Albertville, France, at the 1992 Winter Games, she turned in one of the best performances of her career, winning a silver medal in the downhill.

But the next year brought more frustration for Lindh. While preparing for the world championships, she tore ligaments in her right knee during a fall. She underwent surgery on January 29, 1993. After many months of rehabilitation, she returned for the start of the 1993–1994 World Cup season. At the 1994 Winter Olympics in Lillehammer, Norway, Lindh managed a seventh-place finish in the downhill; she was overshadowed by teammate Picabo Street, who took a silver in the downhill. Much was made of the icy relationship between the two skiers, who had markedly different personalities. Street was extroverted and emotional; Lindh was quiet and introspective, though she bristled when she was described that way.

"I hate being characterized as the strong, silent type," Lindh said. "I'm not silent in personal situations. But I've always disliked people who have to make an impression by being loud. I want to be worthy of respect because I excel at what I do."

Over the next few years, Lindh's relationship with Street improved; although they were not friends, they at least supported each other as teammates. As for Lindh's damaged knee, it seemed to be at full strength by February of 1997, when she captured the downhill title at the world championships in Sestriere, Italy.

Accomplishments

World junior champion, downhill: 1986
U.S. downhill champion: 1986, 1989
U.S. combined champion: 1992
Olympic silver medalist, downhill: 1992

Tara Lipinski

Born June 10, 1982

Tara Lipinski, the youngest world champion in the history of women's figure skating, was born in Philadelphia. An only child, she grew up in Newark, Delaware, and began skating at the University of Delaware Ice Arena at age six. In 1991, when her father, Jack Lipinski, took a job in Sugar Land, Texas, near Houston, the family relocated. Tara's training suffered in the Southwest, however, and soon she and her mother, Pat, returned to Delaware.

Over the next five years, the Lipinski family continued to make sacrifices for Tara's burgeoning career. Jack remained in Texas, while Tara and Pat traveled around the country in search of competition and first-class coaching. In 1994, 12-year-old Tara became the youngest competitor ever to win a gold medal at the Olympic Festival; she also won the novice division of the U.S. championships.

In 1995, after interviewing some of the most highly respected coaches in figure skating, the Lipinskis hired Richard Callaghan to guide Tara through the next phase of her career. Since Callaghan coached at the Detroit Skating Club, Tara and Pat were compelled to move again. Once settled in Detroit, they began working toward their goal: a gold medal at the Winter Olympics in 2002.

But as Lipinski progressed at an astonishing rate, that timetable moved up. In her first appearance at the U.S. Figure Skating Association National Championships, in 1996, she finished third. One month later at the World Figure Skating Championships, she landed seven triple jumps and finished in 15th place—an impressive accomplishment given her age (13) and comparative inexperience.

All that, however, was merely a prelude to what Lipinski achieved in the first few months of 1997. In February the diminutive (4-foot 8-inch, 75-pound) skater with the ever-present smile captured first place at the national championships in Nashville, Tennessee, upsetting defending champion Michelle Kwan. It was a remarkable feat: just one week after losing her last baby tooth, Tara Lipinski landed an unprecedented triple loop/triple loop combination—the first time any skater, male or female, had successfully executed that maneuver—and became the youngest U.S. champion in history.

One month later, at the world championships in Lausanne, Switzerland, Lipinski's ascent continued, as she again upset Kwan to become the sport's youngest world champion, as well as the gold-medal favorite at the 1998 Winter Olympics in Nagano, Japan.

Accomplishments

U. S. national champion: 1997
World champion: 1997
Youngest Olympic Festival gold medalist: 1995

Rebecca Lobo

Born October 6, 1973

Rebecca Lobo, one of the most decorated players in the history of college basketball, was born in Hartford, Connecticut, and grew up in Southwick, Massachusetts. Her parents, Dennis and Ruth Ann Lobo, were educators, and they instilled in her a desire to learn. Ruth Ann also happened to be a former high school basketball star who was nearly 6 feet tall. Her size and her love for the game were passed on to Rebecca, who would be 6 feet 4 inches tall by the time she graduated from high school. Rebecca's brother, Jason, was 6 feet 11 inches tall, and played basketball at Dartmouth College; her sister, Rachel, was 5 feet 11 inches, and played at Salem State College in Massachusetts.

The Lobo children all liked athletics. They played stickball, Wiffle ball, soccer, and volleyball in the backyard, in the street, or on the playground. Rebecca once constructed a homemade catcher's outfit using paper and a football helmet. Jason pitched, Rebecca caught, and Rachel stepped into the batter's box. Jason, the oldest of the children, even dabbled in the promotion business for a while, setting up boxing matches between his two little sisters. He'd have the girls wear mittens stuffed with extra padding, then drop to his knees to act as referee.

All of this fostered competitiveness in Rebecca. She did not like to lose. She believed in working hard and practicing to be the best. She became a fierce competitor, as evidenced by the fact that she endured a series of injuries throughout her career—including a couple of broken noses, a broken finger, and assorted knee problems—most caused by playing with little regard for her body. But she also liked to pull her hair back into a French braid while on the basketball court to diffuse the myth that sport and femininity were incompatible.

When Rebecca Lobo was in the fourth grade she wrote a letter to Boston Celtics president Red Auerbach, declaring her intention to be the first woman to play for his team. She never made it that far, but she did make a name for herself in the world of basketball. She led the University of Connecticut to a 35–0 record and a national championship in the spring of 1995. Lobo, a senior center, was named the Final Four's Most Outstanding Player. In her senior year she averaged 17.1 points per game and was named the National Player of the Year by the Associated Press, the U.S. Basketball Writer's Association, and *College Sports Magazine.* She was awarded the Wade Trophy as the college senior in sports who is the most positive role model for women.

Lobo left Connecticut as the school's all-time leader in rebounds (1,268) and blocked shots (396), and was second in points scored (2,133). She was selected by the New Jersey Turnpikes in the 10th round of the U.S. Basketball League draft; she was the first woman selected that year. Lobo was named to the 1995–1996 U.S.A. Basketball Women's National Team, which spent a year training and touring in preparation for the Summer Olympics in Atlanta. In October 1995, Lobo was named Team Sportswoman of the Year by the Women's Sports Foundation. In 1996 she helped lead the U.S. women's basketball team to an Olympic gold medal.

Accomplishments

Led Connecticut to NCAA Division I basketball
   championship: 1995
Named Most Outstanding Player of NCAA
   Final Four: 1995
College Player of the Year: 1995
Women's Sports Foundation Team
   Sportswoman of the Year: 1995
Olympic gold medalist: 1996

Nancy Lopez

Born January 6, 1957

Nancy Lopez, a four-time Ladies Professional Golf Association Player of the Year, was born in Torrance, California. Her family moved when she was a toddler, and she learned the finer points of golf on the public courses of Roswell, New Mexico. Domingo Lopez, Nancy's father, owned an auto body shop. Both he and his wife, Marina, were avid golfers, and their love for the game was passed on to Nancy, who began playing when she was eight.

Domingo, a 3-handicap, was Nancy's first coach, and he proved to be a wonderful teacher. He was patient, stressing the mental portion of the game above all else. Nancy Lopez was 12 years old when she won the New Mexico Women's Amateur Championship at the University South Course in Albuquerque with a course-record score of 75. In 1972, at the age of 15, she won the United States Golf Association Junior Girls championship; two years later, she won again.

With a wide choice of schools to attend on a golf scholarship, Lopez chose Tulsa University. But after two years she left school. Money in the family was tight, and it was apparent that Nancy, who had finished second in the U.S. Women's Open and first in the NCAA championships in 1976, had an opportunity to make life easier for everyone. In 1977, with the help of a $50,000 loan taken out by her father, Lopez turned professional.

As a rookie on the LPGA tour, Lopez finished second in her first three tournaments. Her mother died shortly thereafter, so she took some time off. When she returned, she was sharper than ever. In 1978, at the age of 21, Lopez dominated the LPGA tour, winning nine tournaments, including the LPGA championship. She was named Rolex Player of the Year, LPGA Rookie of the Year, and Associated Press Female Athlete of the Year.

Lopez was the LPGA's leading money winner in 1978 and 1979. In 1983 she passed the $1 million mark in career earnings. She has been among the tour's leading golfers each year, despite taking time off to raise a family. She was married for a short time in the late 1970s to sportscaster Tim Melton. In 1982 she married baseball star Ray Knight; their first child, Ashley, was born on November 7, 1983; their second, Erinn, was born on May 26, 1986; and their third, Torri, was born on October 30, 1991. As a working mother, Lopez was a pioneer—she was the first woman golfer to take her children on tour with her.

Lopez won her second LPGA championship in 1985, her third in 1989. She was inducted into the LPGA Hall of Fame in 1987 and the PGA World Golf Hall of Fame in 1989. She is a playing editor for *Golf* magazine, which in 1988 selected her as Golfer of the Decade for the years 1978–1987 during the Centennial of Golf in America celebration.

Although she has not won a major tournament since 1989, Lopez remains one of the most successful players on the LPGA tour. She was eighth on the money list in 1992 and still in the top 20 as of 1996. She is fifth on the career money list, with more than $4.5 million.

Accomplishments

  LPGA championship winner: 1978, 1985, 1989
  LPGA Rookie of the Year: 1978
  Rolex Player of the Year: 1978, 1979, 1985, 1988
  NCAA champion: 1976
  Won an LPGA-record five consecutive tournaments: 1978
  Inducted into LPGA Hall of Fame: 1987

Donna A. Lopiano

Born September 11, 1946

Donna A. Lopiano, a softball player who became executive director of the Women's Sports Foundation, was born and raised in Stamford, Connecticut. She was, by her own assessment, a rather typical girl—as much as any little girl who loved stickball and Mickey Mantle and insisted on playing baseball with the boys in her neighborhood could be called typical. Lopiano dreamed of becoming an astronaut or a professional athlete. From the very beginning she was a participant, not a spectator, which led her to have difficulty when she was told that she couldn't play on a Little League team. It was her introduction to gender inequity, and she never forgot it.

When Lopiano was a teenager, she discovered an outlet for her athletic energy—the Connecticut-based Raybestos Brakettes, the finest women's amateur softball team in the United States. Over the years the Brakettes had featured, among others, Joan Joyce, one of the best softball players in history. Lopiano joined the Brakettes when she was 15, and for nearly a decade was among the best players in the game. She not only helped lead the Brakettes to six national championships, but also was named Most Valuable Player of the American Softball Association national tournament three times and first-team All-American nine times.

While playing for the Brakettes, Lopiano attended Southern Connecticut State University, where she received a degree in physical education. She played softball, basketball, field hockey, and volleyball at Southern Connecticut. After graduation she went on to the University of Southern California, where she earned a master's and a Ph.D.

Lopiano became a coach while working on her graduate degrees and later moved into administration. She became assistant athletic director at Brooklyn College when she was only 25; three years later she became an assistant at the University of Texas at Austin. A trace of anxiety might have been understandable, but Lopiano was sure that she could do the job. In fact, her confidence got her the job. "They knew the person they brought in needed a little chutzpah to exist in the same world as Texas football," Lopiano said.

For 15 years Lopiano was director of women's athletics at Texas; during that time women's sports at the university made substantial gains. She had inherited an annual budget of just more than $50,000; when she left in 1992 the budget was $4 million. Texas won 18 NCAA women's titles during her tenure.

As executive director of the Women's Sports Foundation, Lopiano is one of the most influential figures in women's athletics. The goal of the foundation remains unchanged from when it was founded in 1974—to provide opportunities for female athletes, and to recognize and publicize their achievements. Lopiano is an outspoken advocate for gender equity in college athletic programs.

Accomplishments

  Three-time MVP of American Softball Association national tournament
  Nine-time American Softball Association All-American
  Six-time American Softball Association champion
  Named executive director of Women's Sports Foundation: 1992

M

Meg Mallon

Born April 4, 1963

Meg Mallon, who emerged as one of the premier players on the Ladies Professional Golf Association circuit in the early 1990s, was born in Natick, Massachusetts. She was the youngest of six children. Her father, an executive with Ford Motor Co., was transferred several times when Meg was young, but she spent most of her childhood in Birmingham, Michigan. Meg was an athletic child, fond of just about every sport she tried. Little League baseball came first, followed by basketball. Her father did promotional work for the Boston Celtics, and Meg became an avid fan. She played point guard for Our Lady of Mercy High School and to this day considers basketball her favorite sport.

Meg also learned to play golf. Her parents were members of a country club, so she had access to good facilities and private lessons. But she was a 16-year-old high school junior before she began taking golf seriously. She attracted only minor interest from colleges with Division I golf programs and had to pay her own way during her first three years at Ohio State University, where she earned All-Big Ten Conference honors in 1984 and 1985.

Meg Mallon left school 19 credits short of a degree, intent on joining the LPGA tour. "I was ready to try one thing 100 percent," she explained. "I wasn't sure what I wanted to do with my life, but I thought that if I didn't ever try this, I'd regret it."

Mallon was fortunate to have the financial and emotional support of her family, because her first year on tour was a rough one. As a rookie in 1987 she failed to win a single tournament and earned only $1,572. But she gave no thought to quitting. In time, she figured, her game would develop to the point where she would be a competitive player on the LPGA tour. But it was a long, slow climb. In 1988 she earned $25,000; in 1989 she earned $42,574; in 1990 she had four top-10 finishes and broke the $100,000 mark.

Mallon opened the 1991 season in dramatic fashion, winning her first tournament, the Oldsmobile LPGA Classic in Lake Worth, Florida. In June she won her first major tournament, the LPGA championship; two weeks later she captured a second major, the U.S. Women's Open. By year's end she had won four tournaments, finished in the top 10 of a dozen tournaments, and accumulated more than $633,000 in earnings, second only to Hall of Famer Pat Bradley. Mallon was named both *Golf Digest*'s Most Improved Player and the Sudafed Sportswoman of the Year. With her bright smile and pleasant personality, she also became a popular player—in 1991 she was voted friendliest golfer on the tour. Mallon failed to win a tournament in 1992 but still earned more than $400,000. In 1993 she fell to 15th on the money list but won two tournaments. In 1994 and 1995 she was back among the top 10 money winners on the tour.

Accomplishments

    Michigan amateur champion: 1983
    LPGA championship winner: 1991
    U.S. Women's Open winner: 1991
    Sudafed Sportswoman of the Year: 1991

Molla Bjurstedt Mallory

March 6, 1884–November 22, 1959

Anna Margrethe Bjurstedt Mallory, an eight-time U.S. tennis champion, was born in Norway. Nicknamed Molla, she was a playful and competitive child who was fond of snowball fights. She also liked to play tennis, and she was pretty good at it. Mallory won the Norwegian national championship eight times and competed successfully throughout Europe as a young woman. In 1914 she traveled to the United States for the first time and liked it so much that she decided to make it her home.

Just one year later Mallory won the first of four consecutive U.S. titles. Hazel Wightman interrupted her streak in 1919, but in 1920, the last year the nationals were hosted by the Philadelphia Cricket Club, Mallory recaptured the crown. She won again in 1921, 1922, and 1926.

Mallory was an unusually powerful player for her time. She was sturdily built and hit the ball hard. She routinely hit stinging forehands that sent the ball just inches over the net. "I find that the girls generally do not hit the ball as hard as they should," she said. "I believe in always hitting the ball with all my might, but there seems to be a disposition to 'just get it over' in many girls whom I have played. I do not call that tennis." But even though she was a strong player, she did not lack touch; indeed, Mallory could paint the lines.

Mallory's affinity for the serve-and-volley game was not the only attribute that made her unique. When it came to training, she was anything but rigid. She smoked cigarettes and enjoyed a dose of nightlife once in a while. She liked to dance, and sometimes, even when she had a match the next day, she would party well into the night. But there was no questioning her competitive fire. Mallory, nicknamed the Fighting Norsewoman, detested losing. While she was generally pleasant and well-liked off the court, she was a fiercely competitive athlete who swaggered and scowled on the court.

"She was an indomitable scrambler and runner," said Bob Kelleher, a U.S. Ladies Tennis Association former president who was a ball boy when Mallory played. "She was a fighter."

Some of Mallory's most interesting matches were played against Suzanne Lenglen, who won 12 Grand Slam singles titles (six French, six Wimbledon) in her career. The two met in the second round of the U.S. Open in 1921. Mallory won that match when Lenglen defaulted because of illness. Lenglen was sharply criticized for that—it was suggested that she had simply fallen behind and decided to quit rather than face the indignity of losing. Lenglen denied the accusations, but she acknowledged that she had underestimated Mallory.

Lenglen never again played in the United States, but she did gain a measure of revenge in 1922, when she breezed past Mallory in the finals of Wimbledon. Afterward, Lenglen was overhead telling Mallory, "Now, Mrs. Mallory, I have proved to you today what I could have done to you in New York last year." Mallory smiled and replied, "Mademoiselle Lenglen, you have done to me today what I did to you in New York last year; you have beaten me."

Mallory was inducted into the International Tennis Hall of Fame in 1958.

Accomplishments

U.S. Open champion: 1915–1918, 1920–1922, 1926
Wimbledon runner-up: 1922
Eight-time Norwegian national champion
Inducted into International Women's Sports Hall of Fame: 1958

Hana Mandlikova

Born February 19, 1962

Tennis player Hana Mandlikova, a winner of four Grand Slam singles titles, was born in Prague, Czechoslovakia. Her father, Vilem Mandlik, was an Olympic sprinter (in 1956 and 1960) who later became a sports journalist. Early on he recognized his daughter's athletic ability; although the Czech Tennis Federation subsidized much of Hana's training, Vilem put his own time, energy, and money into helping her become a world-class player.

When she was 15 years old, Hana Mandlikova achieved victory in the 16-and-under championships at the Orange Bowl in Miami, Florida. The next year, she finished second to Tracy Austin at the Wimbledon junior championships, and won the International Tennis Federation junior world championship.

In 1979 Mandlikova visited the United States again, this time as a 17-year-old professional. Accompanied by her father, she played almost every tournament on the women's tour, hoping to earn money for her family. She won five tournaments in 1979; she also reached the quarterfinals at the Australian Open and the French Open and the fourth round at Wimbledon. Mandlikova was 5 feet 8 inches tall and 132 pounds, with extraordinary quickness and power. Although a neophyte, she could rally from the baseline or attack the net, and she had a powerful serve.

In 1980 Mandlikova began training with Betty Stove, a former top women's professional. The coaching change seemed to help, because she won the Australian Open—her first major— and reached the semifinals at Wimbledon. In the U.S. Open she played a spectacular match, dazzling the crowd with her athleticism and competitive fire. That she lost to Chris Evert by a score of 5–7, 6–1, 6–1 didn't seem to matter; she was just 18 years old.

At the 1981 French Open, Mandlikova avenged her loss to Evert with a 7–5, 6–4 victory in the semifinals. In the championship she defeated West Germany's Sylvia Hanika. But Mandlikova began to experience back pain during the French Open, and as she continued to play on the tour, the discomfort increased. At Wimbledon, in the spring of 1981, she played well enough to reach her fourth consecutive Grand Slam final, but was thrashed by Evert in straight sets. Afterward, she had trouble walking. Hana was ordered to take several months off.

"I didn't know whether I was going to come back," she said later in an interview. "I didn't know if I would be able to play tennis again."

Mandlikova did return to competition, winning 27 singles events in her career. In 1985 she captured the U.S. Open, and in 1987 she won a second Australian Open title. But she was an erratic player, and questions about her health and commitment persisted over the years. Her back problems continued, and in 1989 she was forced to miss six months because of a hamstring injury. By 1990 Mandlikova had retired from singles competition and turned to coaching.

Accomplishments

U.S. Open champion: 1985
French Open champion: 1981
Australian Open champion: 1980, 1987
Junior world champion: 1978

Carol Mann

Born February 3, 1941

A native of Buffalo, New York, Carol Mann has been one of the most visible women in golf, and not merely because she stands 6 feet 3 inches tall. For many years Mann made her mark with her clubs; later she became an outspoken proponent of higher purses on the Ladies Professional Golf Association Tour. She is a former president of the LPGA and a member of the LPGA Hall of Fame.

Mann's dream of a career in professional athletics began when she was 11 years old. "Theater people close their eyes and see their name in lights," she said. "I'd see mine on a locker-room plaque."

Mann attended the University of North Carolina–Greensboro and turned professional in 1960. Though she was able to earn a living during her first few years on the tour, it wasn't until 1964, at the Western Open, that she picked up her first LPGA victory. The following year she won her first major, the U.S. Women's Open, and by 1968 was the dominant player on the tour. Mann captured 10 tournaments that year and won the Vare Trophy (for lowest average score) with a record average of 72.04. That mark stood for 10 years, until Nancy Lopez broke it in 1978. Mann scored 23 rounds in the 60s in 1968, a record that stood until 1980, when Amy Alcott achieved 25.

In 1969 Mann was the leading money winner on the LPGA tour, with more than $49,000; she was in the top 10 from 1972 through 1975. At the 1975 Borden Classic she played one of the best rounds of her life, carding seven consecutive birdies, an LPGA record that lasted until 1984. In 1976 Mann became president of the LPGA and also won the Babe Didrikson Zaharias Award; the following year she entered the LPGA Hall of Fame.

Mann's last official appearance on the LPGA tour came in 1981, at the Rail Charity Classic. In 1982 she was inducted into the International Women's Sports Hall of Fame. Since then she has remained an active member of the golf community and a supporter of women's sports. She has been a trustee of the Women's Sports Foundation, serving as president from 1985 to 1990. She is the founder of the Female Golf Development Foundation and was appointed to the White House Conference for a Drug Free America. Mann has served as a golf columnist for the *Houston Post* and as a television analyst for ABC, NBC, and ESPN. She wrote the book *The 19th Hole—Favorite Golf Stories.*

Selected by *Golf* magazine as one of the 100 Heroes of American Golf, Mann was elected to the Collegiate Golf Hall of Fame in 1992. She is the president of Carol Mann, Inc., which provides corporate golf programs at LPGA and PGA sites. She also works as a motivational speaker and as a consultant to several golf equipment manufacturers.

Accomplishments

  U.S. Women's Open champion: 1965
  LPGA president: 1975
  Inducted into LPGA Hall of Fame: 1977
  Inducted into International Women's Sports
    Hall of Fame: 1982

Alice Marble

September 28, 1913–December 13, 1990

Four-time U.S. tennis champion Alice Marble, one of the pioneers of women's power tennis, was born in Plumas County, California. Her father worked as a logger and rancher; Marble wrote in her autobiography that one of her first memories was of milking a cow. The family moved to San Francisco when she was six, and shortly thereafter her father died. Alice's older brother, Dan, became head of the household.

It was Dan who introduced Alice to the game of tennis. For several years she had been playing baseball with him and their two brothers. Alice was a natural athlete who could hold her own with the boys. One day in 1927 when she was watching the San Francisco Seals, a minor league baseball team, she was invited down to the field to play a game of catch—one of the players, it seemed, had mistaken her for a boy. She performed so well that the Seals asked her to become the team's mascot and bat girl.

Alice was thrilled but her brother was not. He bought her a tennis racket and suggested she give it a good workout. "Allie, you've got to stop being a tomboy," Dan said. "I want you always to play and enjoy sports, but you must play a ladylike game."

At first, Alice was angry. Baseball was the game she loved. Tennis, she said, was a "sissy sport." But soon her attitude would change. She practiced every day on the public courts at Golden Gate Park. At 5 feet 7 inches and 140 pounds, she was a strong, athletic girl who adapted quickly to the demands of tennis. In 1931, at the age of 17, she played in the U.S. championships for the first time. She lost in the first round but came away from the experience with greater confidence.

With help from a succession of teachers, including San Francisco pro Howard Kinsey and Eleanor Tennant, Alice Marble became one of the best players in the world. She worked hard to develop a game whose foundation was power. She drilled shots from the baseline and attacked the net. She relied on a daring serve-and-volley game that had previously been the

Accomplishments

U.S. Open champion: 1936, 1938–1940
Wimbledon champion: 1939
Associated Press Female Athlete of the Year: 1939–1940
Inducted into International Tennis Hall of Fame: 1964

Conchita Martinez

Born April 16, 1972

C oncepcion "Conchita" Martinez, who emerged as one of the top tennis players in the world in the mid-1990s, was born in Monzon, Spain, a small factory town in the province of Aragon. Her father, Cecilio, was an accountant for Hidro-Nitro, which had an office in Monzon. Conchita grew up in a fourth-floor apartment of a factory housing complex. At the age of eight she began hitting tennis balls with her two older brothers on a pair of concrete tennis courts outside the apartment building. It was little more than a diversion, a break from the tedium of everyday life. "Who could have known that tennis would become her obsession?" Cecilio later said.

Since Conchita did not have early access to tennis clubs and high-priced coaches, she relied on self-discipline and talent to develop her game. She began by practicing for hours against her brothers, then practicing some more by herself, whacking shots against a brick wall. She passed the time by fantasizing that she was beating such luminaries as Martina Navratilova and Chris Evert.

By the time she was 12 years old, Conchita Martinez was traveling 40 miles through the Pyrenees with her father for lessons. She eventually won the Spanish under-12 championship and relocated to Barcelona, where she received a scholarship to attend the Residencia Blume, a government-sponsored athletic training center. Martinez saw her family only on weekends and was quite homesick at first. But she had clearly benefited from her move. In 1985 she reached the championship of the national under-14 tournament, losing to Arantxa Sanchez Vicario. In 1987, at the age of 15, Martinez moved again, this time to a small town near Zurich, Switzerland,

exclusive domain of male players. She possessed a booming serve that had never been seen in women's tennis.

But in 1933 Marble's career was sidetracked. After playing three matches in a single day in 103-degree heat at a tournament on Long Island, she collapsed on the court. Doctors determined that she had suffered from sunstroke and anemia. The following year Marble collapsed again. She was told that she had tuberculosis and was advised never to play tennis again. But in 1936, with the help of her friend and mentor, Eleanor Tennant, Marble returned to the court. The U.S. Ladies Tennis Association, fearing for her safety, at first refused to let Marble play in the national championships. Eventually, though, she was granted entry, and she went on to win the tournament, defeating Helen Jacobs in the final. That was the first of four U.S. titles for Marble (she also won in 1938, 1939, and 1940). In 1939 she also won her first and only Wimbledon title.

Marble was inducted into the International Tennis Hall of Fame in 1964.

where she trained with Dutch coach Eric Van Harpen. Martinez blossomed under Van Harpen's tutelage. She turned professional that year and quickly climbed into the top 50 on the women's computer rankings.

Martinez reached the quarterfinals of the French Open in 1989 and 1990. In 1991 she reached the quarterfinals of both the French Open and the U.S. Open. Two years later she advanced to the semifinals at Wimbledon. Then, in 1994, she defeated Navratilova in the Wimbledon championship. It was a difficult arena in which to capture her first major title, since Navratilova was the most successful player the tournament had ever known. But Martinez withstood the pressure, beating Navratilova in three sets, 6–4, 3–6, 6–3. By the end of the year Martinez was the third-ranked player in the world and had amassed more than $1.3 million in prize money.

In 1995 Martinez reached the semifinals of all four Grand Slam events. She finished the year as the game's second-ranked player. In 1996 she was ranked sixth.

Accomplishments

Wimbledon champion: 1994
Wimbledon semifinalist: 1993–1994
Olympic silver medalist: 1992

Patricia Keller McCormick

Born May 12, 1930

Perhaps no one has dominated the sport of women's diving the way Pat McCormick did in the 1950s. Born Patricia Keller in Seal Beach, California, she and her brother were raised by their mother, a nurse. Keller first became interested in fitness when she was a youngster visiting the famed Muscle Beach near Venice, California. Outdoor activities of all kinds could be found there, including running, weightlifting, swimming, and diving. Keller learned diving basics while practicing from a float in Alamitos Bay. Before long she was winning local competitions, and her talent caught the eye of the coach of the Los Angeles Athletic Club. Struck by the young girl's strength and balance, he invited her to train with his club.

In Los Angeles, Keller trained alongside such Olympic champions as Victoria Draves and Sammy Lee. Far from being awed by these athletes, she used them as barometers of her own improvement and as sources of motivation. She was driven to be the best, and she was able to train to the point of exhaustion. Her routine consisted of more than 100 dives each day, six days a week. Broken fingers and bruised ribs were part of the price she paid to achieve her goal.

Keller's progress in Los Angeles was steady. In 1948, at the age of 18, she finished fourth at the Olympic trials and missed qualifying for the U.S. team. "That defeat was the greatest thing that ever happened to me because all of a sudden I knew I could win the Olympics," she said. "I realized that at Los Angeles I was working with world-class athletes every day."

In 1949 Keller married Glenn McCormick, a pilot. She competed under her married name for the rest of her career. Pat McCormick won the national platform championship in 1949; the following year she repeated as platform champion, and added the 1-meter and 3-meter springboard titles. In 1951 she won three outdoor titles and two indoor titles.

In 1952 McCormick made her first trip to the Olympic Games. In Helsinki she won gold medals in both the platform and springboard events. Four years later, in Melbourne, she defended both titles. Never before had any diver won both gold medals in successive Olympic Games. And not until American Greg Louganis in 1984 and 1988 did anyone match the feat. McCormick's performance at the 1956 Games was particularly impressive because she had given birth to a son just five months earlier.

McCormick was a study in courage and determination, and her efforts did not go unrecognized. In 1956 she became only the second woman to win the Sullivan Award. She was named Babe Didrikson Zaharias Woman Athlete of the Year and Associated Press Woman Athlete of the Year, and was the first woman to be elected to the International Swimming Hall of Fame. In 1984 she was inducted into the International Women's Sports Hall of Fame.

McCormick's interest in diving did not wane after her retirement. She became an avid spectator, primarily because her daughter had become an accomplished diver in her own right. Kelly McCormick won a silver medal at the 1984 Olympics and a bronze in 1988.

Accomplishments

Olympic gold medalist, springboard diving: 1952, 1956

Olympic gold medalist, platform diving: 1952, 1956

First diver to win two gold medals in successive Olympics

Sullivan Award winner: 1956

Inducted into International Women's Sports Hall of Fame: 1984

Floretta McCutcheon

July 22, 1888–February 1967

A member of the Women's International Bowling Congress Hall of Fame, Floretta Doty McCutcheon was born and raised in Ottumwa, Iowa.

McCutcheon didn't begin bowling until she was 35 years old. Though her first game was an embarrassingly low 69, and though she was so frustrated that she nearly gave up the sport after one season of league competition, in just a few years she would become not only one of the best bowlers in the world, but also an athlete who could break barriers.

In 1927 McCutcheon, age 39, made history by beating Jimmy Smith, one of the greatest exhibition bowlers the sport has ever known, in a three-game match. She did this without a handicap, defeating him by a score of 704–697. Smith had never lost to a woman—not head-to-head, anyway—and the victory brought McCutcheon instant celebrity. Among other things, it earned her a spot in *Ripley's Believe It or Not.*

McCutcheon used that victory as a springboard to a successful exhibition career of her own. For the better part of a decade she toured the United States, taking on all challengers, conducting clinics, and generally entertaining fans. Credited with introducing a quarter of a million people to bowling, she had a profound impact on the growth and popularity of the game.

In 1930 McCutcheon opened the Mrs. McCutcheon School of Bowling. That same year, at age 42, she again tried to prove that gender should not be an issue in athletic competition. At the 300 Club Tournament in Cleveland, Ohio, she finished fourth in a field of 254 competitors—she was the only woman. McCutcheon retired from competitive bowling

in 1939, having rolled 10 perfect 300 games, 11 three-game series of 800 or better, and more than a hundred 700-plus series. Making her accomplishments all the more impressive is the fact that she rarely had a chance to familiarize herself with the lanes on which she was competing. She rolled into town, put on a show, and moved on. Strange and unforgiving lane conditions were part of the territory, and she learned to adapt.

Because McCutcheon's greatest achievements came not in sanctioned events but in exhibitions, most of her records are not recognized. But she did record an average of 206 in a sanctioned league during the 1936–1937 season. That mark stood as a record for women bowlers for nearly three decades.

McCutcheon taught bowling in New York until 1954, then settled into a life of quiet retirement in California.

Accomplishments

Bowled 10 perfect games
Averaged 201 for 8,076 career games
Introduced an estimated 250,000 people to the sport of bowling
Inducted into Women's International Bowling Congress Hall of Fame: 1954

Mary Terstegge Meagher

Born October 27, 1964

Swimmer Mary Terstegge Meagher, a three-time Olympian, was born in Louisville, Kentucky. She grew up in a big family, with 10 sisters—including another, older one named Mary—and one brother. The younger Mary, called simply T, could devour an 8,000-meter workout in the morning, break for lunch, then come back and handle another 8,000 meters in the afternoon. At the age of 12 she was breezing through practice sessions worthy of a world-class competitor.

Mary Terstegge Meagher was a gangly eighth-grader with braces on her teeth when she jumped into a pool in San Juan, Puerto Rico, for the 200-meter butterfly at the 1979 Pan American Games. When the race was over she was not only one of the youngest gold medalists at the competition, but also a world-record holder. "The butterfly was always something that came naturally to me," she said.

Meagher's prowess in the butterfly—competitive swimming's most difficult and exhausting stroke—led the media to nickname her Grande Dame and Madame Butterfly. "One of the advantages of childhood achievement," she later said, "is that you really don't understand what's going on." To Meagher, swimming—and swimming fast—was the most natural thing in the world.

Meagher's greatest moment as a swimmer came in 1981, when she was 16 years old. At the U.S. Long Course Championships in Wisconsin, she set world records in the 100-meter butterfly and the 200-meter butterfly. Her records—times of 57.93 and 2:05.96—still stood more than 14 years later. Her 200-meter time was faster than the times of half of the men who competed that day.

Having been forced to miss the 1980 Olympics because of the U.S.-led boycott of the Summer Games in Moscow, Meagher came back four years later with renewed enthusiasm. In Los Angeles, at the 1984 Summer Olympics, she won gold medals in the 100-meter butterfly, the 200-meter butterfly, and the 4 x 100 medley relay. In the spring of her senior year as a University of California student, Meagher called it quits, only to come back two years later for a final Olympic appearance. She wanted the opportunity to compete in an Olympics that featured the finest swimmers from both the East and the West. In 1984 the Soviet Union had led its own boycott of the Los Angeles Games, which had prevented Meagher from swimming against the powerful East German team.

At the 1988 Summer Games in Seoul, South Korea, Meagher was 23 years old and past her prime, but she did win a silver medal in the 4 x 100 medley relay and a bronze in the 200-meter butterfly. She retired with 22 U.S. championships and in 1993 was inducted into the International Women's Sports Hall of Fame.

Accomplishments

Olympic gold medalist, 100-meter butterfly: 1984
Olympic gold medalist, 200-meter butterfly: 1984
Olympic gold medalist, 4 x 100 medley relay: 1984
Inducted into International Women's Sports Hall of Fame: 1993
Winner of 22 U.S. championships

Debbie Meyer

Born August 14, 1952

Debbie Meyer, the first person to win three individual gold medals in Olympic swimming, was born in New Jersey. When she was 12, her father, an executive with the Campbell Soup Co., received a promotion, and the family moved to Sacramento, California. By that time Debbie was already an experienced competitive swimmer. She had learned the basics as a child and was racing by the time she was eight.

In Sacramento, Debbie Meyer joined the Arden Hills Swim Club, where she trained with Sherm Chavoor, one of the best swimming coaches in the country. Chavoor believed in pushing his athletes, even the young ones. Swimmers develop early, and when Meyer began training with Chavoor, she discovered that world-class workouts differed greatly from her customary routine.

"I remember the first time I came out to practice," Meyer said. "Sherm said, 'All right, do 20 laps to warm up.' I couldn't even do four."

But Meyer persevered. She pushed through the pain and embarrassment, becoming one of Chavoor's prized pupils. "With a coach like Sherm, you develop a love-hate relationship," Meyer said. "But you only hate him from time to time when you get tired. You love him all the time when you see what he gets out of you."

By the time she was 14, Meyer had set the first of her 15 world records. In 1967, when she was 15, she won her first national title, capturing the 400-meter freestyle with a time of 4:29. At the 1968 Summer Games in Mexico City, Meyer turned in one of the finest performances in the history of Olympic swimming. She won the 200-meter freestyle with a time of 2:10.5, the 400-meter freestyle with a time of 4:31.8, and the 800-meter freestyle with a time of 9:24. Each time was an Olympic record. Meyer was 16 years old and had already won three gold medals. And she held the world record in every freestyle event from 200 to 1,500 meters. Meyer later expressed regret that she wasn't mature enough to appreciate what she had done.

"The first time I was on the victory stand [at the Olympics]," Meyer said, "I kept thinking,

Memorable Moment: May 17, 1975

Junko Tabei Reaches the Summit of Mount Everest

Mountaineering is one of the most difficult and dangerous sports. Its quirky appeal knows no gender. But for many years, it was difficult for a woman to obtain a spot in a well-financed excursion to any of the great Himalayan peaks. Some males considered women too frail for such demanding work; others simply didn't want to deal with the awkwardness of having a woman in their midst. After all, mountaineering is a raw experience. Members of an expedition work, sleep, and eat together. There is absolutely no privacy, not even when one has to go to the bathroom.

But as with most athletic endeavors, it was eventually demonstrated that women are quite capable of adapting to the rigors of mountain climbing. On May 17, 1975, a woman reached the summit of Mount Everest for the first time—Junko Tabei of Japan. Tabei had climbed her first mountain when she was in the fourth grade. In 1970 she had been part of an all-woman expedition to Annapurna III, another of the great Himalayan peaks.

On Everest, Tabei was part of a 15-woman expedition organized in 1975 by the Japanese Ladies Himalayan Club. Like most expeditions, they were assisted by a large team of Sherpas. Along the way, Tabei and her climbing partners survived a potentially deadly avalanche. On May 15 they established a camp at an altitude of 8,500 meters. At approximately noon on May 16, Tabei and one of the Sherpas reached the summit.

Gee, I wish I was back in my room with my sunflower seeds, washing them down with warm ginger ale and talking with my roomie about boys."

Before 1968 was over, Meyer became the fourth woman to win the Sullivan Award, given annually to the top amateur athlete in the United States. She defended her 400-meter freestyle national title in each of the next three years but grew tired of the routine. In 1972, shortly before the Summer Olympics in Munich, she retired from competitive swimming. She was 20 years old.

Meyer was inducted into the U.S. Olympic Hall of Fame in 1986 and the International Women's Sports Hall of Fame in 1987.

Accomplishments

Olympic gold medalist, 200-meter freestyle: 1968
Olympic gold medalist, 400-meter freestyle: 1968
Olympic gold medalist, 800-meter freestyle: 1968
Sullivan Award winner: 1968
Inducted into U.S. Olympic Hall of Fame: 1986
Inducted into International Women's Sports Hall of Fame: 1987

Ann Meyers

Born March 26, 1955

Ann Meyers, one of the first great female basketball players, was born in San Diego, California. Her brother, Dave, became an All-American forward at UCLA, then played in the National Basketball Association.

Ann Meyers was a versatile high school athlete who earned varsity letters in seven different sports. Her first love was track and field, not basketball. Her dream was to compete in the Olympics as a high jumper. But as a senior she became the first high school player to represent the U.S. women's basketball team in international competition. It was an exhilarating experience for her. From that time on, her athletic career centered around basketball.

In the early 1970s, opportunities for female basketball players were rare. In fact, Meyers was the first woman to receive a scholarship to play basketball. At UCLA she earned All-American status in each of her four years and in 1978, as a senior, was awarded the Broderick Cup as the nation's outstanding woman basketball player. That same year UCLA captured the Association of Intercollegiate Athletics for Women national championship, defeating Maryland by a score of 90–74 in the title game.

While at UCLA, Meyers, a 5-foot 9-inch, 140-pound guard and forward, continued to play in international tournaments. She helped lead the United States to a first-place finish in the Pan American Games in 1975 and 1979, and to a silver medal at the 1976 Summer Olympic Games in Montreal.

After graduating from UCLA, Meyers became the first woman to sign a contract with an NBA team. The Indiana Pacers drafted Meyers; while the gesture was merely a publicity stunt, she did show up at training camp and tried out for the team. As expected, she was cut, but the Pacers offered her a position as a color commentator on televised broadcasts of their games. That same year, Meyers signed a contract to play for the New Jersey Gems of the fledgling Women's Professional Basketball League. She led the league in scoring and won Most Valuable Player honors as a rookie. But the WPBL did not last, and Meyers had to look elsewhere for work. For three years she won the *Women's Superstars* competition, a made-for-TV spectacle pitting various sports stars against each other in a variety of events. She later went into broadcasting.

Meyers, who was married to former Los Angeles Dodgers pitcher Don Drysdale until his death in 1993, is a member of the International Women's Sports Hall of Fame and the Basketball Hall of Fame.

Accomplishments

Four-time All-American in basketball at UCLA
Olympic silver medalist: 1976
College Player of the Year: 1978
Inducted into International Women's Sports Hall of Fame: 1985
Inducted into Basketball Hall of Fame: 1993

Cheryl Miller

Born January 3, 1964

Cheryl Miller, one half of the most famous brother-sister act in the history of basketball, grew up in Riverside, California. Saul and Carrie Miller had five children, all of whom were introduced to sports at an early age. Cheryl's older brother, Darrell, played major league baseball. Younger sister Tammy was a volleyball star at California State University–Fullerton. And little brother Reggie was the trash-talking, smooth-shooting guard who became a college basketball standout at UCLA and an NBA All-Star with the Indiana Pacers.

Cheryl and Reggie, a year apart in age, had much in common. Both were supremely confident—even as children. Both were exceptionally bright, and both loved to play basketball. For them, there was no greater pleasure than an afternoon spent playing pickup.

Brother and sister often went off in search of a game of two-on-two. Reggie would challenge an opponent, maybe make a little wager. When the opposing team saw that Reggie's partner was a girl, they'd naturally take the bet. More often than not, the Millers walked away the winners. "Cheryl was better than most of the guys," Reggie said. "Eventually, we had to get way out of the neighborhood because everyone knew who she was."

Cheryl Miller was 6 feet 3 inches tall, lean, and extremely athletic; she became one of the most heavily recruited high school basketball players in the nation. She was the first player— male or female—to be named to the Parade All-America team during all four years in high school. She had her choice of colleges, but decided to stay close to home and attend the University of Southern California.

As a freshman in 1983, Miller helped USC defeat Louisiana Tech, 69–67, in the NCAA championship game. As a sophomore she not only led the Trojans to a second consecutive national title, but also won the Naismith Award as the most outstanding player in college basketball. When the season was finished, she spent several months training with the U.S. Olympic team; she helped them win

a gold medal at the 1984 Summer Games in Los Angeles.

In 1985 and 1986 Miller won the Naismith Award. In 1985 she was awarded the Wade Trophy, given annually to a player with noteworthy academic and community service accomplishments. In her four years at USC, Miller scored more than 3,000 points and averaged 23.6 points per game. She was inducted into the International Women's Sports Hall of Fame in 1991 and the Basketball Hall of Fame in Springfield, Massachusetts, in 1995. In 1993 she returned to her alma mater as head basketball coach. Two years later she left coaching to pursue a broadcasting career.

Accomplishments

College basketball Player of the Year:
1984–1986
NCAA champion: 1983–1984
Olympic gold medalist: 1984
Inducted into International Women's Sports
Hall of Fame: 1991
Inducted into Basketball Hall of Fame: 1995

Shannon Miller

Born March 10, 1977

Shannon Miller, a two-time world gymnastics champion, was born and raised in Oklahoma. She began taking gymnastics classes at the age of six, though her parents hardly entertained thoughts of Olympic glory. "That wasn't the plan," said Ron Miller, Shannon's father. "We didn't have any goals. Shannon was just tagging along with her older sister."

The Millers believed that exercise was important and that through the discipline of sport a girl could gain confidence as well as fitness. Shannon was only eight years old when her gymnastics club went on a trip to the Soviet Union. The purpose of the trip was to expose the American children to some of the best gymnasts in the world and for the coaches to exchange training tips and philosophies. One of the Russian coaches told Claudia Miller that her daughter had world-class ability. He suggested professional training and guidance. After the family returned to the United States, Shannon joined Steve Nunno's Dynamo Gymnastics in Oklahoma City.

Shannon Miller was 11 years old when she first qualified for the U.S. junior national team in 1988; two years later, at the age of 13, she became the youngest girl ever to qualify for the U.S. senior national team. In 1991 she won a silver medal at the world championships and was named the winner of the Women's Sports Foundation Up and Coming Award. At the 1992 Summer Olympics in Barcelona, 15-year-old Shannon Miller turned in one of the finest performances ever by a U.S. gymnast. The smallest (4 feet 10 inches, 79 pounds) member of the American Olympic team was the most decorated. She won silver medals in the balance beam and all-around competition, and bronze medals in the floor exercise, uneven parallel bars, and team competition.

In 1993 Miller won the all-around title at the world championships in Birmingham, England. She also won gold medals in the floor exercise and the uneven bars. The National March of Dimes named Miller its Female Athlete of the Year in 1993. She was also a finalist for the Jesse Owens Award and the Babe Didrikson Zaharias Award. The next year Miller won three gold medals, including the all-around title, at the world championships in Brisbane, Australia. Later that year, at the Goodwill Games in St. Petersburg, Russia, she won a silver medal in the all-around competition, and two golds and two silvers in individual events.

Back at home, Miller's daily routine involved waking up at 6 A.M., completing a one-hour workout, going to school full-time, and training for five hours in the evening. Despite that hectic schedule, she carried a straight-A average at Edmond North High School in Oklahoma City. Ron Miller, a professor of physics at the University of Central Oklahoma, and Claudia Miller, a bank vice president, stressed academic as well as athletic excellence. "In our family it's understood that you do schoolwork first and then other things," Ron Miller said. "Shannon is an achiever."

In 1996 Shannon Miller became an Olympic gold medalist, helping the United States capture the women's team title at the Summer Games in Atlanta. She also took an individual gold in the balance beam competition.

Accomplishments

Olympic silver medalist, all-around: 1992
Olympic silver medalist, balance beam:
    1992
Gold medalist, Championships of the USA:
    1993
World champion, all-around: 1993–1994
Olympic gold medalist, balance beam:
    1996
Olympic gold medalist, team: 1996

Madeline Manning Mims

Born January 11, 1948

Madeline Manning Mims, who captained three U.S. Olympic track-and-field teams, grew up in a Cleveland ghetto, surrounded by poverty and despair. She was a sickly child who somehow found the strength to rise above her environment. Her courage was passed down from her mother, a woman of deep spiritual faith; her father was an alcoholic who spent little time with the family. Manning overcame a nearly fatal case of spinal meningitis as a child. Because she was a frail, sensitive girl, no one expected her to become an athlete. But one day during gym class at John Jay High School, she impressed the school's track coach with her natural speed and agility. He invited her to join the team. Within a matter of months, Manning was one of the most accomplished runners in the city. She and her John Jay teammates even qualified for a relay race at the national championships in 1964.

In 1966 Manning stepped up to world-class competition. She ran the 800 meters—her specialty—at a meet in Toronto. Although nervous and intimidated, she ran as hard as she could. The pace was faster than any she'd ever experienced, and there was much physical contact. But Manning sprinted to the front of the pack, then crossed the finish line first. The gangly high school girl set a world record.

That performance helped Manning earn a scholarship to Tennessee State University, the alma mater of Wilma Rudolph, which had one of the strongest track-and-field programs in the

country. Manning attended classes, endured exhausting daily workouts on the track, and worked in the college mail room to help pay for her education.

In 1968, to prepare for the Summer Olympics in Mexico City, Manning, like many U.S. athletes, moved to the mountains of New Mexico to train. The high-altitude conditions there were similar to those she would face in Mexico City. Manning's task was daunting. While American runners had traditionally fared well in the sprints, none had ever won a gold medal in the 800 meters. In the Olympic final Manning chose a different strategy—she decided to hang back in the pack during much of the race. Then, in the final 200 meters, she unleashed a devastating kick. Manning reeled in the leaders and captured the gold medal with a time of 2:00.9.

Two years later Manning retired. But before long her competitive juices began to flow again. She qualified for the U.S. Olympic team in 1972 and in 1976. In the latter year she set a U.S. record in the 800 with a time of 1:57.9. After failing to win a medal at the 1976 Games, Manning again tried to step away from the sport. She married and turned her attention to music and charitable work. She regularly visited women in prison and tried to give them a sense of hope. "It's wonderful to see these women, once so bitter and depressed, changing before your eyes," she said.

In 1980, at the age of 32, Madeline Manning Mims again qualified for the U.S. Olympic team. She won the 800 meters at the Olympic trials with a time of 1:58.3, barely missing her own U.S. record. But the U.S.-led boycott of the Moscow Summer Games prevented her from competing in her fourth Olympics. Mims was inducted into the National Track and Field Hall of Fame in 1984, and the International Women's Sports Hall of Fame in 1987.

Accomplishments

Olympic gold medalist, 800 meters: 1968
Inducted into National Track and Field Hall of
    Fame: 1984
Inducted into International Women's Sports
    Hall of Fame: 1987
Captain of U.S. Olympic track-and-field team:
    1972, 1976, 1980

Rosi Mittermeier

Born August 5, 1950

Late in her career, West Germany's Rosi Mittermeier became one of the most popular and decorated women in alpine skiing. Her birth, in the village of Reit Im Winkl, was a difficult one, and she barely survived. Six months later she was nearly crushed when a goat found its way into her baby carriage and sat on her. At the age of two, she ingested some rat poison, which almost killed her.

Having lived through those traumatic experiences, Mittermeier demonstrated by her teenage years that she was an athlete of uncommon ability. As a 17-year-old she qualified for the West German Olympic team in 1968. But at the Grenoble Winter Games, she finished 25th in the downhill and 20th in the giant slalom, and was disqualified in the slalom. Four years later, at the 1972 Olympics in Sapporo, Japan, she took sixth in the downhill, 12th in the giant slalom, and 17th in the slalom. In those years Mittermeier was a fun-loving, personable young woman who was content to get by on her natural ability. It wasn't until she dedicated herself to the sport both physically and emotionally that she blossomed.

Her transformation began shortly after the 1972 Games. But in 1973, during a trip to Hawaii, Mittermeier was injured in a surfing accident and had to sit out most of the season. Two years later she ran into a tourist while skiing and suffered a broken arm—just a short time after recovering from a previous accident in which she collided with a slalom pole and nearly blinded herself.

By 1976 Mittermeier was healthy and determined to prove that she was the finest skier in the world. She finished first in the World Cup slalom standings and second in the giant slalom, and captured the overall World Cup title. But her greatest achievement came at the Olympics in Innsbruck, Austria. Dubbed "Omi" (German for "Granny") because at 25 she was the oldest competitor in the field, Mittermeier became the darling of the Games. First she won the gold medal in the downhill, upsetting American Cindy Nelson and Austrian Brigitte Totschnig.

Mittermeier's performance was all the more stunning because in a decade of international competition, she had never won a downhill race. Three days later she picked up her second gold medal in the women's slalom; later she added a silver in the giant slalom.

Mittermeier retired from competitive skiing after the 1976 Olympics. She published an autobiography, recorded an album of folk songs, and earned a comfortable living as a spokesperson for skiing equipment manufacturers.

Accomplishments

Olympic gold medalist, downhill: 1976
Olympic gold medalist, slalom: 1976
Olympic silver medalist, giant slalom: 1976
World Cup overall champion: 1976

Dominique Moceanu

Born September 10, 1981

Dominique Moceanu, the youngest gymnast ever to win the U.S. national women's all-around title, was born in Hollywood, California. Her parents, Camelia and Dimitry Moceanu, had been gymnasts in Romania; they immigrated to the United States in 1980. Both parents had hoped that their genes and their passion for the sport of gymnastics would be passed on to their daughter, Dominique. When she was only six months old they tested her interest and aptitude. They wrapped some kitchen towels around a clothesline in the backyard, then hoisted little Dominique over their heads, encouraging her to grab on. With her mother on the ground, acting as a safety net, that is precisely what the infant did.

"She was holding her hands so tight," Camelia Moceanu told a reporter. "She just stayed there. She didn't let go. She had a strong grip." As the little girl dangled above them, Dimitry turned to his wife and said that it appeared there was another gymnast in the family.

Three years later the Moceanus placed their first call to Bela Karolyi, one of the finest gymnastics coaches in the world. Among his pupils were Nadia Comaneci and Mary Lou Retton.

Karolyi was sympathetic—he, too, had emigrated from Romania—but he wasn't willing to work with a toddler; he politely told the parents to give him another call when the girl was a bit older. Six years later, when Dominique Moceanu was not quite 10 years old, the family packed up their belongings and moved to Houston, the home of Karolyi's highly regarded gymnastics school.

Almost immediately, Moceanu fit in. She became a member of the U.S. junior national team at the age of 10; she was the youngest person ever to make the team. Three years later, in 1994, she captured the junior national championship. In the spring of 1995 she won her first international all-around title, at the Visa Challenge. Then, on August 18, 1995, at the Coca-Cola National Gymnastics Championships in New Orleans, she enthralled a crowd of over 5,000 with her talent and showmanship, becoming the youngest person to win the women's all-around title. Two weeks later she received the highest score in any individual event at the World Team trials and qualified for the world championships.

Critics argued that Moceanu's success came too quickly and at the expense of a normal childhood. But the gymnast was quick to dispute those claims.

"I love the sport," she said. "It's what I have done since I was little. It's fun. I like competing, and I like to win. When I do something good, I feel proud."

After meeting Moceanu and watching her perform, no less an authority than Comaneci had this to say of the young girl: "A star is born."

In 1996, at the Summer Olympic Games in Atlanta, Moceanu represented the United States despite suffering from a stress fracture in her leg. Although she did not earn a medal in an individual event, she did help the United States win a gold medal in the team competition.

Accomplishments

U.S. junior national all-around champion—1994
U.S. senior national all-around champion—1995
Youngest gymnast to win U.S. national all-around title
Olympic gold medalist, team: 1996

Helen Wills Moody

Born October 6, 1905

Arguably the greatest of all American tennis players, Helen Wills Moody was born in Berkeley, California. Clarence Wills, a physician, gave his daughter her first tennis racket when she was 13. By then she was already an active, athletic girl who liked to ride horses and swim. Tennis captivated her, so her father provided her with a membership at the Berkeley Tennis Club, where she received first-class instruction.

In 1920, during a trip to the West Coast, tennis star Helen Wightman was introduced to 14-year-old Helen Wills. Wightman recognized the girl's talent and began working with her. One year later Wills captured the U.S. junior championship. She was a spectator at the U.S.

Women's Open, where she watched with keen interest the championship match between Suzanne Lenglen and Molla Mallory. In her autobiography, *Fifteen-Thirty*, Wills wrote that after witnessing that match, "I knew the goal for which I hoped to aim, the kind of tennis I wanted to play."

Not long afterward, Wills was playing that caliber of tennis. In 1922 she competed in the U.S. Women's Open for the first time; she lost to Molla Mallory in the final. The following year, at the age of 17, she avenged that loss, defeating Mallory in straight sets, 6–2, 6–1. Wills repeated as U.S. Open champion in 1924 and 1925.

In 1929 Wills married San Francisco stockbroker Freedy Moody. The two often traveled together. Along with playing tennis, Helen Wills Moody wrote freelance newspaper articles, covering fashion shows, gallery openings, and art exhibits. From 1927 to 1933 she won five Wimbledon titles, four U.S. Open titles, and four French Open titles. From August 1926 until 1935, Wills Moody was unbeatable—she did not lose a single match or even a single set. The last of her 19 Grand Slam singles titles came in 1938, when she won Wimbledon for the eighth time.

As successful as she was, Wills Moody was never a crowd or media favorite. Off the court she was aloof; on it, she betrayed no emotion. Strong and stoic, she used her superior stamina and determination to wear down her opponents. As a result, she was given the nickname Little Miss Poker Face.

For all of her achievements on the tennis court, Wills Moody never considered herself solely an athlete. She graduated Phi Beta Kappa from the University of California–Berkeley, and was a socialite whose circle of friends included Lady Astor and George Bernard Shaw. She was an artist whose paintings were exhibited in prestigious galleries. In addition to her autobiography, she wrote mystery novels.

"Tennis is a diversion," she wrote, "not a career." But for more than a decade, Helen Wills Moody was the best female tennis player in the world. She was inducted into the International Tennis Hall of Fame in 1959.

Accomplishments

Wimbledon champion: 1927–1930, 1932–1933, 1935, 1938
U.S. Open champion: 1923–1925, 1927–1929, 1931
French Open champion: 1928–1930, 1932
Inducted into International Tennis Hall of Fame: 1959

Memorable Moment: July 19, 1976

Nadia Comaneci Scores a Perfect 10 in Gymnastics

When 14-year-old Nadia Comaneci of Romania stepped up to the uneven parallel bars at the 1976 Summer Olympics, few people in the Montreal Forum had any idea who she was. And no one knew that she was about to change the sport of gymnastics forever. Most of the fans were simply waiting for Comaneci to complete her routine so that they could see the star of the show, Olga Korbut.

But over the course of the next minute and a half, Comaneci performed flawlessly. With stunning speed and strength, the small, muscular girl with the poker face successfully completed every move in her routine. There was not one slip. Even her dismount and landing were perfect.

Upon witnessing this feat, the crowd went wild. But the greatest drama was yet to come. In the nervous moments before Comaneci's scores were flashed, a buzz filled the Forum. No gymnast had ever been given a score of 10, regardless of how beautiful the performance had been. A 10 represented perfection, and perfection, purists argued, was impossible. It left no room for improvement. But the Montreal judges had never seen a routine such as Comaneci's, and they responded by awarding her the first 10 in Olympic history.

Elisabeth Moore

March 5, 1876–January 22, 1959

Four-time U.S. national singles champion Elisabeth Moore was born in Brooklyn, New York. She competed at a time when women, like men, were required to play five-set matches in the final rounds of tournaments. In fact, she wound up at the center of a controversy regarding that issue.

In 1901 Moore won her second national title, but not until she was on the brink of emotional and physical exhaustion. The format for major tournaments at the turn of the century dictated that the defending champion merely rest and await the winner of the "all-comers" tournament. Moore battled through the all-comers event, defeating Marion Jones in a grueling five-set final, 4–6, 1–6, 9–7, 9–7, 6–3. It was the longest women's final in history, but there was to be precious little rest for Moore. The next day she was back on the court, tired and sore but eager to play in the challenge round. Her opponent was Myrtle McAteer, the defending champion. Again the match lasted five sets. In another epic struggle, Moore emerged with the national title—the scores were 6–4, 3–6, 7–5, 2–6, 6–2. Moore became the first woman to play five-set matches on consecutive days. She played a remarkable 105 games of singles.

Moore was a strong, competitive woman, and the endurance test left no scars on her. Jones, however, staggered through the last few games of the all-comers final; her condition, and the prospect of other women being forced to endure such long matches, so concerned the male-dominated U.S. Lawn Tennis Association that it quickly—and rashly—opted to shorten the finals of all women's matches to best-of-three sets. While perhaps born of good intentions, the decision angered many of the top female players, including Moore. She and many others were particularly miffed that the USLTA neglected to consult any women about the matter—not even the athletes who had been involved in the 1901 marathon.

"I do not think any such change should have been made without first canvassing the wishes of the women players," Moore wrote in a letter to *Lawn Tennis,* the USLTA's publication. "Lawn tennis is a game not alone of skill but of endurance as well, and I fail to see why such a radical change should be made to satisfy a few players who do not take the time or do not have the inclination to get themselves in proper condition for playing."

Despite the protestations of Moore and others, the new rule was put into place. Nearly a century later, despite tremendous changes in training and conditioning, and despite the strides made by female athletes in general, women's tennis matches remain bound to the three-set format.

Moore went on to become one of the most accomplished players of her time, winning national singles titles in 1903 and 1905. She won the U.S. national doubles championship in 1896 and 1903, and the mixed doubles title in 1902 and 1904. She was inducted into the International Tennis Hall of Fame in 1971.

Accomplishments

U.S. national singles champion: 1896, 1901, 1903, 1905
U.S. national doubles champion: 1896, 1903
U.S. national mixed doubles champion: 1902, 1904
Played in last five-set final at U.S. championships
Inducted into International Tennis Hall of Fame: 1971

Angela Mortimer

Born April 21, 1932

Born in Plymouth, England, Florence Angela Margaret Mortimer played in the first all-English final at Wimbledon and later earned admission to the International Tennis Hall of Fame. She did not begin playing tennis until the age of 15. But once she had decided to become an exceptional tennis player, nothing could stop her. Mortimer was neither tall nor quick, and she did not overpower her opponents. Rather, she made the most of her talent and worked harder than the players she faced.

"Every match I ever won had been the result of practice and determination and hard work," she wrote. "Perhaps I had worked harder than most champions. I knew that I was not truly one of the greats."

Mortimer won her first Grand Slam singles title in 1955, defeating Dorothy Knode in a long, hard-fought final by a score of 2–6, 7–5, 10–8. That same year she teamed up with Anne Shilcock to win the Wimbledon doubles title. In 1958 she won the Australian Open championship and reached the Wimbledon singles final for the first time, losing in straight sets to Althea Gibson of the United States. Mortimer was a quarterfinalist at Wimbledon in 1953, 1954, 1956, 1959, and 1960.

But it was in 1961 that Mortimer played the match of her life. At 29 years of age, with a chronically sore arm, she was considered by many tennis observers to be on the downside of her career. But she surprised and delighted the partisan crowds at Wimbledon by advancing to the final for the second time. Her opponent was Christine Truman, another Brit. Six feet tall and only 20 years old, Truman had the physical advantage. But Mortimer was more experienced and was better equipped to deal with the pressure inherent in being a British player in a Wimbledon final. Despite losing the first set and falling behind, 4–3, in the second, Mortimer was able to capture her first Wimbledon crown. She was helped by an unfortunate injury to Truman, who slipped on the wet grass and suffered a pulled hamstring midway through the second set.

Mortimer was a dedicated and prized member of the British Wightman Cup team. She played seven times, and served as captain in 1967 and 1970. Her success was all the more impressive because she was hearing impaired. Mortimer turned an apparent liability into an asset.

"I could hear the applause of the crowd, but not much else," she said. "I think it helped me concentrate, shutting out distractions."

Mortimer later married John Edward Barrett, a British Davis Cup player and a journalist. She was inducted into the International Tennis Hall of Fame in 1993.

Accomplishments

French Open champion: 1955
Australian Open champion: 1958
Wimbledon champion: 1961
Inducted into International Tennis Hall of
    Fame: 1993

Annemarie Moser-Proell

Born March 27, 1953

Annemarie Moser-Proell, who grew up in the Austrian town of Kleinarl, won only one Olympic gold medal; nevertheless, she is regarded as the best woman alpine skier of all time. Annemarie was one of eight children. Her parents were farmers—rugged outdoor types who enjoyed athletic activities in general and skiing in particular. Annemarie was only four years old when she began flying down the slopes on a pair of skis hand-whittled by her father. She was a fearless child who loved the speed and danger of downhill skiing, a fact that was at once distressing and exhilarating to her parents.

Though she never had any formal schooling in the sport, Annemarie Proell became a world-class competitor at a young age. She often skipped school to spend time on the slopes. By the age of 17 she was a powerful athlete who stood 5 feet 6 inches tall and weighed 150 pounds. She had a strong lower body that was ideally suited to withstanding the rigors of downhill skiing; more importantly, she had the courage and determination to challenge any mountain.

From 1971 through 1975 Proell dominated the sport of alpine skiing. In each of those years she was the World Cup overall champion. No other woman has won the title more than twice. In that five-year stretch, Proell won 21 of 33 downhill races and finished second 11 times. In 1972 at the Winter Olympics in Sapporo, Japan, Proell was favored to win a gold medal in the women's downhill. But she was upset by Switzerland's Marie Therese Nadig in both the downhill and the giant slalom, and had to settle for a pair of silver medals.

In 1975, after winning a fifth consecutive World Cup overall title, Proell suddenly decided to retire. She quit skiing, opened a cafe, and married soccer player Herbert Moser. She was 22 years old and probably in her athletic prime. But when the 1976 Winter Olympics were held in her native Austria, Annemarie Moser-Proell was merely a spectator.

By the fall of 1976, Moser-Proell was back on the slopes, training hard to recapture the form that had made her a world champion. It took three years, but by 1979 she was back at the top of her sport, winning a sixth World Cup overall title. One year later, at the 1980 Winter Olympics in Lake Placid, 27-year-old Moser-Proell finally became a gold medalist, defeating Marie Therese Nadig and Hanni Wenzel in the downhill.

After the 1980 Games, Moser-Proell retired again, beginning life as a businesswoman in Austria. In 1982 she was inducted into the International Women's Sports Hall of Fame.

Accomplishments

Olympic gold medalist, downhill: 1980
Olympic silver medalist, downhill: 1972
Olympic silver medalist, giant slalom: 1972
World Cup overall champion: 1971–1975, 1979
Inducted into International Women's Sports
    Hall of Fame: 1982

Shirley Muldowney

Born June 19, 1940

Shirley Muldowney, the first woman to drive a Top Fuel dragster professionally, was raised in Schenectady, New York. She was a rebellious teen who often slipped out of the house late at night to race cars in the streets. Hot rodding was an illegal, dangerous game—and one in which women were rarely allowed to participate. In the 1950s, girls stood by and cheered for their boyfriends, coaxing them down dimly lit streets in the predawn hours.

Shirley Roques was different. She could drive as well as anyone. She was tough and fearless. She also had a boyfriend who shared her passion for drag racing. By the time she was 17, Shirley had dropped out of school, married Jack Muldowney, and given birth to their only child, John. The marriage lasted 15 years, during which time Shirley became a pioneer in the sport of drag racing. She started out with souped-up street cars, moved on to Funny Cars, and then to Top Fuelers, the cream of the quarter-mile drag racing crop.

The world of Top Fuel drag racing can be cruel and dangerous. The automobiles reach 60

miles per hour in less than one second and hit top speeds of 250 miles per hour. Shirley "Cha-Cha" Muldowney, as she came to be known (she later admitted that she hated the nickname), had to deal not only with the possibility of severe injury, but also with the pressure of being the first woman in the sport. Spectators heckled and insulted her, and competitors did nothing to make her feel welcome. To them, she was a woman invading a man's sacred territory. But Muldowney repeatedly demonstrated her talent and toughness. Instead of pretending to be one

of the boys, she accentuated her femininity. She wore makeup and a pink helmet, and drove a pink dragster.

In 1977 Muldowney became the first woman to win the National Hot Rod Association championship. She won a second title in 1980 and a third in 1982. But it wasn't until her third title that she was able to land a major sponsor. Two years later she suffered the worst setback of her career. In a race at Sanair Speedway near Montreal, Canada, she blew a tire while traveling at 247 miles per hour. The car jumped the dragstrip, flipped, and blew into pieces, throwing Muldowney more than 500 feet. When Muldowney, who was 44 at the time, regained consciousness, she was sitting in a farmer's field. She looked down and saw her left foot resting in her lap, dangling by a few arteries. Her right leg, pelvis, and thumb had been fractured. Doctors concluded that she was fortunate to have survived the crash. They gave her little chance of walking again and virtually no chance of racing. But nearly 18 months later, after six operations, she not only was walking, she also returned to the sport she loved.

After the accident, the worst of several during her career, Muldowney ended her feud with rival Don "Big Daddy" Garlits, one of drag racing's biggest stars and a longtime critic of Muldowney. "I resent her sitting in the cab of that truck filing her nails while those turncoat men flog her car for her," Garlits said. But by 1990 the two rivals were working together, with Muldowney driving and Garlits heading her mechanical team.

"The feud settled itself naturally when she crashed," Garlits said. "I was really upset about that."

By the mid-1990s, Muldowney, again having trouble securing sponsorship, was forced to retire.

Accomplishments

First woman to drive a Top Fuel dragster professionally
National Hot Rod Association champion: 1977, 1980, 1982
First woman to break five seconds in a quarter-mile race: 1989

Margaret Murdock

Born August 25, 1942

Born Margaret Thompson in Topeka, Kansas, Margaret Murdock was one of the greatest shooters in history. Although a pioneer throughout her career, she competed in a sport that received little publicity, so few people were aware of her accomplishments. When the International Shooting Union compiled its list of the dozen most accomplished shooters of all time, Murdock was No. 6. She was the only female. Virtually her entire career, Murdock was a pioneer. Shooting was a male-dominated sport. For Murdock, break-

ing down barriers came with the territory. She was the first woman to win an open competition at the world championships and the first woman to win an open competition at the Pan American Games.

The first of Murdock's accomplishments came in 1967, two years after she had graduated from Kansas State University. At the Pan American Games, she captured the gold medal in the small-bore rifle competition. What made her feat even more remarkable was the score—391, a world record. Murdock became the first woman in any sport to break a men's world record. Murdock's achievement went almost unnoticed by the national and international media, which expressed little interest in her or her sport.

Murdock nonetheless continued to compete at the highest levels, winning more medals and trophies, and setting more records. In 1969 she won the national women's small-bore prone position and three-position titles. She also won the prone position title in 1972. At the world championships in 1970, she finished first in the small-bore standing position title—despite being four months pregnant.

In one of her last great international achievements, Murdock finished in a tie with teammate Lanny Bassham in the small-bore three-position event at the 1976 Olympics. Judges spent nearly five hours examining the targets and double-checking the scores to determine the clear winner. They finally decided that Bassham's performance had been marginally better than Murdock's and declared him the gold medalist; Murdock was awarded the silver. Bassham, however, was unhappy with the decision, and during the awards ceremony he embraced Murdock and invited her to join him on the winner's platform while the national anthem was played.

Murdock, a registered nurse, was inducted into the International Women's Sports Hall of Fame in 1988.

Accomplishments

First woman in any sport to break a men's world record
First woman to win an open competition at the world championships
Olympic silver medalist, small-bore three-position: 1976
Inducted into International Women's Sports Hall of Fame: 1988

N

Martina Navratilova

Born October 18, 1956

Martina Navratilova, the all-time leading money winner in women's tennis, began life in Prague, Czechoslovakia. Her mother, Jana Subertova, was a versatile athlete who earned her living as a ski instructor. Her father, Miroslav Subert, was a professional skier. Miroslav and Jana met on the slopes, fell in love, married, and moved into a ski lodge called Martinovka ("Martin's Place")—they later named their daughter after the ski lodge.

When Martina was three years old, Jana divorced Miroslav; mother and daughter moved into a small house in the town of Revnice, near Jana's parents. There Martina was introduced to tennis, a game that was in her blood. Her grandmother had been one of the highest-ranked amateur players in Czechoslovakia, and her mother had been a promising young player. When Jana began playing again at a local club, Martina tagged along. Jana eventually married teaching professional Mirek Navratil, and the family's life began to revolve around tennis. Martina Navratilova was playing regularly by the time she was five, using her left hand to bat balls against a brick wall.

"The moment I stepped onto that crunchy red clay, felt the grit under my sneakers, felt the joy of smacking a ball over the net, I knew I was in the right place," Navratilova said.

Mirek became Martina's tutor as well as her stepfather. Their daily lessons were sometimes a battle of wills—Mirek believed in traditional baseline tennis; Martina was naturally aggressive and wanted to rush the net, to serve and volley. Through compromise, they refined both aspects of her game. Before long Navratilova was quick, strong, and fiercely competitive. In 1972, at the age of 16, despite suffering from a bad cold, she won the Czech national singles championship.

After that, she began competing on the women's tour. In her first season, 1973, she reached the third round at Wimbledon and the quarterfinals at the French Open. Navratilova was having problems adjusting to Western life, most notably Western food. After just one month outside of Czechoslovakia she gained more than 25 pounds. Navratilova battled weight problems for nearly a decade, until conditioning became a priority in her life. At 5 feet 8 inches and 145 pounds, she became one of the healthiest, fittest players ever to pick up a tennis racket.

Memorable Moment: March 5, 1977

Betty Cook Becomes the First Woman to Win a Major Offshore Powerboat Race

Offshore powerboat racing is among the most rigorous of sports. It is fast, dangerous, and demanding. Competitors often have to control their boats in rough seas—10-foot waves are not uncommon. For that reason, among others, powerboat racing was, for the longest time, an exclusively male domain. And Betty Cook seemed an unlikely candidate to invade that world.

Cook was a small woman who didn't begin racing powerboats until after her 50th birthday. She was, in fact, a grandmother before she entered her first race. But she was a strong and determined woman who enjoyed the thrill of competition. She was fearless. Neither the distinct threat of injury nor the snide remarks of traditionalists could dissuade her from competing.

Cook advocated using catamarans in offshore powerboat racing, even though popular theory held that they were not sturdy enough. She eventually proved her theory by winning races in a catamaran.

Cook's first official victory came in the Bushmills Grand Prix off the coast of Newport Beach, California, on March 5, 1977. On that day she became the first woman to win a major offshore powerboat race. And lest anyone dismiss her victory as a fluke, Cook went on to win the world championship that year.

Navratilova defected to the United States while on tour in 1975, the same year she reached the finals of the French Open and the Australian Open. In 1978 she won her first Grand Slam event—Wimbledon. Since then she has won virtually every major title and award in tennis. She won eight more Wimbledon titles, four U.S. Open titles, two French Open titles, and three Australian Open titles; she also won 38 Grand Slam doubles titles. For seven years she was the tour's top-ranked player and, with nearly $20 million in earnings, is the sport's all-time leading money winner. In 1983–1984 she was as dominant as any player in the history of the game, male or female, winning six consecutive Grand Slam titles.

Navratilova was named Female Athlete of the Decade for the 1980s by both the Associated Press and United Press International. In 1984 she was inducted into the International Women's Sports Hall of Fame.

Navratilova's personal life has frequently come under scrutiny, largely because she is one of the few openly gay superstar athletes. She has handled the tumult with style and grace. She donates time and money to many charitable efforts, and remains one of the most admired and respected athletes in the world. Navratilova retired from the women's tour in 1994 but continues to play exhibitions and team tennis.

Accomplishments

Wimbledon champion: 1978–1979, 1982–1987, 1990
French Open champion: 1982, 1984
Australian Open champion: 1981, 1983, 1985
U.S. Open champion: 1983–1984, 1986–1987
Inducted into International Women's Sports Hall of Fame: 1984

Liselotte Neumann

Born May 20, 1966

One of only a handful of golfers to win the U.S. Women's Open as a rookie, Liselotte Neumann was born and raised in Finspang, Sweden, 125 miles south of Stockholm. She was a graceful, athletic child who loved to play sports of all kinds. Neumann said that she was "good at anything played with a ball," including tennis, soccer, and basketball. She also dabbled in ice hockey. It wasn't until she was 10 years old, while accompanying her parents on a trip to a nine-hole course, that she first picked up a golf club. Before long she was hooked. She practiced every day, read all the golf magazines she could get her hands on, and copied the techniques of her favorite players. She became a true student of the game.

Just two years after her introduction to golf, Neumann earned a spot on the Swedish national junior team. At 16 she captured her first Swedish Amateur Championship; a year later she defended her title. That same year, 1983, she won the Swedish Match Play Championship. In 1985 she won the European Open, in 1987 she won the French Open, and from 1986 through 1988 she reigned as German Open champion. Then she turned professional.

When the 1988 U.S. Women's Open began at the Baltimore Country Club, Neumann was just another wide-eyed rookie with a long list of dreams. But by the end of the weekend, she was a 22-year-old champion. By the end of that year she had accumulated nearly $200,000 in earnings and was the Ladies Professional Golf Association Rookie of the Year. Endorsement deals began to roll in, and the distractions mounted.

"Everything happened so fast," Neumann said in an interview several years later. "I wasn't quite comfortable on tour yet. It felt like every person wanted a piece of my time. At first I said, 'Yes, yes,' to everything, but after a while I wanted to say, 'Leave me alone, I want to be by myself.'"

From 1989 through 1993, Neumann won only one tournament, the 1991 Mazda Japan Classic. She fell from 12th on the LPGA money list in 1988 to 57th in 1993. But through persistence and patience, she pulled out of her slump. In a six-month period in 1994, Neumann won five tournaments, including the British Women's Open. At the end of the year she was third on the LPGA money list with more than $500,000, and was first on the European tour. While she failed to win another major tournament that year, she finished third in the U.S. Women's Open, the McDonald's LPGA Championship, and the du Maurier Classic. In 1996 she won three tournaments and more than $625,000, becoming fourth on the LPGA money list.

Although she continues to play both the LPGA and European tours, Neumann spends most of her time in the United States. She is a resident of Boca Raton, Florida.

Accomplishments

Swedish Amateur champion: 1982–1983
U.S. Women's Open champion: 1988
LPGA Rookie of the Year: 1988
Women's British Open champion: 1993

Paula Newby-Fraser

Born June 2, 1962

Paula Newby-Fraser, the most successful female triathlete in history, was raised in South Africa. The sight of soldiers patrolling the streets was common when she was growing up, but she says that she never felt threatened. As a youth she worked hard at her studies; when school was over she devoted herself to ballet and swimming. When Newby-Fraser graduated from high school, she was faced with a decision—join a local dance company or attend the university on a swimming scholarship. She declined to make either choice. Instead, she enrolled at a community college and stopped working out altogether. Having put her social life on hold for so many years, she tried to make up for lost time by eating and partying as much as she wanted. After college, in 1984, she took an office job. In an effort to lose a few pounds and let off a little steam at the end of the workday, she started visiting a gym and going on daily jogs with her boyfriend.

Soon the impulse to train gripped Newby-Fraser again. She ran, took aerobics classes, and lifted weights. Before long she was fit. But the idea of competing in a triathlon did not enter her mind until one morning in late 1984, when she and a few friends were spectators at a local qualifier for the Ironman Triathlon World Championships in Hawaii. At first she thought the competition was insane. She watched the competitors suffer through the grueling event, which consisted of a 2.4-mile ocean swim, a 112-mile bicycle ride, and a full marathon (26.2 miles). She soon found herself training for her first triathlon. Less than a year later, in April 1985, she finished first in the women's division of the Ironman qualifier in South Africa and earned a free trip to Hawaii for the nationals. Newby-Fraser finished third in the women's division of the Ironman in her rookie year.

"That was a turning point for me," she said. "I was looking at girls who were professional tri-athletes and made money out of the sport. I finished only five or six minutes behind the winner, and I'd never done those distances before."

The next year Newby-Fraser returned to Hawaii and won the women's Ironman competition. In 1987 she finished third, and in 1988 and 1989 she was back in the winner's circle. She finished second to Erin Baker in 1990, but for the next four years dominated the event, finishing first each time. In 1992 she became the first woman to break nine hours for the event, clocking 8:55.28.

In 1990 Newby-Fraser, a resident of San Diego, California, was named the winner of the Women's Sports Foundation Professional Athlete of the Year Award.

Accomplishments

First place, Ironman Triathlon World
    Championships: 1986, 1988–1989,
    1991–1994
First woman to break nine hours for the
    Ironman: 1992
Ironman world-record holder
Women's Sports Foundation Professional
    Athlete of the Year: 1990

Betty Nuthall

May 23, 1911–November 8, 1983

Betty Nuthall, a member of the International Tennis Hall of Fame and one of the youngest finalists ever at the U.S. Open, was born in Surrey, England.

She began playing tennis at the age of seven, learning the basics from her father. When she was 16 years old she stepped into the spotlight with a mesmerizing performance at the U.S. Open. She arrived on the scene at a time when spectators were accustomed to seeing the tournament dominated by Americans. In fact, not since Ireland's Mabel Cahill won at Philadelphia in 1891 and 1892 had the winner's trophy of the U.S. Open been captured by a foreign player.

Nuthall's game featured a strong, reliable forehand, superior placement, and an under-handed serve. She was quick and confident enough to become the youngest champion in the history of the U.S. Open. For many years she shared the record for being the youngest finalist with Bessie Moore, who also had been a finalist at the age of 16.

Nuthall was beaten in straight sets in the 1927 final by one of the greatest players the game has ever known—Helen Wills, an older, more experienced player who had already won three U.S. singles titles. It took Nuthall three years to return to the U.S. Open singles final. In 1930, as a wiser, more mature player—and one who had practiced long and hard to develop an overhand serve—she defeated No. 2 seed Midge Morrill in the semifinals, then knocked off No. 1 seed Anna McCune Harper in the championship. That tournament was one of the best Nuthall would ever have; she also teamed up with Sarah Palfrey to win the women's doubles title.

In 1931 Nuthall and Palfrey defended their doubles crown. But in the singles Nuthall fell just short of a second consecutive title, losing in three sets to Eileen Bennett Whitingstall in the semifinals. Nuthall reached the semifinals again in 1933, but lost to defending champion Helen Wills Moody. Although she did not win another Grand Slam singles title, Nuthall came close at the 1931 French Open, where she beat Germany's Hilde Krahwinkel in the semifinals. In the final she lost to another German player, Cilly Aussem, 8–5, 6–1. In doubles, Nuthall and Whitingstall won the French title.

Nuthall was a respected Wightman Cup competitor. In 1927 she was the youngest member of the British team. Twelve years later she played in her eighth and final Cup; that year she served as team captain.

Nuthall later married Franklin Shoemaker and took up residence in New York. She died there in 1983, six years after being inducted into the International Tennis Hall of Fame.

Accomplishments

U.S. Open singles champion: 1930
U.S. Open doubles champion: 1930–1931, 1933
U.S. Open mixed doubles champion: 1929,
    1931
French Open finalist: 1931
Inducted into International Tennis Hall of
    Fame: 1977

Diana Nyad

Born August 22, 1949

Diana Nyad, a record-breaking endurance swimmer, grew up in Fort Lauderdale, Florida. Her Greek-Egyptian father explained to young Diana the meaning of the Greek word *naiad*. According to the dictionary, a naiad is "one of the nymphs in classical mythology living in lakes, rivers, springs, and fountains."

Diana Nyad learned to swim when she was a toddler. By her teenage years, she was the best sprint backstroker in the state of Florida. At age 16, she dreamed of competing in the 1968 Olympic Games in Mexico City. Nyad contracted viral endocarditis, an infection of the heart, which forced her into six months of strict bed rest. After her recovery, having missed a spot on the 1968 Olympic team, she wound up at Emory University but was expelled for parachuting out of a fourth-floor dormitory window. She later went back to school, graduating Phi Beta Kappa from Lake Forest College in Illinois.

Her short-distance career over, Nyad decided to try marathon swims, eventually becoming one of the most accomplished endurance athletes of her time. In 1969, in her first distance race, Nyad was the first female to finish a 10-mile competition in Lake Ontario. Five years later she became the first person to swim across that body of water, from south to north. The 32-mile, 50-degree-water-temperature challenge took her 18 hours, 22 minutes. Over the course of a decade, Nyad conquered many of the world's most difficult lakes, rivers, and seas. In September 1975 she tried to circle Manhattan Island. Strong, unpredictable tides due to a Southern storm made the completion impossible. Nyad swam in place under the Brooklyn Bridge for over an hour until her team decided to try again another day. That day came two weeks later. This time Nyad succeeded, completing the circumnavigation in 7 hours, 57 minutes, easily breaking Byron Sommers' record, which had stood for 48 years.

In August 1978, Nyad attempted her biggest challenge in the water. She set out to break the world record for the longest open-ocean swim in history. Her choice was 103 miles between Cuba and the Florida Keys. Nyad trained intensely, swimming eight hours in the ocean and running an average of 10 miles each day. But all of her preparation could not offset the negative effects of heavy seas and massive jellyfish stings. After more than 40 hours of nonstop swimming, Nyad had covered 79 miles, but her quest was abandoned. The shore was simply not reachable.

A year later Nyad realized her dream. She set the world record for the longest swim in history, for both men and women, when she stroked the 102.5 miles between the island of Bimini in the Bahamas and Jupiter, Florida.

Nyad now works as a television broadcaster, writer, and columnist for National Public Radio. Her autobiography, *Other Shores*, appeared in 1978.

Accomplishments

First woman to swim around Manhattan Island: 1975
World-record holder for longest swim in history, 102.5 miles: 1979

Annie Oakley

August 13, 1860–November 3, 1926

Born Phoebe June Moses in Patterson Township, Ohio, the girl who would become famed markswoman Annie Oakley was the fifth of eight children. Her father, Jacob Moses, died when she was four years old; her mother, Susan, was forced to go back to work as a nurse, and the family was fractured. Phoebe was sent to an orphanage when she was nine. A year later she moved in with a farming family that demanded she work long hours in the field; at 12, having had enough, she ran away and eventually found her mother.

At about the time of the reunion, Phoebe Moses took up hunting to help contribute to the family's finances. Using one of her father's

old rifles, she began tracking and shooting small animals—rabbits and quail, mostly—and selling them at markets in Cincinnati. Her skill as a markswoman was extraordinary for one so young.

When she was 16, Moses was introduced to Frank Butler, an expert marksman who earned his living traveling with a vaudeville show. A mutual friend, knowing of Moses' talent, suggested a shooting contest; the teenage girl beat the 26-year-old man. Less than a year later Phoebe Moses and Frank Butler were married. Shortly thereafter, Moses adopted the name Annie Oakley, and husband and wife traveled together, performing at shows throughout the Midwest. Oakley developed a pleasant stage demeanor, and Frank was an astute business manager. At their peak, they were among the premier attractions on the traveling vaudeville circuit. In 1885 Oakley signed with Buffalo Bill's Wild West Show—one of the first rodeos—and quickly became the main attraction.

It could be argued that Oakley was more performer than athlete, but there is no denying that she had tremendous athletic ability. There were no legitimate athletic arenas where she could display her skill, however. For female sharpshooters in the late 19th century, there were no national championships, no Olympic Games. So, even though Oakley often recorded perfect scores in trapshooting, and even though she won significant prize money in trapshooting contests, she is remembered as an entertainer. Indeed, she was quite good at putting on a show. She shot from a standing position,

from a prone position, and while on horseback. She fired at a cigarette protruding from her husband's mouth. From a distance of 30 paces she punctured a playing card tossed into the air.

Through a combination of skill and personality, Oakley became one of the most famous and admired women in the world. She traveled throughout the United States and Europe, and won a legion of fans wherever she went. She stood 5 feet tall and weighed 98 pounds, prompting the great Sioux chief Sitting Bull—who also traveled with Buffalo Bill—to dub her "My Daughter, Little Sure Shot."

In 1901 Oakley was seriously injured in a train accident. She never performed again. In 1922 she was hurt again, this time in an automobile accident. Four years later, after returning to Ohio, she died, with her husband of 50 years by her side. Three weeks later Butler died.

Humorist Will Rogers said of Oakley, "Her thoughtful consideration of others will live as a mark for any woman to shoot at."

Accomplishments

Member of American Trapshooting Hall of Fame
Star of Buffalo Bill's Wild West Show
Had several perfect scores of 100-for-100 in trapshooting

Margo Oberg

Born September 8, 1953

Margo Oberg (born Margo Godfrey) grew up in the heart of surfing country, in La Jolla Shores, California. A true pioneer in the sport, she rode her first wave at the age of 10 and won her first contest in 1965. Oberg's debut came at the Western Regional Surfing Championships, which included a special "no age limit" women's division for residents of San Diego County. At just 11 years, she was the youngest competitor.

She was also one of the most gifted. By the time the tournament ended, Oberg had captured the women's title and received the Most Promising Surfer award. As impressive as that performance was, it was merely a prelude to what she would accomplish over the next two and a half decades.

Her first national title came at the Menehune Championships in La Jolla Shores. Of the 50 surfers competing in the 12-and-under division, Oberg was the only girl. She soon was the top-ranked women's surfer in the state of California. In 1968, at age 15, she captured the first of seven world championships.

Oberg successfully defended her world title in 1969, but then abruptly retired from competitive surfing. However, in 1975, when surfing became a professional sport, she ended her retirement and quickly took her rightful place at the top of the leader board. She won world championships in 1975, 1976, and 1977, and was runner-up in 1978. She left the pro tour in 1979, but came back to win world championships in 1980 and 1981.

In December of 1982, just three months after the birth of her first child, Oberg finished second in the World Cup at Haleiwa, Hawaii. She won the World Cup in 1983 and finished second in 1984. She was runner-up again in 1988, and in her last World Cup appearance, in 1991, she finished fourth.

The most decorated woman in the history of surfing, Oberg has worked as a television commentator and actor. Primarily, though, she is a teacher. Today she spends most of her time running Margo Oberg's Surfing School in Hawaii.

Accomplishments

Women's world surfing champion: 1968–1969, 1975–1977, 1980–1981
Women's World Cup champion: 1983

Kristin Otto

Born 1966

S wimmer Kristin Otto, the first woman to win six gold medals at one Olympiad, grew up in Leipzig, one of the largest cities in what was then East Germany. Her father taught college physics; her mother was a physical therapist. At that time, children in Communist countries with national athletic programs, such as the Soviet Union and East Germany, were tested and targeted at an early age. So it was with Kristin, whose natural ability in the swimming pool

Memorable Moment:
May 29, 1977

Janet Guthrie Competes in the Indianapolis 500

The sport of auto racing was a boys' club when Janet Guthrie began pounding on the door and demanding admission in the late 1960s. Her credentials were impeccable—she had a pilot's license and a degree in physics, and was a candidate to become one of the first female astronauts—but all that was no match for chauvinism.

Eventually, though, Guthrie proved to be such a first-rate driver and competitor that she was given a chance to compete in some of auto racing's premier events, including the Watkins Glen 500, in which she finished sixth in 1971. But what Guthrie really wanted was an opportunity to race in the grandest event of all—the Indianapolis 500. She tried to qualify for the event in 1976 but failed. Undeterred, she returned the following year. On the last day of qualifying, Guthrie became the first woman to earn a spot in the starting field of the Indianapolis 500. Her average speed was 188 miles per hour, the fastest of any car competing on the last weekend of qualifying.

On Sunday, May 29, 1977, the famous starter's call at Indy was modified: "In company with the first lady ever to qualify at Indianapolis, gentlemen, start your engines." Guthrie did exactly that, but by the 27th lap she was forced out of the race by a broken valve seal. Not finishing the race did not detract from Guthrie's accomplishment. Simply by making it to the starting line, she had shattered a barrier and a stereotype.

caught the eye of a coach. She was 11 years old when she was removed from her conventional school and placed in a special school for gifted athletes. Her life revolved around swimming and studying.

The East German system has been criticized for being abusive of children, but the results were dramatic. By the mid-1980s Kristin Otto was one of the most accomplished swimmers in the world, but a Soviet-led boycott of the 1984 Summer Olympics in Los Angeles prevented her from showcasing her talents on the world's biggest stage. A few months after the Games, she suffered a back injury that left her in a neck brace for the better part of a year. Doctors told her to retire from competitive swimming; they doubted that she could ever return to world-class form and worried that the grueling work-outs common among swimmers of Otto's caliber would aggravate her injury. But she refused to listen to them. By 1986 she was approaching peak form. Otto won six gold medals at the 1986 world championships, including a gold in the 200-meter intermediate medley.

In 1988 Otto finally got the chance to participate in Olympic competition. In one of the most impressive performances in the history of amateur sports, Otto dominated Seoul's Olympic indoor swimming pool. Day after day she stood proudly on the medal stand, a gold medal draped around her neck. First came the 100-meter freestyle, then the 100-meter back-stroke, then the 100-meter butterfly—she won three individual gold medals. Then came gold-medal performances in the 4 x 100 freestyle relay and the 4 x 100 medley relay. And, finally, another gold medal in the 50-meter freestyle. Otto won six gold medals, more than any other woman in Olympic history. The previous record was four, held by another East German swim-mer, Kornelia Ender.

"I didn't come here with a plan to win many gold medals," Otto said. "Just one or two. I'm happy and, quite frankly, astonished."

Skeptics suggested that Otto and many of her East German teammates had benefited from using performance-enhancing drugs. Those allegations were given support years later when an East German Secret Police report was pub-lished in an American swimming magazine in December 1994. *Swimming World* reported that

Otto was one of many athletes who systemati-cally took steroids and that she had more than three times the normal level of testosterone. The magazine quoted Dr. Warner Franke, a German biochemist and a member of a national commission investigating Secret Police files, as saying that the documents "prove without a doubt that every single East German world-class athlete was doped."

Accomplishments

Olympic gold medalist, 100-meter freestyle: 1988

Olympic gold medalist, 100-meter backstroke: 1988

Olympic gold medalist, 100-meter butterfly: 1988

Olympic gold medalist, 50-meter freestyle: 1988

Olympic gold medalist, 4 x 100 freestyle relay: 1988

Olympic gold medalist, 4 x 100 medley relay: 1988

Mary Outerbridge

March 9, 1852–May 3, 1886

Mary Ewing Outerbridge, often called the founder of American tennis, was born in Philadelphia. Many of the details of her life are sketchy, but most tennis historians are con-vinced that she was responsible for introducing the sport to the United States. As the story goes, Outerbridge took a trip to Bermuda to visit some relatives in January 1874. While there she witnessed a strange new game—known as lawn tennis—being played by some British officers stationed on the island. Outerbridge, a smart, athletic young woman, was so intrigued by the sport that she visited the regimental store and bought the supplies necessary for practicing at home—nets, rackets, and balls. She packed up her gear and set sail for New York on the SS *Camina* at the end of January.

Outerbridge thought it would be nice to play the new sport with some of her friends at the Staten Island Cricket and Baseball Club. It wasn't long, however, before tennis was embraced nationwide with a loyalty that bor-dered on fanaticism. Within 13 years the first

U.S. championships were held, and the game's popularity grew with each passing year.

Whether Outerbridge deserves credit for any of this is open to debate. As tennis historian Bud Collins noted in his book *Bud Collins' Modern Encyclopedia of Tennis*, while there is much evidence suggesting that tennis was indeed introduced to the United States in 1874, the first documented game was played in Arizona, not Staten Island. Indeed, the story of Mary Outerbridge seems to be the stuff of folklore. Her life was shrouded in mystery, and her contributions to the sport beyond introducing it to the Staten Island Cricket and Baseball Club are virtually unknown. Outerbridge detractors argue that tennis was not patented until February 23, 1874, meaning that it would have been impossible for Outerbridge to purchase equipment and carry it home a full month earlier.

But Outerbridge apparently has more fans than critics, for in 1981, nearly a century after her death, she was inducted into the International Tennis Hall of Fame in Newport, Rhode Island. A brief biographical sketch provided by the Hall of Fame states that Mary Ewing Outerbridge was the mother of American tennis.

Accomplishments

Introduced the sport of tennis to the United States: 1874
Inducted into the International Tennis Hall of Fame: 1981

Sarah Palfrey

September 18, 1912–February 27, 1996

A two-time U.S. singles champion in tennis, Sarah Palfrey was the fourth of six children. Her father was John G. Palfrey, a prominent Boston lawyer; her mother, Methyl Gertrude Oakes, played tennis and golf at Smith College. Sarah and her sisters were barely walking when they started playing tennis on the private clay court located on the

family's farm in Sharon, Massachusetts. When the Palfreys moved to Brookline, just outside Boston, the girls took lessons at the Longwood Cricket Club from Hazel Hotchkiss Wightman. Each of the five Palfrey girls captured at least one national junior title. "Mrs. Wightman's tennis knowledge was instinctive," Sarah has said. "It came to me, from her mind to my mind."

Sarah Palfrey captained the field hockey team at the Windsor School in Brookline, but tennis remained her true love. She won 39 titles in her career, including a record three consecutive 18-and-under championships. She was a member of the U.S. Wightman Cup team for a decade, starting at the age of 17.

Palfrey was a crowd favorite. At 5 feet 3 inches tall, and with delicate features, she appeared frail on the court. But that was merely an illusion. While smaller tennis players typically rely on a steady baseline game, Palfrey preferred to attack the net. In fact, she was one of the great serve-and-volley players of her time. So adept was she at the net that most of the game's best players solicited her services as a doubles partner; between 1930 and 1941 she captured 13 national women's and mixed doubles titles. She often teamed up with Alice Marble—for four years the two women went unbeaten in doubles competition.

Palfrey was a serious competitor who gave no quarter. At the same time, she was dignified in both victory and defeat, a trait that led *New York Times* tennis columnist Allison Danzig to write, "Sportsmanship has had no truer exemplar than the slip of a Boston blueblood who fought unrelentingly to win, but never at all costs, and ever mindful that it was a game."

Palfrey married Elwood Cooke, another successful tennis player, in 1940. The marriage ended in divorce, but for a time it proved beneficial to Palfrey's tennis game. Cooke tutored his wife, working with her on aspects of her game that needed refining. In 1941, at the age of 28, Palfrey scored a hat trick at the U.S championships. She defeated Pauline Betz for the women's singles title, teamed up with Margaret Osborne for the women's doubles title, and captured the mixed doubles title with Jack Kramer.

Palfrey retired from competitive tennis that same year to raise a family. But she could not stay away from the game. In 1945, by then a 32-year-old mother, Palfrey won her second U.S.

Memorable Moment:
July 22, 1984

Kathy Whitworth Becomes Golf's Biggest Winner

Something about chasing records brings out the best and the worst in a professional athlete. The scrutiny that naturally accompanies such actions can be overwhelming, and one's ability to deal with that pressure reveals as much about the person as any athletic accomplishment. Kathy Whitworth's march through the record books was conducted with style and dignity. In 1982, at the Brookfield West Country Club near Atlanta, Georgia, she broke Mickey Wright's Ladies Professional Golf Association record of 82 career victories. In 1983, at the Women's Kemper Open, Whitworth sank a 40-foot putt on the final hole to tie Sam Snead's record of 84 career victories. For the next year, she dealt with the almost unbearable pressure of eclipsing a legend.

"If I think about it too much, I'll blow it," Whitworth said at the time. "Even the press is getting real quiet about it, I notice. It feels a little funny."

On July 22, 1984, in Rochester, New York, the record watch finally came to an end. Whitworth won the Rochester International for her 85th career victory. No man or woman had ever won that many sanctioned events. Whitworth later won three more tournaments, and her record still stands.

singles title, again defeating Pauline Betz. After that tournament Palfrey stepped away from competitive tennis for good. In 1963 she was inducted into the International Tennis Hall of Fame.

Accomplishments

U.S. Open champion: 1941, 1945
U.S. Open runner-up: 1934–1935
Won 13 national doubles titles

Sandra Palmer

Born March 10, 1941

Born in Fort Worth, Texas, Sandra Palmer became one of the most consistent and enduring performers on the Ladies Professional Golf Association circuit. When she burst upon the scene in the mid-1960s, the media seized upon the fact that her last name was identical to that of one of the greatest male golfers in history—"The Palmer in golf is no longer Arnie," noted *Sport* magazine.

Palmer began playing golf at the age of 13 when she worked as a caddie at a course in Maine. She felt comfortable with the game, saving the money she earned from caddying to buy her first set of clubs, and she was serious from the start. It became an emotional and physical outlet, and she gave herself to it entirely.

"I don't have any secrets," Palmer has said of her own success. "I just love to work hard."

Her hard work first paid off with four West Texas Amateur titles. After graduating from high school Palmer attended the University of North Texas (where she received a degree in education). In 1961 she finished second in the National Collegiate Championships, and two years later she captured the Texas State Amateur. In 1964, after working for a year as a high school biology and physical education teacher, she joined the LPGA tour.

In her first seven years on the tour, Palmer failed to win a tournament. She made a decent living but was unable to reach the top of the leader board. Then, in 1971, she broke through with victories at the Sealy Classic and Heritage Open. She finished fourth on the LPGA money list with $34,035.

The next year, Palmer won her first major tournament, the Titleholders Championship. In 1973 she won five tournaments and climbed to No. 3 on the money list. In 1975 she reached the No. 1 spot with victories at the Colgate Dinah Shore Winner's Circle and the U.S. Women's Open. Palmer's scoring average that year was 72.72, the second best of her career. She won three tournaments in 1976 and two in

1977. That ended an impressive seven-year run in which she managed to win at least two events per season.

At only 5 feet 1½ inches tall, Palmer lacked the power or leverage typically associated with the game's best players. But her timing and coordination were flawless, and her work ethic was incomparable. Although she never again led the LPGA money list, Palmer became a fixture on the tour. In 1986, at the age of 45, she had one of her finest seasons, winning $148,000 and recording a career-best scoring average of 72.71. She was inducted into the Texas State Golf Hall of Fame in 1985 and the National Collegiate Hall of Fame in 1988.

Accomplishments

Titleholders champion: 1972
U.S. Women's Open champion: 1975
Leading money winner on LPGA tour: 1975
Inducted into National Collegiate Hall of Fame: 1988

Dottie Pepper

Born August 17, 1965

Dottie Pepper, one of the most successful players on the Ladies Professional Golf Association tour, was born in Saratoga Springs, New York. Her father, Don Pepper, was a professional baseball player with the Detroit Tigers. Although he spent little time in the majors, he was a talented and competitive athlete whose love for sports was passed on to his daughter. Dottie was a gifted golfer who played on the boys team at Saratoga High School. She could hit the ball off the tee as far as any of them and had a smoother touch on the greens. Her weakness was her temper—she occasionally threw her clubs around the course in disgust. Her burning desire for perfection would both sustain and trouble her throughout her career.

In 1981 Dottie Pepper captured the New York State Amateur title at the age of 16. The following year she was runner-up in the PGA National Junior tournament. In 1983 she was a quarterfinalist at the United States Golf Association Junior Girls Championship. In 1981 and 1983 she was New York Junior Amateur

champion. All of these accomplishments came before she graduated from high school.

At Furman University, Pepper was one of the best collegiate players in the country. She was twice named the school's Female Athlete of the Year and in 1987 was named Athlete of the Year. She was a three-time NCAA All-American and a runner-up at the NCAA championships in 1985. In 1987 she finished fourth in individual scoring, while leading Furman to a second-place finish in the team championship. While at Furman, Pepper was low amateur at the 1984 U.S. Women's Open.

As a rookie on the LPGA tour in 1989, Pepper won more than $137,000 and finished in the top 10 at seven tournaments. She won her first tournament in 1989, the Oldsmobile LPGA Classic, where she defeated Beth Daniel in a five-hole playoff. In 1990 Pepper missed a month of competition because of a torn rotator cuff but still managed to win more than $230,000. Her best year on the tour was 1992, when she not only won her first major tournament, the Nabisco Dinah Shore, but also accumulated $693,335 in prize money, tops on the LPGA tour. She won the Vare Trophy as the player with the lowest scoring average on the tour and was named LPGA Player of the Year.

In 1993 Pepper won the World Championship of Women's Golf, her seventh title. She finished fourth on the LPGA money list with $429,118 and passed the $2 million mark in career earnings. In 1994 she finished third on the money list, and in 1995, despite going through a divorce from her husband, Doug Mochrie, a club professional who had been her caddie and mentor, she won more than $750,000, including a record $290,000 at the LPGA Skins Game.

"I took it as a real career motivation to put the past behind me and dig into my career even more," Pepper said of her divorce. "I know that this is what I'm going to do until I fall over. I'm either going to get into the [LPGA] Hall of Fame or die trying."

Pepper won four tournaments and more than $600,000 in 1996.

Accomplishments

New York State Amateur champion: 1981
Low amateur, U.S. Women's Open: 1984

Nabisco Dinah Shore champion: 1992
LPGA Player of the Year: 1992
Vare Trophy winner: 1992
LPGA Skins Game winner: 1995

Mary Jo Peppler

Born 1940

Mary Jo Peppler, the first great American female volleyball player, was born in Rockford, Illinois, and grew up in Long Beach, California. As a senior in high school she was talented enough to earn a spot on the Long Beach Shamrocks, an amateur volleyball team that captured the national championship. When her parents moved to San Francisco, Peppler chose to stay behind, for Southern California was the hub of the American volleyball scene. She supported herself by, among other things, selling encyclopedias, but she felt that the sacrifices were necessary in order to develop her athletic skills.

In 1964, 6-foot, 155-pound Peppler helped form the Los Angeles Renegades, who won a national title. She represented the United States at the Summer Olympic Games, and four years later she again qualified for the U.S. Olympic team. In 1970 she joined the U.S. national team on an international tour and also competed at the world championships in Bulgaria. The U.S. team finished 11th that year. Nevertheless, there was no mistaking Peppler's talent. She was a dominant player, graceful, athletic, and extremely competitive. Although her team had a disappointing showing, Peppler was named the tournament's outstanding player.

Peppler moved to Houston, Texas, and in 1972 formed another volleyball team—E Pluribus Unum. Peppler was the star player and coach of the team, which captured the national championship in 1972 and 1973. In 1974 the International Volleyball Association was formed. The league represented the first attempt to bring professional coed volleyball to the United States. Each team had four male players and two female players. Peppler signed with El Paso-Juarez, but the league collapsed after a single season.

For all of her talent, Peppler was not one of the most popular players in the game. Her out-

spokenness and independence of mind sometimes got her in trouble. In 1976 the director of the U.S. Volleyball Association informed Peppler that she would not be welcome on the U.S. Olympic team, despite the fact that she was among the best players in the world.

That same year, Peppler turned her attention to another form of athletic competition. She participated in the first *Women's Superstars*, a made-for-TV event featuring athletes from various disciplines competing against each other. The format had succeeded with male athletes, which prompted the ABC television network to offer a similar production for women. The inaugural field included tennis pro Billie Jean King, diver Micki King, gymnast Cathy Rigby, and basketball player Karen Logan. None was any match for Peppler, who walked away with the unofficial title of "world's greatest female athlete," along with almost $50,000 in prize money.

"Women have things we can receive from sport as well as give to it that are different from what men offer and receive," Peppler said. "Finesse and a striving for performance, as opposed to strength and aggressiveness."

Accomplishments

Member of U.S. Olympic volleyball team:
    1964, 1968
MVP of world championships: 1970
Winner of first *Women's Superstars*
    competition: 1976
Player-coach for national champions:
    1972–1973

Marie-Jose Perec

Born May 9, 1968

Marie-Jose Perec, a gifted and graceful runner who won two gold medals at the 1996 Summer Olympics in Atlanta, was born in Guadeloupe and raised by her grandmother after her parents divorced. At the age of 14, Perec was timed by a French track coach during a 200-meter race; to his amazement, she ran fast enough to qualify for the French national team. Not long after that Perec moved to Paris to train and attend school.

Nearly 6 feet tall, Perec combines a long, smooth stride with natural speed—traits that permit her to excel in several events, including the 200 meters, 400 meters, and 400-meter hurdles. Her nickname is La Gazelle. Perec became a national hero in France after winning the 400 meters at the 1991 World Track and Field Championships and at the 1992 Summer Olympics in Barcelona. But two years later she had a falling out with French national team coach Jacques Piasenta over her failure to compete in the European indoor championships.

Perec wound up in Los Angeles, where she began training with John Smith, a former Olympic 400-meter runner and one of the most highly regarded track-and-field coaches. "He has a way of approaching things that is much more positive than I was used to," Perec told the *New York Times* in 1996. "He puts my goals very, very high, and it's worked."

Perec was one of the biggest stars of the 1996 Summer Olympics. In the weeks leading up to the Atlanta Games, much talk centered around Michael Johnson's plan to become the first male sprinter to win the 200 and 400 meters in a single Olympics. But on the night that Johnson completed his historic double, he had to share the stage with Perec.

Like Johnson, Perec had won the 400 earlier in the week. Her time of 48.25 seconds was an Olympic record and the third fastest women's 400 ever run. On August 1 she was on the starting line again, awaiting the gun that would signal the beginning of the women's 200-meter final. Although a bit slow out of the blocks, Perec rallied quickly and ran down Jamaica's Merlene Ottey in the stretch to win the race in 22.12 seconds.

Not since Valerie Brisco in 1984 had a woman swept the 200 and 400 meters in a single Olympiad, and never had it been done under such competitive conditions—in 1984 the Soviet boycott had limited the competition at the Los Angeles Games. Perec beat the world's best in both the 200 and 400, and secured a place in history. Right next to Michael Johnson.

Accomplishments

Olympic gold medalist, 400 meters: 1992, 1996
Olympic gold medalist, 200 meters: 1996
World champion, 400 meters: 1991

Mary Peters

Born July 6, 1939

Olympic gold medalist Mary Peters was born at Halewood, Great Britain. She was a consistent athlete who spent a large portion of her career toiling in the shadow of Great Britain's Mary Rand, who in 1964 became the first British woman to win an Olympic gold medal in track and field. It took the better part of two decades for Peters to receive the credit and respect she had deserved all along.

Peters was 29 years old when she finished eighth in the pentathlon at the 1968 Summer Olympics in Mexico City. After the Games, Peters decided to take a year off in the hope that she would not only recuperate from a variety of nagging injuries but also recapture some of the enthusiasm that had been drained through years of competition.

In 1970, at the Commonwealth Games, Peters captured gold medals for Northern Ireland in the shot put and pentathlon. Her score of 4,524 points firmly established that she was, once again, one of the finest pentathletes in the world. She skipped competing in 1971, just as she had in 1969, and again the rest period rejuvenated her. In 1972 she concentrated on the high jump for the first time, and her improvement in that event helped elevate her point total in the pentathlon. She set a United Kingdom record of 4,630 points in pre-Olympic qualifying and was one of the favorites heading into the Summer Games in Munich.

At age 33, Peters became one of the stars of the Olympic Games. In the first event, the 100-meter hurdles, she clocked 13.3 seconds, the fastest time she had ever run. In the second event, the shot put, she nearly broke her own UK record with a toss of 16.20 meters. In the last event on the first day of competition she set another personal best by clearing 1.82 meters in the high jump. She had 2,969 points, at the time the highest first-day score ever recorded, and a comfortable lead of 97 points.

Peters was not nearly as dominant on the second day, because West Germany's Heide Rosendahl was equally brilliant. Peters needed a superb long jump and a personal best of 24.1 in the 200 meters to hold off Rosendahl and win the gold medal in track and field. She finished with a world-record score of 4,801 points, 10 points better than Rosendahl.

In finishing first, Peters became the third woman from Great Britain to win an Olympic gold medal in track and field. The others were Mary Rand and Ann Packer, a gold medalist at the 800 meters in the 1964 Games in Tokyo.

Accomplishments

Olympic gold medalist, pentathlon: 1972
Set world record in pentathlon: 1972
Commonwealth Games gold medalist,
    pentathlon: 1971
Commonwealth Games gold medalist, shot
    put: 1971

Mary Pierce

Born January 15, 1975

Mary Pierce overcame a distressing family situation to become one of the most promising young players on the Women's Tennis Association tour.

Born in Montreal, Canada, and raised in Florida, Mary, like many tennis professionals, began playing when she was in grade school. Her mentor was her father, Jim, who pulled her out of school in the sixth grade so that she could devote her time to training. The entire family—Jim, his wife, Yannick, and Mary's brother, David—became devoted to Mary's career. They traveled to tournaments as a group, giving the appearance of a healthy, nurturing family.

Jim Pierce worked his daughter furiously, sometimes as much as eight hours a day, even though she was barely in her teens. Occasionally he'd bring in another coach to help with specific aspects of her game, but he was the primary coach. Mary, tall and lean, with a strong, sure groundstroke, developed quickly. She turned professional in March 1989, just a few months after her 14th birthday. She made her debut in a tournament on Hilton Head Island, South Carolina, becoming the youngest American ever to play a professional event (her record was later broken by Jennifer Capriati).

The media viewed Mary Pierce as a prodigy, a girl with a spectacular gift. But she longed for a more common way of life. "I would like to have stayed in school and gone to a prom," she later told a reporter.

Instead, Pierce lived the nomadic life of a budding tennis star. In 1990, while living in Paris, she played in her first Grand Slam event—the French Open. She lost in the second round

but learned from the experience. The next year she reached the third round and in 1992 advanced to the fourth round of the U.S. Open. That same year she received France's Burgeon (Rising Star) Award, as well as the WTA's Most Improved Player Award.

Despite her success on the court, Pierce was an unhappy, troubled young woman. In July 1993 she filed for a restraining order against her father to prevent him from having anything to do with her life or career. She claimed that Jim Pierce, a convicted felon, had physically and emotionally abused her. Her accusations were supported by her mother and brother, and by witnesses who described Jim Pierce's violent behavior at matches. That same year the Women's Tennis Council barred Jim Pierce from attending any events on the women's tour.

Many observers believed that Mary Pierce would blossom once she distanced herself from her father, and that was precisely what happened. By the end of 1993, Pierce had moved up to No. 12 in the WTA rankings; at the end of 1994 she was No. 5. She reached the quarterfinals of the U.S. Open in 1994 and the final of the French Open, where she lost to Arantxa Sanchez Vicario, 6–4, 6–4. In 1995 she won the Australian Open, her first Grand Slam singles title, and finished the year as the fifth-ranked player in the world. In 1996 she fell to No. 34.

Accomplishments

Winner of WTA's Most Improved Player
    Award: 1992
Winner of France's Burgeon Award: 1992
Member of French Olympic team: 1992
French Open finalist: 1994
Australian Open champion: 1995

Memorable Moment:
August 5, 1984

Joan Benoit Wins the First Olympic Women's Marathon

Prior to 1984, female long-distance runners had been largely protected, pampered, and treated with condescension during the Olympic Games. They were not allowed to compete at any distance beyond 3,000 meters because, popular sentiment held, women weren't "meant" to run that far.

But at the 1984 Los Angeles Games all of that changed. For the first time, an Olympic women's marathon was held. It began on a hot, humid morning at Santa Monica College, and featured many of the greatest female distance runners in history—Ingrid Kristiansen, Grete Waitz, Rosa Mota...and Joan Benoit. As an American, Benoit was the crowd favorite, but there was considerable doubt as to whether she could win. She had undergone arthroscopic surgery on her knee prior to the U.S. Olympic Trials, and her conditioning was suspect. But Benoit, one of the toughest athletes her sport has ever known, decided that the best way to win the most important marathon of her life was to take control early. By three miles she had a 20-yard lead; by 12 miles the race was over. Smiling and waving her cap, Benoit entered the Los Angeles Coliseum to thunderous applause from a crowd of 77,000; it was one of the most intensely emotional moments of the Games, validating not only Benoit's performance, but the efforts of female athletes everywhere.

Uta Pippig

Born 1965

Marathon runner Uta Pippig, who emerged as one of the best in her sport with victories at Boston and New York in the mid-1990s, was born in East Berlin, Germany. She felt the restrictions that came with growing up in a Communist country; she also had a strict upbringing. "I did not develop much self-confidence during my childhood," Pippig said. "At our East German youth sports festival one year, I won 10 gold medals and one silver. And my father was angry about the silver. It was the same with my accomplishments in school."

Not only was she a swift and courageous runner, Pippig was also a top-notch student. For many years she was content to have the terms of her athletic career dictated by the East German athletic federation while she pursued a degree in medicine. Her goal was to become a pediatrician.

But Pippig's life changed with the crumbling of the Berlin Wall. On January 5, 1990, she walked through the rubble of the old border between East and West with her coach and companion, Dieter Hogan. Together they established residency in a small town near Stuttgart and began their new life. Pippig transferred to the school of medicine at the University of Tubingen, and became one of the most successful and popular marathon runners in the world. When she showed up in Boston a few months later for the annual marathon, she charmed the media and the spectators. She could speak barely a word of English, but the joy she felt at being free to compete as she pleased and to reap the benefits of her work came through loud and clear.

"Over the years, the desire for victory became more strongly ingrained in me," Pippig said. "It seeps eventually into your flesh and bones. What for many people would be a horror—to compete this hard—is something totally positive, something that makes me happy."

Pippig had run 10 marathons prior to Boston and had a personal best of 2:30.56. She had also run a respectable 32:40 on the track for 10 kilometers. In the 1990 Boston Marathon she shaved more than two minutes off her previous best, finishing in 2:28.03. But she was no match for Portugal's Rosa Mota, who won the race in 2:25.24. In 1993 Pippig finished first in the New York City Marathon with a time of 2:26.24. In 1994 she won the Boston Marathon with a course-record time of 2:21.45.

Accomplishments

New York City Marathon champion: 1993
Boston Marathon champion: 1994

Pam Postema

Born 1954

Pam Postema, one of the first women to work as a full-time umpire in men's professional baseball, grew up in Willard, Ohio. Her father, Philip, was a farmer; her mother, Phyllis, a housewife. The youngest of three children, Pam developed an affection and aptitude for sports when she was a schoolgirl. Hardball, rather than softball, was her game. Her parents and siblings encouraged her to play whatever she wanted. Her brother, Todd, remembers playing some spirited games of catch in the family's backyard. "She used to throw her hardest and try to burn me," Todd Postema said. "It stung, but I'd never say anything. When I burned it in to her, she'd never say anything either."

While visiting her sister in Florida in 1976, Pam Postema heard about the Al Somers Umpiring School in Daytona Beach. Postema, who had never shaken off her fascination with the sport, applied for acceptance. Somers at first turned her down, explaining that his school had never taken a woman; there were no women's locker rooms, no ladies' restrooms. But the rejection only served to make her more determined than ever. Postema wrote a letter to Somers. Among other things, she told him not to be concerned about the bathroom situation. "Don't worry," she wrote. "I have strong kidneys."

Somers relented, and six weeks after her arrival in Daytona Beach, Postema graduated from the school and quickly found work in the Gulf Coast League. Her pay was $550 per month. It was six years before she received a promotion to the Triple-A Pacific Coast League. At that point she was just one step away from the big leagues. She worked as hard as any umpire, working games in Puerto Rico and Colombia during the winter—there she endured threats, insults, and even physical abuse (fans occasionally hurled objects at her).

"It was tough," Postema said. "I really didn't have anyone to confide in. The attitude of the other umpires was, 'If you have to, work with her, but don't help her. Don't make it easy.'"

Despite the obstacles, Postema continued to improve and advance. She worked the Hall of Fame Game in Cooperstown in 1989, and numerous spring training games in 1988 and 1989. Late in 1989, however, Postema was denied a promotion to the major leagues—instead, two men were promoted. After working more than 2,000 games over 13 seasons, Postema was dismissed from her job. An evaluation report by the leagues' Office for Umpire Development stated that her work had deteriorated. This came as a shock to Postema, who only a few months earlier had been rated "better than average" by the same organization.

Postema filed a sex discrimination lawsuit against professional baseball and demanded the first available opening. But as of 1995, neither Postema nor any other female umpire has made it to the major leagues. In 1992 Postema published her autobiography, *You've Got to Have Balls to Make It in This League.*

Accomplishments

Worked as umpire at Baseball Hall of Fame Game: 1988
Worked National League spring training games: 1988–1989

Dorothy Poynton

Born July 17, 1915

Dorothy Poynton, a member of the International Swimming Hall of Fame, was born in Salt Lake City, Utah, and grew up in Portland, Oregon. As a youngster, her interests were divided between dancing and diving; in both endeavors she was a prodigy. Dorothy had an opportunity to dance professionally, but her school's board of education, concerned about the class time she would miss, insisted that her parents hire a private tutor.

The Poyntons responded by moving out of town. They settled in Los Angeles, where seven-year-old Dorothy performed diving and dancing exhibitions at the Ambassador Hotel. "We really packed them in," Poynton later recalled. "We had all kinds of gag acts. They used to put me in this sack and drop me off the 10-foot board. Everyone was sitting there wondering how that little girl was going to get out of that big sack. They didn't know the bag had snaps on the side. Sometimes people would actually jump into the pool to save me."

But Poynton didn't need any help. She was a gifted, confident swimmer and diver. She eventually worked out at the Hollywood Athletic Club, where she benefited from first-rate coaching and training facilities. When she was 12 she finished second in diving at the junior nationals. One year later she traveled to New York to compete in the Olympic trials and qualified for the U.S. team. She was just 13 years old when she boarded a ship for Amsterdam, site of the 1928 Summer Olympic Games. It was a thrilling but difficult experience for Poynton, who was both excited and homesick.

Poynton won a bronze medal in the springboard event. At the time she was the youngest American ever to win an Olympic medal. Four years later, at the 1932 Olympics in Los Angeles, Poynton won a gold medal in platform diving. As she gained strength, if not size (she was only 5 feet tall), she took on that event as her specialty. She won three consecutive national championships in platform diving and never lost a meet.

After her success at the 1932 Games, Poynton had many offers to turn professional. But she was still young—just 17—and she wanted to see how much she could accomplish as an amateur athlete. She trained for four more years, preparing for another trip to the Olympics. Poynton qualified for the 1936 U.S. Olympic team in the springboard and platform competition. She took a bronze in the former and her second consecutive gold in the latter. She remains one of only three women to win four Olympic medals in diving and one of only two to win diving medals in three different Olympiads.

After leaving the sport, Poynton opened a swimming club in West Los Angeles.

Accomplishments

Olympic bronze medalist, springboard diving:
1928, 1936
Olympic gold medalist, platform diving: 1932,
1936
U.S. champion, platform diving: 1933–1935
Member of International Swimming Hall of
Fame

Ana Quirot

Born 1963

Ana Fidelia Quirot, one of Cuba's best runners, was born in Oriente, the same province that was home to Fidel Castro. She was an athletic child who, for a time, had trouble with her weight, which prompted other kids to taunt her with the nickname Gorda ("Fatty"). Eventually, however, her pounds melted away, leaving Quirot with a strong, sleek body ideally suited for competing in track and field.

Even as Quirot developed into the world's fastest runner at the 400 and 800 meters—winning, during one incredible stretch, 39 consecutive races—she remained unknown outside of Cuba. She was too young to compete in the 1980 Olympics. Four years later, when she was emerging as one of the finest runners in the world, Cuba took part in the Soviet boycott of the Summer Games in Los Angeles. Then, in 1988, when the Olympics were held in Seoul, South Korea, Castro ordered another boycott; Quirot, by then 25 years old and approaching her physical peak, was again left to wonder about what might have been. But she expressed no bitterness about Castro's decisions; in fact, she remained one of his most vocal and loyal supporters.

In 1989 Quirot had her greatest season, winning every race she entered. Both the International Amateur Athletic Federation and

Track & Field News selected her as their Female Athlete of the Year. Two years later, at the Pan American Games, she won gold medals in the 400 and 800 meters, setting Pan American Games records in both events. By 1992 Quirot was no longer the fastest 800-meter female runner in the world, but she was still talented and determined enough to make the most of her first Olympic opportunity. She finished third in the 800 at the Barcelona Games; her time of 1:56.8 was more than two seconds off her personal best. But finally she had an Olympic medal. Quirot later discovered that she was several weeks pregnant when she had raced in Barcelona.

Her baby, fathered by Cuban high jumper Javier Sotomayor, was never born. On January 23, 1993, Quirot was seriously injured when a kerosene stove in her home ignited. Third-degree burns covered nearly 40 percent of her body. She survived, but her baby did not. Afterward, rumors about Quirot swept the country, including one that said the accident was a suicide attempt by Quirot, who was supposedly despondent over her breakup with Sotomayor.

"When you're famous, people are always speculating," Quirot said in an interview. "And never in your favor. Sometimes it's good to be famous. Sometimes it's bad."

After seven operations and many months of rehabilitation, Quirot returned to her sport. In late 1993 she finished second in the 800 meters at the Central American and Caribbean Games in Puerto Rico. Her time was comparatively slow—2:05.22—but the performance was perhaps the greatest of her career. "I couldn't tilt my head to the side or up; I looked like a robot," Quirot said. "But a lot of people didn't expect me to run again."

Two years later Quirot took another remarkable step in her comeback by winning the 800 meters at the World Track and Field Championships in Göteborg, Sweden. In 1996, at the Summer Olympics in Atlanta, she won a silver medal in the 800 meters.

Accomplishments

Track & Field News Female Athlete of the Year:
1989
IAAF Female Athlete of the Year: 1989

Once won 39 consecutive races
Olympic bronze medalist, 800 meters: 1992
World champion, 800 meters: 1995
Olympic silver medalist, 800 meters: 1996

Mary Rand

Born February 10, 1940

Mary Rand, the first British woman to win an Olympic gold medal, was born Mary Bignal in Somerset, England. She set her first national record in the pentathlon in 1957 when she was 17 years old, with a score of 4,047 points. The following year she not only won a silver medal in the long jump at the Commonwealth Games, but also finished seventh in the pentathlon at the European championships—a respectable performance considering her age. Because the event is so physically demanding, pentathletes typically peak later than most track-and-field athletes.

Rand qualified for the British Olympic team in 1960. In the trials of the long jump, she set a United Kingdom record of 6.33 meters in the qualifying rounds but inexplicably fell apart in the finals, where she finished ninth. Rand will be remembered as a clutch performer who held up well under pressure, but she acknowledged in 1960 that nervousness had led to her collapse in the long jump. Finishing fourth in the hurdles did little to soothe her damaged ego.

In 1962, only a few months after the birth of her first child, Rand returned to competition. She surprised many people by winning a bronze medal in the long jump at the European championships that year; the following year she helped Great Britain set a world record in a relay event.

"The greatest thing of all would be to do a world record at the Olympics," Rand said on the eve of the 1964 Summer Games in Tokyo. "That would be wonderful."

Not long after issuing that statement, Rand traveled to Tokyo and turned in one of the most astounding performances in the history of women's long jumping. All of her jumps were nearly flawless; each was long enough to win most international competitions. In the end she walked off not only with a gold medal, but also with a world record (6.76 meters). By the time the Games had ended, Rand had two more medals dangling from her neck. The first, a silver, came in the pentathlon, in which her 5,035 points were the second highest total ever recorded. She also helped lead Great Britain to a bronze medal in the 4 x 100 relay.

Two years after her Olympic triumphs, Rand finished first in the long jump at the Commonwealth Games. Injuries began to take their toll, however, and she failed to make the British Olympic team in 1968. She retired from the sport and in 1969 married for the second time, to American decathlete Bill Toomey.

Accomplishments

Olympic gold medalist, long jump: 1964
Olympic silver medalist, pentathlon: 1964
Olympic bronze medalist, 4 x 100 relay: 1964
Commonwealth Games long jump champion: 1966

Judy Rankin

Born February 18, 1945

Judy Rankin, the first woman golfer to earn more than $100,000 in a single year, was born Judy Torluemke in St. Louis, Missouri. She began playing golf at the age of six, taking lessons from her father, Paul. She displayed a natural aptitude for the game and developed quickly; the first time she kept score she needed only 84 shots to complete nine holes. Judy was graceful, and blessed with exceptional hand-eye coordination. Two years later she won the first of many titles, finishing first in a national peewee golf tournament.

There have been many firsts in Judy's career, including a victory in the 1959 Missouri Amateur when she was 14 years old. No one had ever won that tournament at such a young age; as of 1995 her record still stands. In 1960, at the

U.S. Women's Open at Worcester Country Club in Worcester, Massachusetts, she finished as the low amateur. In 1960 and 1961 she was a semifinalist at the United States Golf Association Girls' Championship. In 1961 she won the Missouri Amateur for the second time.

Judy was only 17 when she joined the Ladies Professional Golf Association tour in 1962. Her first few years were difficult, but by 1965 she was a top-five player and capable of earning a comfortable living. She won her first LPGA tour event, the Corpus Christi Open, in 1968, a year after marrying Yippy Rankin. She failed to win a tournament in 1969, but finished 14th on the money list. Over the next decade, Judy Rankin was one of the most consistent players on the tour, winning at least one tournament each season. In 1976 she was named Player of the Year and accumulated $150,734 to become the first woman to crack the $100,000 mark for a single season; she did it again the following year, winning $122,890. In 1977 she won the Vare Trophy as the player with the lowest average score on the tour and was again named Player of the Year.

On the tour Rankin traveled with her husband and her son, Tuey. Their support, she often said, made it possible for her to succeed as a professional athlete. "If you were to ask what's most important in my life," she said, "I'd have to rank golf well behind my other careers as mother and wife."

Rankin succeeded Carol Mann as LPGA president in 1976 and later served on the board of directors. She recorded the last of her 26 tour victories in 1979. Chronic back problems prevented her from touring full-time after 1983. She underwent back surgery in 1985 and later pursued a career in broadcast journalism. Rankin was inducted into the All-American Collegiate Golf Hall of Fame in 1993.

Accomplishments

First LPGA player to win more than $100,000
  in a season: 1976
LPGA Player of the Year: 1976–1977
Vare Trophy winner: 1973, 1976–1977
Inducted into All-American Collegiate Golf
  Hall of Fame: 1993

Betsy Rawls

Born May 4, 1928

Elizabeth Earle Rawls, a member of the Ladies Professional Golf Association Hall of Fame, was born in Spartanburg, South Carolina. She first picked up a golf club when she was 17 years old. Four years later, after studying under legendary teacher and pro Harvey Penick, Rawls won the 1949 Texas Amateur. "Starting later allows you to progress faster, I think," Rawls said. "But if you have the chance, it's better to start young. If I had it to do over, I'd get started at about 10, 11, or 12. You develop a more natural swing if you start as a kid."

Rawls grew up in rural Texas. She was introduced to the game by her father and took to it with ease. She was a competitive and strong-willed young woman who brought a logical, intellectual approach to the game. Rawls graduated Phi Beta Kappa from the University of Texas with a combined degree in math and physics. But she did not play golf in college, because at that time the Southwest Conference had no intercollegiate sports for women.

Rawls joined the LPGA tour in 1951 and won three tournaments, including the U.S. Women's Open. The following year she won the Western Open, and in 1953 she won a second U.S. Women's Open title. In all Rawls won eight majors. The most publicized victory of her career came in 1957, when she won the third of her four U.S. Women's Open championships. That year Rawls actually finished second to Jackie Pung; however, Pung accidentally signed an incorrect scorecard and was disqualified from the tournament, thus allowing Rawls to enter the winner's circle again.

Rawls went on to win the Open again in 1961, and she achieved LPGA championships at the end of consecutive decades—in 1959 and 1969. Competing regularly against such legends as Mickey Wright, Kathy Whitworth, Patty Berg, Louise Suggs, and Babe Didrikson Zaharias, Rawls amassed 55 career victories, third on the all-time list. In 1960, at the age of 32, and only 15 years after she began playing golf, she was inducted into the LPGA Hall of Fame.

Memorable Moment: March 1985

Libby Riddles Becomes the First Woman to Win the Iditarod

The defining moment of Libby Riddles' athletic life came with 300 miles to go in the 1985 Iditarod Trail Sled Dog Race. As her competitors safely slept in the Eskimo village of Shaktoolik while a blizzard raged, Riddles ducked out into the frigid night air. It was a move that was at once daring and foolish. The Iditarod attracts only the most experienced mushers in the world, and not one of them was willing to take a chance in a blizzard.

None except Riddles. "It's impossible," another musher told her. "You'll never make it."

Riddles didn't listen. She roused her team and set off. The weather was brutal—10 degrees, with winds gusting to 40 miles per hour. Visibility was only 25 feet. Riddles didn't care. She had competed in the Iditarod several times, but her highest previous finish was 18th. It was presumed that the honor of being the first woman to win the race would one day go to Susan Butcher, generally regarded as one of the best mushers in the sport—male or female.

After braving the elements for several hours, Riddles gave her dogs a rest. Before long, they were ready to continue. Her bold move had paid off. Riddles cruised into Nome, Alaska, 18 days after leaving Anchorage, and was accorded a hero's welcome.

In 1975 Rawls retired from competition. She was the LPGA's tournament director for six years, during which time the tour experienced unprecedented growth. She later became the first woman to serve on the rules committee of the men's U.S. Open. In 1981 Rawls left her LPGA position to become executive director of the McDonald's LPGA championship, which, under her guidance, became one of the most successful stops on the women's tour. "I look at the LPGA now, playing for $21 million, and I feel like I've had a hand in that," Rawls said. "That's very satisfying. I'd like for people to remember some of those contributions I've made to the game."

In 1986 Rawls was inducted into the International Women's Sports Hall of Fame, and in 1987 she was elected to the World Golf Hall of Fame.

Accomplishments

> U.S. Women's Open champion: 1951, 1953, 1957, 1960
> Western Open champion: 1952, 1959
> LPGA championship winner: 1959, 1969
> Inducted into LPGA Hall of Fame: 1960
> Inducted into International Women's Sports Hall of Fame: 1986

Katherine Rawls

June 14, 1918–April 8, 1982

Katherine Rawls, a member of the International Swimming Hall of Fame, won 28 U.S. national championships in springboard diving and swimming between 1931 and 1938. Born in Nashville, Tennessee, and raised in Florida, she began performing when she was barely in her teens. In 1931, at the age of 13, she won the 220-yard breast stroke competition at the outdoor national championships; that same year she finished second at the Amateur Athletic Union national platform diving championships. She won the 3-meter springboard title three consecutive times (1932 through 1934), and the 1-meter springboard title in 1933 and 1934.

Rawls defended her 220-yard breast stroke title in 1932 (she also won in 1935). She captured outdoor titles in the 440-yard freestyle (1937–1938), the 880-yard freestyle (1932, 1937, 1938), and the 300-meter medley relay (1934). In 1934 she won the 100-yard freestyle indoor championship. Rawls had her greatest success in the 300-meter individual medley. She won this event at the national championships seven times; she was the indoor champion in the 300-meter individual medley for six consecutive years, from 1933 through 1938.

Despite her remarkable accomplishments in the United States, Rawls never won an Olympic gold medal, although she did have her share of success in Olympic competition. She won silver medals in springboard diving at the 1932 and 1936 Games, and a bronze medal in the 4 x 100 freestyle relay in 1936.

After becoming the first woman to win four races at the national championships, Rawls was named Female Athlete of the Year by the Associated Press. She matched her accomplishment again in 1938, then retired in 1939 at age 21. She later married Theodore Thompson and, during World War II, became one of the first female pilots chosen by the Air Transport Command to ferry fighter planes into combat zones.

Accomplishments

Associated Press Female Athlete of the Year: 1937
Inducted into International Swimming Hall of Fame: 1965
Olympic silver medalist, springboard diving: 1932, 1936
Olympic bronze medalist, 4 x 100 relay: 1936
Winner of 28 national championships

Mary Lou Retton

Born January 24, 1968

Mary Lou Retton, the first American to win the all-around title in Olympic gymnastics competition, grew up in Fairmont, West Virginia, in a large athletic family. The youngest of five children, she had to fight for attention and defend herself from the occasional act of sibling terrorism. "I tell her she's got those muscular little legs because she'd do everything for everybody in the family," Mary Lou's mother told a reporter. "They'd say, 'Go get me this, go get me that,' or 'Run upstairs and do that.' She would just run errands for everybody—she was so easygoing. But her brothers would pick on her and fight with her and wrestle with her. It made her tough."

A beaming smile became Mary Lou's signature, but inside she was a fierce competitor. Her coach, Bela Karolyi, noted in his autobiography, "In the beginning I was a bit worried about one aspect of Mary Lou's personality. She was so easygoing in practice. She didn't seem too concerned about the final product, and I thought she might be careless in competitions. I was wrong. Mary Lou was one of the most ambitious gymnasts I have ever worked with. It was just that she had such a damn good disposition."

Mary Lou burst onto the scene unexpectedly in 1983. She had been working with Karolyi for only a few months when she traveled to New York's Madison Square Garden as an alternate for the America Cup meet. Just one day before the competition, an injury sidelined Dianne Durham; that opened the door for 15-year-old Mary Lou. No one knew much about Retton, but when the two-day event was over, she had earned scores of 9.9 or better in six out of eight events and had captured the all-around title. "It was the greatest shock of 1983," Karolyi said. "A complete unknown in the America Cup beating everyone else in the world."

Retton did not fit the typical gymnast's mold. Though she was short (4 feet 9 inches), she was exceptionally muscular. In fact, with her thick legs and square torso, she looked less like a gymnast than a miniature fullback. And her approach was more athletic than artistic. She attacked rather than caressed the equipment, and she took risks.

By the summer of 1984, at the Los Angeles Olympics, 16-year-old Retton was one of the favorites, particularly because the Soviet-led boycott prevented several top gymnasts from competing. Six weeks before the Games, Retton had arthroscopic surgery on her knee, but even that could not stop her. On August 3, 1984, a perfect 10 in the final event—the vault—lifted her past Ecaterina Szabo of Romania and gave her the all-around title. She also won silver medals in the vault and team competitions, and bronze medals in the uneven bars and the floor exercise.

Despite Retton's youth, she became a popular motivational speaker and was sought by advertisers. She was named Sportswoman of the Year by *Sports Illustrated* magazine in 1984 and also Associated Press Athlete of the Year. In 1993 she was inducted into the International Women's Sports Hall of Fame.

Accomplishments

Olympic gold medalist, all-around: 1984
Olympic silver medalist, vault: 1984

Olympic silver medalist, team: 1984
Olympic bronze medalist, floor exercise: 1984
Olympic bronze medalist, uneven bars: 1984
Associated Press Athlete of the Year: 1984
Inducted into International Women's Sports
    Hall of Fame: 1993

Manon Rheaume

Born 1973

Manon Rheaume was the first woman to play in a National Hockey League game. She was born in Lac Beauport, Quebec, and began skating at the age of three on a backyard rink built by her father, Pierre. Like many successful female athletes, Rheaume benefited from growing up in a sports-minded family that included a couple of boys. Older brother Martin and younger brother Pascal played hockey. The boys' favorite activity was to put their sister in the goal, cover her with pads, and fire shots at her for hours. The intent of the sessions was to improve the boys' offensive skills, but it was equally important to Manon, who became a tough little hockey player.

When she was five years old Manon asked to fill in as a goalie during one of her brothers' tournaments. Pierre was the coach; although he initially laughed at his daughter's request, he decided to give her a chance. From that moment on, Manon was like one of the boys. She proved herself at every level, eventually becoming the first girl to play at the Junior A level. Junior A hockey in Canada is highly competitive and just one step below the professional ranks. Manon played goalie for the Canadian National Women's Team, which won a gold medal at the 1992 world championships in Finland. She allowed just one goal in three games and was named the tournament's outstanding goalie.

Her dream was to play professionally. To do that she would have to overcome a significant amount of prejudice, not to mention her own physical shortcomings (she was just 5 feet 6 inches tall and weighed 135 pounds). In the pros, Manon noted, "The players are bigger, the speed is faster, and the shot is harder. It's a big difference."

But when it comes to playing goalie, quick-ness and courage are at least as important as size. So it was on September 23, 1992, in Tampa, Florida, that Rheaume became the first woman ever to play in a professional hockey game. She started as goalie for the Tampa Bay Lightning of the National Hockey League in an exhibition game against the St. Louis Blues. In 20 minutes she had seven saves and gave up two goals. Tampa Bay general manager Phil Esposito, a former NHL all-star, signed Rheaume to a three-year contract with the club's minor league affiliate, the Atlanta Knights. Esposito was accused of using Rheaume as a publicity stunt. He did not deny her marketability, but he also praised her performance.

"She earned the chance to go to Atlanta," Esposito said. "She did well during the preseason, and she earned a spot on the roster."

Rheaume became a celebrity in the months that followed. She was a frequent guest on talk shows and the subject of numerous magazine profiles. She later played for the Nashville Knights of the East Coast Hockey League and the Las Vegas Thunder of the International Hockey League.

Accomplishments

First woman to play in a Canadian Junior A
hockey game: 1991
First woman to play in a National Hockey
League game: 1992
Gold medalist, Women's World
Championships: 1992

Libby Riddles

Born 1956

Libby Riddles, the first woman to win the Iditarod Trail Sled Dog Race, was born and raised in Minnesota. As a child she dreamed of being a cowgirl. She hoped one day to live on a

big ranch, surrounded by animals. When she turned 16 years old, she met a young man who was traveling to Alaska. The tales he told of the frozen North, of living in the wild, seemed extraordinary to Libby, and it wasn't long before she began charting a new course. But rather than simply run away, she completed her high school education, worked long hours in a bank, and saved enough money to finance her dream. Within a short time she had accumulated enough cash to purchase her own plane ticket. Her parents reluctantly offered their blessing, and Libby Riddles set out for Alaska with the

man whose stories had inspired her in the first place, Dewey Halverson.

Riddles and Halverson shared a cabin near Anchorage. He purchased their first sled dogs, and she was relegated to assistant. Frustrated by her limited role, Riddles set out on her own. She began training and racing her own dogs. Like most mushers, she dreamed of competing in the Iditarod, a grueling 1,151-mile race from Anchorage to Nome, Alaska, over a course that follows an old mail route and is named after a deserted mining town along the way.

Riddles finished 20th in the Iditarod in 1981. But she was introduced that year to another competitor, Joe Garnie. They struck up a friendship and decided to live together and pool their resources. Their kennel in Teller, Alaska, about 80 miles from Nome, grew to more than 60 dogs. They lived spartan lives, with the dogs at the center of their universe.

"We're actually living the lifestyle," Riddles said. "I think that's part of the reason Joe and I have done well in the racing business. The dogs kind of know they're being used for an actual purpose, rather than by some guy who's just running a 40-mile loop every night. We haul fish with the dogs, haul firewood with them. We'll go up the beach and haul walrus with them. And the weather up here really toughens the dogs' mental attitude. It toughens the drivers, too."

In 1985 it was presumed that when a woman finally won the Iditarod, it would be Susan Butcher, a perennial contender. But Riddles, whose best previous finish was 18th, took the lead in the middle of that year's race and held on for a stunning upset. Her victory was a tribute not only to her ability to train and sustain a first-class dog team, but also to her own courage and cunning. She had gambled big, leaving an Eskimo village in the middle of the night—during a snowstorm—while the other mushers slept. She braved 40-mile-per-hour winds and single-digit temperatures; she had virtually no visibility. But she pressed on. Three hundred miles later, she was the first one to cross the finish line.

Accomplishments

First woman to win the Iditarod Trail Sled Dog
Race: 1985

Cathy Rigby

Born December 12, 1952

A world-class gymnast who became a successful actress and commentator, Cathy Rigby was born in Long Beach, California. She was a premature baby, weighing only four pounds at birth, and she struggled to survive. With help and love from her mother, a survivor of polio, Rigby eventually thrived, becoming an exuberant child with seemingly boundless energy.

"She was always on top of the refrigerator," Rigby's mother once said. "If she fell off, she just scrambled back up."

Each of the four Rigby children was athletic. Cathy was 18 months old when she learned how to roller-skate and five years old when she began riding a bicycle. At eight she started taking ballet lessons; gymnastics, in the form of somersaults and back flips on a trampoline, followed shortly thereafter. She began working out with the Southern California Acro Team, coached by Bud Marquette. He was the first person to spot Cathy's strength. At 11 years old, with a ponytail and a smile, she was nonetheless strong and determined.

"You can't teach fearlessness," Marquette said. "It has to be inborn. And you can't be a gymnast without it."

As is often the case with the families of gymnasts, the Rigbys made sacrifices for Cathy. Not only did life revolve around the training schedules of Cathy and her sister Paula, but the Rigbys even sold their piano to pay for gymnas-

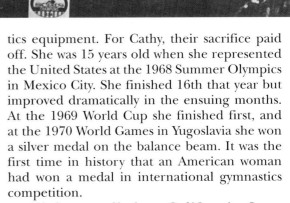

tics equipment. For Cathy, their sacrifice paid off. She was 15 years old when she represented the United States at the 1968 Summer Olympics in Mexico City. She finished 16th that year but improved dramatically in the ensuing months. At the 1969 World Cup she finished first, and at the 1970 World Games in Yugoslavia she won a silver medal on the balance beam. It was the first time in history that an American woman had won a medal in international gymnastics competition.

Rigby enrolled at California State University, Long Beach, after graduating from

Memorable Moment: June 6, 1986

Nancy Lieberman Becomes the First Woman to Play in a Men's Professional Basketball League

In the late 1970s, while a student at Old Dominion University, Nancy Lieberman was the most dominant player in women's college basketball. She was an intensely competitive athlete, with a chip on her shoulder and a wide assortment of playground moves. "She plays like a guy," her opponents said.

When her days as a collegian and an Olympian (she was a member of the silver medal–winning 1976 U.S. Women's basketball team) were over, Lieberman played in two women's professional leagues, both of which quickly folded. At the age of 27, she was not ready to retire, so when an offer came from the Springfield Fame of Massachusetts to play summer ball in the U.S. Basketball League (a men's league), Lieberman jumped at the chance. She understood the reality of the situation—she was, in a sense, a gimmick whose primary purpose was to beef up attendance. Still, she would have a chance to play, and once on the court she would rise or fall on her own.

Her historic opportunity came in Springfield, against the Staten Island Apples. With 3:40 left in the second quarter, Lieberman, a 5-foot 11-inch, 155-pound point guard, entered the game and played the remainder of the half. While slower and smaller than the other players, she held her own. She did not score a point and did not take a shot. But neither did she turn the ball over. In the second half, she did not play.

"I accept my role with the team," Lieberman said after the game. "I just wish I'd been in long enough to break a sweat."

high school, but quickly decided to devote her attention to training. She withdrew from college to become a full-time gymnast. In 1971 she won the all-around title at the World Cup Gymnastics Championships in Miami. Rigby was 4 feet 11 inches tall and weighed just 90 pounds, and she had a bright smile. Crowds loved her, as did the camera. She appeared on the covers of magazines, as well as on network television shows. She earned a spot on the U.S. Olympic team in 1972, despite having had an injury that forced her to miss a portion of the gymnastics competition. At the Summer Games in Munich, Rigby finished 10th in the all-around competition, at the time the highest finish for an American in Olympic gymnastics competition.

Rigby retired after the 1972 Olympics, then married National Football League running back Tommy Mason. She pursued an acting career that included a starring role in a touring version of *Peter Pan*, as well as appearances in a number of television series. She later opened a gymnastics school in Mission Viejo, California, and became a spokesperson for a line of fitness equipment.

Accomplishments

Member of U.S. Olympic team: 1968, 1972
Silver medalist, World Games: 1970
World Cup all-around champion: 1969, 1971

Aileen Riggin

Born May 2, 1906

Aileen Riggin, the first person to win Olympic medals in both swimming and diving, was born in Newport, Rhode Island, and grew up in New York. She became a competitive swimmer as a child and an Olympic athlete when she was in her teens. In 1920 the United States sent its first women's swimming and diving team to the Olympic Games. A handful of European female athletes had competed in swimming and diving at the 1912 Games in Stockholm (World War I wiped out the 1916 Games), but the 1920 Olympiad was to be the first with complete female participation in aquatic events.

"We learned that American women might

participate in the Games in the spring of 1920," Riggin wrote. "The American Olympic Committee and the various affiliated groups were not in favor of sending women at all. In those days women did not participate in strenuous athletics. It was not considered healthy for girls to overexert themselves. And many of the coaches on the Olympic team for men decided that they did not wish to be 'hampered' by having women athletes on the team."

Training was difficult since most pools for women did not have 3-meter or 10-meter springboards. Riggin and her teammates did the best they could and went on to thrive at the Summer Games. Riggin was 14 years old when she traveled to Antwerp, Belgium, for the Olympics. She looked even younger—she stood only 4 feet 8 inches tall and weighed 65 pounds. She had no diving coach—essentially, she was self-taught—but had a respected swimming mentor in Louis B. de Handley, who had worked with such stars as Gertrude Ederle and Eleanor Holm.

In the springboard event, Riggin and teammate Helen Wainwright were essentially even until the final dive. Riggin was the final competitor of the day; she dramatically captured the gold medal by perfectly executing a forward running layout somersault.

Riggin did not train seriously during much of the following year and finished third at the 1921 national championships. But by 1924 she was a more mature, stronger athlete. She won the national outdoor 3-meter springboard championship in 1923; that same year she was a member of the Women's Swimming Association of New York team that finished first in the 4 x 200 relay at the national championships. At the Summer Olympics in Paris, Riggin won a silver medal in the springboard event and a bronze medal in the 100-meter backstroke.

Riggin was a featured performer in the first underwater coaching films made for swimmers. In 1926, after retiring from amateur competition, she began a professional career as a performer, entertainer, and musician. A member of the International Women's Sports Hall of Fame, she continued to swim into her 80s.

Accomplishments

Olympic gold medalist, springboard diving: 1920

Olympic silver medalist, springboard diving: 1924

Olympic bronze medalist, 100-meter backstroke: 1924

Inducted into International Women's Sports Hall of Fame: 1988

Kelly Robbins

Born September 29, 1969

A rising star on the Ladies Professional Golf Association tour, Kelly Robbins was born in Mt. Pleasant, Michigan. She first picked up a club when she was three years old, learning golf basics at the knee of her father, Steve Robbins, a high school biology teacher and golf coach. Steve began providing Kelly with formal instruction when she was in third grade; he remains the only coach she has ever known. "It's hard to separate coach and father sometimes," Kelly said. "We're so close it's scary."

In high school Kelly Robbins was an accomplished all-around athlete. She loved playing basketball, but she truly excelled on the golf course. She received a scholarship from the University of Tulsa, which she helped lead to the NCAA team championship in 1988. Robbins won seven individual titles and twice was named a first-team All-American at Tulsa. In 1991, her final year at Tulsa, she was named NCAA Co-Player of the Year. She left school when her eligibility expired, but before she had earned her degree, a fact that caused her parents some consternation since they both were teachers. But Steve and Margie Robbins were supportive; they realized that their daughter was a talented athlete, and when she wanted to turn professional, they encouraged her.

It helped that Robbins had established herself as a formidable golfer. In addition to her collegiate accomplishments, she was a quarterfinalist at the 1988 U.S. Women's Amateur and survived the cut at the 1991 U.S. Women's Open. She was technically sound and learned her lessons well (her father's master's thesis was on the mechanics of the golf swing). Robbins developed a fluid swing that made her one of the best hitters in the game. It wasn't long before she was consistently hitting the ball more than 250 yards off the tee, a distance surpassed only by perennial long-driving champ Laura Davies.

A bit ragged around the greens when she joined the tour in 1992, Robbins improved both her short game and her putting stroke over the next few years. As a rookie she won $90,405. The next year she won her first event, the LPGA Corning Classic, and earned more than $200,000. In 1994 Robbins finished in the top 10 at three LPGA major events and was eighth on the money list, with $380,770. The fact that she remained modest and good-natured even as the publicity machine kicked into high gear only served to make her more popular.

"Her game is very mature," tour veteran Meg Mallon said of Robbins in 1995. "And so is she."

Professional golf requires as much mental acuity as physical strength, and players often peak in their 30s. But Robbins won her first major tournament, the LPGA championship, when she was 25 years old and in her fourth year on the tour. She did so under extreme pressure, rallying from a three-stroke deficit with seven holes to play to defeat defending champion Laura Davies. Afterward, Davies gave her younger opponent a heartfelt stamp of approval. "I was beaten," she said, "by a great champion."

In 1996 Robbins was sixth on the LPGA money list, with more than $560,000.

Accomplishments

Member of NCAA championship team: 1988
Two-time NCAA first-team All-American
NCAA Co-Player of the Year: 1991
LPGA championship winner: 1995

Betty Robinson

Born August 23, 1911

Elizabeth Robinson, the first American woman to win an Olympic gold medal in track and field, was born in Riverdale, Illinois. She was the youngest of three children—all girls. Her father had been a talented runner, and he believed that his athletic genes, along with his competitive zeal, were passed on to Betty. At picnics and at school, when children raced against each other, Betty Robinson was always one of the fastest. She didn't really know how fast until one day in high school, when she ran for her homeroom teacher, Charles B. Price, who was also a track coach. Price had seen Robinson running for a train one day after school; he was so impressed by her natural speed and graceful stride that he wanted to test her in a time trial. Robinson put on a pair of sneakers and sprinted through the school corridors for Price. When the coach looked at his stopwatch, he was not only pleased—he was shocked. If the watch was right, she had tied a world record for 100 yards. "He was very satisfied," Robinson recalled. "He wanted me to enter a meet."

At first, because there was no girls' track team at her school, Robinson trained with the boys' team. In March 1928, when she was 16, she was asked to join the Illinois Women's Athletic Club. In only her second meet, she tied the world record for 100 meters with a time of 12 seconds. That performance qualified her for the Olympic trials in Newark, New Jersey. Robinson finished second to Elta Cartwright of California in the 100 meters, qualifying her for the Summer Games in Amsterdam, where, for the first time, women would be allowed to compete in track and field.

The Olympic Games were only Robinson's fourth track meet, but her inexperience was evident only during prerace preparations. When she walked onto the infield for her first race, she was stunned to discover that she had brought two left shoes with her. She ran back to the locker room and grabbed a right shoe. "I guess I was kind of nervous and excited," she said. "It was very nerve-racking."

Robinson overcame her nerves in time to run one of the best races of her life. She crossed the finish line first. Still shy of her 17th birthday, she had made history by becoming the first American female to win a gold medal in an Olympic track-and-field event. She also won a silver medal in the 4 x 100 relay.

The following year Robinson won the 50-yard dash and the 100-yard dash at the Amateur Athletic Union national championships; in the former event she set a world record of 5.8 seconds. In 1931 she set world records in the 60-yard dash and the 70-yard dash. That same year she was seriously injured in an automobile accident. Though she was in a coma for nearly two months and needed two years of rehabilitation simply to regain the ability to walk, Robinson eventually returned to the track. She qualified for the 1936 Olympics and won a gold medal in the 400-meter relay.

Accomplishments

Olympic gold medalist, 100 meters: 1928
Olympic silver medalist, 4 x 100 relay: 1928
Olympic gold medalist, 4 x 100 relay: 1936
First American woman to win an Olympic gold medal in track and field
Inducted into U.S. Track and Field Hall of Fame: 1977

Diann Roffe-Steinrotter

Born March 24, 1967

Alpine skier Diann Roffe-Steinrotter, who won an Olympic gold medal in 1994, grew up in Williamson, New York. Her first great athletic love was not skiing; instead, she threw herself into the more genteel sport of horseback riding. As she matured, she discovered that she had the ability to excel in both sports, but there came a time when she had to make a choice. She was 11 years old when she was invited to participate in the U.S. Ski Team camp; at 13 she began to concentrate on skiing. When she was 16 years old she finished second in the giant slalom at the world junior championships in Sugarloaf, Maine, and became the first American to win a medal in that competition.

The next year, 1985, Roffe-Steinrotter captured the giant slalom title at the world championships in Italy. Despite suffering a knee injury that required extensive surgery, she remained one of the most competitive alpine skiers in the world over the next decade. An extremely competitive and energetic woman, she endured in a sport that is not only dangerous, but mentally taxing as well. Her specialty, the giant slalom, may be the most difficult event in skiing. "You have to step out of your comfort zone," she said. "You have to deal with fear of falling, crowds,

speeds…and focus on how to handle the bump that's three turns down."

In 1992, at the Winter Olympics in Albertville, France, Roffe-Steinrotter won a silver medal in the giant slalom. Retirement beckoned but,

like so many athletes that year, she decided to stick around a while longer. A change in the Olympic calendar meant that there would be just a two-year wait until the next Olympiad.

Roffe-Steinrotter went back into training and prepared for one more shot at a gold medal.

In 1994, at the Winter Games in Lillehammer, Norway, she took a gold medal in the super G (a combination of giant slalom and downhill, in which the competitor must negotiate numerous sweeping high-speed turns). She also won the final World Cup race of her career, a super G, in Vail, Colorado.

After the 1994 Olympics, Roffe-Steinrotter became involved in business projects related to skiing. She became a spokesperson for the U.S. Ski Team and introduced her own line of athletic apparel. She settled in Northwood, New York, and began taking classes at Clarkson College, where her husband, Willi, coached skiing and soccer. In 1995 she became the spokesperson for National Women's Ski Week, a promotion designed to "focus attention on the needs of women in a man's sport."

Accomplishments

Silver medalist, giant slalom, world junior
    championships: 1984
Gold medalist, giant slalom, world
    championships: 1985
Olympic silver medalist, giant slalom:
    1992
Olympic gold medalist, super G: 1994

Ellen Roosevelt

August, 1868–September 26, 1954

Tennis champion Ellen Crosby Roosevelt was born and raised in Hyde Park, New York, and was a cousin of President Franklin Delano Roosevelt. Both she and her sister, Grace, were outstanding young athletes. They learned the game from their father, John Roosevelt, a serious-minded fellow who believed that tennis was a sport worthy of respect and commitment. So the girls, unlike many of their friends and opponents, embraced tennis as something akin to a religion.

"Their father coached and treated them as if they were a pair of show ponies," said Ellen Hansell Allderdice, a Hall of Famer who was a contemporary of the Roosevelts. "We nonserious girls giggled at their early-to-bed and food habits."

If John Roosevelt was the prototypical stage father, he was nonetheless a competent teacher. Under his tutelage, on a private court in their backyard, the Roosevelt sisters developed as he hoped they would—it wasn't long before they were among the best players in the game. Ellen won the U.S. singles championship at the Philadelphia Cricket Club in 1890, beating defending champion Bertha Townsend in the challenge round, 6–2, 6–2. In the doubles final, she teamed up with her sister to beat Townsend and Margarette Ballard, 6–1, 6–2. The Roosevelts were one of only two sister teams to win a major doubles title; the other was Juliette and Kathleen Atkinson, who won the U.S. Open in 1897 and 1898.

In 1891 the Roosevelts were not quite as successful. Grace lost to Ireland's Mabel Cahill in the final of the all-comers tournament. Cahill then went on to defeat Ellen in the challenge round, 6–4, 6–1, 4–6, 6–3. In the doubles finals, Cahill and Emma Leavitt Morgan took the crown away from the Roosevelts, 2–6, 8–6, 6–4. For Cahill, the victory was sweet revenge. A year earlier, in the second round of the U.S. singles championships, she had suffered from severe foot cramps and was forced to default to Ellen Roosevelt. Accounts of that match are sketchy and inconsistent. Fans of Roosevelt claim that she tried to give Cahill as much time as possible to recover from her injury; critics argue that she actually insisted that Cahill be given no extra time at all. Either way, there was no great affection between the two women after the 1890 championships. They were later scheduled to meet in the Hudson River Valley Association tournament, but Roosevelt chose to default rather than face Cahill.

Ellen Roosevelt never won another U.S. singles title, but she did win the mixed doubles championship with Clarence Hobart in 1893. Roosevelt died at her home in Hyde Park in 1954. Twenty-one years later, in 1975, she was inducted into the International Tennis Hall of Fame.

Accomplishments

U.S. singles champion: 1890
U.S. doubles champion: 1890
U.S. mixed doubles champion: 1893
Inducted into International Tennis Hall of
    Fame: 1975

Heide Rosendahl

Born February 14, 1947

Heide Rosendahl, who won three medals in track and field for the host country during the 1972 Summer Olympic Games in Munich, was born in Huckeswagen, West Germany. The daughter of a German discus champion, Heide was one of the finest all-around athletes of her generation. She first showed international promise in 1966, when she finished second in the pentathlon at the European championships, a mere 22 points behind the winner. She figured to be among the leaders in both the pentathlon and long jump competitions at the 1968 Summer Games in Mexico City, but she became sick before the start of the Games and could manage only an eighth-place finish in the long jump. Then she pulled a muscle while warming up for the pentathlon and was forced to scratch—without taking part in a single event.

The following year, at the European championships, Heide Rosendahl endured another disappointment when West Germany withdrew from all individual events as a sign of protest over one of its athletes being ruled ineligible to compete. But Rosendahl refused to let any of these setbacks drain her spirit.

She had a superior season in 1970, setting a world record of 22 feet 5½ inches in the long jump, and by 1972 she was again in top form. At the Summer Games in Munich, Rosendahl narrowly captured the gold medal in the long jump, winning by just one-half inch. In the pentathlon, she turned in one of the finest performances of her career, shattering the world record, but Great Britain's Mary Peters was in even better form. Rosendahl challenged Peters with a fierce effort on the second day but fell 10 points shy of a gold medal.

With gold and silver medals to her credit, Rosendahl was the hero of the Games to the West German fans. But her efforts—and those of her fellow athletes—were overshadowed by the massacre of 11 Israelis by terrorists during the Games.

Memorable Moment:
August 23, 1989

Victoria Brucker Becomes the First Girl to Start in the Little League World Series

The Boys of Summer found a girl in their midst in August 1989. Not that there was anything extraordinary about females playing youth baseball—they had, in fact, been members of that fraternity for years. And, on one occasion, a girl had even gotten into the lineup during a Little League World Series game.

But never before had a female player made as much of an impact as Victoria Brucker did. Brucker, who played for San Pedro, California, became the first girl from the United States to play in a Little League World Series game. Not only that, she also became the first girl—from any country—to start a game in the Little League World Series.

Brucker was one of the team's starting pitchers. She also happened to be one of its best hitters, which is why she batted cleanup. On August 23, 1989, she made her historic debut. She scored three runs in leading San Pedro past Tampa, Florida, 12–5. By the end of the day, Brucker had become the first girl to get a hit and score a run in a Little League World Series game.

San Pedro nearly reached the Little League World Series championship game. But in the semifinals, San Pedro lost to eventual champion Trumbull, Connecticut, 6–3. Brucker went hitless in three trips to the plate. But there was no reason for her to feel bad; Trumbull pitcher Andy Paul had allowed just one hit all day.

On the last day of the Olympics, Rosendahl brought the spotlight back to the competitive arena. She ran the anchor leg for West Germany's 4 x 100 relay team. Taking the baton with a one-meter lead on East Germany's Renate Stecher, the world-record holder at 100 and 200 meters—and with more than 75,000 spectators cheering wildly—Rosendahl ran the race of her life. She held off Stecher to win a gold medal with a time that matched the world record.

Accomplishments

Olympic gold medalist, long jump: 1972
Olympic gold medalist, 4 x 100 relay: 1972
Olympic silver medalist, pentathlon: 1972
Set world record in long jump: 1970

Dorothy Round

July 13, 1908–November 12, 1982

Dorothy Edith Round, who dominated British women's tennis in the 1930s, was born in Dudley, Worcestershire. As a child she was graceful and athletic; she enjoyed sports but took few of them seriously. As she grew she became particularly enamored of tennis and decided to dedicate herself to the game. Eventually she became one of the finest players in England. Round possessed a steady right-handed groundstroke and a confident serve-and-volley attack. She had the unusual ability to beat an opponent from the baseline or at the net.

Round reached her first Grand Slam final in 1933, losing to American Helen Wills Moody—the premier player of that time—in three sets, 6–4, 6–8, 6–3. It was a disappointing loss for Round, but she had been the first person in six years to take a set from Wills Moody. In 1934, Wills Moody chose not to defend her Wimbledon title; in the final, Round met another American champion named Helen—Helen Hull Jacobs. But this time Round made sure that the trophy stayed in England. She beat Jacobs, 6–2, 5–7, 6–3. She also won the mixed doubles championship.

In 1935 Wills Moody returned to Wimbledon and recaptured her crown. Round failed to make the final, but that same year she became the first overseas player to win the Australian Open. She defeated Nancye Wynne Bolton, 1–6, 6–1, 6–3, in the final. Two years later, in 1937, Round again took advantage of Wills Moody's absence from Wimbledon. She rolled through the preliminary rounds, defeating, among others, Helen Hull Jacobs and French champion Simone Mathieu. Round met Jadwiga Jedrzejowska of Poland in the championship match. The two women split the first two sets, but Jedrzejowska, a big, strong player, jumped out to a 4–1 lead in the third. Round fought back and won the final set by a score of 7–5. She and Kitty McKane Godfree remain the only British players to win Wimbledon twice since World War I.

Round won the mixed doubles title at Wimbledon three times, and in 1933 she reached the semifinals of the women's singles at the U.S. Open, losing to Jacobs in a rousing three-set match. Round was a six-year veteran of the British Wightman Cup team, though her record—4–7 in singles—was not as impressive as her record in major tournaments. She did defeat Jacobs in the Wightman Cup tournament in 1936, the same year that Jacobs captured the Wimbledon singles title.

Besides being a tennis champion, Round taught Sunday school, and she refused to play any matches on Sunday. She was inducted into the International Tennis Hall of Fame in 1986.

Accomplishments

Wimbledon singles champion: 1934, 1937
Wimbledon mixed doubles champion: 1934–1936
Australian Open singles champion: 1935
Inducted into International Tennis Hall of Fame: 1986

Wilma Rudolph

June 23, 1940–November 12, 1994

Born in the St. Bethlehem section of Clarksville, Tennessee, Olympic track star Wilma Rudolph had a career that was short but brilliant. And something of a miracle. She was the 20th of 22 children fathered by Ed Rudolph, a railroad porter, during two marriages. Wilma was born prematurely and weighed just $4\frac{1}{2}$

pounds at birth. At the age of four she contracted scarlet fever and pneumonia. She survived the illnesses, but her left leg was virtually paralyzed. Wilma's mother, Blanche, massaged her daughter's leg for hours each day, in the hope that she would someday recover. And once a week, on her day off, Blanche Rudolph drove Wilma 90 miles round-trip for physical therapy in Nashville.

Remarkably, at age six, Wilma began hopping on one leg. Two years later she learned to walk with a leg brace, and by 10 she was using only an orthopedic shoe. When Wilma was 11 she shocked her mother by playing basketball in her bare feet. From that day on she never used crutches or braces again.

Basketball remained Wilma Rudolph's favorite game for a while— twice she received all-state honors—but on the track she truly excelled. As a gangly 5-foot 11-inch sophomore, she joined the Burt High School track team. There she first caught the eye of Tennessee State coach Ed Temple, who invited her to one of his summer track camps. She accepted and shortly thereafter began to blossom.

In 1956, as a 16-year-old high school student weighing only 90 pounds, Rudolph qualified for the U.S. Olympic team; she won a bronze medal in the 4 x 100 relay at the Melbourne Summer Games. After graduating from high school she went to Tennessee State University on a track scholarship, while continuing to work with

Temple. She matured physically and emotionally, and by 1960, at the Rome Olympics, she was a strong and graceful 130-pound woman. In one of the most impressive Olympic performances in history, Rudolph won gold medals in the 100 meters, 200 meters, and 4 x 100 relay. In the 100 she equaled the world record in a semifinal heat; in the 200 she set an Olympic record; in the 4 x 100 relay she helped the United States set a world record in a semifinal heat, then overcame a bad baton pass to come from behind and win the final.

The Associated Press named Rudolph its Female Athlete of the Year in 1960. In February 1961 she became the first woman to compete in the Millrose Games at Madison Square Garden, where she tied her own indoor world record for 60 yards. In the summer of 1961, at a meet in West Germany, she set a world record for 100 meters. That same year, she won the Sullivan Award as the top amateur athlete in the United States.

In 1962, having completed her degree in education, Rudolph retired from track and field. Financial opportunities for track-and-field athletes were rare at that time, so she chose another career. Rudolph became an elementary school teacher and coach in Tennessee, and later operated a community center in Indiana. She picked up a handful of endorsement contracts, but most of her time was spent on projects near to her heart, such as the Wilma Rudolph Foundation, which works to motivate children through athletics. Rudolph is a member of the

National Track and Field Hall of Fame, the International Women's Sports Hall of Fame, and the Black Athletes Hall of Fame.

Rudolph, who had married William Ward in 1961, later wed Robert Eldridge, whom she had known since second grade, in 1963. She and Eldridge had four children before divorcing in 1976. In the summer of 1994 Rudolph learned that she had an inoperable brain tumor. She died that fall.

Accomplishments

Olympic gold medalist, 100 meters: 1960
Olympic gold medalist, 200 meters: 1960
Olympic gold medalist, 4 x 100 relay: 1960
Olympic bronze medalist, 4 x 100 relay: 1956
Inducted into National Track and Field Hall of
    Fame: 1974
Inducted into International Women's Sports
    Hall of Fame: 1980

Elizabeth Ryan

February 5, 1892–July 6, 1979

One of the greatest doubles players in tennis, Elizabeth Montague Ryan was born in Santa Monica, California, and spent most of her adult life in England. Nicknamed Bunny, Ryan had a career that spanned more than 20 years. She won more than 650 tournaments, but her status as a runner-up defined her athletic life. She finished second in at least 800 tournaments, and while she accumulated 19 titles at Wimbledon, she never walked away with the singles championship. As gifted as she was at doubles—she was the best partner a player of that era could hope to have—Ryan was always a bit less accomplished, or a bit less lucky, than the women she met in Grand Slam finals.

Ryan, whose favorite shot was a short chop stroke at the net, won the first of her Wimbledon doubles titles in 1914, when, at the age of 22, she teamed up with Agatha Morton. World War I forced the cancellation of Wimbledon until 1919, at which time the tournament resumed and Ryan defended her crown. For the next five years, through 1923, Ryan and Suzanne Lenglen dominated the tournament. Each year they won the doubles title; never were they extended to three sets. After a year away, Ryan and Lenglen returned to the winner's circle in 1925. In 1926 Ryan was back again, this time with a new partner—Mary K. Browne. In 1927 and 1930 Ryan teamed up with Helen Wills Moody, and in 1933 and 1934 her partner was Simone Mathieu.

Ryan won the U.S. Open doubles title in 1926 and the French Open doubles title in 1930, 1932, 1933, and 1934. Her achievements in doubles tend to overwhelm her other accomplishments. Ryan won the British hard court singles title twice and was runner-up in three Grand Slam finals. She often lost to her doubles partners. At Wimbledon in 1921 she was beaten in straight sets by Suzanne Lenglen. Five years later she lost to 42-year-old Molla Mallory in a dramatic three-set final. Ryan led 4–0 in the third set but lost by a score of 4–6, 6–4, 9–7. In 1930, in her last final, 38-year-old Ryan was beaten in straight sets at Wimbledon by Helen Wills Moody.

Those encounters, combined with her experience as a doubles partner, afforded Ryan a unique perspective on the greatest players in history. Some time after her career was over, she was asked to choose from a list that included Alice Marble, Suzanne Lenglen, and Helen Wills Moody. With little hesitation Ryan replied, "Suzanne, of course. She owned every kind of shot, plus a genius for knowing how and when to use them."

There was a genius to Ryan's game as well, but of a quieter sort. She won 50 consecutive doubles matches in a 14-year period at Wimbledon; her 19 titles stood as a record for more than four decades, until it was surpassed by Billie Jean King in 1979. Ryan attended the 1979 tournament, intending to be a witness to the breaking of her own record, but she collapsed and died the day before King teamed up with Martina Navratilova to win the women's doubles title.

Ryan was inducted into the International Tennis Hall of Fame in 1972.

Accomplishments

Wimbledon doubles champion: 1914,
    1919–1923, 1925–1927, 1930, 1933–1934
U.S. Open doubles champion: 1926
French Open doubles champion: 1930,
    1932–1934
Inducted into International Tennis Hall of
    Fame: 1972

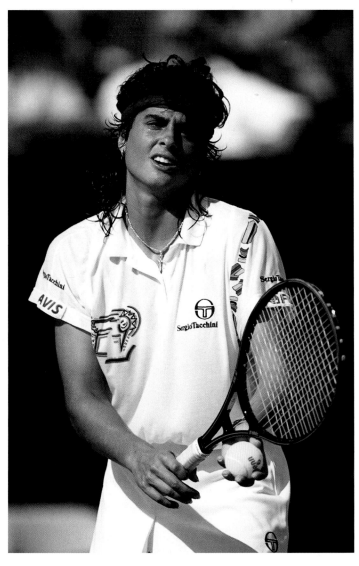

S

Gabriela Sabatini

Born May 16, 1970

Gabriela Sabatini, one of the most popular players in professional tennis during the late 1980s and early 1990s, was born and raised in Buenos Aires, Argentina, a city whose passion for the game is reflected by its more than 1,000 tennis clubs. Gabriela's father, Osvaldo, a General Motors executive, enrolled her in a junior program. By the time she was 13, Sabatini had moved to Key Biscayne, Florida, to train with Patricio Apey, a former Davis Cup player from Chile. Her improvement was dramatic—by the end of 1984 she was the top-ranked junior player in the world. Shortly thereafter she turned professional. In September 1985, Sabatini became the youngest player to reach the semifinals of the French Open (that record was eventually beaten by Jennifer Capriati).

A tall, striking young woman, Sabatini reached the semifinals of the French Open in 1985 and the semifinals at Wimbledon in 1986; endorsement offers flooded in, and soon she was making more money off the court than on. Both abroad and in Argentina, Sabatini was treated like a movie star.

At 5 feet 9 inches tall and 140 pounds, with broad shoulders that gave her powerful ground-strokes, Sabatini had physical gifts rarely seen in women's tennis. But she was unable to become the dominant player she was expected to be. She routinely advanced to the semifinals of Grand Slam events but did not win a major event until the 1990 U.S. Open. By then, tennis insiders had stopped referring to her as "the future of women's tennis"—that role had been assumed by Steffi Graf and Monica Seles.

Sabatini was often regarded as the mystery woman of tennis. She was quiet, almost to the point of being aloof, and rarely displayed any emotion on the court. A consistent top-five player, she was only the fifth woman in the history of the game to surpass $5 million in career winnings. Among fans, the shortcomings in Sabatini's game, along with her inability to win Grand Slam events, seemed to go largely unnoticed. As Mark Preston wrote in *Tennis* magazine in 1988, Sabatini was in "a unique position. She need never equal Graf's on-court achievements to equal Graf's acclaim. Because of her stunning good looks, her enthralling, graceful game, and her unmistakable aura, she doesn't have to be the best in the game to be perceived as the best for the game."

In 1996 Sabatini decided that the game was no longer best for her. At the age of 26

she announced her retirement from competitive tennis.

Accomplishments

U.S. Open champion: 1990
U.S. Open finalist: 1988
Wimbledon finalist: 1991
Olympic silver medalist: 1988
Top-ranked junior player in the world: 1984

Joan Benoit Samuelson

Born May 16, 1957

There are few athletes more resilient and competitive than Olympic marathon champion Joan Benoit Samuelson. Born and raised in Cape Elizabeth, Maine, Joan was the only girl in a family of four children. Though she would become a pioneer in women's distance running, she had little interest in the sport as a child. Her father was an accomplished skier, and she spent considerable time on the slopes. She also played basketball and tennis. Track was merely a diversion, a way to stay in shape between seasons.

Joan Benoit did not stray far from home when she went to college. She chose Bowdoin College in Brunswick, Maine. There she played field hockey and began to blossom as a runner. In the summer of 1976, after her freshman year, Benoit qualified for the U.S. Olympic trials. That taste of success, combined with the chronic soreness she felt in her knees after playing field hockey, prompted her to put away her hockey stick and concentrate on track and field. Benoit trained harder and longer than she ever dreamed possible—she ran road races against world-class competition and logged hundred-mile weeks in preparation for the day she would run in the Boston Marathon.

In April 1979, Benoit, a small woman with a short stride and her baseball cap turned backward, turned in the first major victory of her career. In her second attempt at the distance, she won the Boston Marathon in the American-record time of 2 hours, 35 minutes, 15 seconds. She would win again in 1983, setting a world

record with a time of 2:22.43. But even in the early 1980s, Benoit showed signs of the physical distress that would become part of her life. An appendectomy kept her out of Boston in 1981; later that year she had surgery to remove bone spurs from both feet and had an Achilles tendon repaired. Her career has entailed a cycle of injury, surgery, rehabilitation, intense training, and success, then more injury.

Most long-distance runners, when their training routine is interrupted by injury, turn to other forms of exercise to maintain a high level of fitness. So it was with Benoit, who has known more than her share of aches and pains. When restricted to training indoors, most runners place a stationary bicycle near a window and ride for an hour or more, all the while looking outside, dreaming of what it would be like out on the open road. But Benoit turned the bike toward a wall, preferably in a corner, and pedaled until exhaustion set in. It wasn't much fun, she said, but it helped toughen her mentally.

Benoit's most famous comeback occurred in 1984, when she underwent arthroscopic knee surgery just 17 days before the U.S. Olympic trials. Few expected her to compete in the trials, let alone earn a spot on the U.S. team. "Even as I was jogging to the starting line, I honestly didn't know if I could manage the race," she said. But on August 5, at the 1984 Los Angeles Olympics, she won the first women's Olympic marathon, running away from the pack in the first mile and hanging on despite dangerously high heat and humidity.

A week after her Olympic triumph, Benoit married Scott Samuelson. Over the next several years she continued to suffer from a variety of physical maladies—hip problems, back problems, heel problems. She gave birth to two children, Anders and Abigail. She made numerous comeback attempts along the way, and in more than a few races she showed flashes of being the runner she once was. Today Samuelson lives a quiet life in Maine with her family and friends. She continues to train and, when healthy, race.

Accomplishments

Winner of first Olympic women's marathon: 1984
Boston Marathon winner: 1979, 1983
Set world record in marathon (2:22.43): 1983

Arantxa Sanchez Vicario

Born December 18, 1971

The youngest Spanish woman ever to win the French Open, tennis player Arantxa Sanchez Vicario was born in Barcelona. Her father, Emilio Sanchez, was an engineer; her mother, Marisa Vicario, was a homemaker who raised four children, all talented tennis players. Arantxa's older brothers, Emilio and Javier, became successful on the men's professional tour; her older sister, Marisa, attended Pepperdine University in Malibu, California, on a tennis scholarship. Arantxa was only four years old when she began playing tennis regularly. Eventually she became the most famous and accomplished athlete in her family.

Arantxa Sanchez Vicario, a 5-foot 6-inch, 124-pound bundle of energy and strength, turned professional in 1986, when she was only 15 years old. By the end of the year she was the top-ranked player in Spain and the 124th-ranked player in the world. In 1987 she moved up to No. 47, and in 1988 she was No. 18. In 1989 she not only cracked the top 10 (she was No. 5 at year's end), but also won her first Grand Slam singles title. At the French Open, 17-year-old Sanchez Vicario upset Steffi Graf in a dramatic three-set final to become, at the time, the youngest champion in the history of the French Open.

That victory propelled Sanchez Vicario into the forefront of women's tennis. She was a tireless competitor with a charming personality, admired by fans and competitors. She soon developed a reputation for being one of the most accessible players on the women's tour. She happily signed autographs and patiently conducted interviews. To many she seemed the antithesis of the spoiled, sheltered professional athlete. She became a fixture in the top 10 and in the latter rounds of Grand Slam events. She was a finalist at the French Open in 1991 and at the U.S. Open in 1992. Sanchez Vicario took a bronze medal in singles at the 1992 Summer Olympics and a silver medal (with Conchita Martinez) in doubles. In 1994 she had the finest year of her career, capturing both the U.S. Open and the French Open.

With her victory at the U.S. Open, Sanchez Vicario made it clear that she was no longer content to rely on her formidable groundstrokes. She had made a career out of hugging the baseline and outlasting her opponents, particularly on slower surfaces. But at the Open the surface was faster, and she had to take a less conservative approach. "She has great potential to play the net," her former coach, Sven Groenveld, told a reporter. "She's physically gifted. Quick hands, good hand-eye coordination. She has the natural ability to move, which you normally have to spend a lot of time working on."

Even after she became one of the game's premier players, Sanchez Vicario remained close to her two brothers, and her constant companion on the road was her mother. "I feel good with them," Sanchez Vicario said of her family. "I think I'll always want my mom to be with me."

Sanchez Vicario was a finalist at the Australian Open, the French Open, and Wimbledon in 1995. In 1996 she again reached the finals at Wimbledon and the French Open, and finished the year as the game's second-ranked player behind Steffi Graf.

Accomplishments

French Open champion: 1989, 1994
U.S. Open champion: 1994
Olympic bronze medalist, singles: 1992
Olympic silver medalist, doubles: 1992

Summer Sanders

Born October 13, 1972

Summer Elisabeth Sanders, who won four medals in swimming at the 1992 Summer Olympics in Barcelona, was born in Roseville, California. Her first name became a source of amusement for people who asked if her parents had been hippies. They presumed that her odd moniker was the by-product of some countercultural movement; they assumed that she was a beach girl from Southern California. But Bob Sanders, a dentist, and his wife, Barbara, lived in a quiet area north of Sacramento. When Barbara

was pregnant with the couple's first child, and they discovered that the baby was due on June 21, it occurred to them that "Summer" would be the perfect name for a little girl. But when the child was born, it was a boy. So, they named him Trevor. But they still loved the name Summer, so when their second child, a girl, was born two years later, they named her Summer—despite the fact that she was born in the fall.

The Sanders family built a pool in the backyard, and Summer immediately began working on her strokes. "I was lucky," she said. "Suppose my father had put in a tennis court instead. I can't play tennis at all."

When Sanders was eight years old, her parents divorced; for the rest of their childhood, she and Trevor bounced back and forth between parents. They spent six months with their mother, then six months with their father. It was emotionally difficult, but it forged a bond between brother and sister.

Summer Sanders became one of the top young swimmers in the country. She enrolled at Stanford University, where, as a lithe, 5-foot 9-inch, 125-pound freshman, she was named 1991 NCAA Swimmer of the Year. In the summer of 1992, at the U.S. Olympic trials, she finished first in the 200-meter butterfly, the 200-meter individual medley, and the 400-meter individual medley. She was almost 20 years old when she represented the United States at the Summer Games in Barcelona. There she won gold medals in the 200-meter butterfly and the 4 x 100 medley relay, a bronze medal in the 400-meter individual medley, and a silver in the 200-meter individual medley. No other American swimmer—not even Stanford teammate Janet Evans, the star of the 1988 Summer Games—won four medals in Barcelona.

After the Olympics, Sanders continued to train and compete, but devoted much of her time to speaking engagements, swimming clinics, and television broadcasting. In January 1994, having earned her degree from Stanford, she retired from competitive swimming. Her retirement turned out to be merely a hiatus. In the spring of 1995, Sanders returned to the pool.

Accomplishments

NCAA Swimmer of the Year: 1991
World champion, 200-meter butterfly: 1991

Olympic gold medalist, 200-meter butterfly: 1992
Olympic gold medalist, 4 x 100 medley relay: 1992

Evelyn Sears

September 28, 1881–March 26, 1968

Evelyn Sears, a member of the International Tennis Hall of Fame, was born into a life of privilege in Boston. Her father was Frederick Richard Sears, a real estate and shipping magnate who was intrigued by the sport of tennis and may even have played on the first tennis court constructed in the United States. Her mother, Eleonora Randolph Coolidge Sears, had the bluest of blood—she was the daughter of Thomas Jefferson Coolidge, an ambassador to France, and the great-granddaughter of Thomas Jefferson.

When Evelyn Sears was growing up, tennis was less a sport than an elegant game played casually by the social elite. But she was a competitor, and the energy, enthusiasm, and drive that she brought to other sports she brought to the tennis court. Sears was one of the first accomplished all-around athletes in the United States. Pampered upbringing notwithstanding, she was a woman who enjoyed rolling up her sleeves and playing to win. In her lifetime, she took home nearly 250 trophies in tennis, horseback riding, squash, polo, long-distance walking, swimming, field hockey, and golf.

Sears' athletic career began in Newport, Rhode Island, where she learned to play tennis. She was a casual participant at first, but soon her talent became evident; friends and family encouraged her to test herself in tournament play. Sears' penchant for baring her arms in the heat of competition appalled some spectators, but she didn't care. And if there was criticism of her brazenness, it didn't seem to affect her game. In 1911, when she was 30 years old, Sears won the women's doubles championship at the U.S. Open; her partner was Hazel Hotchkiss, one of the greatest players in the history of women's tennis. The following year Sears reached the finals of the singles competition, only to lose to Mary Browne, 6–4, 6–2. In 1915 Sears and Hotchkiss Wightman teamed up to win another

U.S. Open doubles title; in 1916 and 1917 she captured the doubles title with Molla Mallory.

While she excelled on the tennis court, Sears also proved adept at other sports. She was a national-class equestrian and expert horse breeder. When the National Horse Show stumbled upon hard times, Sears donated the money necessary to keep the event alive. In 1918 she began playing squash; 10 years later, at the age of 46, she won the first national squash championship for women. After that, she became a regular in the U.S. women's squash championships, competing until 1950, when she was 70 years old. Sears became a vocal proponent of physical fitness decades before the fitness craze hit the United States. Through long-distance ocean swims and 50-mile walks along the East Coast, she demonstrated the resiliency of the human body.

Sears was engaged once, to America's Cup yachtsman Harold S. Vanderbilt, but she never married. She died at age 87 after a long battle with leukemia. She is a member of the International Tennis Hall of Fame and the International Women's Sports Hall of Fame.

Accomplishments

U.S. Open doubles champion: 1911, 1915–1918
U.S. Open singles finalist: 1912
First U.S. women's squash champion: 1928
Inducted into International Tennis Hall of
 Fame: 1968
Inducted into International Women's Sports
 Hall of Fame: 1984

Monica Seles

Born December 2, 1973

A native of Novi Sad, Yugoslavia, and a long-time resident of Sarasota, Florida, two-time U.S. Open winner Monica Seles first picked up a tennis racket at the age of seven. She was also a promising young figure skater. Accompanied by her father, Karolj, a cartoonist and documentary filmmaker, and her mother, Esther, a computer programmer, Seles arrived at Nick Bolletieri's tennis academy in Bradenton, Florida, in 1986. Just 12 years old, Seles' frail appearance belied not only an intense desire to compete and succeed, but a sledgehammer of a groundstroke as well. In practice sessions she was relentless, routinely outplaying bigger, stronger opponents—many of them boys—and running for hours in the Florida heat, ripping two-fisted shots until her hands blistered or her legs gave out.

Seles turned professional at 15, and it wasn't long before she was among the top-ranked players in the world. In 1990, at age 16, she became the youngest woman ever to win the French Open; a year later she became the youngest to win the Australian Open. Using two hands on

both sides of the racquet, grunting so loudly that opponents occasionally complained to the chair umpire, and giggling her way through postmatch interviews, Seles became one of the most endearing stars in tennis.

Even when the attention became an annoyance, Seles projected a certain elegance, playing to the cameras and the crowds. At 5 feet 9½ inches and 130 pounds, and blessed with grace and confidence, she landed modeling assignments from such publications as *Vogue, Seventeen,* and *Elle.* Her fame transcended athletics, and eventually there was a backlash. Critics were less than kind when Seles, clearly in peak form, decided to skip Wimbledon in 1991. As it turned out, Wimbledon was the only Grand Slam event she did not win that year.

In 1992 Seles entered 15 events on the women's tour and finished first in 10 of them. Among her titles were the U.S. Open, the Australian Open, and the French Open. She was also a finalist at Wimbledon.

On April 30, 1993, at a tournament in Hamburg, Germany, Seles' brilliant career was tragically interrupted. A man reportedly obsessed with German tennis star Steffi Graf—Seles' chief rival on the women's tour—emerged from the stands and stabbed Seles in the back during a changeover. His intent, he claimed, was not to kill Seles but to injure her so badly that she would be unable to play for a period of time, thus allowing Graf to wrest from Seles the sport's No. 1 ranking.

In the year following the attack, the 19-year-old Seles went into seclusion, allowing Graf to dominate the sport. The Women's Tennis Association declined to protect Seles' ranking during her recovery period, and she quickly tumbled from the top. For Seles, the mental anguish was worse than the physical pain. Long after her wounds had healed, she remained emotionally scarred. She vigorously avoided the spotlight, and there was considerable doubt as to whether she would ever play competitive tennis again.

But in late 1995, Seles resumed her career. She reached the finals of the U.S. Open in her second competitive tournament after returning to the tour. Five months later she capped her comeback with a victory at the Australian Open. Beset by injuries in 1996, she fell to No. 5 in the Women's Tennis Association rankings.

Accomplishments

Australian Open champion: 1991–1993, 1996
French Open champion: 1990–1992
U.S. Open champion: 1991–1992
Youngest player (18 years, 4 months) to
    accumulate 25 tournament victories: 1992

Patty Sheehan

Born October 27, 1956

Patty Sheehan, who grew up in Middlebury, Vermont, is one of the most successful players on the Ladies Professional Golf Association tour. She was raised in the heart of ski country. Her father, Bobo, coached baseball, football, golf, and skiing at Middlebury College. He was also the coach of the U.S. Olympic men's alpine ski team in 1956, the year Patty was born. So she learned to ski about the same time that she learned to walk. Patty Sheehan earned a national ranking when she was only 13—and she

competed against kids three or four years older. She was extremely competitive, in part because she was the only girl in the family; she often found herself playing backyard games against her three older brothers.

"All my friends were boys," Sheehan told *Golf Digest.* "All I did was sports, and I was always better than everybody at football, wrestling, pole vaulting, hockey—everything. At that time it was not the thing to do, for a young girl to be into athletics. There was probably talk behind my back, but you had to buck the system. That's what I loved."

One day Sheehan decided that she was no longer having much fun as a competitive skier, and she almost gave it up on the spot. To her surprise and delight, her father supported her decision. When the family moved to Reno, Nevada, while she was still in high school, she decided to try golf. It didn't take long for her athletic ability and competitive instinct to take over—in 1975, as an 18-year-old, she won the first of four consecutive Nevada State Women's Amateur titles. As a student at San Jose State University, she captured the California State Amateur title in 1978 and 1979.

In 1980 Sheehan turned professional, and by her third year on the tour she was among the LPGA's top five money winners. In the years since, she has been one of the most consistently successful performers in the game, finishing among the top 10 money winners every year. Sheehan won the LPGA championship in 1983, 1984, and 1993. In 1992 she became the first woman to win the U.S. Women's Open and the British Women's Open in the same year. She won a second U.S. Open title in 1994.

As for the secret of her success, Sheehan says she isn't sure. She's always claimed that her only goal in life is to be happy. But she acknowledges a burning desire to win every time she picks up a club. "I have been trying to figure out what that little thing is that makes one person better than another," she said. "The only thing I can think of is that I'm not afraid to lose and I'm not afraid to win. I always have to prove to myself that I deserve to be out there, that I deserve to be on the same playing field as the other greats."

In 1993, at the age of 36, Sheehan won her 30th tournament title and earned induction into the LPGA Hall of Fame. She is also a member of the Collegiate Golf Hall of Fame.

Accomplishments

U.S. Women's Open champion: 1992, 1994
British Women's Open champion: 1992
LPGA championship winner: 1983, 1984, 1993
Inducted into LPGA Hall of Fame: 1993
Top 10 money winner for 13 consecutive years

Pam Shriver

Born July 4, 1962

Pam Shriver reached the final of the U.S. Open when she was only 16 years old and became a consistent winner on the women's professional tennis circuit. But injuries prevented her from fulfilling the immense promise of her rookie season. One of three children born to Sam and Margot Shriver, Pam grew up in Baltimore, Maryland, and attended the McDonogh School. In the late 1970s she was part of a large and influential wave of female tennis players, including Tracy Austin and Andrea Jaeger, whose achievements were stunning in light of their age.

Shriver was a 16-year-old high school junior in the fall of 1978, when she played her first match at the U.S. Open. A gangly 6-foot adolescent with a shock of curly brown hair, Shriver did not look like a world-class athlete. Moreover, she walked onto the court at the National Tennis Center armed with a fat aluminum racket that resembled a snowshoe. But it wasn't long before Shriver's skills became apparent—and it wasn't long before the rest of the world followed her lead and began playing with midsized and oversized rackets.

Although she was still an amateur, Shriver was seeded 16th in the U.S. Open in 1978. The magnitude of the event escaped her, which was probably just as well. "I took it all in with such a laid-back attitude," she said. "I was happy to be there. I was missing a few days of school."

A few of her opponents no doubt wished she had gone back to class. Shriver rolled through the first few rounds, upsetting one established professional after another. Eventually she found herself in the semifinals, facing former champion Martina Navratilova. Shriver was supposed to have no chance, but she stunned Navratilova—and most of the tennis community—by pulling off a 7–6, 7–6 upset. Shriver won the admiration of fans and the respect of her opponent by being gracious in victory. "I didn't go nuts because I felt kind of bad," she said. "A Wimbledon champion going out to a 16-year-old rookie."

That glorious ride ended two days later

when Shriver lost to Chris Evert in the final. She returned to high school and attempted to adjust to the routine of being a typical teenager. But by the time she turned professional in March 1979, she was being lauded as the next great superstar of tennis.

Although Shriver had a solid career and was ranked in the top 10 for nine years, she never again reached the final of a Grand Slam tournament. A year after her dramatic debut, she lost in the first round of the U.S. Open. A nagging shoulder injury forced her to miss much of that season. Her shoulder bothered her throughout her career, and it eventually required surgery.

Despite her inability to win a Grand Slam singles title, Shriver made a significant impact on the game. She teamed up with Navratilova to win three Grand Slam doubles titles, and along with Zina Garrison won the Olympic gold medal in doubles in 1988. Shriver was president of the Women's Tennis Association and vice president of the International Tennis Hall of Fame.

Accomplishments

Olympic gold medalist, doubles: 1988
U.S. Open finalist: 1978
Grand Slam doubles winner: 1983–1984, 1984–1985, 1986–1987

Lydia Skoblikova

Born March 8, 1939

Lydia Skoblikova, who won four Olympic gold medals in speed skating, was born in the city of Zlatoust in the Soviet Union. She grew up in Chelyabinsk, in the heart of Siberia. For her, snow and ice were part of everyday life. So, too, were athletics. She began speed skating when she was 12; not long after she was targeted by the Soviet system as an athlete with great promise. Her father, an engineer, supported her efforts and helped her gain the proper coaching. By the time she was 18, Lydia was married to her coach, Alexander Skoblik. She later became a schoolteacher.

Lydia Skoblikova developed into one of the most decorated and accomplished Olympic athletes in history. In 1960, when she was 20 years old, she competed in her first Winter Olympics, at Squaw Valley, California. Americans who knew little about her and who assumed that most speed skaters—particularly those from Communist Bloc countries—were stocky, rugged types were taken aback by Skoblikova. She was 5 feet 5 inches tall and weighed only 125 pounds; she leaned far over the ice when she skated. When she crossed the finish line, a broad smile would often crease her face, a trait that endeared her to audiences.

The raw beauty and power of her athletic performance proved mesmerizing. The Squaw Valley Games marked the first time that women's speed skating was an Olympic event, and Skoblikova thoroughly dominated the competition. First she won the 1,500 meters, becoming the first woman to win a gold medal in Olympic speed-skating competition. A few days later she won a gold medal in the 3,000 meters. She finished fourth in the 1,000 meters. Although she did not compete in the 500-meter race, Skoblikova demonstrated her versatility less than a month later when she won the 500-meter world championship.

Impressive as she was in her 1960 Olympic debut, Skoblikova was just warming up. Three years later, at the world championships in Japan, she won all four women's races. During the two weeks of the 1964 Innsbruck Olympiad, Skoblikova won four gold medals and set Olympic records in three events. In the 500-meter race she cut five seconds off the existing mark; in the 1,500-meter race she broke her own record by more than half a minute; and in the 1,000 she settled for a one-second improvement. Poor ice conditions prevented her from setting a fourth record in the 3,000 meters.

Skoblikova's accomplishments were historic. No athlete had ever won six Olympic gold medals; none had ever won four in a single Olympiad. In the Soviet Union, Skoblikova was a hero. She was made an official member of the Communist Party and honored, in person, by Premier Nikita Khrushchev. At the 1964 world championships she continued her dominance, finishing first at 1,000 meters, 1,500 meters, and 3,000 meters.

Skoblikova competed in the 1968 Olympics but failed to earn a medal. She then retired from the sport, and turned her attention to teaching and raising a family.

Accomplishments

Olympic gold medalist, 500 meters: 1964
Olympic gold medalist, 1,000 meters: 1960,
1964
Olympic gold medalist, 1,500 meters: 1960,
1964
Olympic gold medalist, 3,000 meters: 1960,
1964

Mary Decker Slaney

Born August 4, 1958

Mary Decker, one of the most accomplished performers in track-and-field history, was born in Bunnvale, New Jersey. She won her first race when she was just 11 and ran a five-minute mile when she was 13. At 14 she was competing internationally; at 15 she began setting world records. Little Mary Decker, as she was known then, was a 100-pound, waiflike girl with a powerful kick.

The career of a world-class runner is often quite short. Injury takes its toll, and the body is unable to withstand the grueling workouts necessary for competing at the highest levels. For a while that appeared to be the fate of Mary Decker. Like a true thoroughbred, she was as fragile as she was fast. In 1974, at the age of 16, Decker suffered her first injury, a stress fracture in the ankle that was complicated by chronic shin splints. For three years she was unable to compete. In 1978 she underwent surgery to correct a problem with her calf muscles; she subsequently became one of the finest middle-distance runners in the world. Decker won a gold medal in the 1,500 meters at the 1979 Pan American Games, and in 1980 set a world record in the mile with a time of 4:21.7. More records followed, despite her ongoing battles with tendinitis and sciatica, and in 1980 she won the 1,500 at the U.S. Olympic trials. But like the rest of her U.S. teammates, Decker's dream of Olympic gold was shattered when the United States boycotted the 1980 Summer Games in Moscow.

Injuries sidelined Decker for the next two years, but in 1982 she was back, setting an

indoor world record for the mile and outdoor records in the 1,500, 2,000, 3,000, 5,000, and 10,000 meters. Decker's stunning display of strength and versatility established her as one of the best runners of her generation. She won the Jesse Owens Award in 1982 and was named Amateur Sportswoman of the Year by the Women's Sports Foundation. In 1983, in the first International Amateur Athletic Federation World Championships in Helsinki, Finland, Decker won gold medals in the 1,500 and 3,000. By the end of the 1983 season, she held every indoor world record from 800 meters to two miles and every outdoor mark from 800 meters to 10,000 meters.

Still, Olympic glory continued to elude her. In 1984, at the Summer Games in Los Angeles, Mary Decker Slaney (she had married British shot putter Richard Slaney) reached the finals of the 3,000 meters. With three laps remaining in the race, 18-year-old Zola Budd, a barefooted runner from South Africa, tried to pass Slaney. As Budd moved into the lead, Slaney's foot clipped Budd's ankle, and both runners lost their balance. Budd managed to stay on her feet and went on to finish seventh; Slaney fell to the track and burst into tears.

"Zola Budd tried to cut in on me without being actually ahead," Slaney later said, with more than a trace of bitterness. "I should have pushed her, but if I had, the headlines would have been MARY PUSHES ZOLA."

Budd was at first disqualified but was later allowed to keep her silver medal.

After the 1984 Games, Slaney retired from the sport to raise a family. She returned in 1988 and earned a spot on the U.S. Olympic team, though she failed to earn a medal. In the years that followed she continued to earn her living on the international track-and-field circuit. She qualified for the U.S. Olympic team in 1992 and in 1996, but neither time did she win a medal.

Accomplishments

World champion, 1,500 meters: 1983
World champion, 3,000 meters: 1983
Jesse Owens Award winner: 1982
Women's Sports Foundation Amateur
    Sportswoman of the Year: 1983

Charlotte Smith

Born 1973

Charlotte Smith, whose overall skill as a basketball player was overshadowed by the fact that she once dunked in a regular-season game, grew up in Shelby, North Carolina. She was the only daughter born to Ulysses and Etta Smith; the couple did, however, have three sons. As is so often the case, Smith, as an athlete, benefited from their presence.

"I think growing up with three brothers made me really tough and competitive," Smith said, "because I always wanted to beat them in everything."

It also helped that her uncle was David Thompson, who not only played professionally with the Denver Nuggets and the Seattle Supersonics, but, having starred at North Carolina State, was also something of a legend in Charlotte's home state. Indeed, basketball was Charlotte's game of choice when she was growing up, just as it is for most kids in North Carolina.

Smith was so athletically gifted that she couldn't help but be drawn into other sports. She was a successful track-and-field performer, winning the state championship in the mile when she was a freshman. She competed on the state level in the 400 meters, 800 meters, high jump, and triple jump. But even as her track-and-field trophies piled up, Smith was thinking about basketball—where she would play in college, what she might accomplish. To her, track was fun but basketball was special.

"I did well in track," she explained, "but I just didn't enjoy it as much as basketball. I guess because of the team unity. That's what I enjoy most—when our team is playing together and we just look awesome."

Like her idol, Michael Jordan, Smith attended the University of North Carolina. When she arrived, she chose his number—23. And, like Jordan, Smith helped lead the Tar Heels to a national championship in dramatic fashion. In the second half of the 1994 NCAA Women's Final Four championship game against Louisiana Tech, Smith had 19 points and 13 rebounds. Her 3-point shot at the buzzer gave North Carolina a

60–59 victory and its first national title. The 6-foot 1-inch junior forward was named the tournament's Most Outstanding Player.

Though she was considered a consummate team player in a program known for unselfishness, Smith will probably best be remembered for one spectacular individual achievement. On December 4, 1994, in a lopsided victory over North Carolina A&T, Smith did something no female player had done in nearly a decade—she dunked during a game. She picked off a pass, dribbled the length of the court, elevated with surprising ease, and slammed the ball home, stunning the crowd in Chapel Hill. Not since West Virginia's Georgeann Wells had dunked twice during the 1984–1985 season had a woman player dunked in a college basketball game.

Accomplishments

> Made winning shot in 1994 NCAA championship game
> Named Most Outstanding Player of 1994 NCAA Women's Final Four

Michelle Smith

Born 1970

The oldest of four children, Michelle Smith grew up in Dublin, Ireland. Improbably, at the comparatively advanced age of 26, she became an Olympic champion and one of the most decorated swimmers in history. Her love affair with the sport began when she was a child. Enrolled in lessons at a modest 25-meter pool at King's Hospital in Dublin by her father, Brian (who wanted no more than to make sure that his kids knew how to swim so that they wouldn't drown), Michelle thrived. Encouraged, though never pushed, by her parents, she became one of Ireland's top young swimmers, qualifying for the 1988 Summer Olympics in Seoul at the age of 18. In Seoul, however, Michelle Smith finished 17th in her best event, the 200-meter backstroke.

Over the next four years Smith continued to train; she attended school in the United States, at the University of Houston. At the 1992 Summer Olympics in Barcelona she carried the Irish flag at the opening ceremonies. But she was not at her best in 1992—a disk problem in her back left her unable to compete at full strength, and she finished 26th in the 400-meter intermediate medley.

While in Barcelona, Smith was introduced to Erik de Bruin, a discus thrower from the Netherlands. The pair fell in love, and soon Smith moved to Rotterdam to train and live with de Bruin. While there, she developed a ferocious appetite for work—she even went so far as to train for several hours on her wedding day, just two months before the 1996 Summer Olympics in Atlanta.

The training paid off. Given little chance of capturing even a single medal, Smith turned in a sensational performance in Atlanta, winning gold medals in the 400-meter freestyle, the 200-meter individual medley, and the 400-meter individual medley, and a bronze medal in the 200-meter butterfly. She became a national hero in Ireland. As Ireland's minister of sport, Bernard Allen, said, "She has surpassed everything that has ever been done in Irish sport."

Smith's stunning improvement (she lowered her personal best in the 400-meter individual medley by more than 13 seconds) prompted some observers to suggest that she had used performance-enhancing drugs. To support their argument they pointed out that Smith's husband (and coach) had been suspended from international competition in track and field in 1993 after testing positive for a banned substance. They also noted that Smith's physique had changed considerably since the Barcelona Games, and that it was almost unheard of for a swimmer to improve so dramatically in her mid-20s. But Smith—who passed all drug tests—vehemently denied the allegations and refused to let the swirl of controversy detract from her accomplishments.

As she said after winning her fourth medal, "This was the greatest week of my life."

Accomplishments

> Olympic gold medalist, 400-meter freestyle: 1996
> Olympic gold medalist, 200-meter individual medley: 1996
> Olympic gold medalist, 400-meter individual medley: 1996
> Olympic bronze medalist, 200-meter butterfly: 1996

Memorable Moment:
September 23, 1992

Manon Rheaume Appears in an NHL Game

Manon Rheaume never thought of herself as a "female" hockey player. She had grown up with the game in Canada and had always found that she fit in well with the boys during pond hockey games. Gender wasn't an issue to her. With every step in her career, she was hailed as a pioneer, but she preferred to concentrate on the game. The way Rheaume saw it, once you were on the ice wearing pads and skates, no one cared whether you were a boy or a girl.

It helped that Rheaume's specialty was protecting the net. While hockey is an extremely physical game, as a goalie she was excluded from the most severe contact. Goalies, after all, don't get slammed into the boards. And goalies almost never throw down their gloves and start fighting.

Still, Rheaume's appearance in a Tampa Bay Lightning uniform on the night of September 23, 1992, was met with a mixture of skepticism and curiosity. To many observers, her record in junior hockey meant nothing. Her quickness meant nothing. To them, her appearance was a cheap stunt likely to turn their game into a circus. But it didn't turn out that way. Rheaume started in goal for the Lightning in a National Hockey League exhibition game against the St. Louis Blues. In 20 minutes she had seven saves and allowed two goals—hardly an embarrassing performance. Shortly thereafter, Tampa Bay general manager Phil Esposito offered Rheaume a three-year contract with the club's minor league affiliate, the Atlanta Knights.

Annika Sorenstam

Born October 9, 1970

Annika Sorenstam, the Ladies Professional Golf Association's Player of the Year in 1995, was born in Stockholm, Sweden, to parents who were lifelong competitive athletes. At the age of five tennis, not golf, first captured her interest. Sorenstam began competing in age-group events in grade school and demonstrated a gift for the sport. But by the time she was a teenager, it was clear that, although she was talented, she would never be a world-class tennis player.

Introduced to golf when she was 12, Sorenstam quickly fell in love with the sport. She liked the fact that she could play and practice by herself; she liked knowing that the course was her opponent. In time she abandoned tennis to devote all of her athletic energy to golf. When she was 16 she was invited to represent the junior national team by the Swedish Golf Foundation. The following year she began a five-year stint as a member of the Swedish National Team.

In 1988 Sorenstam's life began to change. After staying up late one night to watch Liselotte Neumann, a fellow Swede, win the U.S. Women's Open on television, she started to dream of coming to the United States and joining the LPGA tour. A few years later, at an amateur tournament in Japan, Sorenstam competed against a player from the University of Arizona. The young woman was so impressed with Sorenstam that she convinced her coach to offer Sorenstam a scholarship. Sorenstam accepted, and by the time she left Arizona in 1992, she had been named College Player of the Year once and NCAA All-American twice. She was the World Amateur champion and runner-up at the U.S. Women's Amateur in 1992.

In 1993 Sorenstam left Arizona to return to Europe and pursue a professional career. As it had in college, success came quickly for her— She was named the European tour's Rookie of the Year, and she earned nearly $50,000 in three LPGA tour events. The following year Sorenstam joined the LPGA tour; although she did not win an event, she accumulated $127,451 in prize money and was named LPGA Rookie of the Year.

Sorenstam played the finest golf of her career in 1995, winning three tournaments and finishing in the top 10 on 12 occasions. Her first LPGA victory, at the age of 24, came at the U.S. Women's Open. There the usually unflappable Swede was nearly overcome by nerves. She held a three-stroke lead midway through the final round when, suddenly, she began to buckle under the weight of her own expectations. By the 17th hole her lead was down to one stroke, and her hands were shaking on every putt. But Sorenstam somehow regained her composure and held on for a one-stroke victory over Meg Mallon.

Once, as an amateur, Sorenstam had promised that if she ever won the U.S. Women's Open she would retire. "Once you've climbed Mount Everest, what else is there?" she said. But she surely had not intended to win at such a young age. After her victory she went right back to the driving range and then on to the next tournament. By year's end she was the LPGA's leading money winner (with $666,533) and Player of the Year. She was only the second player from outside the United States to win the award.

In 1996 Sorenstam won three more tournaments, including a second straight U.S. Women's Open, and finished as the tour's third-leading money winner, with more than $800,000.

Accomplishments

College Player of the Year: 1991
LPGA Rookie of the Year: 1994
LPGA Player of the Year: 1995
U.S. Women's Open champion: 1995–1996

Hollis Stacy

Born March 6, 1954

Golfer Hollis Stacy, a three-time winner of the U.S. Women's Open, was born in Savannah, Georgia. She developed and refined her game at a very early age; in fact, when she won the 1969 United States Golf Association Junior Girls Championship she was only 15 years and four months old; never had a player that young won the tournament. Stacy won the USGA Junior title again in 1970 and in 1971, becoming only the

second player to win the event three consecutive years. In one of those match-play finals she defeated Amy Alcott, another future Ladies Professional Golf Association star.

Stacy attended Rollins College for two years—and played for the U.S. Curtis Cup team in 1972—before deciding to turn pro. In her first year on the tour, in 1974, she barely scratched out a living, winning just $5,071. But she tripled that figure the following year, and by 1977 she was among the finest players in the world. It was then that Stacy recorded her first tour victory, at the Rail Charity Golf Classic. She later won the Lady Tara Classic and the U.S. Women's Open. The following year Stacy defended her U.S. Women's Open title and won the Birmingham Classic. In 1978 and 1979 she finished among the top 10 money winners on the LPGA tour.

For nine consecutive years Stacy won at least one tournament per season. She became one of the most consistent players in the game. She chugged along, always finishing in the money and occasionally walking off with a first-place check. One of her finest years was 1982, when she won three tournaments—the Whirlpool Championship of Deer Creek, the S&H Golf Classic, and the West Virginia LPGA Classic. In 1983 she repeated at the S&H Classic, and won the CPC International and the Peter Jackson Classic, her third major victory. The next year she won just one tournament, but it was a big one—her third U.S. Women's Open.

Stacy was a popular, affable woman who enjoyed chatting with opponents and spectators. She seemed to save her best performances for the most important tournaments. At the 1978 U.S. Women's Open, Stacy made a difficult high-pressure putt on the 72nd and final hole to defeat JoAnne Carner.

In 1985 Stacy became the 10th LPGA player to surpass $1 million in career earnings. She did not win another tournament until 1991, when she finished first at the Crestar–Farm Fresh Classic. By that time she had begun to pursue other endeavors, including golf course design and coaching. Stacy was the architect behind the Blackhawk Golf Course in Austin, Texas, and she served as an assistant coach at the University of Southern California. At the end of the 1993 season, Stacy had 16 career victories and more than $1.7 million in earnings, 15th on the LPGA's all-time list.

Accomplishments

USGA Junior Girls champion: 1969–1971
Youngest player ever to win USGA Junior
  Girls Championship
U.S. Women's Open champion: 1977–1978,
  1984
Peter Jackson Classic champion: 1983

Renate Stecher

Born May 12, 1950

Renate Stecher, who won six Olympic medals in track and field, was born in Supitz, East Germany. She burst onto the international scene in 1966, at the age of 16. At the European Junior Games that year she captured the gold medal in the 4 x 100 relay. Two years later she proved herself a formidable competitor in individual events, taking silver medals in the 200 meters and 100 meters, as well as the 4 x 100 relay.

By 1969 Stecher had progressed beyond junior competition. Perhaps motivated by the fact that she was a late addition to the East German team, she turned in a memorable performance at the European Senior Championships, winning a silver medal in the 200 meters and helping her team to a first-place finish in the 4 x 100 relay.

In 1970 world records began to fall at Stecher's feet. First came the 100-meter world record (11.0). Then, in 1971, she captured both the 100-meter and 200-meter titles at the European championships. In 1972, on the eve of the Summer Olympics in Munich, she was approaching her physical peak. Her effort in that Olympiad was a surprise to no one who followed the sport of track and field—after all, Stecher had not lost a 100-meter or 200-meter race outdoors in more than two years.

In Munich, Stecher began by winning a gold medal in the 100 meters in 11.07 seconds, a time that approached her own world record. Then she tied the world record of 22.4 seconds in winning a gold medal in the 200-meter final. Finally she capped off the Olympiad by anchoring the East German team to a silver medal in

the 4 x 100 relay. Only a courageous and dramatic run by West Germany's Heide Rosendahl, who edged Stecher at the tape, prevented East Germany from taking the gold.

Stecher's winning streak in the sprints went on for nearly two more years—encompassing 90 races before it ended. In 1973 she went into the record books as the first woman to break 11 seconds for 100 meters, with a hand-held time of 10.8. She lowered the 200-meter world record to 22.1 seconds. Finally, in 1974, at the European championships, Stecher finished second to Irena Szewinska of Poland in the 100-meter and 200-meter finals.

Two years later, at the Summer Olympics in Montreal, the 26-year-old Stecher took a silver medal in the 100 meters and a bronze in the 200 meters. In the 4 x 100 relay she helped East Germany finish first and set an Olympic record. Stecher retired shortly after the 1976 Games.

Accomplishments

Olympic gold medalist, 100 meters: 1972
Olympic gold medalist, 200 meters: 1972
Olympic gold medalist, 4 x 100 relay: 1976
Olympic silver medalist, 100 meters: 1976
Olympic silver medalist, 4 x 100 relay: 1972
Olympic bronze medalist, 200 meters: 1976

Helen Stephens

February 3, 1918–January 17, 1994

A number of fascinating anecdotes can be extracted from the life and career of Helen Stephens, a farm girl from Fulton, Missouri, who went on to become an Olympic champion in track and field. After winning gold medals in the 100-meter dash and 4 x 100 relay at the 1936 Olympics in Germany, Stephens was treated to a personal audience with Adolf Hitler. She described the encounter as follows: "Hitler comes in and gives me the Nazi salute. I gave him a good old Missouri handshake. He shook my hand, put his arm around me, pinched me, and invited me to spend the weekend with him."

Stephens declined the offer.

Even more fascinating was her longtime rivalry with Stella Walsh, a Polish runner whose family immigrated to the United States when she was an infant. Representing Poland, Walsh became an Olympic gold medalist in 1932. She was the best sprinter in the world—until she met Helen Stephens. The two first competed against each other at the 1935 Amateur Athletic Union championships in St. Louis. Stephens, only 17 years old, entered four events—the 50 meters, the 200 meters, the standing broad jump, and the shot put—and won all four. In the 50-meter race she easily defeated Walsh and afterward added insult to injury by stating, quite innocently, that she had no idea who Walsh was. That remark angered Walsh, who reportedly referred to Stephens as "that greenie from the sticks."

Walsh defeated Stephens at the 1936 Olympics, and afterward some Walsh supporters spread a rumor that Stephens was a man masquerading as a woman. But Stephens passed a sex test, and the rumor quickly faded. Many years later the irony of that accusation would be revealed. In December 1980, Walsh was shot and killed during a robbery in Cleveland. An autopsy report revealed the stunning news that Walsh had no female sex organs; she was, in fact, a man.

That revelation served only to magnify the accomplishments of Helen Stephens. She was a remarkably gifted athlete whose talent was evident at a young age. As the story goes, she was only a high school freshman when, in an unofficial early-spring workout, she equaled the world record for the 50 meters. That same year, in gym class, she tied the world record in the standing broad jump. By the time she was a junior in high school, in 1935, Stephens stood 6 feet tall and weighed 135 pounds.

The Associated Press chose Stephens as Best Woman Athlete of the Year after her Olympic victories in 1936. The following year she finished first in the 50 meters, the 200 meters, and the shot put at the AAU championships. Then, only two and a half years after bursting onto the scene, she retired. After that, she earned a living on the barnstorming circuit, competing in exhibition races against Jesse Owens and playing professional basketball. She served in the U.S. Marine Corps during World War II and later worked as a librarian. She coached for a time at William Woods College in Missouri, her alma mater. Stephens suffered a stroke and died in St. Louis in 1994.

Memorable Moment: June 5, 1993

Julie Krone Becomes the First Female Jockey to Win a Triple Crown Horse Race

Julie Krone had long been considered the most talented female jockey in horse racing when she made history at the Belmont Stakes. In fact, she was generally regarded as one of the best riders in the business—regardless of gender. After all, Krone rode her first winner in 1983, at the age of 20, and was among the top five earners in the nation from 1987 through 1989.

Still, the big victory had eluded her. A tremendously competitive athlete, Krone was frustrated by her inability to break through in one of the sport's three major races—the Kentucky Derby, the Preakness Stakes, or the Belmont Stakes. It was difficult enough for a woman to obtain a mount in a Triple Crown race; to get a horse actually capable of winning was almost too much to hope for.

Certainly that was the way Krone felt until 1993, when trainer Scotty Schulhofer assigned Krone to ride Colonial Affair in the Belmont. There was considerable pressure on Krone, for jockeys are often given too much credit when a horse wins and too much blame when it loses. Colonial Affair was a good colt, quite capable of winning the race. A poor effort would likely lead to some criticism of the jockey. Gender was an issue, and Krone knew it. But in the end, she masterfully guided Colonial Affair to victory. For Krone, another hurdle had been cleared.

Accomplishments

Olympic gold medalist, 100 meters: 1936
Olympic gold medalist, 4 x 100 relay: 1936
Winner of 14 national AAU titles
Member of the U.S. Track and Field Hall of Fame

Jan Stephenson

Born December 22, 1951

Jan Stephenson has won more than $2 million on the Ladies Professional Golf Association tour, but she remains most famous for embracing the role of LPGA "glamour girl" in the 1970s. Born in Sydney, Australia, Stephenson displayed not only a gift for the game of golf when she was growing up, but also a taste for competition. In the late 1960s and early 1970s she was easily the finest golfer in New South Wales. She won the first of five straight New South Wales Schoolgirl Championships in 1964; from 1969 to 1972 she was the New South Wales Junior champion. She also won a pair of New South Wales Amateur titles and three Australian Junior titles. In 1971 she was named New South Wales Athlete of the Year.

Stephenson began her professional career in Australia in 1973 and joined the LPGA tour a year later. She finished 28th on the money list and earned LPGA Rookie of the Year honors. But there was more to the Stephenson success story than a long drive and a deft touch around the greens.

The $16,270 that Stephenson earned playing golf represented only a portion of her 1974 income. Along with Laura Baugh she became an instant celebrity, in large part because she chose to take advantage of her stunning physical appearance, rather than downplay it. Stephenson, at 5 feet 5 inches tall, with a slim, athletic build, was an advertiser's dream. Not only could she hit a golf ball, she could sell them as well. She was attractive, talented, and graceful in front of a camera. Unlike many of her counterparts, she was instantly popular with the male portion of the LPGA audience.

Not everyone approved of Stephenson's behavior. Her willingness to pose for calendars and posters while wearing suggestive outfits

angered not only the prudish golf fan, but also a portion of the LPGA community that believed Stephenson's actions detracted from the accomplishments of all women golfers. At a time when women were struggling to achieve respect and recognition purely as athletes, Stephenson welcomed the opportunity to be treated as a sex symbol. It put more money in her pocket and helped her career immensely.

What prevented Stephenson from sinking beneath the weight of the criticism was her talent. She had one of the best fairway games and a steady hand on the greens. Both helped her win her first LPGA event in 1976; that same year, she finished among the top-10 money winners. In 1981 she captured her first major event, the Peter Jackson Classic. The following year she won the LPGA championship. In 1983 Stephenson finished fourth on the money list, winning three tournaments, including the U.S. Women's Open.

Since then, Stephenson's career has been interrupted on several occasions by injuries, but each time she has recovered impressively. She was injured in an automobile accident early in 1987 yet came back to win three tournaments later in the year. In 1990 she suffered a badly broken finger while being mugged in Phoenix, Arizona. Stephenson entered only 13 events that year but returned to the tour full-time in 1991.

Accomplishments

Australian Open champion: 1973, 1977
LPGA Rookie of the Year: 1974
Peter Jackson Classic champion: 1981
LPGA championship winner: 1982

Toni Stone

1921–1996

Born Marcenia Lyle in St. Paul, Minnesota, Toni Stone was the first woman to play in baseball's Negro Leagues. Even as a child her dream was to play professional baseball. She was a tomboy, playing sandlot ball with the boys in her neighborhood and eventually competing in a Little League–style tournament sponsored by Wheaties cereal.

As she matured, Marcenia lost none of her

competitive zeal. In fact, as she improved, her desire to continue playing and to find her place in a world dominated by males became even stronger. Fortunately the encouragement she received prompted her to keep striving toward her goal. One of the people who influenced her strongly was Gabby Street, a former major league ballplayer who managed the nearby St. Paul Saints, a minor league franchise. Street conducted a baseball camp for kids, and one summer Marcenia was the only girl who attended the camp. There and in other recreation leagues, she impressed coaches and opponents with her ability and tenacity.

As an adolescent in San Francisco, Marcenia Lyle became Toni Stone. She joined an American Legion team and later graduated to the San Francisco Sea Lions, a barnstorming outfit made up entirely of black males. But because she was unhappy with her salary, Stone left the Sea Lions and signed a contract with the New Orleans Black Pelicans, another barnstorming team. She spent several seasons as a second baseman with the Pelicans before joining the minor league New Orleans Creoles in 1949. Her salary then was $300 per month. Four years later she got a shot at the majors, in the form of an offer from the Indianapolis Clowns of the Negro American League.

It was a thrilling but difficult time for Stone, who later said that she felt like a goldfish when she first began practicing with the Clowns. All eyes were on her. She was not merely the first woman to play in the Negro Leagues—she was the first woman to play on a major league professional baseball team. But she was aware that her talent was only part of the reason that she was admitted to the Negro Leagues. Jackie Robinson had broken the color barrier in 1947, opening the door for black athletes to play in the major leagues. Since that time the Negro Leagues had seen a depletion of their ranks. They were losing their best players and, consequently, their fans. The signing of Toni Stone was, admittedly, a gimmick, an attempt to draw spectators back to the ballpark.

Stone understood, and accepted, the circumstances of her employment. "There's always got to be a first for everything," she said.

Stone, who earned $12,000 during her season with the Clowns, proved herself a capable player,

batting .243 in 50 games. The next year she signed with the Kansas City Monarchs but played sparingly. She retired from pro ball when the season ended but continued to take part in pickup games well into her 50s. In 1993 she was inducted into the International Women's Sports Hall of Fame.

Accomplishments

First and only woman to play on a major league baseball team
Inducted into International Women's Sports Hall of Fame: 1993

Picabo Street

Born April 3, 1971

Picabo Street, who became a fan favorite after winning a silver medal in downhill skiing at the 1994 Winter Olympics, was born in Triumph, Idaho. Born to free-spirited, countercultural parents, she went without a first name for the first six years of her life. She was known simply as Baby Girl Street. It was only when her parents embarked on an international trip and needed a passport for their daughter that they decided to give her an official name. They settled on Picabo (pronounced "PEEK-uh-boo"), which in the language of the local Native American population meant "shining waters."

Growing up in Sun Valley, Idaho, Street became a recreational skier at an early age, but it wasn't until her high school started a varsity ski team that she began to compete. Even then, Street had trouble taking the sport seriously. She was a fun-loving kid who was not particularly fond of training. She skied for pleasure, and when practice began to feel too much like work she'd disappear.

Nevertheless, by the age of 16, Street was the Western junior champion. At 17 she won the national junior downhill and super G titles. A knee injury in 1989 slowed her progress, but by 1990, at the age of 19, Street was healthy enough to compete in the World Junior Championships.

But, that same year, Street's complacency got her into trouble. After a poor performance at a U.S. skiing summer training camp, in which her attitude was questioned, Street was sent

"These two silver medals mean I don't have to hold my breath anymore, wondering, 'Can I do it?'" she said after the Olympics. "I've shown I can in the big races. Now I want to show I can be more consistent. I want to get back on the podium—and win World Cups!"

That she did the next year, winning four downhill races during the 1994–1995 World Cup season, a feat no American skier had ever accomplished.

Accomplishments

Silver medalist, combined, world
    championships: 1993
U.S. champion, super G: 1993
Olympic silver medalist, downhill: 1994
U.S. champion, downhill: 1994

Kerri Strug

Born November 19, 1977

Gymnast Kerri Strug, who vaulted to fame with a courageous—and gold medal–winning— performance at the 1996 Summer Olympics in Atlanta, was born in Tucson, Arizona. The youngest of three children, she followed in the footsteps of her sister, who was also a gymnast. Kerri began tumbling and bouncing around the family's living room when she was just a toddler. Her father, Burt, a heart surgeon, remembers constantly asking Kerri to "please walk on your feet. You're always traveling upside down." She never listened, though, and by age six was working with Jim Gault, the gymnastics coach at the University of Arizona. She often trained with the older girls and in that way developed advanced skills at an extremely young age.

Bright and exceptionally motivated, Strug asked her parents if she could move to Houston to train with legendary gymnastics coach Bela Karolyi (under whose guidance Nadia Comaneci and Mary Lou Retton had won gold medals) when she was only 12 years old. At first opposed to the idea, the Strugs eventually relented, and Kerri moved to Houston. Within two years she was one of the most promising young gymnasts in the world. In 1991 she became, at 14, the youngest member of the U.S. national team, and in 1992 she was the youngest member of the U.S.

home. Embarrassed by that incident, she dedicated herself to her sport for the first time in her life. She won the North American overall title in each of the next two years, and by 1993 she was a full-time competitor on the World Cup racing circuit. "As my results got better, I got hungrier," Street said. "I just started chomping at the bit a little bit more."

With her outgoing personality and aggressive style on the slopes, Street became one of the stars of the 1994 Winter Games in Lillehammer, Norway. She took a silver medal in the women's downhill. That, combined with a second-place finish in the 1993 world championships, gave Street all the confidence she needed to become one of the top performers in her sport.

contingent that won a bronze medal in the Summer Olympics in Barcelona.

Rather than accept any lucrative offers to compete in exhibitions or sign with an agent, Strug decided to continue competing as an amateur after the Barcelona Games. She finished fifth in the all-around competition at the world championships in 1993 and third at the national championships. After graduating from high school with a perfect 4.0 grade point average in the summer of 1995, she accepted a gymnastics scholarship from UCLA but deferred enrollment for one year so that she could train full-time for the 1996 Summer Olympics in Atlanta.

The 1996 U.S. team was considered a solid contender for team honors in Atlanta; however, Strug was overshadowed by several of her teammates, most notably former national champions Shannon Miller, Dominique Dawes, and Dominique Moceanu. They were the stars—gifted, charismatic athletes expected to contend for medals in the all-around competition. Strug was considered a reliable member of the team, resigned to performing at the edge of the spotlight. But on July 23, events conspired to thrust Strug into a starring role. Moceanu, bothered by injuries throughout the Games, fell twice during the final rotation of the team competition. Her mistakes nearly erased a substantial U.S. lead and set up a scenario in which Strug needed to nail her final attempt on the vault, despite suffering from a severely sprained ankle. Considering that Karolyi had once said Strug had a low threshold for pain, what happened next was remarkable.

On her first vault Strug, obviously in pain and distracted by her swollen ankle, executed a respectable vault but fell on the landing. Rather than withdraw, which seemed a distinct possibility, she decided to attempt a second vault. Strug sprinted down the runway and performed the vault flawlessly. She landed firmly on both feet, hobbled once, and, after thrusting her arms into the air, crumpled to the floor. Moments later, with tears staining her cheeks, Strug heard the roar of the crowd in the Georgia Dome responding to her score of 9.712. Her vault had assured the United States a gold medal.

"I felt pretty good in the air," Strug explained. "Then when I landed, I heard another crack. But I didn't want to be remembered for falling on my butt in my best event."

Instead, Strug is remembered as one of the bravest performers in the history of Olympic gymnastics. She was forced to withdraw from the rest of the competition and even several months later was not able to train or perform at full strength, so severe was her ankle injury. She planned to perform in exhibitions before resuming her academic career in 1997.

Accomplishments

Olympic bronze medalist, team competition: 1992
Fifth place, world championships, all-around: 1993
Third place, national championships, all-around: 1993
Olympic gold medalist, team competition: 1996

Louise Suggs

Born September 7, 1923

Louise Suggs, a charter member of the Ladies Professional Golf Association, was born in Atlanta, Georgia. She honed her skills as a golfer on a course in Lithia Springs, Georgia, that was designed and built by her father, John Suggs, a former professional baseball player.

"I was 10 years old then," Suggs said in an interview. "In those days Lithia Springs was out in the country; there were no neighbors or anything. Since our house almost had the golf course for a backyard, I just started hitting golf balls."

Young Louise had a beautiful, fluid swing, one of the best in the game. She was not big or strong, but she hit the ball with exceptional power. So long off the tee was Louise that comedian Bob Hope dubbed her "Miss Slugs." A winner of 50 tournaments, Suggs went about her business quietly, with dignity and style. Had she come along in another era, she would probably have performed in the glare of the spotlight for years. But she had the misfortune to reach her prime just as Babe Didrikson Zaharias began playing her best golf. So even as Suggs racked up title after title, she walked in the shadow of the more outgoing Zaharias. Suggs was a modest and unemotional woman,

who liked to say that the course was her true opponent.

Before turning professional in 1949, Suggs had a brilliant amateur career. She won the Georgia State Amateur Championship in 1940 and 1942, the Titleholders in 1946, and the U.S. Women's Amateur in 1947. She won the British Amateur in 1948 and was a member of the U.S. Curtis Cup team in 1948. As a professional, it didn't take Suggs long to make her mark. In 1949 she won two majors—the Western Open and the U.S. Women's Open. Three years later, in 1952, she won a second U.S. Women's Open, setting a 72-hole record with her score of 284. She added another Western Open title in 1953; Titleholders Championships in 1954, 1956, and 1959; and the LPGA Championship in 1957.

In 1960 Suggs failed to win a major tournament but remained the tour's leading money winner. Equally notable is the fact that she defeated more than a dozen male professionals—including Sam Snead and Gardner Dickinson—at a tournament in Palm Beach, Florida. Playing from the same tees as the men, Suggs walked off with first place. But she hardly needed that victory to justify her talent. She was already a longtime member of the LPGA Hall of Fame, having been the first official inductee in 1951.

Suggs' last LPGA victory came in 1962, at the St. Petersburg Open; however, she competed for many more years—in 1994, at the age of 71, she was still participating in Sprint Senior Challenge events on the LPGA tour. In 1966 Suggs was elected to the Georgia Athletic Hall of Fame; in 1987 she was inducted into the International Women's Sports Hall of Fame. In 1988 she was named one of *Golf* magazine's "100 Heroes" during the Centennial of Golf in America celebration. She served as LPGA president three times.

Accomplishments

U.S. Women's Open champion: 1949, 1951
Western Open champion: 1949, 1953
Titleholders champion: 1954, 1956, 1959
LPGA championship winner: 1957
First person inducted into LPGA Hall of Fame: 1951
Inducted into International Women's Sports Hall of Fame: 1987

Pat Summitt

Born June 14, 1952

Born Patricia Head in Clarksville, Tennessee, Pat Summitt grew up to become one of the most respected and successful coaches in women's basketball.

Her playing career began at Cheatham County High School in Ashland City, Tennessee. She went on to star in both basketball and volleyball at the University of Tennessee–Martin. While studying for a master's degree in physical education at the University of Tennessee–Knoxville, Summitt became the school's women's basketball coach.

Summitt led the Lady Volunteers to a 16–8 record in her first season. Two years later, in 1977, Tennessee had one of the finest women's programs in the country. The Lady Vols won 28 games and lost just five. For the first seven years of Summitt's tenure, Tennessee played in the Association of Intercollegiate Athletics for Women. In that time the Lady Vols established themselves as a first-rate basketball program. They won four state titles and three regional titles, and advanced to the national semifinals twice. In the 1977–1978 season, Summitt guided Tennessee to a 22–2 season record and a No. 1 ranking in the national polls. The Lady Vols made a charge at the national championship the following year, winning 30 games, but wound up losing in the semifinals. In 1980 they were beaten by Old Dominion in the championship game, and in 1981 they lost to Louisiana Tech.

In 1982 Tennessee reached the Final Four of the NCAA tournament but lost again to Louisiana Tech. The Lady Vols continued to be one of the best teams in the nation over the next few years, but it wasn't until 1987 that they won a national title. They also won titles in 1989 and 1991.

Those championships further boosted the reputation of Pat Summitt. In addition to her success at Tennessee, she had become one of the most respected coaches internationally. She coached the 1979 U.S. national women's team that won a silver medal in the Pan American Games and a gold medal in the world championships. She then led the United States to a silver medal at the 1983 world championships. In 1984 Summitt coached the U.S. Olympic women's basketball team, which won a gold medal.

Heading into the 1995–1996 season, Summitt had compiled an impressive career record of 530-126 at Tennessee. She was second in victories among all active coaches. In 1990 she was inducted into the International Women's Sports Hall of Fame.

Accomplishments

NCAA champion: 1987, 1989, 1991
Olympic gold medalist: 1984
Second winningest active coach in NCAA
Inducted into International Women's Sports
   Hall of Fame: 1990

Katherine Switzer

Born 1947

Katherine Switzer, the first woman to officially enter and finish the Boston Marathon, grew up in Falls Church, Virginia. She attended George Marshall High School and Lynchburg College. After her sophomore year in college, she transferred to Syracuse University, where she studied journalism and English literature. Switzer was an activist as well as an athlete, a woman with great spirit and determination. All her life she had been trying to break down gender barriers. At Lynchburg College she once competed in the mile on the men's track team, an act that some people considered not just defiant and inappropriate but downright despicable. When local newspapers got word of the incident, Switzer began to receive hate mail. Lynchburg is a conservative Southern Christian school, and few people on campus supported Switzer's actions. Even her boyfriend at the time, a cadet at the U.S. Naval Academy who believed that women benefited from participating in sports, wondered whether she was taking things a bit too far.

Switzer wrote an article for the school newspaper declaring her intention to one day run the Boston Marathon, something only one other woman, Roberta Gibb, had ever done. Gibb had been forced to run as an unofficial entrant,

since the Boston Athletic Association did not permit women in its race. Switzer hoped to change all of that. At Syracuse she trained with the men's track team and worked under the supervision of Arnie Briggs, who had been a top-10 finisher at Boston in 1952. Briggs doubted Switzer's resolve. He challenged her, asking for proof that she was serious. She responded by working harder than ever. Together they went on long runs—some more than 30 miles—with Briggs heaping instruction and wisdom on Switzer all the way.

By the spring of 1967 Switzer was ready to run a marathon. But she had to find a way to get in the race. It wasn't enough for her to simply jump in at the starting line and complete the distance. Switzer wanted to be recognized as an official and legitimate competitor. But that wasn't going to happen without a bit of deception. She decided to fill out an application under the name K. Switzer. She underwent the required medical examination. On the day of the race, Briggs picked up her number. Switzer pinned it on her sweatshirt and walked to the starting line.

Switzer ran the first few miles with her boyfriend, hammer thrower Thomas C. Miller. It didn't take long before reporters and photographers noticed that a woman was running, and she seemed to be an official entrant. They were stunned, since they hadn't been informed of any changes in the BAA rules. Jock Semple, a longtime BAA official, tried to physically force Switzer off the course. "Get the hell out of my race and give me that number!" he shouted.

Miller came to Switzer's aid, knocking Semple to the ground with an angry shove. Switzer, nearly overcome by shock and fatigue, struggled to finish the race in approximately 4 hours and 20 minutes, long after the course officials had stopped recording results. Switzer became a celebrity over the following week, as her story appeared in national newspapers and magazines. But the BAA refused to recognize her accomplishment, instead declaring that she had "cheated" by failing to properly identify herself on the entry form.

Switzer ran the Boston Marathon several more times. In 1972, the first year that women were officially allowed to compete, she finished third in 3:29.51. The next year, in a symbolic gesture of acceptance, Switzer's old nemesis,

Jock Semple, kissed her on the cheek moments before the race began.

Switzer went on to become a successful television broadcaster, providing color commentary for many Boston Marathons.

Accomplishments

First woman to officially enter the Boston
    Marathon: 1967
Third-place finisher, Boston Marathon: 1972
Fourth-place finisher, Boston Marathon: 1973
Second-place finisher, Boston Marathon: 1975

Sheryl Swoopes

Born March 25, 1971

Sheryl Swoopes, one of the greatest basketball players in NCAA history, was born and raised in Brownfield, a small farming community in western Texas. Tall and quick, she was blessed with a shooting eye that few of the boys in her school could match. In fact, she proved to be a better basketball player than many of the boys, who gave Swoopes her only competition when she was a youngster. Her game was refined on playgrounds, playing against bigger, tougher males. She never backed down against them; once they saw the way she could play, they welcomed her into their games.

When she played with girls, Swoopes was always the finest athlete in the gym. She was only 16 years old when she was named the Texas state girls' basketball player of the year. By that time people were already comparing her to one of the finest performers in the sport—Michael Jordan. They saw in her a versatility and a competitiveness that was evident in Jordan. They saw a player who was capable of doing virtually anything she wanted with a basketball, a player who was redefining her sport.

But the transition from high school superstar to college student-athlete was difficult for Swoopes. She had grown up in a quiet rural town, and when she went away to the University of Texas in Austin, she felt overwhelmed. She missed her friends and family. Overcome by homesickness, she packed her bags and walked off campus after just three days. But she never stopped playing basketball. She enrolled at South

Swoopes was named 1993 National Player of the Year by *USA Today* and *Sports Illustrated*. The Women's Sports Foundation presented her with its Sudafed Sportswoman of the Year Award.

Success after college was at first elusive for Swoopes. Because professional opportunities for female basketball players in the United States were limited, she signed a contract to play professionally in Italy. But she stayed only a few months and played in just 10 games. Swoopes believed that her employer had not lived up to the terms of their contract. The following year she played with the U.S. national women's basketball team. In 1996 she helped the United States capture a gold medal at the Summer Olympics in Atlanta.

Accomplishments

Junior College Player of the Year: 1991
Most Valuable Player, NCAA tournament:
   1993
National Player of the Year: 1993
Sudafed Sportswoman of the Year: 1993
Olympic gold medalist: 1996

Irena Kirszenstein Szewinska

Born May 24, 1946

Born to Polish parents in Leningrad, in the former Soviet Union, sprinter Irena Kirszenstein Szewinska competed internationally for Poland and won medals in four different Olympics.

Track-and-field athletes typically have short careers. Theirs is a demanding sport, and until quite recently the financial incentive was so small that many chose another line of work after only a few years of world-class competition. Not so with Irena. At the 1964 Tokyo Olympics, she won silver medals in the long jump and the 200 meters, and helped Poland's 4 x 100 relay team win a gold medal with a world-record performance. (The mark was later wiped from the record books after it was revealed that one of the Polish team members had failed a drug test.) By any standard, it was an impressive Olympic debut—Irena Kirszenstein was only 18 years old.

Plains Junior College, which was located close to Brownfield, and fared much better than she had at Texas. She was named the national junior college player of the year and eventually transferred to a four-year school. But her choice this time was Texas Tech in nearby Lubbock. There she became the best player in college basketball, as well as one of the most entertaining.

Swoopes had her best season in 1992–1993, when she led Texas Tech to the NCAA Division I championship. In the Lady Raiders' 84–82 victory over Ohio State in the title game, Swoopes was unstoppable, scoring 47 points. No player—male or female—had ever scored that many points in an NCAA championship game; Swoopes was named the tournament's Most Valuable Player. After averaging 35.4 points and 9.6 rebounds in the NCAA tournament and scoring 53 points in the Southwest Conference Tournament final,

The following year Kirszenstein set world records in the 100 meters (11.1 seconds) and the 200 meters (22.7 seconds). At the 1966 European championships she won the 200 and the long jump, and finished second in the 100. She also helped Poland win the sprint relay. In 1968, at the Mexico City Summer Olympics, Irena Szewinska (she had married her coach the year before) took the gold medal in the 200 meters with a world-record time of 22.58 seconds and the bronze medal in the 100. Her effort in the 100 was a disappointment because she had equaled the world record in a trial heat. In the final she got off to a bad start and lost to Americans Wyomia Tyus and Edith McGuire.

Szewinska gave birth to a son in 1969, took some time off, and came back to win bronze medals at the 1971 European championships and the 1972 Munich Olympics. After that, sensing that her legs were not as quick as they once were, Szewinska moved up in distance. The 400 meters became her specialty; in 1973 she became the first woman to crack the 50-second barrier at 400 meters, setting a world record with her time of 49.9 seconds. That same year, she set a world record in the 200 (22.0 seconds). At the 1976 Olympics in Montreal, Szewinska won the gold medal in the 400 by finishing nearly 10 meters ahead of the competition with a time of 49.29—another world record.

Szewinska announced her retirement after the Montreal Games but attempted a comeback at the 1980 Olympics in Moscow. Time, however, had caught up with her. Even Szewinska could not sprint like a champion at the age of 34. For the first time, her body betrayed her. In a 400-meter heat she ruptured her Achilles tendon and was forced to withdraw. She again announced her retirement, and this time she meant it.

Szewinska has avoided the spotlight in the years since, but her seven Olympic medals and 11 world records stand as testimony to her greatness.

Accomplishments

    Olympic silver medalist, long jump: 1964
    Olympic silver medalist, 200 meters: 1964
    Olympic gold medalist, 4 x 100 relay: 1964
    Olympic gold medalist, 200 meters: 1968
    Olympic bronze medalist, 100 meters: 1968
    Olympic bronze medalist, 200 meters: 1972
    Olympic gold medalist, 400 meters: 1976

T

Jenny Thompson

Born February 26, 1973

Swimmer Jenny Thompson, who won two gold medals at the 1992 Summer Olympics in Barcelona, grew up in Georgetown, Massachusetts. Her parents separated when she was only three years old, leaving her mother, Margrid, to raise four children. Jenny was the youngest; she was also the only girl in the family, which was both a blessing and a burden. As one of her brothers once said, "Jenny was either going to be the meekest person in the world or the most outspoken."

Actually, she fell somewhere in the middle, though she did blast Vice President Dan Quayle after hearing his harsh comments about single mothers. She was fiercely protective of her own mother, who had made tremendous sacrifices to give her children a safe and secure home; Margrid was particularly devoted when it came to her daughter's swimming career. She commuted 30 miles to and from work, then picked Jenny up from school and drove another 40 miles to Dover, New Hampshire, where Jenny worked out with the Seacoast Swimming Association. Jenny also benefited from her brothers' unwavering support. "They built her up and cheered her on," Margrid said.

Jenny Thompson's progress was steady throughout her adolescence. She was a high school All-America team member in 1991; that same year, she won the 100-meter freestyle and the 50-meter freestyle, and was named Swimmer of the Meet at the High School All-Star meet. In 1991, Thompson anchored the U.S. team to a gold medal in the 4 x 100 freestyle relay at the world championships. Offered dozens of college scholarships, she chose Stanford, which traditionally had one of the strongest programs in college swimming.

As a freshman at Stanford, Thompson emerged as not only one of the fastest sprinters in the NCAA, but also one of the fastest in the world. She won collegiate titles in the 50-meter freestyle and the 100-meter freestyle, a prelude to her performance at the Summer Games. Thompson warmed up for the Olympics by setting a world record in the 100-meter freestyle and an American record in the 50-meter freestyle at the U.S. Olympic trials. Then, in Barcelona, she helped the U.S. team set world records in the 4 x 100 freestyle relay and the 4 x 100 medley relay; she also won a silver in the 100-meter freestyle.

In 1993 Thompson was named United States Swimming Association's Swimmer of the Year. She won a pair of NCAA individual titles and a record six gold medals at the Pan Pacific Championships, and was a finalist for the Women's Sports Foundation Sportswoman of the Year Award. In 1994 she won the 100-meter butterfly and the 100-meter freestyle at the world championships in Rome, despite having broken her left arm just a few months earlier. She finished first in the the 100-meter butterfly and 100-meter freestyle at the NCAA championships.

In 1996, at the Summer Olympic Games in Atlanta, Thompson was a member of three winning relay teams, bringing her Olympic gold medal total to five. The only other American woman to win five Olympic gold medals to date is speed skater Bonnie Blair.

Accomplishments

World champion, 4 x 100 freestyle relay: 1991

Olympic gold medalist, 4 x 100 freestyle relay: 1992

Olympic gold medalist, 4 x 100 medley relay: 1992

World champion, 100-meter freestyle: 1994

World champion, 100-meter butterfly: 1994

Olympic gold medalist, 4 x 100 freestyle relay: 1996

Olympic gold medalist, 4 x 200 freestyle relay: 1996

Olympic gold medalist, 4 x 100 medley relay: 1996

Gwen Torrence

Born June 12, 1965

Gwen Torrence, an Olympic gold medalist in track and field, grew up in Decatur, Georgia, and attended the University of Georgia on an athletic scholarship. She was a strong and talented sprinter who had a good deal of success as a youngster, and continued to improve throughout her career. In 1984 the 5-foot 7-inch 123-pound Torrence reached the finals of the 100 meters at the NCAA Track and Field Championships, but finished a disappointing eighth. The next year, she finished second at the NCAA championships. In 1986 she finished second in both the 100 and the 200. In 1987, as a senior, she was one of the outstanding performers at the NCAAs, winning both the 100 and the 200. She also competed in the World Track and Field Championships for the first time, and finished fifth in the 200.

By 1988 Torrence had become one of the premier sprinters in the world. At the U.S. Olympic trials she finished first in the 100 and the 200 meters. But at the Summer Games in Seoul, South Korea, she finished fifth in the 100 and sixth in the 200, and did not compete on the U.S. 4 x 100 relay team.

Torrence was still something of a novice when it came to international competition; she knew there would be other opportunities, so she went back to work, training harder than ever. By 1991 she was once again the top-ranked female sprinter in the United States and one of the best in the world. At the national outdoor championships, Torrence finished first in the 200 and second in the 100. At the world championships in Tokyo, she took silver medals in both the 100 and the 200; in each race she was beaten by German sprinter Katrin Krabbe. At the end of 1991, Torrence was the No. 3–ranked sprinter in the world.

In 1992 Torrence returned to the Olympic Games, having already finished first in both sprint events at the U.S. Olympic trials. In Barcelona she finished fourth in the 100. But in the 200 she ran flawlessly, taking the gold medal with a time of 21.81 seconds. The next year, at the world championships, she took a pair of

individual medals—a bronze in the 100 and a silver in the 200.

In 1995, at the world championships in Göteborg, Sweden, Torrence again ran magnificently, but her achievements were nearly lost in a cloud of controversy. After winning the 100, Torrence prepared for a 200-meter showdown with Jamaica's Merlene Ottey. In the final, Torrence breezed to a lopsided victory over Ottey in the 200 and had, at the age of 30, apparently become the first American woman to win both sprint events at the world championships. But shortly after the race, Torrence was disqualified for running out of her lane, which prompted Ottey to say, "That was cheating. She ran about two meters shorter than everybody else."

Torrence, who admitted to unintentionally stepping on the line, broke into tears when informed of Ottey's comments. Ottey, who was awarded the gold medal, later softened her stance, acknowledging that Torrence was far ahead of the field and would have won the race anyway.

Four years later, at the 1996 Summer Olympic Games in Atlanta, Torrence won a bronze medal in the 100 meters and a gold medal in the 4 x 100 relay.

Accomplishments

NCAA champion, 100 meters: 1987
NCAA champion, 200 meters: 1987
Olympic gold medalist, 200 meters: 1992
World champion, 100 meters: 1995
Olympic gold medalist, 4 x 100 relay: 1996
Olympic bronze medalist, 100 meters: 1996

Jayne Torvill

Born October 7, 1957

British figure skater Jayne Torvill will forever be linked with her partner, Christopher Dean. She was a fine athlete in her own right, but when paired with Dean, she was mesmerizing.

Memorable Moment: February 23, 1994

Tonya Harding vs. Nancy Kerrigan

The sport of figure skating never asked for this kind of publicity. On January 6, 1994, Nancy Kerrigan, one of the favorites in the upcoming Olympic competition, was whacked on the knee by an unidentified man at the U.S. Figure Skating Association Championships. What at first was thought to be a random attack turned out to be a botched attempt to maim Kerrigan on behalf of one of her chief rivals, Tonya Harding. The plot had been hatched by Harding's ex-husband, Jeff Gillooly, and executed with the help of three other men.

With Kerrigan unable to compete in the national championships—which served as the Olympic Trials—Harding finished first. Kerrigan was also granted a spot on the team. In the weeks leading up to the Winter Olympics in Lillehammer, Norway, Harding was implicated in the attack on Kerrigan; however, she maintained her innocence.

On the night of February 23, 1994, millions of people tuned in to watch the dramatic showdown between Kerrigan and Harding. If they hoped for some sort of on-ice confrontation, though, they were disappointed. Instead, they saw Kerrigan skate flawlessly in winning the technical portion of the program; Harding, meanwhile, had numerous problems and reached the halfway point in 10th place. The event drew a 48.5 Nielsen rating, which meant it was the sixth largest audience ever for a television program.

Two nights later, Ukrainian teenager Oksana Baiul won the gold medal, and Kerrigan took the silver. Sordid as it was, the Harding-Kerrigan affair helped introduce figure skating to a vast new audience. Over the next few years a new professional circuit flourished and television ratings soared, as the sport enjoyed greater popularity than it had ever known.

They brought to the sport of ice dancing a sensuality that had never before been seen. It mattered not that Torvill had been an insurance clerk and Dean a police officer—to their millions of fans, they were the most elegant and romantic couple in sports. On the ice, in costume, they were transformed into Torvill and Dean, Olympic champions. They were a fantasy couple, graceful and athletic, their every movement choreographed in such a way as to indicate that the skaters' passion for each other might burn a hole in the ice. Small wonder that the British press speculated for years on the nature of their off-ice relationship. Surely a man and woman who skated like that, pressed so close to each other, staring into each other's eyes while Ravel's *Boléro* echoed through the arena, had to feel something for each other. Surely it wasn't all an act.

"For the two minutes we skated," Torvill said, "we were in love."

Torvill and Dean dominated ice dancing in the early 1980s, winning four consecutive world championships between 1981 and 1984. But it wasn't until the 1984 Winter Olympics in Sarajevo, Yugoslavia, that their fame and appeal transcended the world of figure skating. As their bodies intertwined in a dance that was boldly provocative and unabashedly romantic, they captivated not only the Olympic judges who awarded them the gold medal, but millions of television viewers as well.

After the Olympics, Torvill and Dean retired from amateur competition and began performing in professional shows around the world. Their popularity—and their bank accounts—soared. They were rich and famous beyond their wildest dreams. But something drew them back to Olympic competition in 1994. Torvill was 36 and Dean 35 when they took to the ice at the Winter Olympics in Lillehammer, Norway. No one really understood why they were there. But Torvill offered an explanation. "We've never really hit our peak. This gives us a chance to finish on a high."

While it requires a high degree of technical skill and artistic ability, ice dancing is the least athletic event in figure skating. It is, as the name suggests, a dance on ice. Emphasis is on carefully crafted movements performed to a piece of music. Mood and style are as important as leaps and twists. Hence, a performer is able to stay competitive for a longer period of time. Still, few people expected much out of Torvill and Dean in Lillehammer; in fact, there was some concern that, far from finishing on a high, the duo might be so badly outclassed that the memory of Sarajevo would be forever tarnished.

But once on the ice, Torvill and Dean laid all doubts to rest. While they were not the finest ice dancers in the competition, they were greeted lovingly by the crowd and earned a bronze medal.

Accomplishments

World champion: 1981–1984
Olympic gold medalist: 1984
Olympic bronze medalist: 1994

Bertha Townsend Toulmin

March 7, 1869–May 12, 1909

Bertha Louise Townsend Toulmin, a member of the International Tennis Hall of Fame, was born in Philadelphia. Her mother was Georgiana Lawrence Talman; her father was Philadelphia lawyer Henry Clay Townsend. Bertha, whose nickname was Birdie, was the youngest of the couple's children.

Bertha Townsend was one of the first great left-handed players in tennis. She was also one of the first women to consistently incorporate a reliable backhand into her game. Standing 5 feet 4 inches tall, with a sturdy frame, Townsend was a daring, courageous player. At times her play was spectacular. She was capable of executing shots that few other players would even attempt. But the same boldness that often carried her to victory occasionally cost her a match.

Townsend, a member of the Belmont Country Club, was one of four Philadelphia women who dominated tennis in the 1880s. The others were Louise Allderdice, Ellen Forde Hansell, and Margarette Ballard. Townsend's first big victory came in 1886, when she captured the Chestnut Hill Lawn Tennis Club singles title at the Philadelphia Cricket Club. In 1887 the first U.S. women's singles championship was played, with Hansell emerging as the winner. The death of a family member prevented Townsend from participating in that tournament, but a few weeks later she and Hansell—her Belmont clubmate—met in the finals of the Delaware Field Club tournament. Townsend gained a measure of satisfaction by winning that match. She also teamed up with Milton Works, a well-known bridge player, to win the mixed doubles title.

At the 1888 U.S. championships, Townsend defeated Marion Wright in the finals. She met Hansell in the challenge round and posted a 6–3, 6–5 victory to walk off with her first national title. But neither of those matches was the best of the tournament. Along the way, Townsend posted a dramatic 1–6, 6–5, 6–3 victory over Adeline Robinson of Staten Island, who had never before lost a singles match.

In 1889 Townsend repeated as national champion with a 7–5, 6–2 victory over Louise Voorhes. She also teamed up with Margarette Ballard to win the doubles crown, though it was not yet recognized as a national title. Townsend's bid for a third consecutive national singles championship ended in 1890 with a 6–2, 6–2 loss to Ellen Roosevelt. Townsend and Ballard lost in the doubles final to Ellen Roosevelt and her sister, Grace.

Townsend did not make another serious run at a U.S. championship until 1894, when, as Mrs. Harry Toulmin, she reached the final of the open portion of the tournament before losing to eventual champion Helen Hellwig. In 1895 Toulmin lost in the semifinals, then decided to retire.

In 1974 Bertha Townsend Toulmin was inducted into the International Tennis Hall of Fame.

Accomplishments

U.S. singles champion: 1888–1889
U.S. singles runner-up: 1890
Inducted into International Tennis Hall of
   Fame: 1974

Cathy Turner

Born 1962

Short-track speed skater Cathy Turner grew up in Hilton, New York. She began skating when she was quite young, but it wasn't until she was nearly 30 years old—the age at which most world-class athletes contemplate retirement—that Turner gained international recognition. She had left the sport in 1984 to pursue a variety of career options, including professional cyclist, nightclub performer, and recording artist. But she was eventually drawn back to skating.

In 1992 Turner came out of retirement and earned a place on the U.S. Olympic team. She was excited about the possibility of competing in Albertville, France, where short-track speed skating would make its debut as an Olympic sport. Short-track skating was a strange and new event, a little like traditional speed skating and a little like Roller Derby. The competitors flew around a small, tight indoor track, all the while leaning into the ice, their hands scraping the surface with each turn. Occasionally elbows were exchanged and legs became entangled. It wasn't at all unusual to see the participants go sprawling onto the ice. Sometimes, tempers flared. Purists, of course, hated the sport.

Turner, a fiery, 5-foot 2-inch, 116-pound competitor, fit right in. She loved the sport, warts and all. So she did quite well at Albertville, despite her long layoff. Turner finished first in the 500-meter event and in the relay. But that was merely a prelude to what she would accomplish two years later in Lillehammer, Norway.

Turner's participation in the 1994 Winter Games was something of a surprise. After Albertville, she had once again opted for retirement. This time she tried the Ice Capades. But Turner was still more of an athlete than a performer; she needed to compete, so she returned to the speed-skating oval in time to qualify for one more Olympic appearance.

Brash, driven, and decidedly unapologetic about her style, Turner became one of the most visible—and controversial—figures at the 1994 Winter Games. First she helped the United States win a bronze medal in the relay. Then, in dramatic fashion, she won a gold medal in the 500 meters. But her victory was tainted by vehement protests from her opponents, who charged that she was a dangerous and dirty competitor who needlessly and selfishly tarnished the image of their sport. "Cathy Turner turns our sport into something it's not meant to be," said Nathalie Lambert, a member of the Canadian team. "She is brutal, and the judges overlook her behavior."

The trouble began with two laps remaining in the 4½-lap race, when Turner's hand brushed the leg of the leader, world-record holder Zhang Yanmei of China. Their skates clicked against each other, prompting Zhang to glance up in surprise and surrender the lead. Afterward, Zhang pointed and shouted at Turner; she also filed a formal protest and stormed off the awards stand during the medal ceremony.

But none of that seemed to matter to Turner. "I don't know what's going on and why everybody's mad at me," she said. "But I earned this [medal]. I really earned it. And nobody's taking it away from me."

Accomplishments

Olympic gold medalist, 500 meters: 1992, 1994
Olympic silver medalist, 3,000-meter relay: 1992
Olympic bronze medalist, 3,000-meter relay: 1994

Rebecca Twigg

Born March 16, 1963

Rebecca Twigg, one of the finest cyclists in the world, was born in Seattle, Washington. An exceptionally bright child, she bypassed high school completely and entered the University of Washington when she was only 14 years old. That was when she began training for cycling; she finished third in the road-race competition at the 1977 U.S. championships.

Twigg's bronze medal in the nationals was the first of many honors. In her long career she won 16 national titles. She also won the world championship in the 3-kilometer pursuit in 1982, 1983, 1984, and 1987. No other American had ever won that event. One of her best years came in 1981, when, in an impressive display of versatility, she dominated the U.S. national championships, winning the road race, the junior time trials, and the senior pursuit; the next year she captured the senior pursuit and the senior time trials.

In 1982 the International Olympic Committee announced that women's cycling would be added to the competition schedule at the 1984 Summer Games; Twigg's response was to throw herself into the sport with renewed

fervor. She postponed her plans for graduate school and devoted all of her energy to training. Since cycling in the United States—particularly amateur cycling—was not a sport that attracted significant sponsorship, Twigg packed her bags and moved to Colorado Springs, where she took up residence at the U.S. Olympic Training Center.

In 1984 Twigg won national titles in the individual pursuit, the 1-kilometer, the match sprint, and the points race. But none of those events was contested at the Los Angeles Summer Olympics; the only women's cycling event that year was a

road race. Twigg got off to a great start and seemed to be in control of the race, but wound up losing to Connie Carpenter-Phinney in a dramatic sprint to the finish line.

Twigg continued to compete for the next

few years. She won the national individual pursuit and points race championships in 1985, and in 1986 she set a world record in the 500 meters. After winning three gold medals at the 1987 Pan American Games, Twigg announced her retirement. With her bicycle in storage, she settled into her new life as a computer programmer.

That didn't last, however. She came out of retirement as the decade came to a close and soon was fit enough to compete at the international level. In 1992 she made the U.S. Olympic team and won a bronze medal in the individual pursuit at the Summer Games in Barcelona. In 1993 she won her fifth world title in the pursuit, and in 1995, in Bogotá, Colombia, she not only won a sixth title, but also set a world record. "I felt better and better throughout the rounds," Twigg said. "But I was really surprised that I ended up going so fast."

After the world championships, Twigg moved back to Colorado Springs to train for the 1996 Summer Olympics in Atlanta. She made the U.S. team but did not win a medal.

Accomplishments

World champion, pursuit: 1982, 1984–1985,
  1987, 1993, 1995
Olympic silver medalist, road race: 1984
Olympic bronze medalist, pursuit: 1992

Wyomia Tyus

Born August 29, 1945

Wyomia Tyus, who was born in Griffin, Georgia, was the first person to win two consecutive Olympic gold medals in the 100-meter dash. Athletic success came to her suddenly and belatedly. Tyus was the youngest of four children. Her mother was a laundry worker; her father, a dairy worker, died when Wyomia was 15. By that time she had demonstrated an aptitude for track and field. Wyomia was the only athlete in the family; track was the only sport in which she participated while in high school.

Wyomia Tyus' big break came at a summer camp conducted by Tennessee State coach Ed Temple. There she worked with Temple's prize pupil, Wilma Rudolph, who was five years older

than Tyus. Temple encouraged Tyus and helped her work on training techniques. Eventually the two hooked up again when Tyus graduated from high school and accepted a scholarship to Tennessee State, where Temple had become the track coach.

In February 1964 Tyus set an indoor world record for 70 meters with a time of 7.5 seconds. She wasn't nearly as successful outdoors, where she was often overshadowed by two of her teammates at Tennessee State, Edith McGuire and Marilyn White. But to the surprise of virtually everyone who followed track and field, Tyus turned in a breakthrough performance in the 100 meters at the 1964 Summer Olympics in Tokyo. She chopped three-tenths of a second off her personal best to equal Rudolph's world record of 11.2 seconds in a qualifying heat, then went on to win the gold medal by more than two meters over McGuire. She also helped the United States win a silver medal in the 4 x 100 relay.

Four years later, after ignoring a plea from her mother to retire because running was "unladylike," Tyus returned to the Olympic stage. And this time, though her margin of victory was smaller, she was even more impressive. The 100-meter field was one of the most competitive ever assembled. It included five world-record holders, including Ludmila Samotyosova of the Soviet Union, Irena Szewinska of Poland, and Margaret Bailes and Barbara Ferrell of the United States. Tyus bettered the world record in one of her heats, but the record was disallowed because it had been wind aided. In the final, after being charged with one false start, she got away cleanly and went on to win with a time of 11.0, a new Olympic and world record. Before the Games ended, Tyus also helped the United States take first in the 4 x 100 relay with a world-record time of 42.8 seconds.

Immediately after the 1968 Games, Tyus retired from athletic competition. She went on to become a teacher in, among other places, Los Angeles, where she worked to instill in children a love for both athletics and education.

Accomplishments

Olympic gold medalist, 100 meters: 1964
Olympic silver medalist, 4 x 100 relay: 1964
Olympic gold medalist, 100 meters: 1968
Olympic gold medalist, 4 x 100 relay: 1968

V

Tara Van Derveer

Born June 26, 1953

Tara Van Derveer is one of college basketball's most successful coaches. She was a
starting guard for the Indiana University
Hoosiers for three years in the mid-1970s, but it
wasn't until after her playing career ended that
she truly found her niche. Her first head coaching job was at the University of Idaho, where she
compiled a 42–14 record in two years. From
there she went back to the Big Ten Athletic
Conference, becoming head coach at Ohio State
University. The Buckeyes won 110 games and
lost only 37 during Van Derveer's five-year tenure.
She won four league titles and twice took the
team into the NCAA tournament. Twice she was
named Big Ten Coach of the Year.

Van Derveer moved on to Stanford in 1985.
In the decade since, she has made the Cardinals
one of the premier programs in the nation. At
Stanford, Van Derveer has won two national championships (1990, 1992) and compiled a career
record of 251–62. She was named Pac-10 Coach of
the Year in 1989, 1990, and 1995, and National
Coach of the Year in 1988, 1989, and 1990.

But the biggest honor Van Derveer received
came in the spring of 1995, when she was asked
to coach the U.S. Olympic women's basketball
team the following year in Atlanta. Van Derveer
had led the United States to a gold medal at
the Goodwill Games in 1994, and had been a
head coach at the Olympic Festival and World
University Games. Van Derveer wanted the 1996
Olympic job but was reluctant at first, because it
meant that she would have to take a leave of
absence from Stanford. Eventually, though, she
accepted the position.

"I'm extremely focused on doing the very
best job I can for this team," Van Derveer said.
"When you're representing your country, it's
not something you want to mess up."

With Van Derveer directing from the bench,
the U.S. women's basketball team won a gold
medal in Atlanta.

Accomplishments

Led Stanford to NCAA title: 1990, 1992
Pac-10 Coach of the Year: 1989, 1990, 1995
National Coach of the Year: 1988, 1989,
1990
Coach of Olympic-champion U.S. women's
basketball team: 1996

Amy Van Dyken

Born February 15, 1973

Amy Van Dyken, the first American woman to
win four gold medals in a single Olympics,
grew up in Colorado. That she became one of
the greatest swimmers in Olympic history is testament not only to her talent, but also to her
determination—as a child she was frail and
prone to severe allergic reactions virtually every
time she stepped out the door. "When I was a
kid, I couldn't even go on field trips," she said in
a 1995 interview. "Even a little dust could trigger
an attack. I couldn't stay at friends' houses; I
couldn't even walk up the steps."

Van Dyken eventually learned that she suffered from asthma. At the age of six she was
introduced to a doctor who recommended that
she try swimming in an effort to build up her
lungs. She loved the sport almost from the
start—and, as it turned out, she had talent. In
high school she won state championships in the
50-yard freestyle and the 100-yard butterfly, and
was twice named Colorado Swimmer of the Year.
At the 1990 junior nationals, she finished first
in the 100-yard butterfly and third in the 50-
yard freestyle. In 1991 she captured the 50-
meter freestyle at the Olympic Festival.

Van Dyken failed to make the U.S. Olympic
team in 1992. But by 1994 she was one of the
top swimmers in the world. She finished first in
the 50-yard freestyle and second in the 100-yard
butterfly and 100-yard freestyle at the NCAA
championships, and was named female NCAA
Swimmer of the Year. That summer, at the world
championships, she took a bronze medal in the
50-meter freestyle.

Memorable Moment:
January 1995

A Female Crew Competes in the America's Cup Defenders Series

Women proved themselves capable of handling the roughest of seas in the 1990s. Two all-female crews sailed the 33,000-mile Round-the-World Whitbread, a grueling fleet race. And women routinely competed in international regattas. But the most prestigious yachting event of all, the America's Cup, was an exclusively male event.

That is, until early 1995. Over the course of several days in January, off the coast of San Diego, California, the first all-female crew made history by competing in the America's Cup Defenders Series. The 29-member crew of *America³* had been selected from 678 applicants. The crew included eight Olympic athletes, two veterans of the Whitbread, a world-class weightlifter and football coach, an aerospace engineer, and no less than three mothers. *America³* was captained by Dawn Riley, a Michigan State graduate who wrote the book *Taking the Helm*, the story of the 1993–1994 Whitbread.

This strong and diverse group was selected and supported by William Koch, who had won the 1992 America's Cup. Koch, a multimillionaire with a degree in chemical engineering from the Massachusetts Institute of Technology, was determined to provide the crew of *America³* with the best equipment and training that money could buy. He had spent $68 million to win the Cup in 1992, and he spared no expense in outfitting the first women's crew. Two of his finest yachts were donated for training purposes. Koch's motives were questioned, of course, but he maintained to the end that he was interested only in "showing respect for women's competitive abilities."

In the end, *America³* did not earn the right to represent the United States in the America's Cup. That honor went to Dennis Conner's *Stars and Stripes*. But the women, who were far less experienced than their opponents, did manage to surprise a few people by splitting their first two races with Conner's crew.

Throughout her career Van Dyken endured periodic setbacks caused by her asthma. Under normal circumstances her lung capacity was 35 percent less than that of her fellow competitors. Many asthma medications, which contain ingredients that are considered performance-enhancing substances, are banned in competition. As a result, Van Dyken often resorted to less effective treatments. Occasionally she suffered attacks while training and passed out after workouts.

But Van Dyken was resilient. Considered a contender at the 1996 Summer Olympics in Atlanta, she turned in a stunning performance, winning gold medals in the 50-meter freestyle and the 100-meter butterfly, and helping the United States to victories in the 4 x 100 medley relay and the 4 x 100 freestyle relay. No American woman had ever won so many gold medals in one Olympics. Van Dyken, smiling broadly, punching the water enthusiastically each time she won an event, became one of the most popular athletes at the Games, an inspiration to anyone hoping to overcome a physical problem. Remembering her past as a tall (6 feet), gawky teen who had trouble breathing, Van Dyken dedicated her gold medals to "all the nerds out there." She was named Individual Sportswoman of the Year by the Women's Sports Foundation.

Accomplishments

  NCAA Swimmer of the Year: 1994
  Olympic gold medalist, 50-meter freestyle:
    1996
  Olympic gold medalist: 100-meter butterfly:
    1996
  Olympic gold medalist, 4 x 100 medley relay:
    1996
  Olympic gold medalist, 4 x 100 freestyle relay:
    1996
  Women's Sports Foundation Individual
    Sportswoman of the Year: 1996

Glenna Collett Vare

June 20, 1903–February 10, 1989

The greatest American woman amateur golfer was born in New Haven, Connecticut; she moved to Providence, Rhode Island, when she was six years old. Glenna Collett came from an athletic family—her mother was fond of tennis and her father had been a national cycling champion. Growing up, Glenna dabbled in swimming, diving—even baseball. When she was 14, she was introduced to the game that would become her passion. She went with her father to a golf exhibition conducted by Alexa Stirling, the reigning U.S. Amateur champion. Glenna was bitten by the golf bug that day, and she remained hooked for the rest of her life.

At her father's urging, Collett began taking lessons from Alex Smith, a highly regarded teaching professional whose students included three-time U.S. Amateur champion Jerry Travers. Under Smith's tutelage, Collett began to blossom. Her swing was refined; combined with her natural size and strength (she was 5 feet 6 inches tall and weighed 128 pounds), proper technique made Collett one of the longest hitters in the game. She routinely hit the ball 200 yards off the tee, and once, when she was 18 years old, she even topped the 300-yard mark. At the time, that was the longest recorded drive by a woman. Even today, with high-compression balls and graphite clubs, 300-yard drives are rare. In Collett's era they were unheard of.

Collett won the first of six U.S. Amateur titles in 1922. The Amateur then was a match-play competition that took several days to complete. The 21-year-old Collett overcame her own nervousness and inexperience to defeat Mrs. William A. Gavin of England in the final.

"Even when it was over, and I had won the championship, I couldn't believe it," Collett later wrote. "I had accomplished what I wanted to, when I had only half dreamed that I could, and I suppose I was the happiest girl in the world."

With that victory, Collett became one of the most popular women in sports. Fans loved her, as did the media. Over the years she proved to be not only an accomplished athlete, but the embodiment of sportsmanship as well—a woman who truly enjoyed playing the game and who was gracious in both victory and defeat. Collett captured the U.S. Amateur title again in 1925, 1928, 1929, 1930, and 1935. She was runner-up in 1931 and 1932. No one else has ever won six U.S. Amateur titles. Collett played at a time when women's golf was primarily an amateur pursuit. In 1923 and 1924 she won the Canadian Ladies Open, and in 1925 she won the French Ladies Open. Although she did reach the finals of the British national championship two times, she never won.

Collett married Edward H. Vare in 1931 and continued to play golf while raising a family. She was captain of the U.S. Curtis Cup team in 1934, 1936, and 1948. In 1952 she donated the Vare Trophy, which is now annually presented to the player on the Ladies Professional Golf Association tour with the lowest average score. She also wrote two books about golf.

Accomplishments

U.S. Amateur champion: 1922, 1925,
   1928–1930, 1935
Canadian Ladies Open champion: 1923–1924
French Ladies Open champion: 1925
Curtis Cup captain: 1934, 1936, 1948
Founder of LPGA Vare Trophy
Induced into International Women's Sports
   Hall of Fame: 1981

Margaret Wade

December 30, 1912–February 16, 1995

Margaret Wade, the first woman inducted into the Basketball Hall of Fame, was born in McCool, Mississippi. For three years she was one of the better athletes on the Delta State (Mississippi) Teachers College varsity basketball team; as a sophomore and junior, she was captain of the team. But just before her senior year, the school's administration judged basketball to be far too "strenuous" a sport for ladies and dropped the women's basketball program. Wade and her teammates had no place to play. They protested the school's decision vehemently—even burning their uniforms in public—but the administration did not waver. For the next 41 years, Delta State had no women's basketball team.

After graduating in 1933, Wade played semi-pro basketball with the Tupelo Red Wings for the next two years; she probably would have continued to play even longer, if not for a career-ending knee injury. At 24 years of age she was forced to give up the game she loved.

Unable to play, Wade turned to coaching and became one of the best in the history of the game. Her first great success came at the scholastic level in Mississippi. She held jobs at high schools in Marietta, Belden, and Cleveland. In 21 seasons she compiled a remarkable record of 453 victories and 89 losses.

For many coaches, those would be career numbers, but for Wade they were merely the beginning. In 1959, at the age of 47, she returned to her alma mater and became chairperson of the physical education department. Fourteen years later, in 1973, with Wade's support and determination, women's basketball returned to Delta State. At 60 years of age, when others would consider retirement, Wade returned to the sideline. With an ambitious goal of making Delta State one of the best programs in college basketball, she brought to the job a blend of intelligence, humor, and enthusiasm.

In her first year, Wade led Delta State to a 16–2 record. In each of the next three seasons—1975–1977—the team captured the Association of Intercollegiate Athletics for Women national championship, compiling a record of 93–4. During one fantastic stretch, Delta State, led by another future Hall of Famer, Lusia Harris-Stewart, won 51 consecutive games.

Wade retired from coaching in 1979, with a collegiate record of 157–23. She was inducted into the Basketball Hall of Fame in 1984 and the International Women's Sports Hall of Fame in 1992. Perhaps the most impressive symbol of Margaret Wade's contribution to the game is the fact that each year the outstanding player in women's college basketball is presented with an award—the Wade Trophy.

Accomplishments

Coached Delta State to AIAW national title:
   1975–1977
First woman inducted into the Basketball Hall
   of Fame: 1984
Inducted into International Women's Sports
   Hall of Fame: 1992

Virginia Wade

Born July 10, 1945

A member of the International Tennis Hall of Fame and the winner of one of the most dramatic tennis matches ever played, Sarah Virginia Wade was born in Bournemouth, England. She was the youngest of four children born to clergyman Eustace Holland Wade. When Virginia was almost one year old, Eustace moved his family to South Africa, his wife's native country. During Eustace's tenure as archdeacon of Durban, the Wade children were introduced to tennis—the family lived not far from the Durban Lawn Tennis Club. Virginia was nine when she first picked up a racket. She enjoyed the game from the start, and though she rarely lacked playing partners, on the odd occasion when her siblings weren't around, she would practice alone, whacking shot after shot against a garden wall.

Virginia Wade was blessed with natural talent and athleticism. She was tall (5 feet 7 inches) and muscular (she weighed 135 pounds), traits that helped compensate for the fact that, unlike most world-class tennis players, she never received any long-term formal instruction. She was largely self-taught, though she did work sporadically with such tennis greats as Maureen Connolly and Jerry Teeguarden. But even as she developed, Wade refused to allow herself to be completely consumed by the game. She was an intelligent, well-rounded young woman whose interests extended beyond the boundaries of the tennis court. "I played in tournaments because it was the thing to do and because I wanted a scrapbook," she said.

Wade balanced academics and athletics for several years. In 1966 she not only graduated with honors from Sussex University, but also represented England in the Wightman Cup. For several years she was one of the most wildly inconsistent players in women's tennis. In 1967 she was upset in the first round at Wimbledon; the next year, at the age of 23, she defeated Billie Jean King in the final to become the first Brit since Betty Nuthall in 1933 to win the U.S. Open. Wade was immediately hailed as the savior of British tennis. But she continued to be one of the game's most unpredictable players. In 1970 she failed to win a single tournament; in 1972 she won the Australian Open.

On July 1, 1977, Wade was nine days short of her 32nd birthday and approaching the twilight of her professional career. On that day she walked onto Centre Court at Wimbledon with the weight of the nation on her shoulders. It was not only the silver anniversary of Queen Elizabeth's reign, but also the 100th anniversary of the Wimbledon Tennis Championships. And there was Virginia Wade, playing in the final against Betty Stove of Holland. In front of the queen herself, and with the entire country watching, Wade defeated Stove, 4–6, 6–3, 6–1.

"This means everything to me," Wade said after the match. "I wanted to prove I deserved to be out there with all those champions. I felt I belonged, that I was the best player who hadn't won Wimbledon, and it was wonderful to win it in front of the queen."

Wade never played in another Grand Slam singles final, but her place in history was secure. In 1982 she became the first woman elected to the Wimbledon Committee, and in 1989 she was inducted into the International Tennis Hall of Fame.

Accomplishments

U.S. Open champion: 1968
Australian Open champion: 1972
Wimbledon champion: 1977
Inducted into International Tennis Hall of
    Fame: 1989

Marie Wagner

February 2, 1883–March 30, 1975

Marie Wagner, who won six U.S. indoor singles titles in tennis, was born in New York and grew up in Manhattan. Her parents, Elizabeth Paul Wagner and Adam Wagner, who owned a business manufacturing iron railings, were both born in Germany. Marie began playing tennis on the public courts of Central Park when she was a small girl. She was a steady, indefatigable player who had few weaknesses in her game. As she matured and improved, observers of the New York tennis scene began to take notice. Eventually she was invited to join the Hamilton Grange Lawn Tennis Club in Washington Heights. There, Marie Wagner blossomed into one of the finest indoor players of the early part of the 20th century, winning more than 500 trophies during her career.

Much of her success came at the Seventh Regiment Armory in New York, site of the annual U.S. Indoor Women's Championships. Wagner won her first indoor singles title in 1908, then repeated in 1909. She missed winning a third straight championship, but came back to win again in 1911, 1913, 1914, and 1917.

She finished second in 1907 and 1915. Perhaps the only reason Wagner won only six titles is that, out of modesty, she never again entered the singles competition. She was also a talented doubles player, winning four indoor championships. In 1910 and 1913 she teamed up with Clara Kutroff; in 1916 she won with Molla Mallory; in 1917 she won with Margaret Taylor.

Wagner was not solely an indoor player. In 1908 she reached the finals of the all-comers round at the U.S. championships before losing to Maud Barger-Wallach. In 1914 she won the all-comers division, then lost to defending champion Mary Browne in the challenge round. Wagner was considered one of the best players in the United States for most of her career, regardless of playing surface or venue. When the first U.S. Top Ten was established in 1913, Wagner was No. 6. She remained in that select group for the better part of a decade. In 1914 she achieved her highest ranking—No. 3, behind Browne and Florence Sutton. In 1922, at age 39, she was ranked No. 9.

Even after she was no longer in the top 10, Wagner remained an active member of the tennis community. A social worker, she played in several exhibitions for the Red Cross during World War I and was a longtime member of the national women's tennis ranking committee. Wagner lived virtually her entire life in New York and never married. In 1969 she was inducted into the International Tennis Hall of Fame in Newport, Rhode Island; six years later, while living with her niece on Long Island, Wagner died at the age of 92.

Accomplishments

U.S. indoor singles champion: 1908–1909, 1911, 1913–1914, 1917
U.S. indoor doubles champion: 1910, 1913, 1916–1917
U.S. Open singles runner-up: 1914
Inducted into International Tennis Hall of Fame: 1969

Grete Anderson Waitz

Born October 1, 1953

Born in Oslo, Norway, Grete Anderson Waitz will be remembered as one of the brightest stars in distance running. She was the youngest of three children. Her father worked in a factory, her mother in a grocery store. Like many Norwegian children, Grete enjoyed hiking, skiing, and running, and it wasn't long before she was competing in races. At first she tried sprints of 60 and 100 meters, but found that she lacked the natural leg speed. More often than not, she lost. As she moved up in distance, however, she became more successful. At the age of 16, Grete Anderson was Norway's national junior champion at 400 and 800 meters.

In 1975, at the urging of her new husband—and coach—Jack Waitz, Grete Waitz began training harder and longer and concentrating on cross-country races and marathons. Even though she was working full-time as an elementary school teacher, she found the time to put in 100-mile training weeks.

In 1978, when she was 25, Waitz won the world cross-country championship and the New York City Marathon. From 1978 through 1988 she completed the 26.2-mile race through New York's five boroughs nine times—and nine times she emerged victorious. Her record stands as one of the most remarkable in all of distance running, for New York City, with its hills and potholes, is considered a particularly challenging course. And the career of a marathon runner is typically short and marked by periods of injury and recovery.

Waitz qualified for the Norwegian Olympic team in 1972 and 1976, but because there was no women's marathon in the Olympics then, she had to run the 1,500 meters, a distance she was not suited for. A boycott of the Moscow Games prevented Waitz from competing in 1980, but in 1984, the first year that women were allowed to compete in an Olympic marathon, she finished second behind American Joan Benoit. In 1988, at the Summer Games in Seoul, South Korea, Waitz suffered leg cramps and was forced to drop out.

Wang Junxia

Born 1963

Despite her Olympic disappointments, Waitz had a distinguished athletic career. In her first victory in New York, she lowered the women's marathon record by more than two minutes, with a time of 2 hours, 32 minutes, 30 seconds. In her last New York victory, in 1988, she ran 2:28.07, just three months after having arthroscopic surgery on her knee. A gracious, modest athlete, she was a favorite in New York, as popular as any runner who has ever competed in the marathon. She was a pioneer in the sport of women's marathoning, and her accomplishments helped balance the scales in terms of prize money and recognition.

Accomplishments

New York City Marathon champion:
   1978–1980, 1982–1986, 1988
Olympic silver medalist, marathon: 1984
World cross-country champion: 1978

Wang Junxia was the most talented member of a mysterious team of Chinese distance runners who put together a string of remarkable performances in the early 1990s. They were known as Ma's Army, because their coach, Ma Junren, treated his runners like soldiers. According to Ma, the women routinely trained the equivalent of a full marathon each day. They lived spartan lives, concentrating only on their training. They supplemented their diets with unusual elixirs made of caterpillar fungus and turtle blood, which supposedly gave them the strength to endure their torturous daily workouts.

This revolutionary approach to distance running helped the Chinese runners—Wang in particular—to achieve phenomenal times. Though their rise from obscurity to international dominance occurred over nearly two years, Ma's Army recorded their most startling times during the summer of 1993.

The first records came in August, at the World Track and Field Championships in Stuttgart, Germany. Liu Dong broke the world record in the 1,500 meters; Qu Yunxia broke the world record in the 3,000; and Wang Junxia broke the world record in the 10,000. In each race the Chinese were challenged only by their teammates. Never before had a Chinese runner won a world title or held a world record. But suddenly, in one meet, they exhibited a dominance that the sport had never seen.

The following month, at the Chinese National Games, Wang led Ma's Army to even greater feats. She shattered four world records in six days. Wang won the 10,000 meters with a time of 29:31.78; finished second to Qu Yunxia's world record in the 1,500 with a time of 3:51.92; and won the 3,000 with a record time of 8:06.11, breaking her own record of 8:12.19, set one day earlier during a semifinal heat. These records provoked outrage from runners of other nationalities, who suspected that the Chinese were using performance-enhancing drugs. "Something is wrong, and it seems tragic for the sport," said Lynn Jennings of the United States, one of the world's top distance runners. "It all seems polluted to me now. It is sordid and awful."

But Ma and other Chinese officials denied the accusations of doping, and in fact none of the Chinese runners ever tested positive for drugs. Critics pointed out that there are numerous ways to beat drug testing. They also noted that 11 top Chinese athletes, including several swimmers who had set world records, tested positive for drugs at the 1994 Asian Games, which cast a cloud over the achievements of Wang and the other Chinese runners.

By 1995 Wang and many of her teammates had faded from the international athletic scene. Tired of Ma's dictatorial ways and exhausted by his brutal training regimen, they either left the sport or changed coaches. Wang personally led a revolt that saw 17 of Ma's top runners leave his camp. "We simply can't take it anymore," she said at the time. "We had absolutely no freedom. We were all on the brink of going crazy."

In 1995 Wang withdrew from the 10,000 meters at the national championships and won the 5,000 in a comparatively slow time. She did not compete in the World Track and Field Championships. In fact, at distances between 800 meters and the marathon, China qualified only a single runner for the sport's premier event. But one year later, at the 1996 Summer Olympics in Atlanta, Wang made a triumphant return to international competition, winning the 5,000 meters and finishing second in the 10,000.

Accomplishments

Set four world records in six days: 1993
World champion, 10,000 meters: 1993
World champion, 3,000 meters: 1993
Jesse Owens Award winner: 1993
Olympic gold medalist, 5,000 meters: 1996
Olympic silver medalist, 10,000 meters: 1996

Karrie Webb

Born December 21, 1974

Karrie Webb, who made an astonishing debut on the Ladies Professional Golf Association tour in 1996, was born in the town of Ayr in Queensland, Australia. As a toddler she accompanied her parents to the local nine-hole golf course. Club rules prevented children under the age of eight from playing, but as soon as Webb was eligible, she took club in hand. By the time she was 11, she was a golf fanatic; in fact, her birthday present for 1986 was a trip to the Gold Coast to see fellow Australian Greg Norman compete in a tournament. Norman was at the top of his game that year, having won the British Open and several other tournaments, and Webb was thrilled to see him in person. She came home to Ayr with an autograph and a goal—to become a professional golfer.

In 1991, at the age of 16, Webb won the Australian Junior Championship. She and several other top junior players were given an opportunity to visit Norman at his home in the United States. The younger players spent a week practicing with him and getting tips on how to refine their games. As Norman later told *Golf* magazine, Webb was an impressive student— "She stayed right with me during the workouts and practice. That's when I knew she would be a special player. I didn't have to help her much."

Webb represented Australia in international competition six times from 1992 through 1994. She won the 1994 Australian Strokeplay championship and turned professional late that year. In 1995 she pulled off a stunning upset by winning the Women's British Open. In 1996, at the age of 21, she came to the United States and joined the LPGA tour. (She had hoped to attend school in the United States three years earlier, but her success as an amateur had prompted surprisingly little interest on the part of Division I college coaches.) Despite her limited professional experience, Webb instantly became one of the game's premier players.

In her first event, the Chrysler-Plymouth Tournament of Champions, Webb finished second. In her second tournament she was a winner. Three months later she captured the Titleholders championship, the richest event on the tour. Before 1996 was over she had won four tournaments and amassed more than $1 million in earnings, highest on the LPGA tour. She was named Rookie of the Year.

Accomplishments

Australian Strokeplay champion: 1994
Women's British Open champion: 1995
LPGA Rookie of the Year: 1996
LPGA leading money winner: 1996

Donna Weinbrecht

Born April 23, 1965

Donna Weinbrecht, one of the most accomplished American freestyle skiers, was born in West Milford, New Jersey. As a child, her first love was figure skating. But her family had a vacation home in Killington, Vermont, and during trips there she also developed quite a passion for skiing. In high school she and a friend formed a ski team, but after graduation her alpine career came to an end.

Weinbrecht enrolled in the Ridgewood Art and Design School after high school but lasted only a year. She wanted to test herself as an athlete, and the sport she chose was freestyle skiing. In the freestyle events Weinbrecht was able to combine the courage required in alpine skiing with the grace required in figure skating. Freestyle is as much about art as it is about athleticism, and Weinbrecht fit the sport perfectly.

Her specialty was mogul skiing, one of three freestyle disciplines (the others are ballet and aerials). In mogul skiing, scoring is based on a combination of speed (25 percent), degree of difficulty and the performance of two acrobatic tricks (25 percent), and technique and form through the mogul field (50 percent). Freestyle skiing had been established in the 1970s but did not gain respect until 1988, when the Federation Internationale de Ski, the sport's governing body, voted to allow mogul skiing to be a full medal sport at the 1992 Winter Olympic Games in Albertville, France. Ballet and aerials were added for the 1994 Games in Lillehammer, Norway.

When Weinbrecht moved to Vermont in 1985, she was a 20-year-old who supported her skiing habit by working as a waitress. Having no connections and a slim résumé, she was forced to coach herself. Three years later she finished first in the U.S. championships at Stratton Mountain, Vermont, and was named World Cup Rookie of the Year. She captured the U.S. title in five of the next six years—an injury prevented her from defending the crown in 1993.

In 1991 Weinbrecht prepped for the rigors of Olympic competition by finishing first in the world championships. She traveled to Albertville carrying the burden of being a favorite to win a gold medal. In the weeks leading up to the event, she had been put through the media wringer, thanks to the fact that she was an attractive, well-spoken woman—with a trademark two-foot-long ponytail—and because she was the best in the world in an event that practically no one understood. Weinbrecht handled the pressure well. In front of a crowd of 10,000 spectators who had braved a cold, snowy day, she performed flawlessly. As the penultimate skier, Weinbrecht knew precisely what was required to win; she could have skied conservatively but did not. Instead, she attacked the bumpy course and thrilled the crowd by winning the sport's first Olympic gold medal.

A knee injury wiped out her 1993 season, but Weinbrecht won another U.S. championship in 1994. At the 1994 Olympics in Lillehammer, she finished seventh. Afterward she announced her retirement, but quickly changed her mind and returned to competition. In 1996 she finished first in the final World Cup standings in the moguls competition.

Memorable Moment: August 1, 1996

The United States Wins the First Olympic Women's Soccer Championship

Although soccer has long been considered the most popular sport in the world—and although millions of girls and women are involved in the game as both spectators and participants—it wasn't until 1996 that women's soccer became an Olympic sport.

In front of a crowd of 76,481 at Sanford Stadium in Athens, Georgia, the United States defeated China, 2–1, in the women's soccer final to capture the gold medal at the Atlanta Summer Games. The winning goal was scored in the 68th minute by Tiffeny Milbrett, on a beautiful assist from right halfback Joy Fawcett.

The women's final stood as testament to the rising popularity of women's sports in general, and to soccer in particular. Never before had a women's soccer game attracted such a large audience; despite ticket prices that topped out at more than $130, it was the largest crowd ever to see a women's sporting event of any kind in the United States. Unfortunately, those who weren't lucky enough to attend the Olympics saw precious little of the women's final, since NBC decided to devote less than 20 minutes of airtime to the game. As Hank Steinbrecher, executive director of the U.S. Soccer Federation, said, "NBC must think the world is full of divers."

By the time the Atlanta Games ended, it was clear that the world is full of soccer fans. And if the women's game continues to prosper, the 1996 Olympic champions—most notably Mia Hamm, Michelle Akers, and Julie Foudy—will one day be considered pioneers.

Accomplishments

U.S. champion: 1988–1992, 1994
World champion: 1991
Olympic gold medalist: 1992
World Cup champion, moguls: 1996

Priscilla Welch

Born 1945

Long-distance runner Priscilla Welch, the oldest woman ever to win the New York City Marathon, grew up in a small rural town near Beford, England, about 80 miles north of London. For the first 12 years of her life, Welch lived in a house with no indoor plumbing and no electricity. Contact with the outside world was maintained through a battery-powered radio. "We children didn't know anything different," Welch said. "So we just got on with life as we knew it—no messing."

That attitude has served Welch well throughout her life, even as she has made some extraordinary transformations. At the age of 35 she was a member of the British military. Her fiancé, Dave (who later became her husband), had decided to take up distance running; he encouraged her to join him on his workouts. Eventually she relented, at first because she thought daily exercise might help her kick her heavy smoking habit. "I was looking to do something different," Welch said. "The only thing I ever did in those days was work, and my body was forever stiff."

Progress was slow at first. Dave challenged her to up her mileage, which, over time, she did. She began entering local road races to fuel her competitive fires. She began to win. Still, Welch never entertained the idea of becoming a world-class athlete—until she finished second in a major 10K race in Oslo, Norway, in 1980. Before the year was over she had also successfully completed her first marathon. In 1984, at the age of 39, she turned in one of the most inspiring performances at the Summer Olympics, finishing sixth in the women's marathon with a time of 2:28.54.

As it turned out, that was the fastest marathon Welch ever ran. But there were other accomplishments, including a third-place finish at the America's Marathon in Chicago in 1986 and a stirring victory at the New York City Marathon in 1987. At 42 years of age, she was the oldest winner—male or female—in the history of the race.

Welch continued to compete internationally for several more years, until she was diagnosed with breast cancer in the winter of 1993. She underwent a radical mastectomy and received chemotherapy treatment for several months. By the fall of 1993 she had resumed training and racing, though on a reduced schedule.

"I'll never go back to hammering my body the way I've done the last 10 years," she said. "In the time I've got left, I'll approach running more sensibly. I also hope this has made me a better person—that I'm a bit more compassionate, that I listen to people and that I appreciate life a bit more."

Accomplishments

Sixth-place finish, Olympic marathon, at age 39: 1984
Runner-up, London Marathon: 1984
Third place, Chicago Marathon: 1986
Oldest runner (age 42) to win New York City Marathon: 1987

Joyce Wethered

Born November 17, 1901

Joyce Wethered was the finest golfer of her time, a shy woman with a perfect swing who played the game so well that many considered her an artist. She was born in Maldon, Surrey, England, and began playing golf during family vacations in northern Scotland. Her father, H. Newton Wethered, was a talented player who introduced the game to both Joyce and her older brother, Roger, who would one day win the British Amateur. Joyce had little formal training; rather, she learned to play by watching such great players as Bobby Jones and Harry Vardon. She studied their mannerisms and techniques, and mimicked them perfectly. It was an unusual strategy, but it seemed to work.

Joyce Wethered entered her first tournament, the Surrey County championship, in 1920, and reached the semifinals. It was a surprising

debut, but nothing compared to her performance a few months later in the English Ladies Closed Amateur Golf Championship. There the unknown Wethered advanced to the finals, where she met defending champion Cecil Leitch. Wethered, perhaps a victim of nerves, fell behind early and was 6-down after 20 holes of the 36-hole tournament. But she came back and eventually evened the match with three holes remaining, and went 1-up with two holes left. With a train rumbling nearby, she calmly knocked in the winning putt on the 35th hole. Later, when reporters asked her if the noise of the train had disturbed her, Wethered said, "What train?" It was a deadpan reply that helped establish her reputation as an unflappable competitor.

Over the next few years, Wethered dominated European golf and became the best player of her generation, winning five British championships and four British Open Amateur victories. In an era when tournaments adhered to a match-play format, Wethered lost only two individual matches. She retired from competition in 1925, when she was 24 years old. In 1929 she staged a brief comeback, defeating American Glenna Collett Vare in the final of the British Open Amateur at St. Andrews.

Wethered forfeited her amateur status in 1930 when she took a job selling sporting goods in a London department store. In 1935 she appeared in a series of exhibition matches in the United States, playing with the likes of Gene Sarazen and Babe Didrikson Zaharias. She received a reported $35,000 for the tour. Two years later, in 1937, Wethered married Sir John Heathcoat Amory and settled into a quiet life, continuing to play golf regularly.

Wethered often said that what she liked most about golf was the solitude of the game, the simplicity. Even in her most important matches, she said that her opponent was the course, not the woman standing next to her. That attitude allowed her to concentrate fully on her game. Indeed, she seemed to be at one with her equipment and the course whenever she played, and the rhythm of her game left even the greatest players in awe. As Bobby Jones, who shared a round with Wethered at St. Andrews, observed: "She did not miss one shot; she did not even half miss a shot; and when we finished, I could not help saying that I had never played golf with anyone, man or woman, amateur or professional, who made me feel so utterly outclassed."

Accomplishments

British Women's Amateur champion: 1922, 1924, 1925, 1929
Runner-up, British Women's Amateur: 1921
Six-time English Ladies Championship winner

Willye White

Born January 1, 1939

Long jumper Willye White, the only American woman ever to compete in five Olympic Games, was born in Money, Mississippi, and grew up on a Mississippi Delta plantation. She was sent to work in the fields at a very young age; by the time she was eight, White was toiling in a cotton field for the sum of $8 a day. Despite growing up in poverty and hardship, White succeeded in athletics. She was a gifted girl, capable of competing against older, bigger children in a variety of sports. In elementary school, White tried out for her high school varsity basketball team—and qualified. She was only 16 years old when she went away to Tennessee State University, where she became one of the best in a long line of runners coached by Ed Temple, whose Tigerbelles were among the most successful college track-and-field programs in the nation.

White was still just a girl when she began running at Tennessee State, but she had the strength and speed of a grown woman. She qualified for the U.S. Olympic team in 1956 and won a silver medal in the long jump at the Melbourne Summer Games. White went on to dominate that event in national competition over the next 15 years.

White was one of the most consistent and successful long jumpers in U.S. history. In 1960 she won her first national outdoor championship. Her second came in 1962. Others followed in 1964, 1965, 1966, 1968, 1969, and 1970. She also won national indoor long-jump titles in 1962 and 1968. She won a gold medal at the 1963 Pan American Games and set an American record of 21 feet 6 inches in 1964.

White was also a fine sprinter who won a silver medal as a member of the United States' runner-up 4 x 100 relay team at the 1964 Olympic Games in Tokyo. She was so consistent that people began to take for granted her Olympic appearances. From 1956 through 1972, White was a participant in every Olympics. But she rarely turned in her best performances at the Games. She finished 16th in the long jump in 1960, 12th in 1964, 11th in 1968, and 11th again in 1972. But that could not detract from her accomplishments, which, in addition to her 12 national titles, included lengthening the national long-jump record seven times.

White retired from track-and-field competition after the 1972 Olympics and studied nursing. She worked as a health administrator in Chicago, and in 1976 was named to the President's Commission on Olympic Sports. She was inducted into the U.S. Track and Field Hall of Fame in 1981, and the International Women's Sports Hall of Fame in 1988.

Accomplishments

Olympic silver medalist, long jump: 1956
Olympic silver medalist, 4 x 100 relay: 1964
Only U.S. woman to compete in five Olympic Games
Winner of 12 national long-jump titles
Inducted into U.S. Track and Field Hall of Fame: 1981
Inducted into International Women's Sports Hall of Fame: 1988

Kathy Whitworth

Born September 27, 1939

Kathy Whitworth, the winningest player in the history of golf, was born in Monahans, Texas, and raised in Jal, New Mexico. In 1959, her first season on the Ladies Professional Golf Association tour, what Whitworth seemed to lack in athleticism she made up for in motivation. In the days when even the LPGA's biggest stars could not afford the luxury of air travel, Whitworth was a barnstorming champion, bouncing from city to city, living out of the trunk of her car, stopping whenever the green of a golf course beckoned.

Eventually, Whitworth, a gentle, soft-spoken woman, became something of a living legend,

Memorable Moment:
August 4, 1996

Teresa Edwards Wins a Third Olympic Gold Medal in Basketball

Although overshadowed by such high-profile teammates as Lisa Leslie, Rebecca Lobo, and Jennifer Azzi, Teresa Edwards was the heart and soul of the U.S. women's basketball team that captured the gold medal at the 1996 Summer Olympics.

Edwards was born in Atlanta and had played basketball at the University of Georgia, so the Atlanta Games were of particular importance to her. It was an opportunity to play in her hometown, in front of friends and family. It was also a chance to make history. No basketball player, male or female, had collected more Olympic hardware than Edwards. She had led the United States to gold medals in 1984 and 1988, and to a bronze medal in 1992. Now, in Atlanta, she was attempting to become the first person to win a third Olympic gold medal in basketball.

On August 4, 1996, the United States defeated Brazil, 111–87, in the championship game of the women's tournament. Typically, Edwards was not the offensive star of that game (Leslie had 29 points); instead, she played the role that had come to define her 1996 Olympic experience—floor leader. Edwards led all women with an average of 7.7 assists in the Olympics, including a team-high 10 in the gold medal game. At 32 years of age she was the oldest player on the U.S. team. And the most decorated.

though she cringed whenever that expression was used in her presence. She was the LPGA's leading money winner eight times and Player of the Year seven times. In 1981 she became the first woman golfer to reach the $1 million mark in career winnings. The following year she took over the LPGA lead for most career victories, and in 1985, with her 85th career title, she surpassed Sam Snead as the winningest player in the history of the sport—male or female.

In 1986 the Golf Writer's Association of America presented Whitworth with the William Richardson Award as "an individual who has made consistently outstanding contributions to golf." Only two other women had ever won that award—Patty Berg in 1959 and Babe Didrikson Zaharias in 1954. In 1993 the LPGA, in an unprecedented display of respect and admiration, dedicated its championship tournament to Whitworth. Although Whitworth failed to win

the U.S. Women's Open, that did not prevent her from gaining entrance into the World Golf Hall of Fame, the Texas Golf Hall of Fame, and that most exclusive of clubs, the 13-member LPGA Hall of Fame.

Through good times and bad, Whitworth conducted herself with grace and dignity, a trait that helped carry her through a particularly rough time in 1986. In the twilight of her career, she discovered that she had been swindled out of most of her life savings by an unscrupulous financial adviser. Rather than wallowing in self-pity, she polished her irons and stepped up her playing schedule. Against women half her age, Whitworth began rebuilding her life and her bank account. By 1993, at the age of 53, she was able to settle into a life of semiretirement, serving as an ambassador for the sport she loves.

Accomplishments

LPGA Player of the Year: 1966–1969,
   1971–1973
LPGA leading money winner: 1965–1968,
   1970–1973
LPGA championship winner: 1967, 1971, 1975
Inducted into LPGA Hall of Fame: 1975
Inducted into International Women's Sports
   Hall of Fame: 1984

Hazel Hotchkiss Wightman

December 20, 1886–December 5, 1974

Tennis player Hazel Hotchkiss Wightman, a four-time winner of the U.S. national singles title, was born in Healdsburg, California. She was a fragile child but was also a bundle of energy, and her parents, William and Emma Hotchkiss, encouraged her interest in sports. Hazel spent time playing football and baseball with her four brothers; while the experience sometimes took its toll on her, it also helped prepare her, both physically and mentally, for a career in competitive sports: At a time when women were rarely afforded athletic opportunities, she was a pioneer.

Hazel Hotchkiss entered her first tennis tournament in 1902, at the age of 16. In 1909 she won the first of her 44 titles. In that year Hotchkiss captured the singles, doubles, and mixed doubles titles at the U.S. Lawn Tennis Association championships—later known as the U.S. Open. It was an astounding feat, but for Hotchkiss, it was only the beginning. In each of the next two years she repeated that accomplishment, becoming the first person—male or female—to win singles, doubles, and mixed doubles titles at the U.S. Open in three consecutive years.

In 1912 Hotchkiss graduated from the University of California–Berkeley and married George Wightman. Shortly after giving birth to a son one year later, Hazel Hotchkiss Wightman, by then a resident of Chestnut Hill, Massachusetts, returned to competitive tennis. In 1915 she reached the finals of the national singles championships, losing in three sets to Molla Mallory. By 1919 Wightman was again on top of the tennis world. She defeated Marion Zinderstein in straight sets to win the national singles title.

After that, Wightman's role was as much ambassador as athlete. In late 1919, after winning the national title, she approached officials of the International Tennis Federation and suggested that the time might be right to form a women's team competition patterned after the Davis Cup. It took a few years for her plan to take shape, but eventually her vision was realized. The first Wightman Cup match, between teams from the United States and Great Britain, was played in 1923 at the West Side Tennis Club in Forest Hills, New York; the United States won by a score of 7–0. Wightman herself played that year, as well as in 1924, 1927, 1929, and 1931. Often she served as team captain.

With Helen Wills Moody as her partner, Wightman won the national doubles championship in 1924 and 1928—at the age of 42. She won Olympic gold medals in doubles and mixed doubles in 1924, as well as the mixed doubles title at Wimbledon. Three years later, at age 45, she won the women's singles title in the national squash championships and finished second in the national badminton mixed championships. She later wrote an instructional book on tennis.

In 1940 Hazel and George Wightman were divorced. She continued to live in Chestnut Hill and was elected to the International Tennis Hall of Fame in 1957. In 1973 she was named an honorary commander of the British Empire by Queen Elizabeth II. Wightman is remembered not only as the woman who introduced the aggressive serve-and-volley approach now common in women's tennis, but also as the woman who introduced sensible tennis attire. At a time when women were expected to wear corsets and blouses—even in the heat of athletic competition—Helen Hotchkiss Wightman wore sleeveless dresses.

Accomplishments

U.S. national singles champion: 1909–1911,
   1919
U.S. national doubles champion: 1909–1911,
   1915, 1924, 1928
Olympic gold medalist, doubles and mixed
   doubles: 1928
U.S. national squash champion: 1928

Venus Williams

Born June 17, 1980

Tennis prodigy Venus Williams grew up in Compton, California. Her father, Richard Williams, saddled her with the moniker Cinderella of the Ghetto, which turned out to be a fair assessment. Venus and her younger sister, Serena, began playing tennis on the courts of a public park in Southern California. Theirs was a rough neighborhood, but the girls were so talented that, according to their father, they were sheltered from the violence of the city. Gang members would surround the courts when the two girls practiced, ensuring their safety.

In this urban environment Venus began to hone the skills that would make her one of the top young players in the sport. When she was only 10 years old, she won the Southern California Girls 12-and-Under Championship. Not long after that, Richard Williams, realizing his daughter's potential, moved his family to Florida. Venus and Serena began training under tennis guru Rick Macci, who had previously worked with such stars as Mary Pierce and Jennifer Capriati. Richard Williams could not afford the many thousands of dollars required to groom a world-class tennis player, but Macci was so impressed by Venus and Serena that he offered scholarships to both girls.

Venus Williams played for only a year on the hypercompetitive junior circuit before her father pulled her out. From 1991 until 1994 her career was shrouded in secrecy. She left her public school in Delray Beach, Florida, and received instruction from her parents at home. She continued to practice tennis for several hours a day but rarely competed. In November 1994, in Oakland, California, she made her professional debut at the Bank of the West Classic. At the age of 14 she met, and defeated, the 59th-ranked player in the world, Shaun Stafford, in straight sets. She also took a set off No. 2–ranked Arantxa Sanchez Vicario. In that tournament the 6-foot 1-inch, 150-pound teenager displayed a stunning all-court game. Her serve was powerful, her volleying confident.

As quickly as she appeared on the scene, however, Williams faded away. Her father, citing the burnout that affects so many young tennis players—most noticeably Capriati—refused to allow his daughter to play another professional tournament in 1994. His schedule for her called for a maximum of three more pro events in 1995. Critics accused Richard Williams of being overly protective and manipulative; he said he was merely looking out for his daughter's best interests. "I'm very concerned that what happened to Jennifer [Capriati] could happen to Venus," he said. "I'm afraid we could fall into that same doggone trap. Venus would love to play all the Grand Slams. But she's not going to. No way."

Despite her limited experience, Williams signed a multi-million-dollar endorsement deal with Reebok when she was only 14 years old. Her father predicted that she would be the No. 1 player in the world by the time she was 18.

Accomplishments

- Southern California Girls 12-and-Under champion at age 10
- Played first professional tournament at age 14
- Signed multi-million-dollar endorsement deal with Reebok at age 14

Katarina Witt

Born December 3, 1965

Katarina Witt, winner of two Olympic gold medals in figure skating, was born in Karl-Marx-Stadt, East Germany. Each day, when she walked to kindergarten, Katarina passed an ice rink. The little girl was fascinated by the skaters and often asked her mother when she would be old enough to join them. Kathe Witt, a physical therapist, relented early on, and at the age of five, Katarina laced up a pair of skates for the first time. Coaches and friends later described her as a natural athlete who floated across the ice with uncommon grace.

Katarina Witt was targeted for stardom from the beginning. Bernd Egert, head coach of the Karl-Marx-Stadt sports club, recruited the young girl for one of East Germany's special training programs. It was common in those days for East German children with unusual athletic ability to be plucked from the routine of family life and

placed in an environment that stressed athletic excellence above all else. Katarina Witt thrived in this system. At nine years of age she began working with Jutta Mueller, one of the best figure skating coaches in the world. Under Mueller's tutelage, Witt landed a triple jump in practice when she was just 11 years old—an extraordinary accomplishment. She cracked the top 10 at the world championships at the age of 14, and one year later she placed fifth. At the 1982 European championships, when she was 17, Witt finished first. At the world championships she was second.

All of that was a prelude to the 1984 Winter Olympic Games in Sarajevo, Yugoslavia, where Witt became more than just a champion—she became a celebrity. Talented, glamorous, and charismatic, she won a gold medal and millions of new fans. That same year she finished first at the European and world championships. She repeated at both events in 1985. Witt lost her

world title to American Debi Thomas in 1986, but recaptured the crown in 1987 and 1988.

Witt brought to the sport of figure skating a style and a charm that had never been seen before. She was, by her own admission, a flirt on skates. It was part of her act. Critics accused her of taking advantage of her beauty, rather than relying strictly on athletic ability. But Witt believed that figure skating was as much theater as sport, and she knew how to please both crowds and judges. The 1988 Winter Olympics in Calgary marked the zenith of Witt's career. Both Witt and Thomas skated to the music from the opera *Carmen* during their long programs. Witt's was the more dramatic interpretation: she fell to the ice in tears—like the dying Carmen—at the end of her program. The gold medal was hers again. She became the first female figure skater since Sonja Henie some 50 years earlier to capture gold medals in two consecutive Olympics.

Witt turned professional after the 1988 Olympics. She toured in ice shows, performing regularly with Brian Boitano of the United States. At the 1992 Olympics in Albertville, France, she worked as a color commentator for CBS. Two years later, when professional athletes were allowed to compete in the Olympics, Witt returned to the ice. She failed to win a medal at the 1994 Lillehammer Olympics, but her appearance added a touch of nostalgia to the Games, and the crowd responded with warmth and respect.

Accomplishments

Olympic gold medalist: 1984, 1988
World champion: 1984–1985, 1986–1988

Lynette Woodard

Born 1960

Lynette Woodard, the first woman to play for the Harlem Globetrotters, was raised in Wichita, Kansas. On January 16, 1965, a U.S. Air Force tanker plane crashed in Woodard's neighborhood, destroying several houses. For five years the crash site was nothing more than a vacant lot. But eventually it became Piatt Park, a public playground where Woodard learned to play basketball.

As a 14-year-old freshman at Wichita's North High, Woodard played on the junior varsity. The following year she led North to its first state championship. The tournament that year was held in Lawrence, which made it convenient for University of Kansas coach Marian Washington to do a little scouting. Woodard went into the tournament as a virtual unknown; by the time it was over, she had moved to the top of Washington's recruiting list—even though she had two years of high school remaining. "When I saw how gifted she was," Washington said, "I was scared to death."

At the University of Kansas, Woodard was a pioneer. At 5 feet 11 inches tall, she had the size to play forward. But she also had the ball-handling ability of a guard. She was one of the first great entertainers in women's basketball, a player with stunning improvisational ability. She was the leading rebounder in the country as a freshman; for the next three years she was the leading scorer. She was a four-time All-American who set a career collegiate scoring record with 3,649 points. In 1981 she was named Women's Collegiate Player of the Year.

After graduating from Kansas, Woodard played professional basketball in Italy for a year but suffered from homesickness. She returned to Kansas to work as an assistant coach at her alma mater. In 1984 she was captain of the U.S. team that won a gold medal in women's basketball at the Los Angeles Summer Olympics.

Woodard's most memorable accomplishment came in 1985, when she beat out 25 women for a chance to wear the uniform of the most famous basketball team in the world—the Harlem Globetrotters. At the time, it was suggested that the Globetrotters, whose attendance had been sagging, were merely using Woodard as a publicity stunt. After all, she was a cousin of Geese Ausbie, himself a Globetrotter for more than two decades. And, of course, she was a woman, which made her so unique that she was certain to attract a few curiosity seekers. As it turned out, Woodard was much more than a sideshow attraction. She not only helped boost attendance by 20 percent in her first year with the team, but she also proved herself an exceptional player. And she never looked at the experience as something less than "real" basketball. Woodard loved the showmanship associated with Globetrotters basketball.

"I always say, playing with the Globetrotters is like playing jazz," Woodard told a reporter. "You get to be as creative as you want to be."

Woodard played with the Globetrotters for two years before leaving to play professional basketball in Japan.

Accomplishments

Four-time All-American
Collegiate Player of the Year: 1981
Olympic gold medalist: 1984
First woman to play for the Harlem
  Globetrotters: 1985

Mickey Wright

Born February 14, 1935

Mary Kathryn Wright, a member of the Ladies Professional Golf Association Hall of Fame, grew up in San Diego, California, and received her first set of clubs at the age of nine. Her father, an attorney, gave Mary her nickname, Mickey, which stemmed from the fact that he had hoped to have a son named Michael.

His daughter would become one of the best players on the LPGA tour.

Mickey Wright's greatest asset was her strength. At 5 feet 9 inches tall and 150 pounds, she was a powerful player, averaging better than 225 yards off the tee and occasionally sending the ball nearly 300 yards down the fairway. Wright won the 1952 U.S. Girls' Junior Championship when she was 17 years old; two years later she won the World Amateur and was low amateur at the U.S. Women's Open. By that time she had decided to leave Stanford University to become a professional golfer. It wasn't long before she was the most dominant player in the game.

Wright won her first tournament in 1956, kicking off a streak of 14 consecutive years in which she won at least one tournament each year. From 1961 through 1964 she was the leading money winner on the LPGA tour. She won the U.S. Women's Open four times—in 1958, 1959, 1961, and 1964; she was runner-up in 1968. She took the LPGA title in 1958, 1960, 1961, and 1963; in 1964 and 1966 she finished second. Five consecutive times—from 1960 through 1964—she won the Vare Trophy for having the lowest average score on the LPGA tour.

In a 10-year span, from 1959 through 1968, Wright accumulated 79 of her 82 career victories, averaging 7.9 victories per year. She won a remarkable 13 events in 1963—a record that still stands. Wright's finest year on the tour was 1961, when she captured three of the LPGA's four major tournaments—the U.S. Women's Open, the LPGA championship, and the Titleholders championship. She is the only golfer to twice win the LPGA championship and the U.S. Women's Open in the same year. No golfer, not even Kathy Whitworth, was more prolific.

Wright stopped playing regularly in 1969, when she was 34 years old. Reasons for her premature semiretirement included problems related to overexposure to sunlight, an aversion to flying, and chronic foot problems. In 1979, 10 years after she had left the LPGA tour, Wright—wearing sneakers the entire time—finished second to Nancy Lopez at the Coca-Cola Classic. She has played sporadically since, including an appearance at the 1993 Sprint Senior Challenge, where she finished fifth.

Wright, who now lives in Port Saint Lucie, Florida, was elected to the LPGA Hall of Fame in 1964 and to the International Woman's Sports Hall of Fame in 1981.

Accomplishments

U.S. Women's Open champion: 1958–1959, 1961, 1964
LPGA championship winner: 1958, 1960–1961, 1963
Titleholders champion: 1961–1962
Western Open champion: 1962–1963, 1966
LPGA Hall of Fame: 1964

Kristi Yamaguchi

Born June 12, 1971

Figure skater Kristi Yamaguchi was raised in Fremont, California. She grew up to become an Olympic gold medalist, but as a child she suffered from serious physical problems. She was born clubfooted, which made it necessary for her to wear special casts that had to be changed twice a month. After more than a year, her feet had straightened, but doctors told Kristi's parents that, as a precautionary measure, she should wear corrective shoes for at least three years.

Kristi was one of three children born to Jim and Carole Yamaguchi. Her mother was a medical secretary, her father a dentist. Kristi began taking dance lessons when she was four. Two years later, after seeing an ice skating show at a shopping mall, she convinced her mother to let her try figure skating. She fell hard and often for quite some time, but eventually joined a junior program and, with the help of private lessons, became an accomplished young skater.

At the age of 12, Kristi Yamaguchi entered her first serious event, the California state regionals. The next week she won the Pacific Coast championships, which automatically qualified her for the U.S. junior nationals. There

senior nationals for the first time. She was only 16 years old, so her 10th-place finish was not a disappointment. She viewed it as a learning experience; the following year, she told herself, things would be different. In 1989, at the nationals, Yamaguchi and her partner, Rudy Galindo, finished first in the pairs competition; Yamaguchi then took a silver medal in singles. Despite spending more than half of her time training for the pairs competition, she was one of the best individual figure skaters in the United States.

After graduating from high school in June 1989, Yamaguchi moved to Canada to board with her singles coach, Christy Kjarsgaard. Several days each month she returned to Fremont, California, to train with Galindo. But the strain became too much for her, so in early 1990 Yamaguchi decided to concentrate exclusively on singles. She embarked on a serious weight training program for the first time in her life, in an effort to add strength to her small (5-foot 3-inch, 93-pound) frame. "Kristi is her own toughest critic," Kjarsgaard said. "She may not show it on the outside, but inside is a woman burning with the desire to be the best."

Yamaguchi became one of the best skaters in the world. She finished first at the world championships in 1991. A year later she won the U.S. and world championships, and captured a gold medal at the Winter Olympics in Albertville, France.

After her Olympic success, Yamaguchi became a prized commodity among advertisers. She signed several lucrative endorsement deals and became a performer in professional skating events.

Accomplishments

U.S. national champion, pairs: 1989
U.S. national champion, singles: 1992
World champion, singles: 1991–1992
Olympic gold medalist: 1992

Sheila Young

Born October 14, 1950

Born in Birmingham, Michigan, Sheila Young was a world champion in both speed skating and cycling. The passing of time and the obscure nature of Young's sports have conspired

she finished fourth. She also finished fifth in the pairs competition at the world junior championships. The next year, as a freshman in high school, Yamaguchi returned to the world junior championships and performed spectacularly, winning gold medals in the singles and the pairs competitions.

In 1988 Yamaguchi competed in the U.S.

against her, as many sports fans don't even recognize her name. But her accomplishments were remarkable—she became a world champion in two separate sports at the same time. Even the great Babe Didrikson Zaharias put away her track-and-field spikes before picking up a golf club. Sheila Young, who held championships in speed skating and cycling in 1973 and 1976, was one of the most versatile athletes in history.

Young grew up in a large family devoted to athletics. Her parents cycled and skated; their affection for sports was passed on to their daughter, who began skating at the age of two. When Young was 12, her mother died of cancer. Shortly thereafter her family moved to Detroit, where her father had taken a new job. Young felt isolated in her new environment and decided to throw herself into sports to combat her loneliness. With the help of her family, she became a serious competitive speed skater. "Going skating went with raising the kids," her father said. "I couldn't afford a baby-sitter, so everybody had to come along."

Despite a lack of adequate training facilities, Young progressed as a skater. At the 1972 Winter Olympics she just missed a medal, taking fourth place in the 500 meters. A year later, at the age of 22, she was more mature, both physically and emotionally. She began working with a new coach, Peter Schotting, who had much more international experience than her previous coach (her father). In 1973 Young, considered primarily a sprinter, demonstrated her versatility at the U.S. championships by finishing first in three events—the 500, the 1,000, and the 3,000 meters. Later that season she set a world record in the 500 meters, and in February, at the world championships, she won a gold medal in the 500.

In the spring of 1973, Young turned her attention to cycling. She had cycled for recreation and to supplement her skating. But now she wanted to test herself against world-class cycling competition. She qualified for the world championships in San Sebastián, Spain, and shocked the cycling community by becoming the first American—male or female—to win. Inexperienced, anxious, and nervous, Young crashed twice in the preliminary heats of the sprint championship but came back in the final

to upset heavily favored Galina Ermolasva of the Soviet Union.

After that, it was back to the ice. Young won another world title at 500 meters in 1975. By 1976 she was ready to stake her claim to an Olympic medal. At the Winter Games in Innsbruck, Austria, Young won a gold medal in the 500 meters, a silver medal in the 1,500, and a bronze in the 1,000. Never before had an American athlete won three medals in one Winter Olympics. Young capped her brilliant skating career by winning another 500-meter world championship in 1976. A few months later she hopped back onto her bicycle and won sprint-cycling titles at the U.S. and world championships.

Accomplishments

Olympic gold medalist, speed skating, 500 meters: 1976
Olympic bronze medalist, speed skating, 1,000 meters: 1976
Olympic silver medalist, speed skating, 1,500 meters: 1976
World champion, speed skating, 500 meters: 1973, 1975–1976
World champion, sprint cycling: 1973, 1976

Babe Didrikson Zaharias

June 26, 1911–September 27, 1956

Born Mildred Ella Didriksen (she changed the spelling of her last name as an adult), the Texas Babe is considered by many to be the greatest female athlete in history. She earned that title through hard work, talent, ambition, and charisma. Babe Didrikson was raised in Beaumont, Texas, the sixth of seven children. Her love for performing was evident as early as the age of seven, when she excelled as a tap dancer and a harmonica player. At the same time, she was interested in sports. As a girl, Babe worked out in a makeshift gymnasium set up by her father in the backyard. She used a hedge to refine her hurdling technique.

Because opportunites for girls to participate in high school and college sports were rare in those days, Didrikson's career in organized athletics did not begin until 1930, when she took a job with the Employers Casualty Insurance Co. of Dallas. She was supposed to be a typist, but in truth, she was hired as an athlete. Didrikson had been spotted by M.J. McCombs, head of the company's athletic program, which featured a well-known basketball team. Didrikson averaged 42 points per game to lead Employers Casualty to the 1930 Amateur Athletic Union women's championship.

Later that same year the company launched a track program. Didrikson signed up, and despite having had no previous formal experience, she soon became one of the most accomplished track-and-field performers in Texas. In 1932 she led Employers Casualty to the women's team title at the AAU nationals—a stunning performance because she was the only member of the team. At the 1932 Olympics in Los Angeles, Didrikson competed on a world stage for the first time, and her results were no less impressive. She won gold medals in the javelin and the 80-meter hurdles, and a silver medal in the high jump.

After the Olympics, Didrikson toured with a coed basketball team, pitched for a barnstorming men's baseball team known as the House of David, and put together a vaudeville-style act in which she played the harmonica, whacked plastic golf balls, and ran on a treadmill. She also

received money for commercial endorsements. All of these activities caused Didrikson to lose her status as an amateur athlete, and she was ruled ineligible to compete in the 1936 Olympics.

In the late 1930s Didrikson married former wrestler George Zaharias. Babe Didrikson Zaharias then asked to be reinstated as an amateur athlete. The battle lasted for several years, and virtually every athletic governing body refused her request. In 1944, however, Zaharias was granted amateur status by the United States Golfing Association. She won the U.S. Amateur in 1946, and in 1947 she became the first American to win the British Amateur. In 1948 the Ladies Professional Golf Association was founded; Zaharias was the tour's premier attraction. She competed as a professional for eight years, winning 31 LPGA tournaments, including the U.S. Women's Open three times.

In 1950 Zaharias was chosen by the Associated Press as the Greatest Female Athlete of the First Half of the 20th Century. A tough, outspoken competitor, Zaharias won the last of her U.S. Women's Open titles by 12 strokes in 1954, one year after being diagnosed with colon cancer. The disease took her life in 1956.

Accomplishments

Olympic gold medalist, 80-meter hurdles: 1932
Olympic gold medalist, javelin: 1932
Olympic silver medalist, high jump: 1932
U.S. Women's Amateur golf champion: 1946
Women's British Amateur golf champion: 1947
U.S. Women's Open golf champion: 1948, 1950, 1954

Bibliography

In researching this book, I consulted a wide variety of sources, including newspaper and magazine articles, book-length biographies, media guides, encyclopedias, electronic databases, and assorted reference books.

Included in the following bibliography are the most frequently consulted sources.

Aaseng, Nathan. *Florence Griffith Joyner: Dazzling Olympian*. Minneapolis: Lerner Publications, Co., 1989.

Benoit, Joan, with Sally Baker. *Running Tide*. New York: Alfred A. Knopf, 1987.

Carlson, Lewis H., and John J. Fogarty. *Tales of Gold*. Chicago: Contemporary Books, Inc., 1987.

Celzic, Mike. *Courage*. New York: Carrol & Graf Publishers, 1991.

Clark, Judith Freeman. *Almanac of American Women in the 20th Century*. New York: Prentice Hall Press, 1987.

Clark, Patrick. *Sports Firsts*. New York: Facts on File, 1981.

Coffey, Frank, and Joe Layden. *Thin Ice: The Complete Uncensored Story of Tonya Harding*. New York: Windsor Publishing Corp., 1994.

Coffey, Wayne. *Katarina Witt (Olympic Gold!)*. Woodbridge, Conn.: Blackbirch Press, 1992.

Collins, Bud, and Zander Hollander. *Bud Collins' Modern Encyclopedia of Tennis*. Garden City, N.Y.: Doubleday, 1980.

Condon, Robert J. *Great Women Athletes of the 20th Century*. Jefferson, N.C.: McFarland & Co., Inc., 1991.

Derderian, Tom. *Boston Marathon: The History of the World's Premier Running Event*. Champaign, Ill.: Human Kinetics Publishers, 1994.

Emert, Phyllis Raybin. *Jane Frederick: Pentathlon Champion*. New York: Harvey House, 1981.

Freedman, Lew. *Iditarod Classics*. Fairbanks, Alaska: Epicenter Press, 1992.

Frayne, Trent. *Famous Women Tennis Players*. New York: Dodd, Mead & Co., 1979.

Glenn, Rhonda. *The Illustrated History of Women's Golf*. Dallas, Tex.: Taylor Publishing Co., 1991.

Goldstein, Margaret J., and Jennifer Larson. *Jackie Joyner-Kersee: Superwoman*. Minneapolis: Lerner Publications Co., 1994.

The Good Housekeeping Woman's Almanac. New York: Newspaper Enterprise Association, Inc., 1977.

Guttmann, Allen. *Women's Sports: A History*. New York: Columbia University Press, 1991.

Hart, Stan. *Once a Champion: Legendary Tennis Stars Revisited*. New York: Dodd, Mead & Co., 1985.

Hickok, Ralph. *A Who's Who of Sports Champions: Their Stories & Records*. New York: Houghton Mifflin, 1995.

Hollander, Phyllis. *100 Greatest Women in Sports*. New York: Grosset and Dunlap, 1976.

Johnson, Susan E. *When Women Played Hardball*. Seattle: Seal Press, 1994.

Karolyi, Bela, and Nancy Ann Richardson. *Feel No Fear: The Power, Passion, and Politics of a Life in Gymnastics*. New York: Hyperion, 1994.

Kieran, John, and Arthur Daley. *The Story of the Olympic Games*. Philadelphia: J.B. Lippincott Co., 1973.

King, Billie Jean, with Cynthia Starr. *We Have Come A Long Way: The Story of Women's Tennis*. New York: McGraw Hill, 1988.

King, Billie Jean, with Frank Deford. *Billie Jean*. New York: Viking Press, 1982.

Knudson, R.R. *Martina Navratilova: Tennis Power*. New York: Viking Penguin, Inc., 1986.

Krebs, Gary M., ed. *The Guinness Book of Sports Records*. New York: Facts on File, 1995.

Laklan, Carli. *Golden Girls*. New York: McGraw-Hill, 1980.

Libby, Bill. *Stars of the Olympics*. New York: Hawthorn Books, 1975.

Littlefield, Bill. *Champions: Stories of Ten Remarkable Athletes*. Boston: Little, Brown & Co., 1993.

LPGA Player Guide. Daytona Beach, Fla.: Ladies Professional Golf Association, 1996.

Mallon, Bill, and Ian Buchanan. *Quest for Gold: The Encyclopedia of American Olympians*. New York: Leisure Press, 1984.

McWhirter, Norris. *Guinness Book of Women's Sports Records*. New York: Sterling Publishing Co., 1979.

Meserole, Mike, ed. *The 1995 Information Please Sports Almanac*. Boston: Houghton Mifflin, 1995.

Messner, Reinhold. *Everest: Expedition to the Ultimate*. London: Kay & Ward, 1979.

Morrissete, Mikki. *Jennifer Capriati*. New York: Time, Inc., 1991.

Navratilova, Martina, with George Vecsey. *Martina*. New York: Alfred A. Knopf, 1985.

Nelson, Rebecca, and Marie J. MacNee, eds. *The Olympic Factbook*. Detroit: Visible Ink Press, 1996.

Phillips, Louis, and Karen Markoe. *Women in Sports: Records, Stars, Feats & Facts*. New York: Harcourt Brace Jovanovich, Inc., 1979.

Savage, Paul. *Kristi Yamaguchi: Pure Gold*. New York: Dillon Press, 1993.

Searle, Caroline, and Bryan Vaile, eds. *The IOC Official Olympic Companion 1996*. London: Brassey's Sports, 1996.

Sherman, Eric. *365 Amazing Days in Sports*. New York: Time, Inc., 1990.

Wade, Paul, and Tony Duffy. *Winning Women: The Changing Image of Women in Sports*. New York: Times Books, 1983.

Wallechinsky, David. *The Complete Book of the Olympics*. New York: Viking, 1988.

Wallechinsky, David. *Sports Illustrated Presents the Complete Book of the Summer Olympics*. Boston: Little, Brown & Co., 1996.

Ward, Geoffrey C., and Ken Burns. *Baseball, an Illustrated History*. New York: Alfred A. Knopf, 1994.

Watman, Mel. *Encyclopedia of Athletics*. New York: St. Martin's Press, Inc., 1977.

WTA Media Guide. St. Petersburg, Fla.: Women's Tennis Association, 1996.

Zaharias, Mildred Babe Didrikson, *This Life I've Led: My Autobiography*. New York: A.S. Barnes, 1955.

Abbreviations

Following is a list of the most commonly used abbreviations and acronyms in *Women In Sports*.

AAU—Amateur Athletic Union
ABL—American Basketball League
AIAW—Association of Intercollegiate Athletics for Women
AP—Associated Press
BAA—Boston Athletic Association
ESPN—Entertainment and Sports Programming Network
IAAF—International Amateur Athletic Foundation
IOC—International Olympic Committee
LPGA—Ladies Professional Golf Association
MVP—Most Valuable Player

NAIA—National Association for Intercollegiate
  Athletics
NBA—National Basketball Association
NCAA—National Collegiate Athletic
  Association
NHL—National Hockey League
NYRA—New York Racing Association
PGA—Professional Golf Association
TAC—The Athletics Congress
UPI—United Press International
USFSA—United States Figure Skating
  Association
USGA—United States Golf Association
USLTA—United States Lawn Tennis
  Association
USOC—United States Olympic Committee
USTA—United States Tennis Association
WBL—Women's Basketball League
WIBC—Women's International Bowling
  Congress
WNBA—Women's National Basketball
  Association
WTA—Women's Tennis Association

Photo Credits

Index

R 920 LAY

Layden, Joseph.
Women in Sports.

$29.95

DATE			